WITHDRAWN

PURCHASED FROM
MULTNOMAH COUNTY LIBRARY
TITLE WAVE BOOKSTORE

Sexuality in America

Understanding Our Sexual Values and Behavior

Edited by

PATRICIA BARTHALOW KOCH and DAVID L. WEIS

Preface by

PATRICIA BARTHALOW KOCH and DAVID L. WEIS

with contributions by

Diane Baker, Sandy Bargainnier,
Sarah C. Conklin, Martha Cornog,
Richard Cross, Marilyn Fithian,
Jeannie Forrest, Andrew D. Forsythe,
Robert T. Francoeur, Barbara Garris,
Patricia Goodson, William E. Hartman,
Robert O. Hawkins, Jr., Linda L. Hendrixson,
Barrie J. Highby, Ariadne Kane,
Sharon King, Robert Morgan Lawrence,
Brenda Love, Charlene L. Muehlenhard,
Raymond J. Noonan, Miguel A. Pérez,
Timothy Perper, Helda L. Pinzón,
Carol Queen, Herbert P. Samuels,
Julian Slowinski, William Stackhouse,
William R. Stayton, and Mitchell S. Tepper

Foreword by

ROBERT T. FRANCOEUR
General Editor of
The International Encyclopedia of Sexuality

Sexuality in America

Understanding Our Sexual Values and Behavior

Robert T. Francoeur, Ph.D., General Editor

Patricia Barthalow Koch, Ph.D., and David L. Weis, Ph.D.
Editors

CONTINUUM • NEW YORK

1998

The Continuum Publishing Company
370 Lexington Avenue
New York, NY 10017

Copyright © 1998 by Robert T. Francoeur

All rights reserved. No part of this book may be reproduced,
stored in a retrieval system, or transmitted, in any form or by any means,
electronic, mechanical, photocopying, recording, or otherwise, without
the written permission of The Continuum Publishing Company.

Typography, Design Coordination, and Computer Graphics by
Ray Noonan, ParaGraphic Artists, NYC [http://www.paragraphics.com]

Printed in the United States of America

Library of Congress Cataloging-in-Publication Data

Sexuality in America : understanding our sexual values and behavior /
    Robert T. Francoeur, general editor ; Patricia Barthalow Koch and
    David L. Weis, editors ; [preface by Patricia Barthalow Koch and
    David L. Weis ; with contributions by Diane Baker . . . et al. ;
    foreword by Robert T. Francoeur].
        p. cm.
    Includes bibliographical references (p.   ) and index.
    ISBN 0-8264-1003-0 (Hbd : alk. paper)
        1. Sex—United States.   2. Sexual behavior surveys—United States.
    I. Francoeur, Robert T.   II. Koch, Patricia Barthalow.   III. Weis, David L.
    HQ18.U5S517   1998
    306.7'0973—dc21   98-4020
                                                                           CIP

CONTENTS

Foreword

Robert T. Francoeur, Ph.D., A.C.S., F.S.S.S.S.

Sexuality in America is unique because of the way it grew as a carefully constructed mosaic. Unlike other books that have attempted to present a panoramic view of American sexual behaviors and values, this volume was not written by one or two authors who are expert in their own field of sexology and must then wrestle with a vast amount of research information and data outside their usual interests and research. Drs. Patricia Barthalow Koch and David L. Weis, the editors, met this challenge by making their contributions on specific areas in which they have had a long-standing special interest and expertise. To fill in the gaps, they judiciously recruited a team of thirty American sexologists who were asked to write chapters or sections of chapters that would complete this panorama of American sexuality. This approach gives Sexuality in America unique authority, since these thirty experts provide a combination of "insider," or emic, and "outsider," or etic, views of complex issues. Adding to this balance, the editors invited sixteen other scholars to review sections in which they have expertise. The result: a panoramic mosaic created by forty-six American sexologists working together under the editorial leadership of Drs. Koch and Weis. This approach enabled the editors to deal comfortably with the ethnic, racial, and religious complexity of American sexuality, as well as with the wide range of complex topics and sensitive issues that are part of sexuality in America today.

My own role was to advise based on the lessons I learned in compiling similar but less extensive chapters on thirty-one other countries on six continents. These appear in the first three volumes of *The International Encyclopedia of Sexuality*, for which I am general editor.

In this present volume, Koch and Weis add new information and perspectives to the substantial text that originally appeared in the three-volume *International Encyclopedia*. This single-volume, expanded publication makes this authoritative and critical review of American sexual values and behavior more available to the general public, as well as to students and other scholars interested in the complex mosaic that is *Sexuality in America*.

Among our contributors, the reader will encounter professionals from a variety of disciplines including: anthropology, biology, gender studies, health-care, health education, nonverbal behavior, social, clinical, and evolutionary psychology, cultural and evolutionary sociology, activism, and advocacy. Each contributor was more or less strongly influenced by her or his professional background and training. Because the editors are very much aware of and sensitive to the diversity of our contributors and their varied and rich perspectives, they decided to let each contributor speak for her- or himself. In respecting this freedom and diversity, we feel a strong responsibility to comment on the consequences of this decision for the reader.

Thus, the reader should *not* expect to find in this volume a single, consistent picture of sexual attitudes and behaviors in the United States. In some sections, the reader will encounter an insider's or emic view of a particular aspect, e.g., Ariadne Kane offers an insider's view of cross-gender issues and Mitchell Tepper writes about sexuality and people with physical and developmental disabilities from both his personal experience and professional perspective. Other contributors write from an etic or outsider view as researchers or observers. To appreciate critically these various views, the reader should consider the perspective of the individual writer.

The reader will also encounter research theories and statistics. These data may represent the results of studies conducted by researchers who might have been constrained by popular interests, political restrictions, or the biases of funding agencies. Thus, they may have had to devote their expertise to more limited and perhaps chic or politically safe research than was warranted in providing a more comprehensive and well-balanced understanding of sexuality.

The panorama of American sexuality presented here represents a mosaic that is not always consistent, nor could it be, given the diversity of American sexologists, the funding and support for sexology, and the ever-changing complexity of American sexual attitudes, values, and practices. This volume does, however, present a solid picture of what American sexologists do when they summarize the research and data available on topics in their own domain of interest and specialization. This volume also gives an unparalleled picture of what a team of scholars have learned from years of studying the many intriguing mysteries of *Sexuality in America*.

Preface

Patricia Barthalow Koch, Ph.D., and David L. Weis, Ph.D.

The August 1997 publication of the three-volume, 1,750-page *International Encyclopedia of Sexuality* was greeted with critical acclaim both in the United States and abroad. The *Encyclopedia* was the recipient of the 1997 Citation of Excellence for "an outstanding reference work in the field of sexology" awarded by The American Foundation for Gender and Genital Medicine and Science at the Thirteenth World Congress of Sexology in Valencia, Spain. The three volumes were also endorsed by the World Association of Sexology as "an important and unique contribution to our understanding and appreciation of the rich variety of human sexual attitudes, values, and behavior" in 32 countries around the world.

Because the cost of these three volumes limits their availability to many scholars and students, as well as general readers, Continuum, our publisher, decided to publish an expanded, updated version on the United States from the third volume as a volume of its own. The result is an in-depth presentation of American sexual values and behaviors, unlike any other scholarly work created by individual scholars. We hope this publication of *Sexuality in America: Understanding Our Sexual Values and Behavior* will make this authoritative and comprehensive picture of American sexuality and sexology available to a wider audience of students, scholars, and general readers.

In *The International Encyclopedia of Sexuality,* sexologists from 32 countries prepared an analysis of sexuality within their respective countries, following a common outline of topics. These topics, arranged in fourteen sections, covered demographics and a historical perspective; basic sexological premises; gender, religious, and ethnic factors affecting sexuality; formal and informal sources of sexual knowledge and education; autoerotic, heterosexual, homosexual, and bisexual patterns of sexually relating; transgendered persons; unconventional sexual behaviors (sexual abuse, rape, incest, prostitution, and pornography); contraception, abortion, and population planning; sexually transmissible diseases; HIV/AIDS; sexual dysfunctions and therapies; and sexological research and advanced education. Structuring material from each country in this way facilitates the reader making cross-cultural comparisons. This original format was retained in the structure of the material presented in this volume. As you read through the fourteen chapters or sections that follow, you will encounter an occasional note advising you of additional information on a particular topic to be found in Section 15, Current Developments, where we explore some new topics and update our mosaic picture of sexuality in America. Page cross-references and a supplementary bibliography are provided in both the original sections and the new section on Current Developments.

In the first chapter, Weis examines the general theme of social changes in sexuality that occur in a process of conflict between diverse and frequently competing social groups. That theme is explicitly noted by several authors of particular chapters. Even when it is not explicitly discussed, this theme is apparent in the coverage of a wide array of sexual values and practices by our diverse group of contributors. Koch returns to this theme in her concluding chapter (written for this USA-only edition) and reviews a number of examples appearing throughout the book. We hope that this approach will help the reader to understand the systemic nature of the processes that constitute sexuality in American society. In fact, this focus will be important to sexual scientists and students as they continue to explore and attempt to understand the continuing evolution of American sexuality.

We hope that professionals, students, and the public at large will find this book useful in providing meaning and context, as well as information, concerning various aspects of sexuality in the United States. We would encourage the reader to savor and digest the entire text in order to receive the most benefit of the breadth and depth of this carefully integrated mosaic.

American Demographics and a Sketch of Diversity, Change, and Social Conflict

DAVID L. WEIS

A. A Demographic Overview

In one sense, great diversity is virtually guaranteed by the sheer size of the United States. The U.S.A. is a union of fifty participating states. It is one of the larger nations in the world, with the forty-eight contiguous states spanning more than three thousand miles across the North American continent, from its eastern shores on the Atlantic Ocean to its western shores on the Pacific Ocean, and more than two thousand miles from its northern border with Canada to its southern border with Mexico and the Gulf of Mexico. In addition, the state of Alaska, itself a large landmass covering thousands of square miles in the northwest corner of North America, and the state of Hawaii, a collection of islands in the mid-Pacific Ocean, are part of the union.

The U.S.A. has a population of more than 260 million racially and ethnically heterogeneous people (Wilkinson 1987; *World Almanac and Book of Facts, 1993*). A majority, about 161 million or two thirds, are white descendants of immigrants from the European continent, with sizable groups from Great Britain, Ireland, Italy, Germany, and Poland. The second-largest group, roughly 29 million or 12 percent, is African-American, most of whose ancestors were brought to North America as slaves before the twentieth century. The third-largest group, 22 million or 9 percent, is comprised of Hispanic-Americans, whose ancestors emigrated from such places as Mexico, Puerto Rico, Cuba, Haiti, and the Dominican Republic, as well as other Central and South American nations. Hispanics represent the fastest-growing minority group in the U.S.A. There are also more than two million Native Americans—Eskimos, Aleuts, and those mistakenly at one time called Indians—whose ancestors have occupied North America for thousands of years, and whose residence within the boundaries of what is now the U.S.A. predates all of the other groups mentioned.

Another group experiencing rapid growth in recent decades is Asian-Americans; there are now more than three million residents of Asian heritage. Substantial populations of Japanese and Chinese immigrants have been in the U.S.A. since the nineteenth century. More recently, there has been an increase from such nations as India, Vietnam, Korea, the Philippines, Cambodia, Indonesia, and Pakistan. Finally, there are smaller groups of immigrants from virtually every nation, with growing numbers of Moslems in recent decades. The size of the various nonwhite minority groups has been increasing in the last thirty years, both in terms of real numbers and as a percentage of the total U.S.A. population (Wilkinson 1987; *World Almanac 1993*).

It is fair to conclude that the U.S.A. is generally a nation of former immigrants. Moreover, one continuing feature of American history has been the successive immigration of different groups at different points in time (Wells 1985).

Approximately two thirds of the population lives within one hundred miles of one of the coastal shorelines. Most of the largest metropolitan areas lie within these coastal areas, and it is worth noting that most sexologists in the U.S.A. also reside in these same areas.

The U.S.A. is somewhat unique among the world's economies in that it is simultaneously one of the largest agricultural producers as well as one of the largest industrialized nations, exporting manufactured goods and technology to the rest of the world. Historically, the northeast and upper midwest have been the principal industrial centers, and the southeast and the central Great Plains have been the agricultural centers.

One of the economically richest nations in the world, America, nevertheless, has an estimated 500,000 to 600,000 individuals and 125,000 to 150,000 families homeless on any night. Overall, 15 percent of Americans—30 percent of the poor—are without health insurance. Infant-mortality rates and life-expectancy rates vary widely, depending on socioeconomic status and residence in urban, suburban, or rural settings. Fifty-two million American married couples are paralleled by 2.8 million unmarried households and close to 8 million single-parent families.

In summarizing aspects of sexuality in America, it is helpful to keep in mind that the United States of the twenty-first century will look profoundly different from the nation described in this chapter. Four major trends for the future have been detailed in *Population Profile of the United States* (1995), published by the U.S. Census Bureau.

- The average life expectancy for an American in 1900 was 47 years. An American born in 1970 had a life expectancy of 70.8 years. This rose to 76 years in 1993 and is projected to reach 82.6 years by 2050.
- The median age of Americans is currently 34; early in the next century, it will be 39. There are currently 33 million Americans over 65; this number will more than double to 80 million in 2050.
- America's ethnic minorities will continue to grow far more quickly than the majority white population, due to immigration and higher birthrates. In 1994, for the first time, more Hispanics than whites were added to the population. If current trends hold, the percentage of white

Americans will decline from 73.7 percent in 1995 to 52.5 percent in 2050.
- In 1994, 24 percent of all children under age 18 (18.6 million) lived with a single parent, double the percent in 1970. Of these single parents, 36 percent had never been married, up 50 percent from 1985. Meanwhile, the number of unmarried cohabiting couples increased 700 percent in the past decade.

There is also great diversity in religious affiliation in the U.S.A. (Marciano 1987; see Section 2A). To a considerable degree, the choice of religious denomination is directly related to the ethnic patterns previously described. The overwhelming majority of Americans represent the Judeo-Christian heritage, but that statement is potentially misleading. Within the Judeo-Christian heritage, there are substantial populations of Roman Catholics, mainstream Protestants (Lutheran, Methodist, Baptist, Episcopalian, and others), and a growing number of fundamentalist Christians. There is no great uniformity in religious practice or sexual mores shared by these various groups. In addition, there is a relatively small percentage of Americans who are Jewish and range from ultra-orthodox to conservative, reformed, and liberal. In recent decades, as immigration from Asia has increased, there has been a corresponding growth in the Moslem and Hindu faiths.

Several trends related to the practice of religion in the U.S.A. have become a source of recent social concern. These trends include: the declining attendance at the traditional Protestant and Catholic churches, in what has been labeled the growing "secularization" of American culture; the "religious revivalism" reflected by the growth of fundamentalist churches; the growth of religious cults (e.g., Hare Krishna and the Unification Church); the growing power of the conservative Christian Coalition; and the emergence of the "Electronic Church" (religious broadcasting) (Marciano 1987). Throughout the history of this nation, diversity of religious beliefs and the separation of church and state have been central elements in conflicts over sexual morality.

The subcultures and peoples of the United States are as varied, diverse, and complex as any other large nation. The unique feature of sexuality in the United States is that we have far more information and data on American sexual attitudes, values, and behaviors than is available for any other country.

B. A Sketch of Recent Diversity, Change, and Social Conflict

A few examples will illustrate some of the issues that have been affected by this complex of influences.

- The dominant news story in the U.S. through much of 1998 concerned the alleged extramarital sexual practices of President Bill Clinton.

Stories about Clinton's sexual experiences with a number of women routinely surfaced throughout his presidential term. Certainly, no American president has ever been subjected to as much speculation about extramarital sex while still in office. As early as his first presidential campaign in 1992, Gennifer Flowers alleged that she had had a long-term affair with Clinton while he had been governor of Arkansas. Clinton initially denied her specific allegations. He did admit in a televised interview that he had had extramarital experiences, claiming that he and his wife had resolved their marital problems. Later, after his election, he admitted to an affair with Flowers. In 1994, Paula Jones, a former Arkansas state employee, revealed at a press conference sponsored by a fundamentalist Christian group that she believed Clinton had sexually harassed her in 1991, while he was governor. Later that year, Jones filed a civil suit charging the President with sexual harassment. Jones claimed that Clinton invited her to his hotel room (using a state trooper as an intermediary), exposed himself, and asked her to perform fellatio (Isikoff and Thomas 1997; Taylor, 1997). The U.S. Supreme Court ruled unanimously in 1997 that the suit could proceed while Clinton was still in office (Isikoff and Thomas 1997).

Enter Kenneth Starr. Starr, a Republican judge, had been appointed as a special prosecutor early in the Clinton presidency to investigate possible improprieties in an Arkansas business deal involving the Clintons, that had come to be known as the Whitewater investigation. By November 1996, having spent three years and roughly $30 million and failing to generate credible evidence of wrongdoing by the Clintons, Starr's investigators began questioning women who may have had sexual encounters with Clinton (Isikoff and Fineman 1997). With the Supreme Court ruling that the Jones lawsuit could proceed, Jones's lawyers also began a search for women who could testify that they had been approached by the President while working for him. Members of the American press followed leads along the same lines. By early 1997, these separate lines of inquiry led all three groups to Linda Tripp, Monica Lewinsky, and Kathleen Willey.

Kathleen Willey, a former volunteer in the White House social office, was initially called to testify in the Jones case. She made charges that Clinton had kissed and fondled her in the White House Oval Office in 1993, when she met with him there seeking a full-time job. Upon leaving Clinton's office, Willey saw Linda Tripp in the hallway. According to Tripp's affidavit, Willey had left that meeting looking disheveled and told her that the President had made sexual overtures toward her. Clinton's attorney, Robert Bennett, called the charges a lie and attacked Tripp (Fineman and Breslau 1998; Isikoff and Thomas 1998). Tripp claimed that Willey had been pleased and "joyful" about the experience. Willey later claimed that she was distraught and upset by the incident. However, a friend of Willey's claimed that Willey had instructed her to lie about being distraught over the incident. According to the friend, Willey had not been upset (Isikoff 1997). The Willey allegations did not become public until a "60 Minutes" television interview in March 1998. Clinton denied the charges.

In January 1998, President Clinton and Monica Lewinsky each signed affidavits in the Paula Jones case that they had never had sexual relations with each other. However, throughout 1997, Lewinsky had told a friend of hers on numerous occasions that she had been having an affair with the President. The friend was Linda Tripp. Believing that she would be called to testify about what Lewinsky had told her and fearing that she would be attacked by Clinton's defense team, Tripp began taping her phone calls with Lewinsky. A week after the Lewinsky affidavit denying any sexual involvement with Clinton, Tripp approached Kenneth Starr's investigators with her story. They proceeded to wire her for subsequent conversations with Monica Lewinsky. Roughly a week later, the story hit the headlines that Clinton may have had an affair with Lewinsky, that he may have perjured himself in the Jones case by denying it, that there was taped evidence of Lewinsky telling a friend about the affair, and that Clinton and his associates may have obstructed justice by urging Lewinsky to lie under oath (Fineman and Breslau 1998; Isikoff and Thomas 1998). There seemed to be little else in the news besides this ongoing saga.

As we go to press, it is not yet clear how these allegations will turn out. On April 1, 1998, the suit by Paula Jones was thrown out of court. The federal judge in the case ruled that Clinton had not committed a crime of either sexual assault or sexual harassment, even if Jones's claims were factual. Two thirds of American adults had indicated months earlier that they did not believe the Jones incident constituted sexual harassment (Isikoff and Thomas 1997).

In an ironic twist, President Clinton's approval ratings increased to their highest levels ever in the months since the Lewinsky story became national news. There has been considerable speculation in the press about what this means. It seems clear that the majority of the American public does not want to see Clinton removed from office for the charges that have surfaced thus far. Many interpret the polls as indicating that most Americans believe that a person's sex life—even the President's—is a private matter and should not be subjected to public investigation unless it is specifically criminal itself. The message from the American public seems to be, "Stay out of our bedrooms."

Another ironic consequence of these collected stories is that, at least for the time being, discourse about sexuality has never been freer or more open. Americans in general and the American media now routinely discuss the President's sex life, extramarital sex, oral sex, and the like. As a culture, we seem to be talking about sex more than ever.

- In late 1993, *Private Parts* by radio disc-jockey Howard Stern (1993), the inventor of "Shock Rock" radio, was published. Stern's radio shows had had a large audience across the U.S.A. for more than a decade. He had been strongly condemned by some for the sexual explicitness of his shows and criticized by others for the sexist nature of those same shows. On several occasions, his shows had been investigated by the Federal Communications Commission. *Private Parts*, a lurid account of Stern's shows and his sexual fantasies, was roundly criticized. However, it also became the best-selling book in the U.S.A. in 1993 (Adler 1994). By 1998, Stern had a nationally syndicated television show, in addition to his nationally syndicated radio show. *Private Parts* was released as a movie in 1997 to critical acclaim and huge audiences. A compact disc of the soundtrack to the movie was also a national hit in 1997.
- Dr. Joycelyn Elders was fired in late 1994 as the Surgeon General of the United States for saying that children perhaps should be taught in school about masturbation. Elders, who was called the "Condom Queen" by conservatives in the United States, had become what the press described as a "political liability" to President Bill Clinton for expressing her views on controversial social issues, such as abortion, condom education for youth, and drug legalization (Cohn 1994). However, her firing was a direct reaction to comments she made about including masturbation as a part of sex-education programs for children. Elders made her comments on December 1, 1994, in an address to a World AIDS Day conference in New York City. In response to a question from the audience about her views on masturbation, Elders said, "I think that is something that is a part of human sexuality, and it's a part of something that perhaps should be taught. But we've not even taught our children the very basics." She added, "I feel that we have tried ignorance for a very long time, and it's time we try education" (Hunt 1994). In announcing her dismissal, the Clinton administration pointedly indicated that the President disagreed with her views.
- By the middle of the 1990s, seven physicians and clinical staff members had been killed by anti-abortion activists. Over 80 percent of abortion providers in the U.S.A. have been picketed, and many have experienced other forms of harassment, including bomb and death threats, blockades, invasion of facilities, destruction of property, and assaults on patients and staff. The most recent tactic adopted by abortion opponents is to locate women who have had a bad experience with an abortion in order to persuade them to file a malpractice suit against the physician who performed the abortion.
- The term "sexual harassment" did not appear in American culture until around 1975. In the years since, there has been a tremendous growth in research on the problem and growing social conflict over its prevalence and definition. As late as 1991, when Anita Hill testified against Supreme Court nominee Clarence Thomas, only 29 percent

of Americans believed her claims (Solomon and Miller 1994). Yet the number of women filing claims doubled in the 1990s, and the U.S. Supreme Court ruled in 1993 that harassment could be determined if a worker demonstrated that the workplace environment was "hostile" or "abusive" to a "reasonable person" (Kaplan 1993). Workers would no longer have to demonstrate that severe psychological injury had occurred as a consequence. Similar controversies over definitions, prevalence, and credibility of claims have emerged with the issues of incest, child sexual abuse, and date or acquaintance rape.

- In June 1997, the Southern Baptist Convention, the nation's second largest religious denomination, called for a boycott of Walt Disney Company stores and theme parks to protest its "anti-Christian and anti-family trend" in extending health benefits to the same-sex partners of employees. The Baptists declared that such policies constituted an overly permissive stance toward homosexuality (Morganthau 1997). Gay activists were outraged by the decision, regarding it as mean-spirited.
- In April 1997, Ellen DeGeneres, star of the sitcom "Ellen," publicly announced that she was gay. On April 30 of the same year, her television character also came out of the closet, making Ellen the first leading lesbian in an American sitcom (Marin and Miller 1997). By early 1998, the ABC network canceled the show because of sagging ratings, a problem that had begun before the television "coming out."
- Some years ago, the Iowa state legislature passed a bill outlawing nude dancing in establishments that serve alcohol. The activity moved to "juice bars." In 1997, the legislature decided to make nude dancing illegal in any establishment holding a sales-tax permit, except businesses devoted primarily to the arts. As a result, the Southern Comfort Free Theater for the Performing Arts opened in Mount Joy, Iowa. Patrons are asked for "donations" and are described as "students." In a similar story in Orlando, Florida, a ban on nude dancing has been circumvented by the establishment of "gentlemen's clubs," where patrons pay membership dues (*Newsweek* 1997).
- After decades of explicitly banning homosexuals from the military, President Clinton proposed ending the ban shortly after he assumed office in 1992. The policy put into place, popularly known as "Don't ask, don't tell," was one in which the military agreed that they would stop asking recruits to report their sexual orientation. However, gays and lesbians can only serve in the armed forces if they keep their orientation private (*Newsweek* 1993, 6). By mid-1998 the Servicemembers Legal Defense Network reported violations of the policy not to ask, pursue, or harass homosexuals had soared from 443 violations in 1996 to 563 violations in 1997. Reported cases of physical and verbal harassment of gay servicemembers rose 38 percent from 1996 to 1997, while cases of illegal asking by military authorities increased by 39 percent. In 1996, an airman at Hickham Air Force Base had his life

sentence for forcible sodomy reduced to 20 months in return for outing 17 other allegedly gay servicemen. All the accused airmen were discharged, while the rapist served less than a year.

• There is a growing wave of censorship being engineered by grassroots far-right organizations targeting in particular sexuality education textbooks and programs in local school districts throughout the country. Fear of personal attacks, disruption, controversy, and costly lawsuits have resulted in more teachers, administrators, and school boards yielding to the demands of vocal minority groups. In more than a third of documented incidents, challenged materials and programs were either removed, canceled, or replaced with abstinence-only material or curricula (Sedway 1992). In 1996, the U.S. Congress overwhelmingly passed the Communications Decency Act (CDA), a bill intended to regulate "indecent" and "patently offensive" speech on the Internet, which included information on abortion. In mid-1996, a three-judge federal panel in Philadelphia declared unconstitutional major parts of the new law. Even as the judges described attempts to regulate content on the Internet as a "profoundly repugnant" affront to the First Amendment's guarantee of free speech, the government planned an appeal to the U.S. Supreme Court. Both the Senate and House of Representatives had overwhelmingly passed the CDA, and the President signed into law the bill that included it (Levy, 1997). The law was finally ruled unconstitutional by the Supreme Court on June 27, 1997, although various government efforts continue to try to circumvent the decision (Noonan 1998).

• In the mid-1990s, a broad-based evangelical-revivalist movement, modeled in part on the Million Man March, which brought hundreds of thousands of African-American men to Washington, packed athletic stadiums across the country with men confessing their failures as husbands and fathers, and promising with great emotion to fulfill their Christian duties as men, husbands, fathers, and the heads of their families. The Promise Keepers, like the Million Men Marches, were criticized and denounced by feminists and others for their alleged devotion to traditional patriarchal and sexist values.

Each of the above events serves as an intriguing indicator of the state of sexuality in the United States, and each also reveals much about the interaction of politics and sexual issues as we approach the end of the twentieth century. They demonstrate that, despite the immense social changes that have occurred during the twentieth century, a strong element of religious fundamentalism and conservatism remains active within the culture. In fact, a full explanation of sexuality in the United States requires an understanding of the diverse sexual, social, and political ideologies characterizing the culture and the ongoing conflict between various groups over those ideologies.

In this respect, there is a rather schizophrenic character to sexuality in the United States. On the one hand, the U.S.A. is a country with a multibillion-dollar-a-year erotica/pornography business; a mass-media system where movies, television, books, magazines, and popular music are saturated with sexually titillating content alongside serious educational material; a high rate of premarital sex (nearly 90 percent by the 1990s); one of the most active and open gay-rights movements in the world; and a continuing public fascination with unusual sexual practices, extramarital sex, and gender-orientation issues, including, most recently, bisexuality.

On the other hand, federal, state, and local governments have invested heavily in recent years in prosecuting businesses for obscenity, allowed discriminatory practices based on sexual orientation, largely failed to implement comprehensive sexuality-education programs in the schools, and refused to support accessibility to contraceptives for adolescents. The consequences of these failures include one of the highest teenage-pregnancy and abortion rates in the world and increasing incidents of gay-bashing that reflect the prevalence of homonegative and homophobic attitudes in the U.S.A.

These examples illustrate one of the major themes in this chapter: the changing nature of sexuality in the U.S.A. throughout the twentieth century. Although accounts of changing sexual norms and practices are frequently portrayed as occurring in a linear process, we would suggest that the more-typical pattern is one reflected by ongoing conflicts between competing groups over sexual ideology and practice. Each of the examples cited is an illustration of how those conflicts are currently manifested in the social and political arenas in the U.S.A.

A focus on the conflict between groups with contrasting ideologies and agendas over sexual issues will be a second theme of this chapter. This process of changing sexual attitudes, practices, and policies in an atmosphere that approaches "civil war" is a reflection of the tremendous diversity within American culture. In many respects, the widespread conflict over sexual issues is a direct outcome of the diversity of groups holding a vested interest in the outcomes of these conflicts, with some groups seeking to impose their beliefs on everyone.

The diversity of these groups will be the third major theme of the chapter. One example that will be apparent throughout this chapter is the question of gender. There is growing evidence that men and women in the U.S.A. tend to hold different sexual attitudes and ideologies, to exhibit different patterns of sexual behavior, and to pursue different sexual lifestyles—frequently at odds with each other (Oliver and Hyde 1993). In some ways, it may even be useful to view male and female perspectives as stemming from distinct gender cultures. In reviewing sexuality in the U.S.A., we will frequently attempt to assess how change occurs in a context of conflict between diverse social groups.

1. Basic Sexological Premises

DAVID L. WEIS

This overall theme of social change occurring in a process of conflict between diverse groups is woven throughout the history of the U.S.A. itself. There are at least two ways in which a study of history is important to an understanding of contemporary sexological premises and sexual patterns in the U.S.A. First, there is a specific history of sexual norms and customs changing over time. To the extent that sexual attitudes and practices are shared by the members of a social group or population in a particular time period, they can be viewed as social institutions. Unfortunately, it is exceedingly difficult to describe such sexual institutions in the U.S.A. prior to the twentieth century, because there are few reliable empirical data sets available for that period. To a large extent, we have to rely on records of what people said about their own or others' sexual attitudes and practices, and such statements may be suspect. Still, it seems reasonable to suggest that current sexual norms and customs have been shaped, at least in part, by earlier patterns.

In addition, there is a second way in which the general social history of the U.S.A. is important to understanding changing sexual institutions. Sexuality, like other social institutions, does not operate in a vacuum. It is related to and influenced by other social institutions, such as the economy, government, marriage and the family, religion, and education, as well as social patterns such as age distributions and gender ratios. As we will discuss in Section 2, a good deal of research evidence indicates that such social institutions are often related to various sexual variables. Researchers have not consistently tested these associations, but the point is a crucial one theoretically for explaining the dynamics of sexual processes in a culture as large and diverse as the U.S.A.

A. From Colonial Times to the Industrial Revolution

In 1776, at the time of the War for American Independence, the U.S.A. became a nation of thirteen states located along the shore of the Atlantic Ocean. Most of the inhabitants of the former British colonies were of English descent, and they tended to be Protestant. Although the first Africans had been brought to America as indentured servants as early as 1620, the practice of slavery quickly evolved. By the time of independence, an active slave trade involving hundreds of thousands of Africans and Caribbeans was well established. Of course, the Africans and Caribbeans brought their own customs with them, although they were frequently prevented from practicing them. West of the thirteen original states, the remainder of the North American continent within the area now constituting the nation was inhabited by several million Native Americans representing hundreds of tribes, each with its own set of customs.

At its birth, the U.S.A. was essentially an agrarian society. More than 90 percent of the population were farmers. There were few cities with as many as 5,000 residents. Boston was the largest city with 16,000, and New York was the second largest with 13,000 (Reiss 1980). The Industrial Revolution had yet to begin. Few men, and virtually no women, were employed outside the family home. Although it has become common to think of the twentieth-century pattern of role specialization, with the man serving as the family provider and the woman as the housekeeper and child-care provider, as the traditional American pattern, it did not characterize this early-American agrarian family. Family tasks tended to be performed out of necessity, with both men and women making direct and important contributions to the economic welfare of their families. Sexual norms and practices in early America arose in this social context.

The images of early-American sexuality in folklore are those of antihedonistic Puritanism and sexually repressed Victorianism. In popular culture, these terms have come to be associated with sexual prudishness. This view is oversimplistic and potentially misleading. Recent scholars (D'Emilio and Freedman 1988; Robinson 1976; Seidman 1991) tend to agree that sexuality was valued by the eighteenth-century Puritans and nineteenth-century Victorians within the context of marriage. To the Puritans, marriage was viewed as a spiritual union, and one that tended to emphasize the duties associated with commitment to that union. Marriage involved mutual affection and respect, and the couple was viewed as a primary social unit. Spouses were expected to fulfill reciprocal duties. One of these was sexual expression. No marriage was considered complete unless it was consummated sexually. The Puritans accepted erotic pleasure, as long as it promoted the mutual comfort and affection of the conjugal pair. The reciprocal duties of marital sexuality were justified, because they were seen as preventing individuals from becoming preoccupied with carnal desires and the temptation to practice improper sex outside of marriage (Seidman 1991). Of course, one of the principal functions of marital sex was reproduction. Pleasure alone did not justify sexual union. Instead, the regulation of sexual behavior reinforced the primacy of marital reproductive sex and the need for children (D'Emilio and Freedman 1988).

Within this context, it is certainly true that the early English settlers tried to regulate nonmarital forms of sexual expression. However, even this point can be exaggerated. Reiss (1980) has noted that Americans have always had a courtship system where individuals were free to select partners of their own choice. To some extent, this may have been due to necessities imposed by immigration to frontier territories, but it also was a consequence of the freedom settlers had from the institutions of social control found in Europe. Elsewhere, Reiss (1960; 1967) has maintained that such autonomy in courtship is associated with greater premarital sexual permissiveness.

In this regard, it is interesting to note that the settlers in New England developed the practice of bundling as a form of courtship. In colonial New

England, settlers faced harsh winters. They commonly faced fuel shortages, and mechanized transportation forms had yet to be developed. Single men would travel miles to visit the home of an eligible female. Typically, they would spend the night before returning home the next day. Few New England homes of the period had multiple rooms for housing a guest, and few could heat the house for an entire twenty-four-hour day. At night, the woman's family would bundle the man and the woman separately in blankets, and they would spend the night together talking to each other as they shared the same bed. It is worth noting that the practice of bundling was restricted to winters. Reiss (1980) has argued that the implicit understanding that the couple would avoid a sexual encounter was not always honored. In fact, a study of marriages in Groton, Massachusetts, from 1761 to 1775 found that one third of the women were pregnant at the time of their weddings (cited in Reiss 1980). This system was acceptable because betrothals were rarely broken at the time and because it served to produce the marital unions the Puritans valued so highly. Eventually, bundling was replaced by visits in the sitting parlors of nineteenth-century homes and by the practice of dating outside parental supervision in the twentieth century (Reiss 1980).

Around 1800, the Industrial Revolution began changing this world, albeit gradually. In the two centuries since, virtually every aspect of American life has been transformed. The nineteenth century was marked by social turmoil, a frontier mentality open to radical change, and a resulting patchquilt of conflicting trends and values. Among the events that left their mark on American culture in the nineteenth century were the following:

- The century started with 16 states and ended with 45 states; the 1803 Louisiana Purchase doubled the country's size. Victory in the War of 1812 with England and a war with Mexico also added territory.
- A Victorian ethic dominated the country. Preachers and health advocates, like Sylvester Graham and John Kellogg, promoted a fear of sexual excesses, such as sex before age 30 or more than once in three years, and a paranoia about the dangers of masturbation.
- Despite a dominant conservative trend and three major economic depressions, small religious groups pioneered a variety of marital and communal lifestyles, and had an influence far beyond their tiny numbers. The Perfectionist Methodists of the Oneida Community (1831-1881) endorsed women's rights and group marriage; the Church of Latter-Day Saints (Mormons) practiced polygyny; Protestant Hutterites celebrated the communal life; and the Shakers and Harmony Community promoted a celibate lifestyle.
- In 1837, the first colleges for women opened.
- In 1848, the first women's rights convention was held in Seneca Falls, New York.
- A midcentury California gold rush and completion of the transcontinental railroad opened the west to an explosive growth. San Francisco,

for example, doubled its population from 400 to 810 between 1847 and 1857; four years later, its population was 25,000. A major shortage of women led to importing thousands of women from Mexico, Chile, China, and the Pacific islands, with widespread prostitution.

- In 1861-1865, a devastating Civil War led to the abolition of slavery, as well as to new opportunities for employment, such as secretaries using the new mass-produced typewriters, and nurses using the skills they developed when they took care of the wounded in the Civil War.
- In 1869, the Territory of Wyoming gave women the vote.
- In 1873, the Comstock Law prohibited mailing obscene literature, including information about marital sex and contraception; it was finally declared unconstitutional a century later.
- In the latter part of the 1800s, a few thousand Americans were part of an influential "free love" movement, which advocated sexual freedom for women, the separation of sex and reproduction, the intellectual equality of women and men, self-health and knowledge of one's own body and its functions, and women's right to the vote, to enjoy sex, and to obtain a divorce.

Pankhurst and Houseknecht (1983) have identified five major trends that they maintain began to change and shape the modern institutions of marriage and the family in the nineteenth century and have continued to impact American culture in the twentieth century. The author of this section suggests that they have had a similar influence on sexual institutions. These trends are:

1. Industrialization, with its consequent process of urbanization and the eventual emergence of suburbs surrounding metropolitan areas;
2. A shift in the family from an economic-producing unit to that of a consumer;
3. The entry of men, and later of women, into the paid labor force;
4. The elongation and expansion of formal education, especially among women and minorities; and
5. Technological change.

We do not have the space to explore fully the impact of each of these trends. However, relevant effects would include increased life spans, decreased maternal and infant mortality at childbirth, the development of effective contraceptives, the emergence of a consumer culture that allows families to purchase most of their goods and services, the creation of labor-saving household technologies, increased leisure time, the development of modern forms of transportation, especially automobiles and airplanes, an increasing divorce rate, the increasing entry of wives and mothers into the labor force, decreasing birthrate and family size, increasing rates of single-parent families and cohabitation, increasing

;es of adults living alone, and increasing proportions of married
;ith no children currently living at home (Coontz 1992). Many
hanges have resulted in greater personal autonomy for individuals. As Reiss (1960; 1967) has argued, such autonomy may be a major
factor underlying several changes in sexuality throughout American
history.

It should be stressed that these changes have not necessarily been linear
or consistent throughout the period of the Industrial Revolution. Many
began to emerge in the nineteenth century, but accelerated and became
mainstream patterns only in the twentieth century. For example, as late as
1900, a majority of Americans were still farmers. The 1920 census was the
first to show a majority of the population living in towns and cities. By 1980,
only 4 percent of Americans still lived on farms (Reiss 1980). Similarly,
women began entering the labor force in the early nineteenth century.
However, it was not until 1975 that one half of married women were
employed. By 1990, 70 percent of married women between the ages of 25
and 44 were employed (Coontz 1992). Yet another example is provided by
the divorce rate. It had been gradually increasing for decades. That rate
doubled between 1965 and 1975, and for the first time, couples with
children began divorcing in sizable numbers at that time (Coontz 1992;
Reiss 1980; Seidman 1991).

Seidman (1991) has described the principal change in American sexuality during the nineteenth century as the "sexualization of love." It could
also be described as a shift to companionate marriage. Marriage came to
be defined less as an institutional arrangement of reciprocal duties, and
more as a personal relationship between the spouses. The modern concept
of love as a form of companionship, intimacy, and sharing came to be seen
as the primary justification for marriage. As this process continued, the
erotic longings between the partners, and the sexual pleasures shared by
them, became inseparable from the qualities that defined love and marriage. By the early part of the twentieth century, the desires and pleasures
associated with sex came to be seen as a chief motivation and sustaining
force in love and marriage (Seidman 1991). This view has come to be so
dominant in the contemporary U.S.A. that few Americans today can envi-
sion any other basis for marriage.

D'Emilio and Freedman (1988) have argued that what they call the
liberal sexual ethic described in the previous paragraph has been the
attempt to promote this view of the erotic as the peak experience of
marriage while limiting its expression elsewhere. However, as this view
became the dominant American sexual ideology of the twentieth century,
it also served to legitimate the erotic aspects of sexuality itself (Seidman
1991). Eventually, groups emerged which have sought to value sex for its
inherent pleasure and expressive qualities, as well as for its value as a form
of self-expression. In effect, as the view that sexual gratification was a critical
part of happiness for married persons became the dominant sexual ideol-

ogy of twentieth-century America, then it was only a matter of time until some groups began to question how it could be restricted only to married persons (D'Emilio and Freedman 1988).

B. The Twentieth Century

The social turmoil and the pace of social change that marked the nineteenth century has accelerated exponentially in the present century. American culture in the twentieth century has been increasingly complicated and changed by often-unanticipated developments in technology, communications, and medicine. Among the events that have been identified as significant in twentieth-century United States are the following:

- In the early 1900s, Sigmund Freud and Havelock Ellis helped trigger the emergence of a more-positive approach to sexuality, especially in recognizing the normal sexuality of women and children, and the need for sex education.
- In 1916, spurred by Havelock Ellis, Margaret Sanger, a New York nurse, launched a crusade to educate poor and immigrant women about contraception, and established the first Planned Parenthood clinics.
- World War I brought women out of their Victorian homes into the war effort and work in the factories; shorter skirts and hair styles were viewed as patriotic fashion and gave women more freedom. American soldiers encountered the more-relaxed sexual mores of France and Europe.
- The "Roarin' Twenties" were marked by the invention of cellulose sanitary napkins, the mobility of Henry Ford's affordable automobiles, new leisure and affluence, the advent of movies with female vamp stars and irresistible sex idols, and the appearance of the "Charleston," the "flapper," and cheek-to-cheek, body-clutching dancing.
- From 1929 to 1941, the Great Depression brought a return to sexual conservativism.
- World War II opened new opportunities for women, both at home and in the military support. Interracial marriages set the stage for revoking miscegenation laws later in 1967.
- In the 1940s, the advent of antibiotics brought cures for some sexually transmitted diseases.
- In 1948 and 1953, Alfred Kinsey and colleagues published *Sexual Behavior in the Human Male* and *Sexual Behavior in the Human Female*. They brought sexual topics into widespread public discussion.
- In the 1950s, Elvis Presley became the first major rock 'n' roll star; television became a major influence on young Americans. Senator Joseph McCarthy portrayed sex education as part of a Communist plot to take over the U.S. Coed dormitories appeared on college campuses and bikini swimsuits swept the nation. Motels became popular, provid-

ing comfort for vacationing Americans, as well as for Americans seeking privacy for sexual relations.

- In 1953, the first issue of *Playboy* magazine was published.
- In 1957, the Supreme Court decision in *Roth v. U.S.* set new criteria for obscenity that opened the door to the works of D. H. Lawrence and Henry Miller, and other classic erotic works.
- In the 1950s and 1960s, the beatniks, hippies, flower children, and drug culture emerged.
- In the early 1960s, the hormonal contraceptive pill became available.
- In 1961, Illinois adopted the first "consenting adult" law decriminalizing sexual behavior between consenting adults.
- In 1963, Betty Friedan's *Feminine Mystique* was published, giving voice to the modern feminist movement.
- In 1968, William Masters and Virginia Johnson published *Human Sexual Response.*
- Following the 1969 Stonewall Inn Riot in Greenwich Village, New York City, homosexuals rebelled against police harassment, and launched the gay-rights and gay-pride movement.
- In the 1970s, television talk shows popularized discussions of alternative lifestyles, triggered by the publication of Nena and George O'Neill's *Open Marriage* in 1972.
- In 1970, the White House Commission on Pornography and Obscenity found no real harm in sexually explicit material. President Richard Nixon refused to issue the report.
- In 1972, the first openly gay male was ordained to the ministry of a major Christian church.
- In 1973, the U.S. Supreme Court legalized abortion.
- In the 1980s, openly gay legislators appeared in federal and state governments, and in professional sports.
- In 1983, AIDS was recognized, leading to a new advocacy for sex education in the schools and general public.
- In the late 1980s, conservative Christian activists, including the Moral Majority, the Christian Coalition, Focus on the Family, and similar organizations, emerged as politically and socially powerful groups.

These and other events too numerous to list, let alone analyze here, both contributed to and reflect the tension between the two ideologies mentioned above—one viewing sex as legitimate only in marriage, but as a necessary component of marital happiness, and the other viewing sex as a valid and important experience in its own right. The attempt to reconcile them can be seen as an underlying dynamic for many sexual practices and changes in the twentieth century. These broad-based trends include:

1. The emergence in the 1920s of dating and in the 1940s of "going steady" as courtship forms (Reiss 1980);

2. The rising percentage of young people having premarital sexual experiences (D'Emilio and Freedman 1988; Kinsey, et al., 1948; 1953; Reiss 1980; Seidman 1991);

3. The greater equality between the genders (D'Emilio and Freedman 1988; Reiss 1980; Seidman 1991);

4. The eroticization of the female, including a decline in the double standard and an increased focus on female sexual satisfaction (D'Emilio and Freedman 1988; Seidman 1991);

5. The emergence of professions devoted to sexuality—research, education, and therapy;

6. The expansion of marital sexuality, including increases in frequency, satisfaction, and variation in behavior (Hunt 1974);

7. The emergence of a homosexual identity and subculture, including a gay-rights movement (D'Emilio and Freedman 1988; Seidman 1991);

8. The passage of consenting adult laws;

9. The commercialization of sex, by which we mean the appearance of an "industry" providing sexual goods and services (D'Emilio and Freedman 1988; Seidman 1991).

Reactions to these trends, and the continuing tension between the two major ideologies we have outlined above, lie at the very heart of the ongoing conflicts over sexual issues today. Robinson (1976) has characterized this conflict as a battle between nineteenth-century romanticism and what he calls sexual modernism. Romanticism affirmed the essential worth of the erotic, but only within the context of an intense interpersonal relationship transformed by a spiritual and physical union. Modernism reaffirms this romantic ideal, but also transforms it by acknowledging the value of "an innocent physical need" (p. 194). Although the modernist is glad to be rid of Victorian repression and anticipates the promise of a greater sexual freedom, there is a concomitant fear of a future of emotional emptiness.

Reiss (1981) has characterized this as a conflict between what he calls the traditional-romantic and modern-naturalistic ideologies. He maintains that this distinction can be used to explain current conflicts over such issues as abortion, gender roles and differences, pornography, definitions of sexual exploitation, concepts of sexual normality, and even accounts of sexual history itself. This perspective is useful in interpreting mass-media claims about sexuality in the U.S.A. Thus, Lyons (1983), reporting for *The New York Times*, proclaimed that the "sexual revolution" was over by the 1980s and that America was experiencing a return to traditional values and lifestyles. To support his argument, he claimed that there was a recent decrease in the number of sex partners and a shift away from indiscriminate, casual sexual behavior (Lyons 1983). In contrast, Walsh (1993), writing for *Utne Reader*, proclaimed that the 1990s have been characterized by a renewed sexual revolution (second-wavers), with pioneering new philosophies and techniques employing technology (latex, computer imaging, computer networks, virtual reality sex, phone sex, cathode rays, and group safe sex) to achieve sensual pleasure in a safe way.

From 1970 to 1990, as these social processes continued, Americans witnessed: (1) a decrease in the marriage rate; (2) an increase in the divorce rate; (3) an increase in the birthrate for unmarried mothers (although the overall adolescent birthrate decreased); (4) an increase in single-parent families; and (5) an increase in married couples without children at home (Ahlburg and DeVita 1992). In the next section, we consider the impact of religious, ethnic, and gender factors on such changes.

2. Religious, Ethnic, and Gender Factors Affecting Sexuality

Social scientists have demonstrated an association between human behavior and such social factors as religion, race, gender, social class, and education. This is as true of sexuality as of other forms of behavior. Although sexuality researchers have not always incorporated a recognition of this principle in their designs and analyses, there is still abundant evidence that sexual practices in the U.S.A. are strongly related to social factors. In this section, we examine several examples. First, we review the general influence of the Judeo-Christian heritage in the U.S.A. and describe the sexual culture of a particular religious group within this tradition, the Church of Jesus Christ of Latter-Day Saints (Mormons). Then we review the sexual customs of two of the largest minority groups in the U.S.A., African-Americans and Hispanic-Americans. Finally, we review the emergence of feminist ideology in the U.S.A., a view constructed around the concept of gender. These reviews are by no means exhaustive or complete, but should serve to illustrate both the diversity of social groups within the U.S.A. and the influence that membership in such groups exerts on sexual customs and practices.

A. Sources and Character of Religious Values

General Character and Ramifications of American   ROBERT T. FRANCOEUR
Religious Perspectives on Sexuality   AND TIMOTHY PERPER

Sexual science in America is a mid- to late-twentieth-century discipline. By contrast, Western religious thought about love, sexuality, marriage, the social and familial roles of men and women, and the emotions and behavioral patterns associated with courtship, pair bonding, conception, and birth have textual bases in the Jewish *Pentatuch* and other biblical writings. In pre-Christian Hellenic thought, the first great document of sexology is Plato's *Symposium* (ca. 400 B.C.E.). Because Judaic and Hellenic thought have strongly influenced the sexual views of Christianity and all of Western culture, one must acknowledge that the theological, religious, and secular writings that permeate American conceptions of sexuality are embedded in this 3,500-year-old matrix that gives sexuality its place in life (and unique meanings). This section will explore the sources and character of religious values in the U.S.A. and their impact on sexual attitudes, behaviors, and policies.

Religious Groups in the U.S.A. Statistically, Americans are 61 percent Protestant—21 percent Baptist, 12 percent Methodist, 8 percent Lutheran, 4 percent Presbyterian, 3 percent Episcopalian, and 13 percent other Protestant groups, including the Church of Latter-Day Saints (see Section 2 below for a more in-depth discussion of the sexual doctrines and practices of this religious group), Seventh-Day Adventists, Jehovah's Witnesses, Christian Scientists, and others. Roman and Eastern-rite Catholics account for 25 percent of Americans, Jews 2 percent, 5 percent other religious groups, and 7 percent are not affiliated with any church. Therefore, the two largest denominations in the U.S.A. are the Roman Catholic Church with a membership of over 50 million and Southern Baptist Conventions with between 10 and 15 million members (Greeley 1992). There are also 2.5 million Muslims in the U.S.A.

Because Americans tend to cluster geographically according to both their religious and ethnic heritages, local communities can be much more strongly affected by a small but highly concentrated religious or ethnic tradition than the above percentages might suggest at first sight. With recent public debate focusing on sexual morality (e.g., contraception, abortion, and homosexuality), a paradoxical realignment has occurred, with liberal Roman Catholics, mainstream Protestant churches, and liberal and reformed Jews lining up on one side of these issues, and conservative (Vatican) Roman Catholics, fundamentalist Protestants, including the televangelists and Southern Baptists, Orthodox Jews, and fundamentalist Muslims on the other side.

A Basic Conflict Between Two Worldviews. American religious institutions on the national level, their local religious communities, and individual members are caught in a pervasive tension between the security of traditional unchanging values and the imperative need to adapt perennial religious and moral values to a radically new and rapidly changing environment. This tension permeates every religious group in the United States today, threatening schism and religious "civil war" (Francoeur 1994).

At one end of the spectrum are fundamentalist, evangelical, charismatic factions that accept as word-for-word truth the writings of the Bible as the word of God and advocate the establishment of the United States as a Christian nation. For them, living under God's rule would be evidenced by the man firmly established as the head of each family in the U.S.A. and the woman in her God-given role as submissive wife and bearer of children for the Kingdom of Heaven. Similar fundamentalist strains in the United States are apparent among ultra-orthodox Jews and radical Muslims (LeHaye and LeHaye 1976; Marty and Appleby 1992, 1993, 1994; Penner and Penner 1981; Wheat and Wheat 1981). These embody an absolutist/natural law/fixed worldview.

On the conservative side, books about sexuality written by married couples dominate the market and sell millions of copies without ever being noticed by the mainstream publishing industry. *Intended for Pleasure* (Wheat and Wheat 1981) and *The Gift of Sex* (Penner and Penner 1981)—the latter couple having been trained by Masters and Johnson—provide detailed information on birth control and express deep appreciation of sex as a gift to be enjoyed in marriage. Tim and Beverly LeHaye's *The Act of Marriage* celebrates marital sexual pleasure, but disapproves of homosexuality and some sexual fantasy. All books in this category stress mutual pleasuring and the importance of female enjoyment of marital sex.

At the other end of the spectrum are various mainstream Protestants, Catholics, Jews, and Muslims who accept a processual/evolutionary world-view (Fox 1983, 1988; Curran and McCormick 1993; Heyward 1989; Kosnick et al. 1977; Nelson 1978, 1983, 1992; Nelson and Longfellow 1994; Ranke-Heinemann 1990; Spong 1988; Thayer 1987; Timmerman 1986) rather than the fixed fundamentalist worldview. In this processual worldview, the sacred divinely revealed texts are respected as

> the record of the response to the word of God addressed to the Church throughout centuries of changing social, historical, and cultural traditions. The Faithful responded with the realities of their particular situation, guided by the direction of previous revelation, but not captive to it. (Thayer et al. 1987)

The most creative and substantive analysis of the evolution and variations in biblical sexual ethics over time is William Countryman's *Dirt, Greed, and Sex: Sexual Ethics in the New Testament and Their Implications for Today*. (For a full annotated list of sexuality texts, see Cornog and Perper 1995.)

The tension between the values and morals derived from fixed world-views and those derived from processual worldviews is evident in official church debates about sexual morality and is also experienced by church members as they struggle to find their way through the confusion resulting from these two views. But it also affects the lives of secular Americans with no connection with a church, mosque, or synagogue, because the religious debate over sexual values permeates all levels of American society, and no one can escape the impact of this debate and conflict on politics, legislation, and social policies. Table 1 is an attempt to describe in a nondefinitive way the two divergent sets of values derived from the processual and fixed worldviews. Table 2 lists some religious traditions in both the fixed and processual worldviews in the major religions around the world.

Table 1

A Cognitive and Normative Continuum of Sexual Values Derived from Two Distinct Worldviews, Fixed and Process, Within the Christian Tradition

	Christian Religions Type A	Christian Religions Type B
Basic vision	*Cosmos*—a finished universe	*Cosmogenesis*—an evolving universe
Typology	The universe, humankind is created perfect and complete in the beginning.	The universe, humankind is incomplete and not yet fully formed.
	Theological understanding of humans emphasizes Adam.	Theological emphasis has shifted to Christ (The Adam) at the end of time.
Origin of evil	Evil results from primeval 'fall' of a perfect couple who introduce moral and physical evil into a paradisical world.	Evil is a natural part of a finite creation, growth, and the birth pains involved in our groping as imperfect humans struggling for the fullness of creation.
Solution to the problem of evil	Redemption by identification with the crucified Savior. Asceticism, mortification.	Identification with the Adam, the resurrected but still fully human transfigured Christ. Re-creation, growth.
Authority system	Patriarchal and sexist. Male-dominated and ruled. Autocratic hierarchy controls power and all decisions; clergy vs. laity.	Egalitarian—'In his kingdom there is neither male nor female, freeman or slave, Jew or Roman.'
Concept of truth	Emphasis on one true Church as sole possessor of all truth.	Recognition that other churches and religions possess different perspectives of truth, with some elements of revelation clearer in them than in the "one true Church."
Biblical orientation	Fundamentalist, evangelical, word-for-word, black-and-white clarity. Revelation has ended.	Emphasizes continuing revelation and reincarnation of perennial truths and values as humans participate in the creation process.
Liturgical focus	Redemption and Good Friday, Purgatory, Supernatural.	Easter and the creation challenge of incarnation. Epiphany of numinous cosmos.
Social structure	Gender roles clearly assigned with high definition of proper roles for men and women.	There being neither male nor female in Christ, gender roles are flexible, including women priests and ministers.
Goal	Supernatural transcendence of nature.	Unveiling, Revelation of divine in all.

continued

Table 1 continued

	Christian Religions Type A	Christian Religions Type B
Ecological morality	Humans are stewards of the earth, given dominion by God over all creation.	Emphasis on personal responsibility in a continuing creation/incarnation.
Self-image	Carefully limited; isolationist, exclusive, Isaias's 'remnant.' Sects.	Inclusive, ecumenical, catalytic leader among equals.
Human morality	Emphasis on laws and conformity of actions to these laws.	Emphasis on persons and their interrelationships. We create the human of the future and the future of humanity.
Sexual morality	The 'monster in the groins' that must be restrained.	A positive, natural, creative energy in our being as sexual (embodied) persons "Knowing" (*yadah*), Communion.
	Justified in marriage for procreation.	An essential element in our personality in all relationships.
	Genital reductionism.	Diffused, degenitalized sensual embodiment.
	Heterosexual/monogamous.	"Polymorphic perversity," "paneroticism."
	Noncoital sex is unnatural, disordered.	Noncoital sex can express the incarnation of Christian love.
	Contraceptive love is unnatural and disordered.	Contraception can be just as creative and life-serving as reproductive love.
	Monolithic—celibate or reproductive marital sexuality.	Pluralistic—sexual persons must learn to incarnate *chesed/agape* with *eros* in all their relationships, primary and secondary, genital and non-genital, intimate, and passionate.
Energy conception	Competitive.	Synergistic.
	Consumerist.	Conservationist.
	Technology-driven and obsessed.	Concerned with appropriate technologies.

Modern America is a ferment of discourse and debate concerning relationships between sexuality and religion. This occurs on the local and personal level among church members, as well as on the administrative level among the church leadership. The vast majority of local church debates are not reported in the popular press. These debates center on the interpretations of revelation, religious truths, and the nature and place of sexuality within a particular absolutist/natural law/fixed worldview or processual/evolutionary worldview. From time to time, denominational leaders and assemblies issue authoritative statements in denominational

Table 2

A Spectrum of Ethical Systems with Typical Adherents in Different Religious Traditions

This table is an attempt to visualize the range of sexual moralities in different religious traditions and relate them in terms of their basic worldviews. There is often more agreement between different Jews, Protestants, and Catholics at one or the other end of the spectrum, than there is between Protestants, or Catholics, or Jews who disagree in their worldviews. Protestants in the covenant tradition, for instance, have more in common with liberal Catholics who disagree with the Vatican's opposition to such practices as contraception, masturbation, premarital sex, abortion, divorce, and homosexuality, than they do with their fellow Protestants who are members of the fundamentalist Christian Coalition, Eagle Forum, or Focus on the Family.

	A Spectrum or Continuum	
Tradition Source	**Fixed Philosophy of Nature**	**Process Philosophy of Nature**
Roman Catholic tradition	Act-oriented natural law/ divine law order ethics expressed in formal Vatican pronouncements	A person-oriented, evolving ethics expressed by many contemporary theologians and the 1977 Catholic Theological Society of America study of human sexuality.
Protestant nominalism	Fundamentalism based on a literal interpretation of the Bible, as endorsed by the Moral Majority and the religious New Right: Seventh-Day Adventists, Jehovah's Witnesses, and Church of Latter-Day Saints	An ethic based on the covenant announced between Jesus and humans—examples in the 1970 United Presbyterian workstudy document on Sexuality and the Human Community, Unitarian/Universalists, and the Society of Friends (Quakers)
Humanism	Stoicism and epicurean asceticism	Situation ethics, e.g., the 1976 American Humanist Association's "A New Bill of Sexual Rights and Responsibilities"
Judaism	Orthodox and Hasidic concern for strict observation of the Torah and Talmudic prescriptions	Liberal and reformed application of moral principles to today's situations
Islam	Orthodox; observance of female seclusion (*purdah*) and wearing of the veil (*chador*); ritual purifications associated with sexual activities	Secular; more or less adoption of Western gender equality; flexible/lax observance of sex-associated purification rituals

continued

Table 2 continued

While Eastern religions may, in some cases, fit in with this dualism of worldviews, the ascetic traditions of the East are positive traditions and lack the negativism towards sexuality that permeates the history of Christian asceticism and celibacy. Eastern asceticism is seen as a positive balance to the Eastern's embrace of sexuality as both a natural pleasure to be greatly enjoyed and a path to the divine union. Also, the relationship with the dichotomous weltanschauungs evident in Western traditions needs to be explored and explicated.

Tradition Source	A Spectrum or Continuum	
	Fixed Philosophy of Nature	Process Philosophy of Nature
Hinduism	Ascetic tradition of monks with world-denying sexual abstinence; Yoga; ritual taboos and purification rites associated with sexual activities	Sacramental view of sex with worship of male lingam and female yoni; the *Kama Sutra*
Buddhism	Ascetic tradition of monks with sexual abstinence	Tantric traditions in which sexual relations are a path to divine union

position or workstudy papers. These formal statements are designed to answer questions of sexual morality and set church policy. However, contradictory majority and minority positions rooted in the opposing fixed and processual worldviews accomplish little beyond stirring heated debate and deferring the problem to further committee study (Francoeur 1987, 1994).

However, there is often a great difference between official church doctrine and worldview and the views and practices of its members. For example, the most erotophilic religion in America may be grassroots Roman Catholicism as expressed and lived by the laity. Many rank-and-file American Catholics express great and amused doubt and scorn for the sexual pronouncements of the Vatican (Greeley 1995). Peter Gardella (1985) has made a strong case for the thesis that Christianity has, in fact, given America an ethic of sexual pleasure.

The Conservative Christian Coalition. Among the major forces in the American religious scene that affect public sexual mores is the conservative Christian Coalition. Among the fundamentalist Christians, one finds an extraordinary heterogeneity. There exists a large and virtually unstudied mixture of Pentecostal, fundamentalist, and evangelical/charismatic churches whose preachers expound on sexuality, marriage, family, and morality. Their opinions are diverse, and poorly known or understood by those outside their domain, especially sexologists. Two examples illustrate this: A religious pamphlet published by the Rose of Sharon Press in Tennessee, the buckle of the so-called Bible Belt in the U.S.A., extols the clitoris as the "cradle of love," and the Reverend Timothy LeHaye reminds his followers that God indeed created the delights of oral sex for married couples (only) to enjoy. No statistical data exist concerning these groups, and we know nothing about sexual behavior among individuals within these churches.

The current strength of the power of the American religious right is evident in the wide-reaching branches of Pat Robertson's political machine, the Christian Coalition, and the "electronic churches," including Robertson's cable television Christian Broadcasting Network (CBN), with annual revenues of $140 million (Roberts and Cohen 1995). A parallel conservative culture is James Dobson's multimedia empire, Focus on the Family, which includes ten radio shows, eleven magazines (including speciality publications for doctors, teachers, and single parents), best-selling books, film strips, and videos of all kinds, curriculum guides, church-bulletin fillers, and sermon outlines faxed to thousands of pastors every week. The popularity of Dobson's first book, *Dare to Discipline*—more than 2 million copies sold in 1977—inspired his formation of Focus on the Family, which now has an annual budget of $100 million and a staff of 1,300 workers who answer more than 250,000 telephone calls and letters a month (Roberts and Cohen 1995).

In the late 1980s, Protestant fundamentalist televangelists from the South were reaching millions of listeners. Their influence was weakened by several major sex scandals, but they continue to play a major role in the anti-abortion movement and are part of the Christian Coalition. In the same era, the National Conference of Catholic Bishops tried to establish a cable television network to bring the Catholic faith to the masses. Where they failed, a determined Catholic fundamentalist-charismatic, Mother Angelica, from Mobile, Alabama, succeeded with the Eternal Word Network, which brings ultraconservative interpretations of Catholic sexual and social morality to devoted listeners twenty-four hours a day.

In the southern states, on the east and west coasts, and in the populous midwest states are several hundred "mega-churches," which draw upwards of 5,000 to 20,000 faithful every week to each church. Congregations seated in upholstered theater seats are inspired by the style of a professional theater with a large choir, orchestra, large screens displaying hymn verses for congregational singing, interpretive dance, bible lessons with soft-rock concerts, and morality plays that rival anything on music television (MTV). These mega-churches are usually huge glass and steel shopping-mall-like complexes with large theater-stage sanctuaries, scores of meeting and classrooms for a variety of activities, including aerobics, multimedia Bible classes, counseling centers, and even bowling alleys, accompanied by acres of parking space. Sermons delivered by skilled "teaching pastors" include such topics as: how to find joy in a violent world, create a "happy day" each week, find rhythm between work and rest, handle teenage children, and discipline one's mind to a biblical perspective. Youth, in particular, are attracted to the instant intimacy of this large-group, Disney-World environment. Weekly contributions from 15,000 members at one mega-church averaged $228,000, giving the church an annual budget of almost $12 million (Roberts and Cohen 1995). With the mainstream small local churches suffering a steady decline in attendance and contributions, many of the more-traditional pastors are turning to the mega-churches for pastoral retraining. Thus, the mega-churches are establishing smaller, local congregations. It appears that the way these churches deal with sexual issues may have a major impact on American sexuality because of the large memberships they are attracting.

Emergence of a Sex-Positive Individual-Based Value System. Diotima of Mantinea, Socrates' instructress in the art of love in the *Symposium,* explained that the god Eros provides an avenue or way by which human beings reach upward to the Divine—a view modern classical scholars chauvinistically attribute to Socrates and call the "Erotic Ascent." Historically, Diotima's argument became the basis of the later Christian idea that God is Love. In Eurocentric Christianity, the first great flowering of Eros came between 1050 C.E. and 1200 C.E., when Ovid's *The Art of Love* reached Europe from Arab-Spanish sources. The synthesis of sexuality and spirituality quickly assumed major status as a popular doctrine expressed in the music of the troubadours of "courtly love."

Its most ardent opponents were the faculty of the medieval universities led by Thomas Aquinas, who developed a full and coherent alternative to the theology of the Platonic Erotic Ascent in the thirteenth century. The Thomistic synthesis, with its denunciation of the Erotic Ascent and analysis of the essence and goals of human sexuality in terms of a "natural law," became the official Catholic view. This synthesis is the basis on which the modern magisterium and hierarchy of the Roman Catholic Church grounds its absolute condemnation of contraception, abortion, and the practice of homosexuality. By contrast, Protestantism has been much more accepting of sexuality and sexual pleasure, and more flexible with and accommodating to such issues as divorce, contraception, abortion, masturbation, premarital sex, and even homosexuality.

However, it was not the theory of Thomistic Aristotleanism that ultimately superseded late medieval and Renaissance beliefs in Eros. These dwindled as Europe, staggered under waves of the Black Death, which ultimately killed one quarter of Europe's population; the Crusades, during which 22,000 people were killed in the Provençal city of Bezier alone; endless local wars among nobles, kings, and petty brigands where the peasants were invariably victimized; Turkish invasions; the epidemic of syphilis in 1493; peasant uprisings in Germany and England in the 1300s and 1400s; and the Inquisition, that specifically targeted women as its victims.

Protestant reformers from Luther through Calvin, Knox, and Zwingli, not only rejected the "natural law" approach to sexual morality; but extended, strengthened, and normalized the nuclear family and the blessing of marital sex. This type of marriage was a valuable social institution for assuring the distribution of new wealth from father to son. For example, in northern European merchant families, it replaced the older, southern European models of inheritance by name, and social status by membership in a "house" (e.g., the "house of the Medici"), with this type of lineage system.

An important characteristic of the Renaissance was appreciation and acceptance of individual control of one's own life. Thus, the late 1500s and early 1600s saw a new struggle of the young to wrest control over their love affairs and marriages from their parents and families. Shakespeare's *Romeo and Juliet* epitomizes what was to become the central issue of the modern-American religious debate about sexuality and spirituality. Who is to control the sexuality of the young? Older and more powerful individuals, who have vested interests in the outcome of youthful sexuality, . . . celibate church leaders still convinced of the unchangeable patriarchal sexual values expressed in the Genesis story of creation, . . . or young people, who claim for themselves the right to find the right mates and express their erotic passion in a way that, for them, brings sexuality and transcendence together?

Of growing significance in the 1990s in the U.S.A. is the question of the sacred nature of Eros. Among the liberal religious best-sellers pioneering a new synthesis of sexuality and spirituality are: *Human Sexuality: New Directions in American Catholic Thought* (Kosnick et al. 1977), which was sponsored by the Catholic Theological Society of America, but was condemned by the Vatican; *Original Blessing* (1983) and *The Coming of the Cosmic Christ* (1988) by the Dominican Matthew Fox (censured and expelled from his community by the Vatican); sociologist and erotic-novel author Father Andrew Greeley's *Sex, The Catholic Experience* (1995); lesbian theologian Carter Heyward's 1989 *Touching Our Strength: The Erotic as Power and the Love of God*; Presbyterian seminary professor James Nelson's books *Embodiment* (1978), *Between Two Gardens: Reflections on Sexuality and Religious Experience* (1983), and *Body Theology* (1992); James Nelson and Sandra Longfellow's anthology on *Sexuality and the Sacred* (1994); William Phipps' *Recovering Biblical Sensuousness* (1975); Catholic feminist theologian Joan Timmerman's *The Mardi Gras Syndrome: Rethinking Christian Sexuality* (1986); and Episcopalian Bishop John Shelly Spong's 1988 *Living in Sin? A Bishop Rethinks Human Sexuality*. In addition, some Christians have turned to Eastern religions, particularly in the Tantric and Taoist traditions, to seek the nexus between sexuality and spirituality (Francoeur 1992).

Current and Future Religious Debate. During the 1980s, the most virulently debated issue was abortion. In 1994, between U.S. Supreme Court decisions and violence and murder by extreme anti-abortionists, support for anti-abortion stands stalled. For the majority of Americans, abortion appeared to fade as the central moral dilemma and joined the list of unresolved moral issues that includes war, drugs, crime, capital punishment, discrimination, and related social ills. Certain far-right religious leaders, who still have a devoted and vocal following and claim to speak for Christ, even conceded reluctantly that they could not win their war against abortion, and seemed to refocus their crusade on homosexuality and "the danger of homosexual rights" as their mobilizing issue.

However, with the mid-1995 success of the Republicans' conservative hundred-day Contract with America, the Christian Coalition announced its own Contract with the American Family. Two-dozen legislative proposals were introduced into Congress, including an unprecedented attempt to ban and criminalize some now-legal abortions. A bill to reinstate a ban on abortions at American military hospitals overseas was passed. Other proposed bills would ban family planning programs from including abortion counseling for low-income women and adolescents; refuse funding to institutions that favor requiring obstetric/gynecology programs to provide training in abortion procedures; overturn an executive order lifting a ban against using foreign-aid money for abortion counseling or referrals; end or restrict support for agencies, including the United Nations, that offer family planning programs with abortions funded by private money; limit federal Medicaid money for abortions to situations where the woman's life is threatened and ban it in cases of incest or rape; ban fetal-tissue research; ban clinical testing of RU-486; restore a ban on counseling women about abortion at clinics that receive any federal money; and prohibit the federal employee's health benefit plan from covering abortion. The ultimate goal is to make all abortions under all circumstances a crime.

The list of controversial sexual issues that are religiously debated with little hope of being resolved in the near future includes:

1. Individual sexual choice: Who should be in control of one's sexuality? Should it be church leaders or people themselves, who claim the right to express their sexuality with those of their own choosing in ways that would bring them mutual pleasure, eroticism, and spirituality?
2. Contraception: Should minors have access to contraception? Should condoms be distributed in the schools? Does education about contraception and sexual behaviors outside of marriage promote "promiscuity"? Should people be free to choose the best method of contraception for themselves without religious restriction?
3. Abortion: Should women have control of their own reproductive faculty? Is the embryo/fetus a person with inalienable rights at the moment of conception or does fetal personhood develop over the nine months of gestation? When do fetal rights transcend those of pregnant women, if at all?

4. Nonmarital sexuality: Can sex outside marriage be morally acceptable? If so, under what circumstances? How can it be reconciled with
traditional Judeo-Christian morality that limits sexual expression to
the marital union?

5. Sexual orientation: Are homosexuality and bisexuality natural and
normal states of being? Should sexually active gays, lesbians, and
bisexuals be welcomed into church membership? Should they be
ordained into the ministry? Should variation in orientation be presented in sex-education curricula as normal, moral, and socially acceptable?

6. Masturbation: Is self-loving and autoeroticism a natural, normal, and
morally acceptable expression of human sexuality? (See the first item
in Section B of American Demographics at the beginning of this
chapter for an illustration of the impact this issue has had on American
politics.)

The American religious, and consequent social and political, debates
over each of these issues are not likely to be resolved in the near future.
The dichotomy of the two worldviews is too deeply embedded in the
American culture to allow for a quick resolution. The more likely prognosis
is for continued, tension-filled confrontations within the churches, denominations, and political/legislative arenas throughout the United States.

The Religious Right's social and political agenda deeply divides American society. Although 40 percent of Americans express concern about the
Democrats' ties to radical liberal groups, 39 percent are worried by Republican ties to conservative special-interest groups like the Religious Right,
the Family Research Council, Focus on the Family, Eagle Forum, and the
Christian Coalition (Roberts and Cohen 1995). These results reflect the
continuing diversity of worldviews within the Judeo-Christian tradition.
They also indicate that these religious differences not only result in contrasting sexual ideologies, but also have an important impact on political
processes in the U.S.A. more broadly. As such, religion continues to be a
major American social influence.

Church of Jesus Christ of Latter-Day Saints   JEANNIE FORREST*

Mormon Origins and Polygyny. One example of a particular religious group
within the general Judeo-Christian heritage is provided by the Church of
Jesus Christ of Latter-Day Saints (LDS), which is the fastest-growing religion
in the world today. The over seven million members are known colloquially
as the Mormons. They base their belief system on the Bible and additional

---

*Additional comments by Mark O. Bigler, Ph.D., a lifelong member of the Church of Latter-Day
Saints, a graduate of New York University's doctoral program in sexuality, and director of
community education programs at the Utah AIDS Foundation, are enclosed in brackets with his
name [. . . (Bigler)].

scriptures, most significantly the Book of Mormon, which is understood to be a record of God's dealings with an ancient population of the American continent. The Mormons believe this book came from gold plates revealed to the church founder, Joseph Smith, in Ontario County, New York, in 1823. The church was officially organized in 1829.

The early Mormons were persecuted because their founder claimed the Bible had not been translated properly, that all other religions were false, that religious leaders did not have God's authority—the priesthood—to act in God's name, and finally that the practice of polygyny was a part of the divine plan. There was also the political reality that the tight-knit Mormon communities exercised considerable local power. Interestingly, the term "polygamy" as used in LDS church history and old doctrine means the "condition or practice of having more than one spouse." A more-accurate definition of the Mormon practice of that century lies in the word "polygyny," meaning having more than one wife at one time. The role of polygyny in the church is a source of some embarrassment to mainstream modern-day Mormons, who may discuss the practice somewhat wryly as a revelation designed to build the church population at a time when they literally had to forge new communities under hardship. After several attempts to settle in an area and build a sectarian community, the Mormon pioneers ultimately settled in the Salt Lake City area of Utah, where the church is now headquartered.

Modern Mormon doctrine does not include the practice of polygyny. Church prophet and leader, Wilfred Woodruff, officially eliminated polygyny from doctrine in the Manifesto of 1890 (Ludlow 1992). This proclamation against plural marriage ended a decade of hardship and persecution against the church members, particularly by the Republican Party that had as part of its platform elimination of the "immoral practice of multiple wives." While mainstream Mormons are not held accountable for not practicing plural marriage, they still must "suffer the curse of monogamy." Today, small fundamentalist splinter groups still practice polygyny, despite state laws against it and lack of official church acknowledgment. Even before the church abandoned its practice of plural marriage, only a small fraction of Mormon men, between 3 and 15 percent, had more than one wife (Murstein 1974, 350-364).

Perhaps the persecution faced by the early members of the LDS regarding their marital patterns has contributed to a unique and paradoxical tension around sexuality. On one hand, there is nothing more sacred than sex within the bounds of church-sanctioned marriage. On the other hand, rarely is there found a modern-American subculture more prohibitive and repressive about sexuality.

Salvation and Sex. To further understand this tension, one needs a basic understanding of the Mormon Plan of Salvation. Before birth, the Mormons believe, the soul is alive as an intelligence in a spirit world. During this preexistence, a variety of situations are possible, including acts of valor that would allow the soul to be born into a family of Mormons where opportunities for service abound. At birth, the soul passes through a veil of forgetfulness where all memory of the preexistence is lost (Church of Jesus Christ of Latter-Day Saints, 1989 (Moses 3:5, p. 7; Abraham 3:21-23, pp. 35, 38; Talmage 1977).

During life on this earth, individuals face choices throughout the course of their lives that determine in which of three kingdoms they will spend eternity. The highest kingdom, the Celestial Kingdom, is reserved for those Latter-Day Saints who meet all the requirements of doctrine, one of the most important of which is marriage to another Saint in special temple rites. The exaltation and eternal life in the highest degree of the Celestial Kingdom are achieved only by faithful Mormons through the achievement and building of an eternal marriage, discussed later. (Other good people can only hope to reach the Terrestrial Kingdom, a kind of heaven on earth, while unrepented adulterers, practicing homosexuals, murderers, and other sinners are limited to the Telestial Kingdom, which some describe as a Mormon version of the Christian hell.

[According to Mormon tradition, "hell" is not a place, but rather a state of mind. Those who do not achieve the highest degree of glory (the Celestial Kingdom) will recognize the reward they might have had and live out their eternities with the knowledge of this lost potential. However, the Telestial Kingdom, though typically described in less-than-positive terms, is not generally thought of as the fire and brimstone of the traditional Christian hell. In fact, one prominent Mormon Church leader described the Telestial Kingdom as follows: ". . . all who receive any one of these orders of glory are at last saved, and upon them Satan will finally have no claim. Even the telestial glory 'surpasses all understanding; And no man knows it except him to whom God has revealed it'" (Talmage, 1977, 92-93). (Bigler)]

In Mormon belief, one's marital status is decisive for the life hereafter. Without marriage one can only become a servant angel ministering to those who are far more worthy of glory, the truly married. But most of those who have married on earth are married for *time only* (until death), and not truly married unless they have their marriage sealed in the temple. In heaven, those who are married only for this life will be single, no better than bachelors and spinsters. (In the Mormon view of heaven, one can enjoy all the pleasures of sex, food, and other sensual delights.) Those who are married by a prophet in the temple are sealed to each other and married *for time and eternity*. Couples in a sealed marriage will remain married for eternity, and enjoy reigning in separate kingdoms. It is also possible to marry for eternity and not for time. Thus a kindly man may marry a spinster for eternity but not for time, leaving her to her celibate lifestyle here, but destined for all the delights of the Celestial Kingdom as his mate in eternity (Murstein 1974, 350-362).

Gender Roles. As with all societies, gender roles among Mormons are scripted very early in life. The LDS church plays a distinct role in gender definition and scripting. Church activities segregate children at around the age of 12: boys are guided into vigorous endeavors, such as scouting and outdoor gamesmanship, whereas girls learn household activities and crafts.

[To clarify Forrest's comment above, it is important to note that Mormon adolescents frequently participate in mixed-gender activities. Although young men and young women generally meet separately as a part of the official church youth program (known variously as Mutual Improvement Association (M.I.A.), Mutual, and Young Men's/Young Women's Program), males and females come together for Sunday School and the Mormon worship service known as Sacrament Meeting. In addition, LDS seminaries—religious study programs for high-school-age teens (grades 9 through 12) that operate in virtually every location around the world where congregations of Mormons are found—are always conducted with male and female students meeting together. Furthermore, Mormon youth regularly attend church-sponsored dances and participate together in community activities, including school proms, holiday celebrations, and cultural events. Young Mormon women and men are encouraged to interact, though care is usually taken to provide chaperons or to direct young people into activities where the possibility of sexual contact is limited (e.g., Mormon youths are strongly encouraged by their church leaders and parents to date in groups, and establish curfews that will not keep them out past midnight). (Bigler)]

It is not unusual for a preadolescent girl to have an LDS-designed poster on her bedroom wall urging her to remain "temple worthy," or reminding her of gospel precepts that will keep her safe from worldly situations. For example, one poster is of a young girl looking into a mirror in whose reflection is a vision of herself as a young woman in a bridal scene with a handsome man. The caption says, "looking forward to a temple marriage." Young men are also urged to bridle their carnal urges. Masturbation is expressly forbidden, and moral cleanliness, a requirement for any temple ceremony, essentially equates to abstaining from sexual activity before marriage.

[In Mormon practice, "moral cleanliness" at its most basic level is understood as abstaining from sexual activity before marriage and remaining faithful to one's spouse. It is not at all equated with celibacy, as the author has implied. A pamphlet for youth, recently published by the church, makes this position clear: "Our Heavenly Father has counseled that sexual intimacy should be reserved for his children within the bonds of marriage. . . . Because sexual intimacy is so sacred, the Lord requires self-control and purity before marriage as well as full fidelity after marriage" (Church of Jesus Christ of Latter-Day Saints, 1990, 14-15). (Bigler)]

Gender roles become even more firmly established during transitions into adulthood. Church officials clearly define the position, duties, and destiny of women in the divine plan. Women are to be "copartners with

God in bringing his spirit children into the world" (Tanner 1973); this is generally understood metaphorically without any sexual connotation. Rather than focus on the erotic element of this distinction (having babies does require first having sexual intercourse), the LDS leaders instead urge women to stay home in order to love and care for children to ensure a generation of Mormons who learn about their "duty as citizens and what they must do to return to their Heavenly Father." Women are regarded as sacred vessels, with important roles not only in childbearing, but also as positive influences on men's lives. A "general authority" in the church, Hugh B. Brown, suggests that "women are more willing to make sacrifices than are men, more patient in suffering, and more earnest in prayer" (Relief Society 1965). Women in the Mormon community are indeed known for their good works. The Relief Society is the oldest women's group in the United States and is remarkably active with community support of all kinds.

[Most Mormons, female and male alike, continue to hold traditional views concerning gender and gender roles. In general, Mormon women today still view motherhood and caregiving as fundamental traits of a "righteous" woman. However, it is also fair to say that the beliefs of church officials and the broader membership regarding gender roles have liberalized somewhat since President Hugh B. Brown's statement in 1965. For example, in a recent general conference of the church, Chieko N. Okazaki, First Counselor in the Relief Society General Presidency, urged LDS women to obtain an education and career training:

> [Each year it becomes increasingly important for women to improve their abilities to take care of themselves and their children economically, if circumstances should require. . . . If anything, [the counsel of Elder Howard W. Hunter] has become even more relevant in the almost twenty years that have passed as the national economy has made it increasingly difficult for one wage to support a family, as more mothers are left alone to raise their children, and as more women spend lengthy portions of their lives single. He is telling all of us to use the oar of study to prepare ourselves professionally for worthy and rewarding activities, including paid employment. (Okazaki, 1994) (Bigler)]

LDS men have a clearly defined role as well. Men bear the responsibility and the privilege of the Priesthood, which is a spiritual calling and connection to God specifically not given to women. An exception to this is found in LDS mission work, where young women on evangelical missions for the church have a type of "priesthood calling" on a temporary basis, lasting only for the duration of the mission.

[Throughout the church's history, Mormon women have served missions for the church. Today, young women (typically in their early 20s) are embarking on proselyting and church service missions in ever-increasing numbers. Although Mormon men are encouraged much more strongly

than are women to go on missions, teaching and preaching are not restricted to priesthood holders (males) in the church today. In fact, the
priesthood is not a prerequisite for participation in most church positions,
all of which are filled by lay members. Nevertheless, church leadership at
its highest levels, both locally and generally, remains a function of the
priesthood (male members). (Bigler)]

Through the priesthood, God governs all things. Priesthood power is
considered a vital source of eternal strength and energy; a responsibility
delegated to men for the well-being of mankind. Holding the priesthood
means having authority to act as God's authorized agent, which includes
some church organizational duties. The right of worthy priesthood holders
is to preside over their descendants through all ages, achieving its highest
function in the family. As the presiding priesthood holder in the home,
decisions relating to discipline often fall to the man, and the role of
providing for the household is ultimately his, in spite of the presence of
more employed Mormon women. Giving righteous advice, loving family
members, and the laying-on-of-hands for healing purposes are all rights of
the man of the house.

[In the ideal Mormon household, discipline, family decisions, and the
day-to-day management of the home are seen as a shared responsibility
between a unified husband and wife. Although Mormon fathers have been
designated the presiding authority in the family (once again a function of
the priesthood), it is the mother who is typically responsible for managing
the home and children. However, male church members are counseled
against the misuse of their designation as leader in the home, and men
have been encouraged by the prophet and president of the church himself
to share in parenting and home management:

> [A man who holds the priesthood accepts his wife as a partner in the
> leadership of the home and family with full knowledge of and full
> participation in all decisions relating thereto. . . . You share, as a loving
> partner, the care of the children. Help her to manage and keep up your
> home. Help teach, train, and discipline your children. (Hunter, 1994,
> 5-7) (Bigler)]

Body Theology. The Mormon doctrine about the body is worth noting since
it creates another element of sexual tension. In many Christian religions,
the body is considered simply a vessel housing the spirit/soul for the
duration of life. For the Mormons, the body itself is highly revered and
serves an eternal function. At the point of resurrection, the body of an
individual is returned to "perfection," ridding it of all the faults and defects
of this life. A Mormon friend of mine often queries, "Just whose version of
perfection will I get in Eternity? I have a list of modifications right here."

One indication of the importance of the body is manifested by the
wearing of "garments." During the Temple marriage, a couple is given

special "garments" to wear. This special underwear (manufactured by the Mormon church) is designed to serve as a reminder of the sanctity of the covenants made in the temple and to protect the body from harm. A quiet Mormon joke about the garments refers to them as "Mormon contraceptives," since they must be worn next to the skin at all times and are notoriously unsexy in appearance. Women wear their foundation garments, such as brassieres and slips, over the Mormon garments. Because of the design of the garments, only modest clothing can be worn. However, the modern garments are much more relaxed and functional than traditional ones. The old versions are still available, with the tops extending just below the elbows and the bottoms below the knee, but most younger Mormon women opt for the cap sleeve and midthigh cotton versions for comfort and more choice in clothing.

[Mormon garments (which are worn by both women and men) serve as a constant reminder of sacred covenants made in temple ceremonies. Mormons also believe that these undergarments help protect the wearer against physical and spiritual harm. In addition, the design of the under-clothing encourages the wearing of modest clothing. Although temple garments are to be worn day and night under normal circumstances, church members are not required by either doctrine or dictum to keep their underclothing on during activities such as bathing or while participating in sporting events. Nor are faithful Mormons required to wear their garments during sexual activity. (Bigler)]

Adolescent Dating. Adolescent dating rituals are very similar to those of other conservative American cultural groups. As LDS children grow older, the church plays more of a role in their lives, interweaving doctrinal and social activities. The transitions through church steps for adolescents are made in tandem with all their church peers. For instance, at 8 years old, children reach the "age of understanding" and are baptized into the church. Many of their peers are also taking this step, which takes on social significance in the form of family gatherings and informal parties. Later, dating is encouraged in group settings around church activities, since this context is most likely to encourage an interfaith marriage. Teens are often told, "if you don't date outside, you won't fall in love outside, and you won't marry outside the faith."

[Dating among Mormon teens is not restricted solely to church activities, although local congregations do often sponsor teen-oriented events, such as dances, firesides (discussions of religious topics especially relevant to teens), and cultural activities (plays, concerts, art exhibits, etc.). While dating outside of the church is not strictly forbidden, it is, as the author states, discouraged by church leaders and parents in an effort to reduce the chances that a member will marry outside of the church. Families of particularly staunch members are likely to view the marriage of a child to someone from outside of the church as a lamentable and perhaps even shameful event. Although Mormons who are married to nonmembers are not excluded from church activity or normal religious practice, one's relationship to the church is undoubtedly affected by the "part-member" status of the family. (Bigler)]

At Brigham Young University, a Mormon-owned and operated institution in Provo, Utah, approximately 45 miles south of Salt Lake City, a subculture of dating reigns. Known to be an ideal place for Mormon youth to find a same-faith marriage partner, it is also a hotbed of sexual exploration. Mormon coeds fine-tune their "NCMOS," (pronounced "nick-moes"), which is an acronym for "noncommittal make-out sessions." These sexual forays include "everything but intercourse": extensive kissing, petting, and "dry humping" (rubbing bodies) is common, but touching of the genitals is typically off-bounds, as is penetration of any kind.

[Brigham Young University, the oldest private university west of the Mississippi River, boasts a student body of more than 30,000, comprised almost entirely of young Mormons who come from every state in the country and many nations outside of the United States. The amount and types of sexual activities that the author reports occur among BYU students are not all that atypical of young college students in general. However, given the strict code of sexual conduct that Mormons have for themselves, even nongenital sex play and sexual activity short of intercourse give BYU the appearance of a "hotbed of sexual exploration." At the same time, such activity also suggests that young Mormons have healthy sexual appetites, and perhaps are not as peculiar as it may first appear when compared to their peers on other American campuses. (Bigler)]

Marriage, Sex, and the Celestial Kingdom. In order to access the Celestial Kingdom, a couple must marry in the temple. These temple rites seal the two partners together not just for life, but for all eternity. When a couple is in the Celestial Kingdom together, they can enjoy the full experience of their resurrected and eternally perfect bodies. The purpose of the sealed marriage is primarily to ensure the eternal connection between partners, allowing them to procreate and populate their own worlds (eternal procreation). An essential precept, "As man is, so God once was; as God is, so man can become," guides heterosexual couples through life with the promise that they, as the God they worship has done, will become creators of their own world (Murstein 1974).

Although not formally prohibited, birth control is regarded with clear reservation by church members, since large families are viewed favorably. Women who leave the Mormon church often refer, "with tongue in cheek," to their loss of opportunity to bear children during the afterlife. One woman commented, "At least I know I won't be barefoot and pregnant through time and eternity."

[While birth control is regarded with reservation by many church members and authorities, various forms of contraception are commonly practiced, even by active, faithful members. Today, the decision to use birth control is left to the discretion of the couple. (Bigler)]

The gender roles established early in the life of the couple are metaphorically established again during the marriage ceremony. The order of the Plan of Salvation is clearly outlined during the ceremony, as is the order of the household that symbolically supports the Divine Order when it is in accord with the Plan of Salvation. An interesting element of the temple marriage is the giving of a name to the bride, known only to her husband. This name is for the use of the husband in calling his wife to him in the afterlife. She does not have access to his secret name—the calling of partners in eternity is purely a masculine prerogative. The giving of the name to the bride is kept secret from outsiders, as is much of the rest of the ceremony, which is closed to all those without special church endowments. Mormon church weddings are different from typical American weddings in that only worthy LDS family members and friends are allowed into the temple to observe the ceremony itself. If a family member is an inactive church member or a nonmember, they will be excluded from the wedding ceremony, joining the party outside the temple or at the reception.

In the face of the lack of sexuality education, the first act of sexual intercourse for a good Mormon is likely to be ill-informed. One contemporary of mine recalls her first sexual experience, which took place after an LDS temple marriage: "We were both virgins, and it literally took us several weeks to consummate the marriage by having intercourse. We had been raised to believe sex was a sacred thing, so we just sat in bed, prayerfully, kissing gently and waiting for something to happen. Obviously, something finally did, but I was dreadfully disappointed. It not only didn't feel sacred, it didn't even feel good." This particular couple did not seek therapy for support or education, relying instead on the Holy Spirit, a decision common among LDS couples.

Because the church operates with a lay ministry, the local bishop has an enormous influence on how issues of sexuality are handled. In most instances in which married couples face difficulty with sexual relations or general marital dissatisfaction, the bishop is the first and most likely source of comfort and counsel. Often the bishop is just a kindly intentioned neighbor with limited or no training. Many times, his response is based on his own experience, attitudes, aversions, and parental training. Some extremely compassionate bishops give forgiving responses to an individual who has erred sexually. Some bishops advise specifically against such behaviors as oral or anal sex. Others, repulsed by the vulgarity of even discussing the topic of sexuality, take refuge in esoteric spiritual or academic language or avoid the topic altogether. Still others may be open-minded and suggest that either the lay ministry has an extremely limited role in the bedroom of other folks or advise liberal measures, such as doing whatever works best for the couple involved. If marriage counseling is clearly needed, a referral may be made by the bishop to the LDS Social Services or to an LDS therapist, who can give professional advice with an empathy for the doctrinal requirements. In sharp contrast, other bishops respond with an injunction to leave the fellowship if someone has premarital intercourse, commits adultery, or engages in homosexual relations, all of which are forbidden by church doctrine.

[Problems that result from limited sexuality education coupled with well intentioned but poorly trained lay clergy are compounded for Mormons by a dearth of LDS therapists and other mental-health professionals who have specific training and experience in the area of sexuality. (Bigler)]

Divorce is discouraged, but not uncommon. The divorce rate in the state of Utah, in spite of a predominantly LDS population, matches those of many states. Even marriages sealed in the temple are now relatively easy to unseal. Remarriage from a doctrinal standpoint is difficult to comprehend in light of the eternal marriage concept, but temple divorces will officially separate the couple for the purposes of the Celestial Kingdom.

[If a temple divorce has been granted, a second marriage can be sealed in a Mormon temple. Marriages that take place outside of the temple are officially recognized by the church as legal and valid, with the understanding that these unions will not carry on into the eternities. (Bigler)]

The Mormon Family. An ideal Mormon family works together, putting the sense of "family" first, honoring the doctrine that families will endure throughout eternity. It is a rare LDS home that lacks some visible reminder of this doctrine in an embroidered or otherwise handcrafted item proclaiming, "Families are Forever." The cultural value placed on family as a priority distinctly impacts those who choose not to have children, making those couples at least the object of social curiosity, if not censure.

Utah, the Mormon Mecca, is culturally oriented toward family because of the LDS church influence. Exemplifying this is Enid Waldholtz, the Republican congresswoman elected to office in 1994 from Utah, who is only the second member of Congress to bear a child while in office. This choice on the part of LDS Congresswoman Waldholtz clearly cemented her popularity among her Mormon constituents. She made a clear statement about her support for family life by meeting one of the most basic expectations of a Mormon couple with this childbirth.

Sex Education. Children are taught about sexuality more by implicit measures than direct and overt messages. Sexual exploration at a very early age is treated with quiet but firm repression. Mormon adults often describe their sense of guilt at their developing sexuality, often beginning at a very early age. These ideas are often disseminated by parents during "morality lessons," which might include the suggestion of singing hymns if "impure thoughts" enter one's mind, or using affirmative reminders that one's primary objective is to reach the Celestial Kingdom, which demands the purity of the body temple. "Impure thoughts" are usually not specifically defined, but are so pervasively assumed to be sexually related that many Mormon adults still claim to equate words such as "purity" and "morality" with specific sexual connotations.

In spite of the importance placed on having babies in a married state, very little formal education is done regarding sexuality and pregnancy. Countless times after I have made a simple junior- or high-school presentation on HIV prevention, students have lined up to ask me other "related" questions, often regarding basic body functioning, for example, "I haven't started my period. . . . How do I know if I'm pregnant? . . . Can I get pregnant from kissing?"

[Mormon families are counseled by their leaders to hold a weekly Family Home Evening each Monday night. This is a specially designated time during the week for the family to join together to study religious topics, enjoy activities outside of the home, or address important family issues. Family Home Evening, as it has been outlined, provides LDS families with a perfect opportunity to provide sexuality education in the home within the framework of the family's own value system. After observing this practice among Mormon families, Dr. Ruth Westheimer and her colleague Louis Lieberman noted:

> [In particular, we have been impressed by the manner in which the Church of Jesus Christ of Latter-day Saints (the Mormons) has approached the difficult task of teaching moral and ethical precepts in the area of sexuality. If Jews, Italians, Chinese, and Japanese, among other groups, may be said to be child-centered societies, the Mormons must be said to be family-centered, par excellence. There appears to be a structured, systematic, integrated and total approach to morality through the family. Thus, sexual morality is taught as part of a system and way of life that focuses on the goal of eternal or celestial marriage. The church reaches out to the family through many media: songs, family meetings, family resource books, television, videos, etc., to provide the Mormon perspective on all aspects of sexuality for all family members. (Westheimer & Lieberman 1988, 109)

[Unfortunately, all too often, Mormon families fail to take advantage of this valuable resource, and miss an obvious opportunity to educate their children about matter related to human sexuality. (Bigler)]

Many couples marry with limited information even about the act of intercourse. If they have been properly parented in the faith, they will have been protected from exposure to sexual or "perverted" images. A Mormon church leader, Dallin Oakes, in a speech at Brigham Young University, said "We are surrounded by the promotional literature of illicit sexual relations on the printed page and on the screen. For your own good, avoid it." He added, "Pornographic or erotic stories and pictures are worse than filthy or polluted food. The body has defenses to rid itself of unwholesome food, but the brain won't vomit back filth."

Biological information about menstruation is disseminated clinically. Some women recall this clinical information as imbued with a sense of shame, in which menstruation is described as a sickness or something one does not discuss in polite company. For example, I dated a Mormon man who was so unfamiliar with menstrual issues and women's bodies—in spite of having several sisters—that he did not know what the purpose of a tampon was or how it functioned.

Abortion. Abortion is considered a most venal sin. Since Mormon doctrine regards the bearing of children as an opportunity to bring "spirit" children into an earthly form, abortion is not only considered murder, but in addition, a denial of a body for a predestined soul.

Gay Culture. Both the San Francisco and New York gay cultures take special note of the Brigham Young University gay underground, famous for its size and covert scope. Many of the returning missionaries come back to BYU to find a mate and resolve the same-sex desires often stirred on the two-year LDS mission strongly encouraged by the Church with strictly enforced male-only companionship.* Sometimes that resolution does not come easily. Support groups for Mormon homosexuals in the Provo and Salt Lake area around BYU give voice to the pain of these men. Lesbians face the same dilemma, since they are surrounded by the cultural pressure to marry and have families.

The divine mandate of heterosexual marriage regards homosexuality as a repudiation of the gift and giver of life. Thus, homosexuality is regarded as a direct violation of God's plan, which is that men should cleave to women. Sexual relations between any nonmarried persons is considered sinful and homosexuality falls into this category. According to Dallin Oaks, one of the church apostles, "Eternal laws that pertain to chastity before marriage and personal purity within marriage apply to all sexual behavior. However, marriage is not doctrinal therapy for homosexual relationships" (Ludlow 1992). Since so much of the restored gospel hinges upon the legally and temple-wedded heterosexual couple, practicing homosexuals are excommunicated.

[*A note on LDS missionary services. Mormon men are strongly encouraged (*not* required) to serve a two-year mission at the age of 19. Formal sanctions are not imposed on those males who choose not to go on a mission. However, in a strong Mormon family or LDS community, social sanctions can be quite severe. The status of "Returned Missionary" is a valuable asset to a young man's marriage potential. In contrast, the decision not to serve a mission—or worse yet, leaving on a mission and returning home early—often brings shame to both the young man and his family. Mormon women, on the other hand, can choose to go on an 18-month mission at the age of 21. However, the expectation of service is not nearly as great for females as it is for males, and the decision not to go, particularly if a young woman opts to get married instead, results in few, if any, negative repercussions. (Bigler)]

Often the feelings of a gay person meet responses of incredulity on the part of parents and church leaders. One parent counseled his son not to act on his "supposed" same-gender feelings, "to date young women seriously, to wait and see" (Schow et al. 1991). Because homosexual couples cannot reproduce, this parent urged his son to "choose otherwise." The church offers "counseling to those who are troubled by homosexual thoughts and actions" in order that they might become acceptable to God. Repentance is offered in these circumstances. "Homosexuality and like practices are deep sins; they can be cured; they can be forgiven" (*Church News* 1978). In order to remain a Mormon in good standing, homosexuals must remain celibate and refrain from all same-gender eroticism. Acceptance is not advocated at any level.

[The current Mormon position on homosexuality can be described as one of limited tolerance. Because sexual activity is reserved for marriage, and same-sex relationships are not recognized by most legal bodies or by the church, homosexual activity is therefore forbidden. As the author correctly notes, to continue to be a Mormon in good standing, homosexual men and women must remain celibate and refrain from all same-sex sexual activity. The church's position officially allows for individuals who are sexually attracted to members of the same gender to remain fully involved in church activities, so long as there is no sexual activity. This stance, though still extremely restrictive, is quite a departure from past policy and practice when virtually any indication of same-sex attraction could be used as grounds for excommunication. However, despite the apparent shift in thinking toward greater acceptance, it remains difficult, if not impossible, for members who feel a same-sex attraction to continue to actively practice Mormonism. Unfortunately, homophobia is often a more-powerful emotion for many church members than the New Testament challenge to "Love thy neighbor as thyself." Frequently, this homophobia is internalized and, despite Ludlow's declaration that "marriage is not doctrinal therapy for homosexual relationships," many gay, lesbian, and bisexual Mormons follow the traditional course that has been set for them by getting married and starting a family. Some carry on with a heterosexual life and take the secret of homosexuality to the grave. Others find their true sexual feelings too powerful to deny and may have clandestine same-sex relationships or seek out friendly advice, often from a bishop or other church authority. For those who acknowledge same-sex attraction, reparative or reorientation therapy is a common recommendation. These programs have demonstrated little lasting success in changing sexual orientation. Participation in reparative or reorientation therapy is often experienced as the ultimate failure, since the promise of change is directly linked to the sincerity and worthiness of one's efforts.

[Change-orientated therapy, therefore, is commonly the final step for many gay, lesbian, and bisexual Mormons before leaving the church or being asked to leave. In the end, homosexual Mormons are often left with a choice between their church and their sexuality. Because the two are diametrically opposed, there is little room for compromise. (Bigler)]

Summary. The Mormon culture is distinct in many ways. Known for hard work, loyal families, and abstinence from alcohol and tobacco, the Mormons are steadfast in their maintenance of traditional family values. Sexually conservative and repressive, Mormon doctrines may be the ideal for people disillusioned with or anxious about the liberalization of sexual attitudes and practices occurring in the United States in recent decades. According to the 1995 United States census, Utah—with a 70 percent Mormon population—ranks first in fertility and last in teen pregnancy. The Mormons, long considered remarkable for their nearly anachronistic traditional values, may actually be on the cutting edge of the Christian Right's abstinence- and morality-based vision of American family life.

B. Racial, Ethnic, and Feminist Perspectives

In addition to the religious factor, two other social factors continue to exert considerable influence on American sexual ideologies and practices, race/ethnicity and gender. In this section, we examine the sexual customs of two of the largest racial and ethnic minority groups in the U.S.A., African-Americans and Latino-Americans, and the effects of feminism and feminist perspectives on sexuality in America and sexological research.

African-Americans   HERBERT SAMUELS

The term African-American is widely and often carelessly used to suggest or imply that the more than 30 million African-Americans constitute some kind of homogeneous community or culture. This is both contrary to reality and dangerous, as the term properly includes a rich diversity of very different, and often distinct, subcultures, each with its own set of sexual values, attitudes, and behavioral patterns. Included under the rainbow umbrella of African-Americans are urban African-Americans in the northeast, ranging from Boston south to Washington, D.C., African-Americans in Los Angeles on the West Coast, and African-Americans in urban centers in the southern states. Rural African-Americans are often quite different from urban African-Americans, even in nearby metropolitan centers. Socioeconomic and educational differences add to the diversity of African-American subcultures. This perspective is essential to avoid overgeneralizations about the observations provided here.

Historical Perspective. A review of the past record reveals that many white Americans have regarded the majority of African-Americans as representing the sexual instinct in its raw state. This belief that African-American sexual behavior is somehow more sordid and crude than the sexual behavior of white Americans is by no means a new concept. Reports dating from the mid-sixteenth century depict the sexual behavior of Africans as bestial. The same descriptions were later applied to the Africans brought to the New World by the slave trade.

Moreover, the folk view of the sexuality of blacks is often hard to distinguish from what appears in the scientific literature. In the guise of science, some investigators have presented such conclusions as: (1) African-American men and women are guided by "bestial instinct" (DeRachewiltz 1964; Jacobus 1937; Purchas 1905); (2) the black man is more animalistic in bed (DeRachewiltz 1964; Jacobus 1937; Purchas 1905); (3) the black man's penis is larger than the penis of the white man (DeRachewiltz 1964; Edwardes and Masters 1963; Jacobus 1937); (4) the black man is a sexual superman whose potency and virility is greater than the white man's (DeRachewiltz 1964; Jacobus 1937; Jefferson 1954); (5) the black man's reproductive capacity is colossal (Jacobus 1937); (6) black men are obsessed with the idea of having sex with white women (Edwardes and Masters 1963; Fanon 1967); (7) all black women want to sleep with anyone who comes along (DeRachewiltz 1964; Jacobus 1937; Rogers 1967); and (8) black women respond instantly and enthusiastically to all sexual advances (DeRachewiltz 1964; Jacobus 1937). Blacks have also been characterized as holding more-permissive attitudes regarding extramarital affairs (Bell 1968; Christensen and Johnson 1978; Houston 1981; Reiss 1964, 1967; Roebuck and McGee 1977; and Staples 1978). This simplistic notion may well misrepresent the complexity of African-American sexual values. According to Robert Staples (1986, 258),

> Blacks have traditionally had a more naturalistic attitude toward human sexuality, seeing it as the normal expression of sexual attraction between men and women. Even in African societies, sexual conduct was not the result of some divine guidance by God or other deities. It was secularly regulated and encompassed the tolerance of a wide range of sexual attitudes and behaviors. Sexual deviance, where so defined, was not an act against God's will but a violation of community standards.

Gender, Gender Role, Sex, Love, and Marriage. Gender and gender roles are culturally defined constructs that determine the boundaries of acceptable and unacceptable behavior for men and women. These notions are often based on stereotypes—a fixed, oversimplified, and extremely distorted idea about a group of people. In the general American culture, the traditional stereotyped female is gentle, kind, dependent, passive, and submissive. The traditional stereotyped male is tough, brutal, independent, aggressive, and intractable. Any deviation from one's expected gender role may be met with skepticism about one's psychological health. For example, the traditional view of the black male—as it relates to gender-role identification—is that he has been emasculated by the experience of slavery and is suffering from gender-identity problems because of absent or inadequate male role models. Moreover, because of these two problems, he has a more-feminine gender identity than white males (Grier and Cobbs 1968; Glazer and Moynihan 1964; Pettigrew 1964; Wilkinson and Taylor 1977). Grier and Cobbs (1968, 59) suggest that:

> For the black man in this country, it is not so much a matter of acquiring manhood as it is a struggle to feel it his own. Whereas the white man regards his manhood as an ordained right, the black man is engaged in a never ending battle for its possession. For the black man, attaining any portion of manhood is an active process. He must penetrate barriers and overcome opposition in order to assume a masculine posture. For the innermost psychological obstacles to manhood are never so formidable as the impediments woven into American society.

Pettigrew (1964) supported the notion that black males are more feminine than white males because of certain responses to items in the masculinity-femininity scale on the Minnesota Multiphasic Personality Inventory (MMPI). Two items that Pettigrew noted were the statements, "I would like to be a singer" and "I think I feel more intensely than most people do." Black males responded more positively to these statements than did white males. This pattern was interpreted to mean that black males are more feminine than white males. Pettigrew based his conclusion regarding the black male's gender identity on two studies. One study included a sample of Alabama convicts; the other was a group of veterans with tuberculosis! As Pleck (1981) notes, these are hardly representative samples.

In contrast to the emasculated, feminine, black-male hypothesis, Hershey (1978) argues that black males have a stronger masculine identity than white males. In her study of sex-role identities and sex-role stereotyping, the black men's mean masculinity score was significantly higher than the mean masculinity score of the white men in her sample.

To the extent that African-American males have been emasculated by gender-role stereotyping, African-American females have been de-feminized by gender-role stereotyping. The so-called black matriarchy has been historically blamed for the deterioration of the black family, because black women have greater participation in family decision making in a society where male control is the "normal rule." Because white stereotyped norms are violated, African-American women are seen as being domineering. By virtue of the historical legacy of slavery and discrimination against African-American men, African-American women were in the labor market, received education, and supported their families.

According to Staples,

> Sex relations have a different nature and meaning to black people. Their sexual expression derives from the emphasis in the black culture

on feeling, of releasing the natural functions of the body without artificiality or mechanical movements. In some circles this is called "soul" and may be found among peoples of African descent through the world. (Cited by Francoeur 1991, 90-92)

In a practical sense, this means that black men do not moderate their enthusiasm for sex relations as white men do. They do not have a history of suppressing the sexual expression of the majority of their women while singling out a segment of the female population for premarital and extra-marital adventures (Staples 1977, 141-42).

The major problem with such studies is that few have questioned the stereotyped assumptions regarding gender-role socialization upon which their conclusions are based.

Views and Practices of Sex Education. Black males and females are socialized very early into heterosexual relations by their culture and extended-family system. The less-stringent age and gender-role orientations that are evident in the black community exposes children at an early age to a more permissive sexual ethos. Many African-Americans perceive sex as a natural function; thus, children are not hidden from discussions of a sexual nature.

Academically, many sexuality- or family-life-education programs employ the Health Belief Model, not only as a way to predict sexual behavior, but to facilitate behavior change. This model has certain assumptions that are based on Euro-American social norms. These norms may not be consistent with the beliefs and values of many African-Americans. Mays and Cochran (1990) correctly maintain that such attitude-behavior models

> assume that people are motivated to pursue rational courses of action. They further assume that people have the resources necessary to proceed directly with these rational decisions. . . . Black Americans confront an environment in which much of their surrounding milieu is beyond their personal control. Models of human behavior that emphasize individualistic, direct, and rational behavioral decisions overlook the fact that many blacks do not have personal control over traditional categories of resources—for example, money, education, and mobility.

For many African-Americans, educational models that place emphasis on social norms and the extent of commitment to social responsibilities, rather than those that value individualistic rational reasoning, may be better predictors of future behavior.

Masturbation. Most studies indicate that African-American men and women masturbate less than do white men and women. In a recent national study, *The Social Organization of Sexuality* (Laumann et al. 1994), one third of white men and 56 percent of white women reported that they had not masturbated at all in the past year. However, black men were almost twice as likely to report that they had not masturbated at all during the past year, and about 68 percent of black women reported that they did not masturbate the past year. However, those African-Americans who do masturbate demonstrate the same childhood, adolescent, and adult patterns as their white counterparts. Blacks may not acknowledge that they masturbate as readily as whites, because of the belief that admitting that one masturbates means one is unable to find a sex partner.

Children and Sex. African-American children, according to Staples (1972), are socialized very early into heterosexual relations by their culture and extended-family system. This socialization pattern exposes them at an early age to a more permissive sexual ethos. Thus, African-American children may have a knowledge of sexual intercourse, masturbation, condom usage, and other sexual practices at a younger age.

Adolescents and Sex. Compared to white teenagers, African-American teenagers begin coitus about two years earlier, on the average, and are more likely to progress directly from light petting to sexual intercourse (Brooks-Gunn and Furstenburg 1989). Consequently, African-American females may be at greater risk of pregnancy.

Black men start dating earlier, are more likely to have a romantic involvement in high school, have the most liberal sexual attitudes, and are most inclined to have nonmarital sex without commitment (Broderick 1965; Larson et al. 1976; Johnson and Johnson 1978). (See Section 5B for additional data comparing black and white adolescent sexual patterns).

Adults. In the aftermath of the Civil War, blacks married in record numbers because, under the inhumane institution of slavery, legal marriage had been denied to them. Three out of four black adults were living in intact nuclear families by the early part of the twentieth century, and the overwhelming majority of black children were born to parents who were legally married. Today, an African-American child has but a one-in-five chance of being raised by two parents (Chideya et al. 1993). Out-of-wedlock births have risen since the 1960s, particularly among African-Americans. Two out of three first births to African-American women under the age of 35 are now out of wedlock.

Traditionally, women in American society have tended to marry men in their own social class or to "marry up" to a higher socioeconomic group. This pattern has been substantially disrupted among African-Americans, largely because of a distorted gender ratio among blacks. This imbalance in the proportion of males and females of marriageable age has been present for several decades, but has become exacerbated in recent years. By the 1990s, there were roughly fifty adult African-American women for every forty-two African-American men, largely because of abnormally high rates of black-male mortality and incarceration (Staples and Johnson, 1993). Because the proportion of African-American women who attend college and earn degrees is much higher than the rate for men, this problem is even more severe for higher-status women. As a result, increasing numbers of black women are remaining single or marrying partners from lower-status groups (i.e., less education and/or income). There is no evidence that large groups of black women are choosing to marry outside their race (Staples and Johnson, 1993)

Joseph Scott (1976) has argued that these social conditions are largely responsible for the emergence of a pattern he calls "mansharing." Mansharing is a lifestyle where a number of African-American women, each of whom typically maintains her own separate residence, "share" a man for intimate relationships. Typically, he splits time living with each of the women. Scott (1976) argued that mansharing represented the appearance of a new, polygamous family form in the African-American community. However, we want to stress that this does not mean that black women like or prefer this lifestyle. Cazenave (1979) has noted that lifestyles can sometimes be imposed by external social constraints. There is some evidence (Allen and Agbasegbe 1980) that most black women do not approve of mansharing as a lifestyle, but feel they have reduced options in an environment with few eligible male partners. Scott concluded that:

> Until there is some way to correct the sex ratio imbalance and until blacks control the economic and welfare institutions in such a way to stop the breaking up of black monogamous relationships we cannot be too harsh on black men and women who find some satisfactory adjustments in sharing themselves and their economic resources in a new, at least for this society, family form which meets their most basic needs. (Scott 1976, 80)

Homosexuality and Bisexuality. Attitudes within the African-American community reflect those in the majority culture. According to Staples (1981), homosexuality may be tolerated in the black community but will not be approved openly. Bell and Weinberg (1978), in their study of homosexuality, found that black male homosexuals tended to be younger than their white counterparts, had less education, and were employed at a lower occupational level. Moreover, black male gays more often expressed the belief that their homosexuality and homosexual contacts had helped more than hurt their careers.

Compared to black gay males, black lesbians had fewer transient sexual partners. Most reported that the majority of their sexual encounters were with women for whom they cared emotionally.

Coercive Sex and Pornography. The incidence of rape among African-Americans has been subject to some controversy. According to the Department of Health and Human Services, 683,000 adult women were raped in 1990. By contrast, the National Victim Center estimated that there were 130,236 rapes in 1990 and 207,610 in 1991. Although earlier reports indicated that African-American women were more likely to be sexually assaulted than white women, newer studies do not find any statistically significant difference between African-American and white samples. The historical notion that most rapists are black men is totally without merit; indeed most rapists and their victims are members of the same race or ethnic group.

There is an important difference between the attitudes of those whites who support the antipornography movement in the United States and the lack of interest this issue stirs among African-Americans. For African-Americans, as Robert Staples (1986, 258) argues, issues of poverty, education, job opportunities, and teenage pregnancy are far more pressing concerns than the crusade against pornography.

> Rather than seeing the depiction of heterosexual intercourse or nudity as an inherent debasement of women as a fringe group as [white religious conservatives and] feminists claim, the black community would see women as having equal rights to the enjoyment of sexual stimuli. It is nothing more than a continuation of the white male's traditional double standard and paternalism to regard erotica as existing only for male pleasure and women only as sexual objects. Since that double standard has never attracted many American blacks, the claim that women are exploited by exhibiting their nude bodies or engaging in heterosexual intercourse lacks credibility. After all, it was the white missionaries who forced African women to regard their quasi-nude bodies as sinful and placed them in clothes. This probably accounts for the rather conspicuous absence of black women in the feminist fight against porn.

Contraception and Abortion. Since the early 1970s, many in the African-American community have viewed contraceptive use as a form of genocide advocated by whites. Thus, control over reproduction has had political and social implications.

The majority of women having abortions are white. Although 12 percent of the population is of African-American ancestry, black women constitute approximately 31 percent of the women who seek abortions. There is a history of forced sterilization against African-Americans, which many perceive as a form of genocide similar to contraception.

STDs and HIV/AIDS. In 1932, the United States Public Health Service recruited 600 African-American men from Tuskegee, Alabama, to participate in an experiment involving untreated syphilis. The aim of this study was to determine if there were any racial differences in the development of syphilis. The Tuskegee participants were never informed that they had syphilis. This wanton disregard for human life allowed the disease to spread to the sexual partners of these men, as well as their offspring. This experiment continued until 1972! The repercussions from the "Tuskegee Experiment" still resonate strongly through African-American communities, and negatively impact on HIV/AIDS prevention programs.

HIV was the eighth-leading cause of death for all Americans in 1990, but it was the sixth-leading cause of death for African-Americans. It is the leading cause of death for African-American men between the ages of 35 and 44, and the second-leading cause of death for black men and women between 25 and 35. Again this raises the specter of genocide among many members of the African-American community, in that many believe that the virus was man-made!

Sexual Dysfunction. The stereotyped notions about the sexual experiences of African-Americans not only influence the attitudes that whites may have about African-Americans, but also affect the way in which African-Americans perceive themselves. For example, the willingness of an African-American male who is experiencing difficulty in maintaining an erection or ejaculatory control to seek help may be dependent on how closely he identifies with the myth of the "super potent" black man. Any man may feel embarrassment about a sexual problem, but for the African-American male, the embarrassment that he may feel is compounded by the images of the myth.

For clinicians, an awareness of this historical legacy is essential to the treatment process. A key component in the treatment of many sexual problems is the use of self-pleasuring exercises. These exercises are an effective method for a person to learn more about his or her own sex responses. Many African-Americans have negative feelings about masturbation that may infringe on the treatment process. First, changing these negative feelings may take more time than is typical for other clients. Second, African-Americans who do masturbate may be more reluctant to discuss this issue because, for many, admitting that they masturbate indicates that they cannot find a sexual partner.

Latino Perspectives on Sexuality   MIGUEL A. PÉREZ AND HELDA L. PINZÓN

Latinos, like most other ethnic/racial groups residing in the United States, exist in a distinct social environment, have developed a unique culture, and are often disfranchised from mainstream society. The terms "Latino" and "Hispanic" are used interchangeably in this section to describe a heterogeneous group of people representing a kaleidoscope of experiences, educational attainment, acculturation levels, and citizenship status. The term "Latina" pertains specifically to Hispanic women. The heterogeneity of the Latino population residing in the United States of America can be observed in each group's unique culture, beliefs, language, socio-

economic background, family name, racial ascription, and culinary preferences (Castex 1994; Neale 1989; Williams 1989). Although Latinos can be
found in almost every state, more than half of them live in Texas and
California (National Council of La Raza 1992).

Latinos are one of, if not the fastest-growing population groups in the
United States. According to census data, in the last decade, the United
States Latino population increased by 54 percent, a rate of increase more
than twice that of the general population (U.S. Bureau of the Census
[USBC] 1993). Currently, almost nine percent of the U.S. population is
classified as being of Hispanic or Latino descent; this figure is expected to
increase to 21 percent by the year 2050. High fertility rates, high levels of
immigration to the United States, and the relatively young population, are
often cited as reasons for this increase (Brindis 1992). Among Latinos,
persons of Mexican origin form the largest population group, with a
population total of approximately 13.5 million people; Puerto Ricans place
at a distant second with over 2.7 million (USBC 1993).

Overall, U.S. Latinos are a relatively young population with a median
age of 26 years compared to 34 years for non-Latinos; conversely, less than
5 percent of Latinos are aged 65 or older compared to 13 percent for
non-Latinos (USBC 1993). Among U.S. ethnic groups, only Native Americans have a younger population. Further differences among Latinos can
be observed in the age distribution of different Latino groups. Census data
show that Mexican-Americans have the youngest population, with a mean
age of 24 years, and Cuban-Americans have the oldest population—mean
age 40 years (Claude 1993).

The following material describes relevant sexological concepts among
United States Latinos. Although it does not seek to report all sexual-related
knowledge, it will highlight relevant sexological issues and hopefully dispel
some of the stereotypes related to Latino sexuality. Comparisons presented
here represent general data for Latinos, thus the reader needs to understand that there are differences between Latino subpopulation groups. The
truth is that the variety of sexual practices and patterns among Latinos in
the United States, and for that matter in Latin America, are only surpassed
by the limits of human imagination.

Family Issues. Several authors (de la Vega 1990; Lifshitz 1990; Fennelly 1988)
have emphasized the importance of recognizing the differences in family
and cultural expectations regarding sexual behavior for females and males
in the Latino culture. The acknowledgment of these differences allows for
the understanding of the complexity of sexuality-related issues within this
population group. Traditionally, Latinos have placed a high value on the
family, the entity which shapes their earlier views on sexuality (Brindis
1997). Latinos frequently place family over an individual's needs. It is,
therefore, not uncommon for Latinos to reside in multigenerational households with members of their extended families (Alberda and Tilly 1992;

Garcia 1993). This arrangement permits the division of labor, sharing of economic and domestic responsibilities, and most importantly, allows extended-family members to participate in the rearing of children (Kutsche 1983; Leaper-Campbell 1996).

Latino culture has been described as being patriarchal in nature. However, although men are traditionally the family's representative before society, women are the primary caregivers at home; in fact, women in the Latino culture are seen as the base of the family structure. Latinas, according to de la Vega (1990), have an important non-public and non-verbal authority within the family. Females are expected to maintain the equilibrium and smoothness of family relationships. In this role, Latinas traditionally tend to pay more attention to the family's needs than their own. This expectation is most often noted in young women taking care of older relatives, while their male counterparts seek to forge their own future, albeit not too far from the family unit.

Along with family orientation, Latinos often show the closely related concept of *simpatía*. The latter refers to Latinos' willingness to go along with items which may not be understood or that they may disagree with. Szapocznik (1995) has suggested that familism and *simpatía* may now be liabilities for Latinos in the United States, particularly for gay men who attempt to conceal their true HIV-status from their families and friends.

Sexological Concepts: Acculturation and Sexual Practices. Until the advent of the AIDS epidemic, few researchers had systematically documented sexual practices and knowledge among Latinos. Inappropriate application of methodological issues, language difficulties, and cultural insensitivity have all been identified as barriers to data collection among U.S. Latinos (Ford and Norris 1991).

Sexuality is an important life element among Latinos. However, Latino sexuality is not limited or circumscribed to coital activity, but it is rather expressed through a variety of life attitudes which reinforce male and female sexual identities. In the United States, sexual patterns are not only affected by culture, but also by the individual's degree of acculturation and assimilation (Spector 1991).

Acculturation and education also play a pivotal role in the acceptance of new expressions of sexuality. In a 1990 study, Marín, Marín, and Juárez found that Latinas with higher levels of acculturation reported more multiple sexual partners than those with lower acculturation levels. The same study found that less-acculturated males were more likely to carry condoms and report fewer sexual partners. A follow-up study found that less-acculturated Latinas were less likely to carry condoms and experienced higher levels of sexual discomfort (Marín, Gomez, and Hearst 1993). More-acculturated and educated Latinas are also more likely to adopt a leading role during heterosexual activities.

Acculturation notwithstanding, sexuality continues to be a taboo topic for many Latinos, particularly for older, Spanish-speaking Latinos.

Sexual Stereotypes. It is perhaps significant that general knowledge of Latino sexuality is denoted more by stereotypes than factual information. De la Vega (1990) concluded that numerous myths and stereotypes are found among Latinos, as within any group of individuals. It is important that these subtle cultural forms of differentiation not be missed by North American service providers, as they may be the nuances that allow for the development of educational strategies that will effectively reach the Latino "population."

Perhaps the most widely accepted stereotype for Latino males is that of the proverbially promiscuous "Don Juan." This eternally charming individual is known for his ability to sexually conquer and satisfy a large number of females. A second stereotype deals with the erotic nature of some Latino groups as contrasted with more-conservative norms found among more-educated Latinos. Finally, the submissive and passive female stereotype continues to overshadow realities of contemporary Latinas.

Gender and Gender Roles. Worth and Rodriguez (1987) reported that despite the fact some Latinos in the United States have non-traditional lifestyles, they continue to adhere to traditional gender roles. Fennelly (1992) reported on cultural double standards and suggested that, whereas males are encouraged to develop strong self-reliant identities and explore their sexuality, females are taught the value of *etiqueta*, or proper and expected forms of feminine sexual behavior. These, sometimes-conflicting cultural norms contribute to what has been called the "cult of virginity" (Garcia 1980). This "cult of virginity" has its roots in the Catholic Church's teachings and is seen as a sign of purity for women. The basic premise of virginity until marriage has been found to decrease a number of sexual health problems, such as unplanned pregnancies, and to decrease the number of STDs. The primary problem with this concept, at least as practiced among Latinos, is that it is not applied equally to both genders. The literature suggests that these double standards result in either females postponing sexual activities, underreporting of sexual contacts (Taggart 1992), and in some cases, denial of other sexual behaviors, such as anal sex, in order to preserve the "cult of virginity" basic premises. This, however, does not prevent sexual innuendo from taking place.

Coquetería is a term used to describe a group of female behaviors aimed at reinforcing sexual attraction. Some of these behaviors include the use of sexually appealing clothing, the adoption of manners that stimulate sexual attraction, and the use of verbiage that indicate sexual interest. Latinas are not the only ones to discreetly express their sexual or personal interests. *Piropos* are statements generally expressed by men that include a sexual connotation within the context of respect and value for females. Cultural sexual standards are also denoted in language which arbitrarily classifies females as either suitable for marriage, *novias*, or those who can be pursued for sexual conquests, *amantes* (Alexander 1992; Carballo-Diéguez 1989). This dichotomy of sexual and gender roles may explain the reason sexual discussions seldom take place among spouses, since *esposas* (wives) are expected to possess little knowledge about their own sexuality, and even less about their spouse's. It has been suggested that, in some cases, the only Latinas totally in charge of their own sexuality are commercial sex workers, as they can be less constricted to express and fully explore their sexuality.

De la Vega (1990) suggested that sexual double standards are based on the erroneous belief that males are less able than females to control themselves sexually. It is believed that women exercise greater control over their sexual impulses while males appear to be guided by their instincts. In this context, male infidelity is more easily tolerated than female infidelity. Research indicates that Latinos who have poor sexual communication skills engage in extramarital affairs more often then those who have fewer difficulties communicating with their sexual partners. A 1994 study found that infidelity rates were higher among those who attended church infrequently than regular church attenders (Choi, Catalnia, and Docini 1994).

Machismo and Marianismo. *Machismo* has been described as a strong force in most Latino communities, which encourages males to be sexually dominant and the primary providers for their families; it stresses male physical aggression, high risk-taking, breaking rules, and casual, uninvolved sexual relations (de la Vega, 1990). In contrast, *Marianismo* refers to Latino cultural expectations that include the spiritual and moral superiority of women, and encourage Latinas to be virginal, seductive, privately wise, publicly humble, fragile, and yet, provide the glue that holds the family together. It has been argued that while these standards lead to womanizing, they also foster the tenet among males that they are responsible for their family's welfare.

Sexual Education. The AIDS epidemic has spearheaded an emphasis on the need to investigate sexuality education and communication patterns among Latinos in the United States. Family bonds, moral values, *machismo*, *Marianismo*, *etiqueta*, as well as profound religious beliefs, combine to prevent U.S. Latinos from openly discussing sexuality with family members. In some cases, just saying sexual words in front of family members may be difficult for some Latinos (Medina 1987).

The secrecy surrounding sexuality prevents Latinos from receiving adequate, if any, information about sexuality, contraceptives, and HIV/AIDS and other STDs (Amaro 1991; Carrier and Bolton 1991; Mays and Cochran 1988). In 1992, only 67 percent of Latinos said they had communicated with their children about AIDS, as compared to 77 percent of European-Americans and 74 percent of African-Americans (Schoenborn, Marsh, and Hardy 1994).

In traditional Latino families, sexuality education may come from extended-family members rather than nuclear-family members. Aunts, uncles, and grandparents may assume the role of sexuality educators for younger generations. For instance, Marín, Marín, and Juárez (1990) reported that Latinos were more willing than non-Hispanics to discuss certain sexual topics (i.e., drug use and sex) with an older family member. Similarly, data from the National Health Interview Survey found that less than two thirds (59 percent) of Latino parents had discussed AIDS with their children aged 10-17, compared to 72 percent of African-American and 68 percent of European-American parents (Dawson 1990).

In a study of first-generation immigrant adolescents employed in agriculture, Pérez (in press) found that Latino parents failed to adequately educate their children about sexuality-related matters. However, not all Latino parents hesitate to address sexuality-related issues with their offspring. Some researchers have found that 57 percent of Latino parents do communicate with their children about sexuality. In those cases, home-based sexuality education is the primary responsibility of the mother (Biddlecom and Hardy 1991; Dawson and Hardy 1989).

Supporting our earlier assertion that not all Latinos are created equal, Durant (1990) reported that Mexican-American females where less likely than non-Latinas to have communicated with their parents about contraception, sex, and pregnancy. Dawson (1990) found that Mexican-Americans were less likely to broach these topics with their children (50 percent) than were Puerto Ricans (74 percent) and other Latinos (64 percent). In those instances where parents educate their children about sexuality, the responsibility most often lies with the mother. The data suggest that some Latino parents rely on the schools and, in some cases, mass media to educate their children about sexuality-related issues. In a 1994 study, Schoenborn, Marsh, and Hardy found that 46 percent of Latinos had received AIDS information through radio public service announcements (PSAs), compared to 36 percent of European-Americans and 44 percent of African-Americans. An additional 14 percent of Latinos said they had received information through store displays or brochures, compared to 7 percent of European-Americans and 12 percent of African-Americans. Marín, Marín, and Juárez (1990) concluded that this lack of sexual education may contribute to higher rates of childbearing among Latinos. This is among the greatest paradoxes encountered among Latinos, since research suggests that home-based sexuality education plays a key role in decreasing pregnancy rates among Latino adolescents (Brindis 1997) and increasing condom use (Moran and Corley 1991).

Contraception. Throughout Latin America, the number of children in a household assists in establishing a male's role in the community. A large number of children, especially among low-income populations, are sometimes necessary for economic survival; the more hands available for work, the greater the family's income. It is, therefore, not surprising that contraceptive methods are skeptically viewed by some Latinos. This is further compounded by the fact that contraception among Latinos is primarily the responsibility of the woman.

Research indicates that contraceptive use among Latinos is dependent on a number of factors. Attitudes toward contraceptives, religion, condom use during first sexual experience (Marín, Marín, and Juárez, 1990), sexual orientation (Rotheram-Borus et al. 1994), education, and income (Fennelly 1992) have all been identified as being involved with attitudes and likelihood of using contraceptives. Other studies have found that Latino males are less likely to use condoms with their spouses or other primary partners than with other sexual partners (Pérez in press; Sandoval et al. 1995).

In a survey of urban adolescents, Sonestein, Pleck, and Ku (1989) found that Latino males have more-negative attitudes towards condom use than their non-Hispanic counterparts. Although 42 percent of Latina females reported they had used condoms during their first intercourse, Marín, Marín, and Juárez (1990) reported that males still exert a great deal of influence on the decision to use contraceptives. The researchers found that males' attitudes towards condom use determined the likelihood of using them. Latina women whose sexual partners opposed condom use were less likely than those whose partners did not oppose them or voiced no opinion. In a study of 131 bisexual youth in New York City, Rotheram-Borus and colleagues (1994) found that males were more likely to use condoms with a male than with a female sexual partner. The data indicate that more and more Latino men tend to share the decision on whether or not to use contraceptives with their sexual partners. The couple's acculturation and assimilation level, their adherence to Catholic Church doctrine, and their desire for large or small families also play a key in their decision to use contraceptives (Marín, Marín, and Juárez 1990). Furthermore, the data indicate that the proportion of European-Americans who use contraceptive methods at first intercourse is higher than that of Latinos (69 percent and 54 percent, respectively) and that the decision to use condoms during intercourse will be affected by male attitudes towards prophylactics (Forrest and Sing 1990).

Adolescents and Sexuality. One of the pivotal stages in a Latina woman's life is the *quinceañera* celebration—an event that is analogous to the traditional "sweet sixteen" observed in North America. The *quinceañera* party marks a woman's ability to seek a spouse and announces her ability to bear children. During this joyous time, the female is formally introduced to society and is recognized as having achieved full womanhood.

Studies investigating sexual behaviors among Latino adolescents have yielded mixed results. Brindis (1992) found that coital activity rates for Latino youth fall somewhere between that of African-Americans and European-Americans. In contrast to self-reports of lower sexual-activity levels among Latino youth, a national survey found no differences among the proportion of Latino and non-Latino Anglo-American young men who engaged in sexual activities before age 13 (4 percent and 3 percent, respectively) (Sonestein, Pleck, and Ku 1991). Similarly, Forrest and Sing (1990) found that among never-married females 15-19, 49 percent of Latinas reported being sexually active compared to 52 percent of European-Americans and 61 percent of African-Americans.

Differences, however, have been found based on attitudes towards premarital sex (Ginson and Kempf 1990; Padilla and Baird 1991). The data suggest that among adolescents, Latino males tend to engage in sexual intercourse at an earlier age than do females (13 and 15 years of age, respectively). In cross-cultural comparisons, Latino adolescents have been found to have higher sexual risk-taking behaviors (i.e., unprotected sex) than their non-Latino counterparts (Brindis, Wolfe, McCater, Ball, et al. 1995). Brindis (1997) concluded that "acculturation is a key variable influencing adolescent attitudes, behavior, and knowledge about reproduction and contraception" (p. 8).

Latino youths in the United States balance conflicting messages from two cultures regarding their sexuality (Brindis 1992). While the dominant culture appears to promote high levels of non-marital sexual activities, Latino youths, particularly females, must also deal with the more-conservative Latino cultural norms towards sexuality and the "cult of virginity." Some very conservative families see teenage pregnancy, and in some cases pregnancy before marriage, as a "failure." These views are expressed in the often used phrase *fracazó la muchacha*. It is important to clarify that this "failure" does not represent a rejection of the newborn, but rather the woman's limitation to pursue educational goals, employment opportunities, and her possibilities for marriage. Educational level and formal instruction play a role in parental willingness to discuss and educate their adolescent offspring about sexuality. Those with more education have been found to be more willing to educate their children about sexuality-related issues.

Adults and Sexuality. To date, we lack reliable data on the frequency and sexual preferences, masturbatory frequency and techniques, use of pornography, and sexual dysfunctions among Latinos in the United States. Although dialogs about sexual issues are often avoided, Latinos have other more socially acceptable forms to express their sensuality and sexual desire. Some of these mediums include music, dance, art, and poetry. Research indicates that Latino males learn about their sexuality through practical experience rather than through sexual education. Anecdotes suggest that it is not uncommon for young Latinos to lose their virginity through an experience with a sex-industry worker; usually encouraged by older relatives in what could be termed a "sexual rite of passage." Sexual discussions among Latino men tend to occur within same-gender groups while they are under the influence of alcohol, with sex-industry workers, and in the context of jokes (Carrier and Magaña 1991; de la Vega, 1990; Hu and Keller 1989).

In a national survey of sexual behaviors, Billy, Tanfer, Grady, and Klepinger (1992) found that Latino men reported a median of 6.1 sexual partners over a lifetime as compared to 8.0 for African-Americans and 6.4 for non-Latino white males. The same study found that Latinos were more likely than non-Latinos to report four or more sexual partners in the last eighteen months. In a survey of over 1,500 Latinos, Marín, Gomez, and Hearst (1993) found that 60 percent of single Latino males reported multiple sexual partners in the previous 12 months.

Pregnancy. Researchers have identified acculturation level, parental communication, low education, language, and country of origin as a determinant for pregnancy among Latino women (Durant 1990). Given the cultural significance of motherhood, it is not surprising that in the United States Latinas experience more per-capita births than their non-Latina counterparts. In 1990, the average number of children per Latino family was 3.76 compared to 3.43 for African-Americans and 3.11 for European-Americans (USDC 1991). Brindis (1997) has suggested that the higher number of children among Latinas may be a residual effect of an intrinsic belief that developed among immigrants based on economic needs and high mortality rates in their countries of origin.

Garcia (1980) suggested that motherhood serves to secure an identity for the Latino woman. In a 1991 survey, Segura found that the meaning of motherhood among Latinas differed, depending on their country of birth. In his study, Segura surveyed Mexican-born women and American-born Chicanas; the findings indicate that while Mexican-born women viewed motherhood as all-encompassing, Chicanas gave greater meaning to child rearing. Among Latinas, Puerto Rican females have the highest rate of pregnancies. Among Mexican women, those born in Mexico experience more pregnancies than those born in the U.S. (Aneshensel, Becerra, Fiedler, and Schuler 1990). Darabi and Ortiz (1987) concluded that "one plausible explanation of these findings could be that Mexican-origin women marry at very early ages" (p. 27). Further differences were reported by Fennelly (1992), who found birth rates among Latino adolescent females ranging from a high of 21 percent among Mexican-Americans to a low of 6 percent among Cuban mothers. Fennelly-Darabi and Ortiz (1987) reported that Latino women were more likely than non-Latino women to have a second birth shortly after the first, and were less likely to have positive attitudes towards abortions.

Despite higher birth rates than other ethnic groups, lower socioeconomic backgrounds, and fewer prenatal visits to physicians, Latinas as a group have fewer low-birthweight babies. This finding has confused experts who would expect the opposite to be true based on socioeconomic factors. Several explanations have been offered, such as better nutrition in the form of complete proteins, less use of alcohol and other psychoactive drugs during pregnancy, and increased family support during the months preceding childbirth. Other researchers have attempted to link higher birthweights with religiosity and spirituality of Latinas in the United States (Magaña and Clark 1995).

Marriage. Marriage is highly valued among Latino groups; however, in some cases, no difference is made between legal unions and long-term cohabitation. Fennelly-Darabi, Kandiah, and Ortiz (1989) reported that it is not possible to determine the number of couples in informal unions. In a later study, Landale and Fennelly (1992), reported that while the number of non-marital unions has decreased on the island of Puerto Rico, they have greatly increased among Puerto Ricans living on the U.S. mainland.

According to the Census Bureau, in the U.S., Latino marriage rates (62.3 percent) are almost the same for non-Latino whites (64 percent) and are higher than that of African-Americans (46.3 percent). On the other hand, National Council of la Raza data indicate that "The number of Hispanic single parents has increased at a faster rate than Black or White female-headed families" (1993, p.12). According to the U.S. Census Bureau, in 1991, 60 percent of Latino families with a female head-of-household with children under 18 lived under the poverty line (USBC, 1993).

Fennelly, Kandiah, and Ortiz (1989) argued that "A woman's marital status at the time she bears a child is important because of the implications for her later fertility, and for her own and her children's economic and social status" (p. 96). The social and legal implications of out-of-wedlock births have then been used to explain the reasons why there are more premarital pregnancies than premarital births in the Latino culture. It has been a time-honored tradition among some Latinos to marry while the woman is pregnant, in order to provide a stable and legal union for the newborn.

Rape. Few studies have been conducted to investigate sexual activities among Latinos in the United States; however, research findings seem to suggest that acculturation and gender, not culture, are key determinants of attitudes towards forcible sexual activities. In a study of attitudes towards date rape among college students, Fischer (1987) found that Latino students held more-traditional gender roles and had a more-positive attitude towards forcible intercourse under certain circumstances. These included spending a lot of money on the woman, the length of time they had dated, the female "leading" the man on, and the perceived female's previous sexual history.

Acculturation and gender was also found to play a role in the views of college students towards forcible sexual encounters. According to Fischer (1987), "Bicultural and bilingual Hispanic women are less rejecting of forcible rape than assimilated Hispanic and majority women are, while Hispanic males, regardless of degree of acculturation, are less rejecting of forcible date rape than are majority males" (p. 99). Lefley and colleagues (1993) reported that Latinos not only had different definitions of sexual coercion, but also were more likely to blame the victim than were their Anglo-American counterparts. A review of the literature did not support the notion of espousal rape. Males under the influence of alcohol may force their spouses to engage in sexual activities. Forcible sexual intercourse may not be perceived as a violation of a female's body if it happens within the context of marriage. As a result, espousal-rape reports among Latinos in the U.S. are more likely to occur among the acculturated, assimilated second generation, and those with higher educational levels.

Same-Gender Sexual Activities. In a study of African-American, Latino, Asian/Eurasian, and Caucasian gay adolescent males, Newman and Muzzonigro (1993) found that traditional families were less accepting of homosexuality than low-traditional families. Bonilla and Porter (1990) found that Latinos did not differ significantly from their African-American and white counterparts on attitudes toward homosexuality; however, they were less tolerant in their perceptions of civil liberties. This lack of acceptance may force males to hide their sexual orientation or to pursue heterosexual lifestyles (i.e., marriage) while secretly engaging in same-gender sexual activities.

Family acceptance is only part of the equation explaining Latino views toward same-gender sexual activities. Same-gender sex has different meanings and connotations for Latinos than for the non-Latino population in the United States. As a general rule, same-gender relationships are heavily stigmatized among Latinos, even among highly acculturated groups (Fischer, 1987). Homosexuality is not a topic easily discussed among males (Pérez and Fennelly 1996).

Magaña and Carrier (1991) suggested that it is not totally uncommon for Latino males to turn to "effeminate" males to satisfy their sexual needs under certain conditions. They identified lack of a female sexual partner and/or lack the economic resources to visit a sex worker as an acceptable reason for male-male sexual activities. Same-gender sexual behaviors are also more likely to appear while under the influence of alcohol. Same-gender sexual activity perceptions are also affected by Latino cultural norms. Latinos do not necessarily classify the penile inserter during male-male anal sex as homosexual (Amaro 1991; Carrier 1976). As a result, Latino males engaging in same-gender sexual activities may not perceive themselves, or be perceived as, "homosexual" or "bisexual," as long as they play the appropriate dominant sexual role—a role which tends to mirror that of the male in a heterosexual couple (CDC 1993). Carrier (1976) reported that unlike their American "gay" counterparts, Mexican males engaging in same-gender sex prefer anal intercourse over fellatio or other forms of sexual gratification. Also, in contrast to their Anglo-American counterparts, Latino males are more likely to assume only the passive or receptive role during same-gender encounters. Ross, Paulsen, and Stalstrom (1988) concluded that it is not the sexual act itself, but rather the cross-gender behavior which gets labeled and heavily stigmatized among Latinos.

The lack of identification with the homosexual community may explain the inability of Latino men who engage in sex with other men to identify or respond to educational programs targeting homosexuals. But, most importantly, it emphasizes the need for researchers to concentrate more on behaviors than labels when studying sexual interactions (Alcalay et al. 1990; Carrier and Magaña 1991). The labeling-versus-behavior distinction is important in light of the fact that 45 percent of AIDS cases among Latinos are the result of same-gender sex, and that an additional 7 percent of AIDS cases are related to same-gender sex with intravenous drug users (CDC 1994).

Bisexuality. De la Vega (1990) discussed three bisexual patterns among Latino men in the United States. The first type he labeled the closeted, self-identified, homosexual Latino. He described this type as a male with homosexual tendencies, but who lives a heterosexual lifestyle. The second type discussed by de la Vega, is the closeted, latent-homosexual Latino; this type is characterized by a male who describes himself as a heterosexual, but who engages in same-gender sex while under the influence of mind-altering substances, primarily alcohol. Finally, de la Vega described the "super-macho" heterosexual Latino. This man allows himself to have sexual contacts with other males since he considers them to be "pseudo-females." This last type of male will not admit, even to himself, that he may express homosexual tendencies.

HIV/AIDS. Keeling (1993) described the minority experience with AIDS in the United States as follows:

> The factors of social and economic class, poverty, and urban despair
> . . . will continue to result in an increasingly disproportionate impact
> of the epidemic on African-American and Hispanic people during the
> second decade of HIV; it is worth emphasizing as strongly as possible
> that these disproportions occur not because of biologic reality of race,
> but because race is a "front" for class, socioeconomic status, and poverty
> in this context. (p. 264)

This fact could not be of greater truth among Latinos in the United States of America.

The Latino community in the United States has been disproportionately affected by HIV infection. In 1996, Latinos accounted for 17.3 percent of all male AIDS cases in the United States, some 78,926 cases among this population group (CDC 1996). Intravenous drug use (IVDU) is second only to same-gender sex as a transmission mode among Latino males. Latina women account for 20.5 percent of all AIDS cases, a cumulative total of 11,909 Latinas (CDC 1996). Among Latinas, 45 percent contracted AIDS through heterosexual contact, whereas 44 percent of AIDS cases are contracted from IVDU (CDC 1996). Weeks and colleagues (1995) concluded that, although the number of heterosexual cases are increasing among Latinas, the number of AIDS-prevention programs geared towards them continues to be inadequate.

Among Latinos, Puerto Ricans have the highest incidence of HIV infection. Puerto Ricans also have the fourth-highest rate in the nation (NCLR, 1992). According to the Centers for Disease Control and Prevention (1993), up to 70 percent of AIDS cases are related to IVDU in Puerto Rico.

Latino awareness of the disease does not vary greatly from other ethnic groups. Dawson (1990) reported that 41 percent of Latinos said they had some knowledge about AIDS, compared to 39 percent for African-Americans and 48 percent for European-Americans. However, less than half (48 percent) of Latinos understood the connection between HIV and AIDS, compared to 69 percent among European-Americans. These figures did not vary greatly two years later, when Schoenborn, Marsh, and Hardy (1994) reported that 40 percent of Latinos, 47 percent of European-Americans, and 39 percent of African-Americans had "some" knowledge about AIDS.

Latinos are less likely than other ethnic groups to accurately identify HIV-transmission modes. Alcalay, Sniderman, Mitchell, and Griffin (1990) found that Latinos were more likely (36 percent) than European-Americans (15 percent) to believe they could get AIDS from blood donations. The same study found that Latinos were more likely than non-Latinos to believe that HIV transmission could occur through casual contact (e.g., hugging or from water fountains). Dawson (1990) found that 7 percent of Latinos believed it was "very likely" they could become infected with HIV by eating at a restaurant where the cook had AIDS, compared to 5 percent of European-American respondents. The researchers also found that 19 percent of Latinos believed they could catch AIDS from an unclean public toilet, whereas only 8 percent of the European-American respondents and 10 percent of African-Americans believed this to be an exposure category.

Knowledge about AIDS seems to be related to language preference among some Latinos. Research indicates that Spanish-speaking Latinos are more likely than bilingual Latinos to believe AIDS is spread through casual contact (Hu and Keller 1989). Another survey found that 24.1 percent of Spanish-speaking Latinos answered positively to the question, "Do you believe that one can catch AIDS from shaking hands with someone who has AIDS?" in comparison to 1.7 percent of English-speaking Latinos (Alcalay, Sniderman, Mitchell, and Griffin 1990).

Dawson and Hardy (1989) found that Mexican-Americans tended to be less knowledgeable about HIV/AIDS than other Latino groups. Only 50 percent of Mexican-American respondents in their study indicated it is "definitely true" that "AIDS is an infectious disease caused by a virus" compared to 62 percent of other Latinos. Only 46 percent of Mexican-American respondents said they knew that blood transfusions are routinely tested for HIV antibodies, compared to 55 percent of other Latinos, 72 percent of European-Americans, and 53 percent of African-American respondents.

Hu and Keller (1989) found that, despite their lesser knowledge about AIDS, Spanish-speaking Latinos reported a higher interest in learning about AIDS (88 percent) than English-speaking groups (83 percent). Pérez and Fennelly (1996) found that Latino farmworkers are willing to learn about AIDS, even though their reluctance to discuss sex has not decreased. One might expect that lower levels of knowledge about HIV/AIDS among Latinos in the United States would lead to more discrimination towards persons with AIDS. Instead, Alcalay et al. (1990) found no differences between Latinos and non-Hispanics in their likelihood to support AIDS victims' rights.

Summary. Latinos in the United States represent a wide range of educational attainment, socioeconomic levels, and skin color. Sexual practices and knowledge among this population have been found to be heavily influenced by strict cultural norms largely shaped by the Catholic Church. However, the data suggest that Latino sexual norms and behaviors are as varied as the heterogeneous group they represent. Further research is needed to properly investigate sexual attitudes and behaviors among the individual groups.

Feminism and Sexuality in the United States   PATRICIA BARTHALOW KOCH

A Brief History of the Feminist Movements. Earlier in this section, we discussed groups that illustrate ways in which religion and race or ethnicity operate as social factors defining subcultures within the U.S.A. and influence sexuality. Gender can be regarded in a similar manner. Here, we now consider feminist perspectives as reflections of a distinct social group or subculture.

Feminism is defined and implemented in various ways by different people. In its broadest interpretation, feminism represents advocacy for women's interests; in a stricter definition, it is the "theory of the political, social, and economic equality of the sexes" (LeGates 1995, 494). Although the terms "feminism" and "feminist" are only about a hundred years old, advocates for women's interests have been active for centuries throughout the world. As Robin Morgan (1984, 5) wrote in *Sisterhood Is Global,* "An indigenous feminism has been present in every culture in the world and in every period of history since the suppression of women began." Throughout history, women have protested, individually and collectively, against a range of injustices—often as part of other social movements in which gender equality was not the focus of the activity and women were not organized to take action on behalf of their gender.

However, stress on the ideologies of liberty, equality, and emancipation of men in the eighteenth-century political revolutions in Britain, France, and the United States laid the groundwork for these ideologies to be championed in women's lives also. In addition, the Industrial Revolution of the nineteenth century provided educational and economic opportunities supportive of a feminist movement in many societies.

Actual women's movements, or organized and sustained activities for gender equality supported by a relatively large number of people over a period of years, have occurred since the mid-1800s in many countries throughout the world. The United States, as well as most European societies, experienced extensive women's movements in the closing decades of the nineteenth century, with another wave of feminism occurring in the 1960s.

The beginning of an organized women's movement in the United States has been traced to the Seneca Falls Convention of 1848 where a Declaration of Principles called for gender equality (Chefetz and Dworkin 1986). Issues addressed included women's legal rights to property, children, and to their own earnings; equal educational and employment opportunities; the changing of negative feminine stereotypes; and increased opportunities for women to improve their physical fitness and health. These early feminists also addressed more-explicit sexual issues, including the abolition of the sexual double standard of expecting men to be "promiscuous" and women to be "pure"; equality between sexual partners; and the right of married women to refuse sexual activity with their husbands. Yet, although feminist ideology was well developed during these pre-Civil War years, the progressive feminist leaders had few followers. "In the nineteenth and early twentieth centuries the United States was not ready for a mass movement which questioned the entire gender role and sex stratification systems" (Chefetz and Dworkin 1986:112).

Only when the issues were narrowed to focus upon women's right to vote did the movement gain mass following. By 1917, about two million women were members of the National American Woman Suffrage Association, and millions more were supporters of the women's suffrage campaign (Kraditor 1965). The reasons for supporting a woman's right to vote, however, were varied. For some, it was an issue of basic human rights and gender equality. Many others, who believed in gender-role differentiation, supported suffrage on the basis that women would bring higher moral standards into governmental decisions. This more-conservative perspective dominated the movement. After achieving the right to vote in 1920 with the passage of the Nineteenth Amendment to the U.S. Constitution, this first wave of feminism dissipated.

A second wave of feminism developed within the United States, as well as worldwide, in the 1960s. At this time, many women were finding that, while their participation in educational institutions and the labor force was increasing, their political, legal, economic, and social status was not improving. This American feminist movement came on the heels of the black civil rights movement, which had already focused attention on the immorality of discrimination and legitimized mass protest and activism as methods for achieving equality (Freeman 1995). The contemporary women's movement was organized around many interrelated issues, including: legal equality; control over one's own body, including abortion rights; elimination of discrimination based on gender, race, ethnicity, and sexual orientation; securing more political power; and the ending of institutional and social roadblocks to professional and personal achievement. By the mid-1970s, this issue became a mass movement, with over half of American women supporting many of its principles and demands (Chefetz and Dworkin 1986).

The second women's movement had two origins, from two different strata of society, with different styles, values, and forms of organization (Freeman 1995). Although the members of both branches were predominantly white, middle-class, and college-educated, there was a generation gap between them. The younger branch was comprised of a vast array of local, decentralized, grassroots groups that concentrated on a small number or only one issue, rather than the entire movement. Members tended to adjure hierarchical structure and the traditional political system. Some of the activities in which they engaged included: running consciousness-raising groups; providing educational conferences and literature; establishing woman-supporting services (bookstores, health clinics, rape-crisis centers, and battered-women shelters); and organizing public-awareness campaigns and marches. This branch was responsible for infusing the movement with new issues, strategies, and techniques for social change. Many of its projects became institutionalized within American society (e.g., rape-crisis centers) through government funding and entrepreneurship.

These feminists also took their particular perspectives into other arenas, including the prochoice, environmental, and antinuclear movements. They also impacted academia, establishing women's centers and women's studies departments, programs, and courses on campuses throughout the country. By the early 1980s, there were over 300 women's studies programs and 30,000 courses in colleges and universities, and a national professional association, the National Women's Studies Association (Boxer 1982). Many periodicals devoted exclusively to scholarship on women or gender were begun; Searing (1987) listed ninety-four such journals.

The second branch of the women's movement was the older, more-traditional division that formed top-down national organizations with officers and boards of directors, and often paid staffs and memberships. Most of these organizations sought support through contributions, foundations, or government contracts to conduct research and services. Some of these feminist organizations included: the Women's Legal Defense Fund, the Center for Women's Policy Studies, the Feminist Majority Foundation, and the National Coalition Against Domestic Violence; with other previously established groups taking on a more-feminist agenda, such as the National

Federation of Business and Professional Women and the American Association of University Women.

The National Organization for Women (NOW), an action organization devoted to women's rights, was the primary feminist group to develop a mass membership. NOW focused its attention at the national level to become politically powerful. One of its major campaigns was the passage of an Equal Rights Amendment (ERA) to the U.S. Constitution guaranteeing legal equality for women. The ERA was endorsed by the U.S. Congress and sent to the states for ratification in 1972. In 1978, over one hundred thousand people marched in Washington D.C. in support of the Equal Rights Amendment. But the ERA and feminism were to meet with strong opposition from well-organized conservative and right-wing political and religious groups that depicted feminist goals as "an attack on the family and the American way of life" (Freeman 1995, 525). Stop-ERA campaigns were adeptly organized by these politically savvy groups and, by 1982, the ERA had failed to pass within the allotted timeframe by seven votes in three states.

Yet, it cannot be said that the feminist movement failed. Many states passed equal rights amendments of their own, and many discriminatory federal, state, and local laws were changed with the Supreme Court unanimously ruling in favor of interpreting constitutional law to provide equal opportunity for women. In addition, a powerful women's health movement had been spawned, and efforts for reproductive freedom, including abortion rights, would be continued to combat anti-abortion groups throughout the 1980s and 1990s. As Freeman (1995, 528) concluded: "The real revolution of the contemporary women's movement is that the vast majority of the [United States] public no longer questions the right of any woman, married or unmarried, with or without children to work for wages to achieve her fullest potential."

Although feminists agree there are still many strides to be made in achieving the goals of legal, economic, political, and social equality for women in the United States, they are often divided over philosophy, goals, and strategies for achieving equality in these areas. Feminism is not a monolithic ideology. There is "not a single interpretation on what feminism means but a variety of feminisms representing diverse ideas and perspectives radiating out from a core set of assumptions regarding the elimination of women's secondary status in society" (Pollis 1988, 86-87).

Feminism and Sexuality. Sexuality has always been a critical issue to feminists, because they see the norms regarding "proper" and "normal" sexual behavior as functioning to socialize and suppress women's expression and behavior in an effort to control female fertility as socioeconomic and political assets (Tiefer 1995). "The personal is political," the feminist rallying cry, applies particularly to sexuality, which is often the most personal, hidden, suppressed, and guilt-ridden aspect of women's lives. MacKinnon (1982:515) captures this essence well in the analogy that: "Sexuality is to feminism what work is to Marxism: that which is most one's own, yet most taken away."

Although women are now being seen as sexual beings in their own right, not simply as reproducers or sexual property, Tiefer (1995, 115) describes how women's sexual equality is still constrained by many factors, including:

> Persistent socioeconomic inequality that makes women dependent on men and therefore sexually subordinate; unequal laws such as those regarding age of sexual consent and rights in same-sex relationships; lack of secure reproductive rights; poor self-image or a narrow window of confidence because of ideals of female attractiveness; ignorance of woman-centered erotic techniques, social norms about partner choice; and traumatic scars from sexual abuse.

In general, feminists believe that both women's and men's sexuality is socially constructed and must be examined within its social context (McCormick 1994). Gender-role socialization is viewed as a very powerful process creating unequal power relationships and stereotypic expectations for appropriate sexual feelings and behaviors of women and men. Male gender-role socialization based on male political, social, and economic dominance is likely to result in male sexual control, aggression, and difficulties with intimacy. On the other hand, female gender-role socialization based on political, social, and economic oppression of women is likely to result in disinterest and dissatisfaction with sex, as well as passivity and victimization. Feminists question the assumption of a binary gender system and challenge traditional concepts of masculinity and femininity (Irvine 1990). They politicize sexuality by examining the impact that power inequalities between men and women have on sexual expression.

Although most feminists may agree upon the relevance of socialization and context in the creation of male and female sexuality, they may vehemently disagree about the nature of sexual oppression and the strategies for its elimination (McCormick 1994). This has resulted in the emergence of two major feminist camps: radical feminists and liberal feminists.

As described by McCormick (1994, 211), radical feminists have polarized male and female sexuality—often demonizing men and idealizing women in this process. They view women as victims who must be protected. They use evidence showing girls and women as the predominant victims and boys and men as the perpetrators of rape, sexual harassment, prostitution, domestic violence, and childhood sexual abuse to support their views.

Radical feminists are vehemently opposed to pornography, "likening erotic images and literature to an instruction manual by which men are taught how to bind, batter, torture, and humiliate women" (McCormick 1994, 211). They have spearheaded many efforts to censor pornographic/erotic materials, often joining with right-wing organizations in these efforts. Another goal of radical feminists is the elimination of prostitution, which they view as trafficking in women's bodies. They believe that all women in the sex trades are being victimized.

Because of these beliefs, radical feminists are criticized as treating women as children who are incapable of giving true consent to their choice of sexual activities. In response, these feminists argue that it is our sociopolitical system that treats women as second class and has robbed them of the equality needed for consensual sexual expression. Until this system is changed, true consent from women is not possible. In fact, orthodox radical feminists do not recognize the possibility of consensual heterosexuality, finding little difference between conventional heterosexual intercourse and rape, viewing both acts as representing male supremacy (McCormick 1994, 211). Radical feminists are accused of advocating "politically correct sex" by idealizing monogamous, egalitarian, lesbian sex and celibacy, and rejecting any other forms of consensual relationships or activity.

On the other hand, liberal feminists defend women's rights to sexual pleasure and autonomy. They believe that, if women are viewed only as victims, they are stripped of their adult autonomy and their potential to secure joyous and empowering sexual pleasure and relationships on their own behalf (McCormick 1994, 211). These feminists do not view all erotic material as harmful and believe in women's right to create their own erotic material. They differentiate between the depictions of forced sex in pornography and actual violence against women. Although not always pleased with all types of pornographic material, they believe in the right of free speech and choice, and acknowledge that censorship efforts could never eliminate all pornographic material anyway. In addition, who is to decide what is pornographic and what is erotic? Regarding prostitution, they view sex work as a legitimate occupational choice for some, and acknowledge the tremendous range of experience with sex work primarily based on social class.

Liberal feminism dominated the first phase of the women's movement of the 1960s. The emphasis was on women's empowerment to achieve professional and personal, including sexual, potentials. The expansion of sexual possibilities was explored, with pleasure being emphasized. The strategies of consciousness-raising, education, and female-centered care were used to help eliminate sexual shame and passivity, with women being encouraged to discover and develop new sexual realities for themselves (Tiefer 1995, 115). However, beginning in the 1970s, the pendulum began to swing away from an emphasis on the power of self-definition towards the agendas of the radical feminists who emphasized issues of sexual violence against women, including rape, incest, battery, and harassment. Thus, during this current feminist movement, much more time and emphasis has been devoted to women's sexual victimization, danger, and repression than to women's sexual equality, pleasure, and relationship enhancement.

Today, many in the general public, professionals, and even sexologists fail to distinguish between differences within feminism. They are most aware of and react primarily to the radical-feminist ideologies and strategies. Thus, feminism has become stereotyped by the extreme positions of the radicals and seems to have lost much of its overt mass support, with many trying to distance themselves from these extreme positions. For example, it is not unusual to hear someone today say, "I believe in women's rights but I'm not a feminist."

Feminist Critiques of and Contributions to Sexology. Feminist sexology is the scholarly study of sexuality that is of, by, and for women's interests. Employing diverse epistemologies, methods, and sources of data, feminist scholars examine women's sexual experiences and the cultural frame that constructs sexuality. They challenge the assumptions that sexuality is an eternal essence, arguing "that a kiss is not a kiss and a sigh is not a sigh and a heterosexual is not a heterosexual and an orgasm is not an orgasm in any transhistorical, transcultural way" (Tiefer 1995, 597). These theories and approaches have resulted in an enormous body of work during the last two decades reexamining theories, methods, and paradigms of gender and sexuality, and contributing to social change (Vance and Pollis 1990).

During this time, feminists and others have challenged the preeminence and validity of traditional science, particularly as it has been applied to human beings and their behaviors. They have argued that traditional science, rather than being objective and value-free, takes place in a particular cultural context (one that is often sexist and heterosexist), which thus becomes incorporated into research, education, or therapy (McCormick 1994). For example, research on unintended and adolescent pregnancy is focused almost exclusively on females, reflecting a double standard requiring women to be the sexual gatekeepers while relieving men of such responsibilities.

Another example comes from therapy. Numerous studies have determined that relationship factors, including intimacy, nongenital stimulation, affection, and communication, are better predictors of women's sexual satisfaction than frequency of intercourse or orgasm. Nevertheless, the dominant therapeutic paradigm, as enforced by the *Diagnostic and Statistical Manual of Mental Disorders*, uses physiologically based genital performance during heterosexual intercourse as the standard for determining women's sexual dysfunctions (Tiefer 1995).

Feminist scholarship uses the following principles in overcoming the deficits in understanding of women's experiences, gender and gender asymmetry, and sexuality:

1. Acknowledgment of the pervasive influence of gender in all aspects of social life, including the practice of science;
2. A multifaceted challenge to the normative canons of science, especially the tenet of objectivity, which splits subject from object, and theory from practice;

3. Advocacy of consciousness raising as a research strategy that elevates and legitimates experience as a valid way of knowing, essential to uncovering meaning structures and diversity among individuals;
4. Conceptualization of gender as a social category, constructed and maintained through the gender-attribution process, and as a social structure;
5. Emphasis on the heterogeneity of experience and the central importance of language, community, culture, and historical context in constituting the individual; and
6. Commitment to engage in research that is based on women's experience and is likely to empower them to eliminate sexism and contribute to societal change (Pollis 1986,88).

Sexology has been criticized for being reticent to integrate feminist perspectives and scholarship into its establishment for fear of being perceived as unscientific and radical (Irvine 1990). However, in recent years feminist perspectives have become more visible in the scholarly journals, conferences, and among the membership and leadership of professional sexological organizations. Future goals for feminist sexologists include more attention to understanding the intersections of race, class, and culture within gender, and making the results of their work more usable.

General Summary of Social Factors

This discussion of social factors influencing sexuality in the U.S.A. has selectively focused on religion, race/ethnicity, and gender. Essentially, we have taken the view that such social variables exert influence largely through membership in corresponding social groups. Our review examined the general tradition of the Judeo-Christian heritage of the U.S.A., membership in the Mormon church, African-American, and Latino minority groups, and identification with feminist perspectives as specific examples.

We recognize that this approach omits other important social factors such as education, social class, and size of city of residence. Our purpose has not been to provide an exhaustive review of all pertinent social groups within the U.S.A. Rather, we wished to demonstrate the abundant evidence that a full understanding of sexuality in American culture eventually will require a recognition of the diverse social groups that reside in this nation. As we proceed to examine what sexuality researchers have learned about specific forms of sexual attitudes and behavior, the authors will report, where possible, the results of research which documents an association between sexuality and social variables.

Unfortunately, a recognition of these associations has not always been incorporated into investigations of sexual practices. For example, much of the existing research has been conducted with predominantly white, middle-class, college-educated populations. Researchers have frequently failed to adequately describe the demographic characteristics of their samples, and they have often failed to test possible correlations with social variables. One consequence is that American sexual scientists have yet to develop a full understanding of the very diversity of social groups we have tried to describe. Closing such gaps in our knowledge remains one of the principle tasks of sexual science in the U.S.A.

3. Sexual Knowledge and Education
PATRICIA BARTHALOW KOCH

According to the National Coalition to Support Sexuality Education,

> Sexuality education is a lifelong process of acquiring information and forming attitudes, beliefs, and values about identity, relationships, and intimacy. It encompasses sexual development, reproductive health, interpersonal relationships, affection, intimacy, body image, and gender roles [among other topics]. Sexuality education seeks to assist children [people] in understanding a positive view of sexuality, provide them with information and skills about taking care of their sexual health, and help them to acquire skills to make decisions now and in the future. (SIECUS 1992)

A. A Brief History of American Sexuality Education

Sexuality education in the United States has always been marked by tension between maintaining the status quo of the "acceptable" expression of individual sexuality, and change as precipitated by the economic, social, and political events of the time. The major loci for sexuality education have shifted from the family and the community (in earlier times being more influenced by religion, and in modern times, by consumerism and the media), to schools. Much of the education has been developed by and targeted towards middle-class whites. As will be described in more detail, the two major movements to formalize sexuality education in the United States were spearheaded for the advancement of either "social protection" or "social justice." Throughout history, the goals, content, and methodologies of sexuality education in these two movements have often been in opposition to one another.

According to D'Emilio and Freedman (1988), young people in colonial America learned about sexuality through two primary mechanisms. In these agrarian communities, observation of sexual activity among animals was common. Observation of sexual activity among adults was also common, since families lived in small, often-unpartitioned dwellings, where it was not unusual for adults and children to sleep together. Second, more formal moral instruction about the role of sexuality in people's lives came from parents and clergy, with lawmakers endorsing the religious doctrines. The major message was that sexual activity ought to be limited to marriage and aimed at procreation. However, within the marital relationship, both the man and woman were entitled to experience pleasure during the procreative act.

Ministers throughout the colonies invoked biblical injunctions against extramarital and nonprocreative sexual acts, while colonial statutes in both New England and the Chesapeake area outlawed fornication, rape, sodomy, adultery, and sometimes incest, prescribing corporal or capital punishment, fines, and in some cases, banishment for sexual transgressors. Together, these moral authorities attempted to socialize youth to channel sexual desires toward marriage (D'Emilio and Freedmen 1988,18)

A small minority of colonists also were exposed to a limited number of gynecological and medical-advice texts from London. These underscored the primary goal of sexuality as reproduction, with pleasure only to be associated with this goal.

After the War for American Independence, small autonomous rural communities gave way to more-commercialized areas, and church and state regulation of morality began to decline. Individual responsibility and choice became more emphasized. Thus, instruction on sexuality changed from community (external) control to individual (internal) control. For example, between the 1830s and 1870s, information about contraceptive devices and abortion techniques circulated widely through printed matter (pamphlets, circulars, and books) and lectures. However, peer education was the primary source of sexuality education, with more-"educated" people, especially women, passing along their knowledge to friends and family members.

Increasing secularization and the rise of the medical profession spawned a health-reform movement in the 1830s that emphasized a quest for physical, as well as spiritual, perfection. With advances in publishing and literacy, a prolific sexual-advice literature, written by doctors and health reformers of both genders, emerged. The central message was that, for bodily well-being (as well as economic success), men and women had to control and channel their sexual desires toward procreative, marital relations. "Properly channeled, experts claimed, sexual relations promised to contribute to individual health, marital intimacy, and even spiritual joy" (D'Emilio and Freedman 1988, 72). The popularity of these materials demonstrated Americans' need for and interest in sexuality education. Much of the self-help and medical-advice literature directed at men emphasized the dangers of masturbation. Women were taught that they had less sexual passion than men, and their role was to help men to control their sexual drives. In other words, a standard of female "purity" was the major theme of the sexuality education of the time.

Two studies of women's sexuality conducted in the early 1900s provide insight into the sources of sexual information for women during the nineteenth century. Katharine B. Davis (1929) studied one thousand women (three quarters born before 1890) and Dr. Clelia Mosher (1980) surveyed forty-five women (four fifths born between 1850 and 1880). Over 40 percent of the women in Davis' study and half in Mosher's reported that they received less-than-adequate instruction about sex before marriage. Those who indicated that they had received some sexual information identified Alice Stockham's advice manual, *Tokology*, about pregnancy, child-birth, and childrearing as their chief source.

In the later nineteenth century, a combined health and social-reform movement developed, that attempted to control the content of and access to sexuality education. Middle-class reformers organized voluntary associa-tions, such as the Women's Christian Temperance Union (WCTU), to address issues, including prostitution and obscenity. The social-purity move-ment in the late nineteenth century added the demand for female equality and a single sexual standard to the earlier moral-reform movements. The WCTU spearheaded a sex-education campaign through the White Cross to help men resist sexual temptation. Social-purity leaders authored marital advice books that recognized women's sexual desires and stressed that women could enjoy intercourse only if they really wanted it. Women's rights and social-purity advocates issued the first formal call for sex education in America. They argued that women should teach children about sex: "Show your sons and daughters the sancties and the terrors of this awful power of sex, its capacities to bless or curse its owner" (D'Emilio and Freedman 1988, 155). They demanded a public discourse of sexuality that emphasized love and reproductive responsibility rather than lust.

An example of the restricted character of sexuality education at the time was the enactment of the 1873 "Comstock Law" for the "Suppression of Trade in, and Circulation of Obscene Literature and Articles of Immoral Use." This revision of the federal postal law forbade the mailing of infor-mation or advertisements about contraception and abortion, as well as any material about sexuality. The Comstock Law was in effect until being overturned by a federal appeals court in 1936 in a decision about contra-ception: *United States v. Dow Package.*

Yet, the turn of the century ushered in a more "progressive" era fueled by industrial capitalism. Progressive reform provoked by the middle class called upon government and social institutions, including schools, to in-tervene in social and economic issues, such as sex education. One of the major movements for sex education was the social-hygiene movement spearheaded by Dr. Prince Morrow to prevent the spread of syphilis and gonorrhea. In 1905, he formed the Society of Sanitary and Moral Prophy-laxis in New York City, later renamed the American Social Hygiene Asso-ciation. This society was joined by the WCTU, YMCA, state boards of health, and the National Education Association in an "unrelenting campaign of education to wipe out the ignorance and the prejudices that allowed venereal diseases to infect the nation" (D'Emilio and Freedman 1988, 205).

They held public meetings and conferences, published and distributed written materials, and endorsed sex education in the public schools. While insisting on frank and open discussions of sexual-health matters, they promulgated the traditional emphasis of sexuality in marriage for reproductive purposes and the avoidance of erotic temptation (like masturbation). More-conservative Americans considered such openness to be offensive. Former-President Howard Taft described sex education as "full of danger if carried on in general public schools" (D'Emilio and Freedman 1988, 207). Others considered this type of education to be too restrictive. For example, Maurice Bigelow, Professor of Biology at Columbia University Teachers' College, objected to the terms "sex" and "reproduction" being used synonymously. Not until after 1920 would these activists see any progress towards the goal of having some basic sex (reproductive) instruction integrated into any school curriculum.

The early 1900s found American minds being expanded by the writings of Sigmund Freud and Havelock Ellis, among others. These psychologists helped popularize the notion of sexuality as a marker of self-identity and a force permeating one's life, which, if repressed, risks negative consequences. In addition, socialist and feminist ideologies and the industrial economy created an environment fertile for the demand of birth-control information and services. These events spearheaded the second major movement for sexuality education, which was based on social-justice issues, particularly for women and the poor.

In 1912, Margaret Sanger began a series of articles on female sexuality for a New York newspaper, which was confiscated by postal officials for violating the Comstock antiobscenity law. Later, to challenge the constitutionality of this law, she published her own magazine, *The Woman Rebel*, filled with information about birth control. She was charged with nine counts of violating the law, with a penalty of forty-five years in prison, after writing and distributing a pamphlet, *Family Limitation*. To avoid prosecution, she fled to Europe; but in her absence, efforts mounted to distribute birth-control information. By early 1915, activists had distributed over 100,000 copies of *Family Limitation*, and a movement for community sexuality education was solidified. Public sentiment in favor of the right to such information was so strong that charges were dropped against Sanger when she returned to America. Community education about and access to birth control, particularly for middle-class women, began to become accepted, if not expected, as a matter of public health, as well as an issue of female equality (social justice).

Premarital experience became a more-common form of sexuality education among the white middle-class, beginning in the 1920s and accelerating as youth became more autonomous from their families (through automobiles, attendance at college, participation in more leisure activities like movies, and war experiences). Dating, necking, and petting among young peers became a norm. "Where adults might see flagrantly loose behavior, young people themselves had constructed a set of norms that regulated their activity while allowing the accumulation of experience and sexual learning" (D'Emilio and Freedman 1988, 261).

Courses on marriage and the family and (sexual) hygiene were being introduced into the college curriculum. Marriage manuals began to emphasize sexual expression and pleasure, rather than sexual control and reproduction, with more-explicit instructions as to how to achieve satisfying sexual relationships (such as "foreplay" and "simultaneous orgasm"). By the end of the 1930s, many marriage manuals were focusing on sexual "techniques." In addition, scientific reports, such as *Sexual Behavior in the Human Male* by Alfred Kinsey and his associates (1948) and the corresponding *Sexual Behavior in the Human Female* (1953), were major popular works primarily read by the middle class. These books provided sexuality education about the types and frequencies of various sexual expressions among white Americans to more than a quarter of a million people. They also are considered landmarks in sexuality education:

> What they [Americans] have learned and will learn may have a tremendous effect on the future social history of mankind. For they [Kinsey and colleagues] are presenting facts. They are revealing not what should be, but what is. For the first time, data on human sex behavior is entirely separated from questions of philosophy, moral values, and social customs. (D'Emilio and Freedman 1988, 286)

As scientific information on sexuality became readily available to the American public, more-explicit presentation of sexual material in printed and audiovisual media became possible through the courts' decisions narrowing the definition of obscenity. The proliferation of such sexually explicit materials was encouraged by the expansion of the consumer-oriented economy. For example, advertising was developing into a major industry, beginning in the 1920s. Sex was used to sell everything from cars to toothpaste. Gender-role education, in particular, was an indirect outcome of the advertising media. A "paperback revolution" began in 1939 placing affordable materials, such as "romance novels," in drugstores and newsstands all over the country.

In December 1953, Hugh Hefner published the first issue of *Playboy*, whose trademark was a female "Playmate of the Month" displayed in a glossy nude centerfold. The early *Playboy* philosophy suggested males should "enjoy the pleasures the female has to offer without becoming emotionally involved" (D'Emilio and Freedman 1988, 302). By the end of the 1950s, *Playboy* had a circulation of 1 million, with the readership peaking at 6 million by the early 1970s. Many a man identified *Playboy* as his first, and perhaps most influential, source of sex education.

By the 1970s, sex manuals had taken the place of marital advice manuals. Popular books like the 1972 *Joy of Sex* by Dr. Alex Comfort encouraged sexual experimentation by illustrating sexual techniques. Sexual references became even more prolific in the mainstream media. For example, the ratio of sexual references per page tripled between 1950 and 1980 in magazines, including *Reader's Digest, Time,* and *Newsweek.* In addition, Masters and Johnson's groundbreaking book, *Human Sexual Response,* emphasizing that women's sexual desires and responses were equal to those of men, was published in 1966. The media were influencing Americans—female and male, married and single—to consider sexual pleasure as a legitimate, necessary component of their lives.

Yet, even with the explicit and abundant presentation of sexuality in the popular media, parents were still not likely to provide sexuality education to their children, nor were the schools.

In 1964, a lawyer, a sociologist, a clergyman, a family life educator, a public health educator, and a physician came together to form the Sex Information and Education Council of the United States (SIECUS). SIECUS is a nonprofit voluntary health organization with the aim to help people understand, appreciate, and use their sexuality in a responsible and informed manner. Dr. Mary Calderone was a co-founder and the first executive director. SIECUS soon became known all over the country as a source of information on human sexuality and sex education.

This private initiative for sexuality education was followed by a governmental one in 1966 when the Office of Education of the federal Department of Health, Education, and Welfare announced its newly developed policy supporting

> family life and sex education as an integral part of the curriculum from preschool to college and adult levels; it will support training for teachers . . . it will aid programs designed to help parents . . . it will support research and development in all aspects of family life and sex education. (Haffner 1989, 1)

In 1967, a membership organization, first called the American Association of Sex Educators and Counselors, was formed to bring together professionals from all disciplines who were teaching and counseling about human sexuality. The organization later expanded to include therapists, and is known today as the American Association of Sex Educators, Counselors, and Therapists (AASECT). Opposition to sexuality education from conservative political and religious groups grew quickly. In 1968, the Christian Crusade published, "Is the Schoolhouse the Proper Place to Teach Raw Sex?" and the John Birch Society was calling sex education a "Communist plot." In response, over 150 public leaders joined the National Committee for Responsible Family Life and Sex Education.

In 1970, Maryland became the first state to mandate family-life and human-development education at all levels in their public schools. However, the new "purity" movement by conservatives was under way, coordinating over 300 organizations throughout the country to oppose sex education in the public schools. Several states passed antisexuality-education mandates, with Louisiana barring sex education altogether in 1968. By the late 1970s, only half-a-dozen states had mandated sex education into their schools, and implementation in the local classrooms was limited.

In 1972, AASECT began developing training standards and competency criteria for certification of sexuality educators, counselors, and therapists. A list of the professionals who have become certified in these three areas is provided in a published register so that other professionals and consumers can locate people who are trained. (Currently this list identifies over 1,000 certified professionals.) AASECT also has developed a code of ethics for professionals working in these fields.

In 1979, the federal government through the Department of Health, Education, and Welfare conducted a national analysis of sex-education programs in the United States. The researchers calculated that less than 10 percent of all students were receiving instruction about sexuality in their high schools. The report's overall conclusion stated:

> Comprehensive programs must include far more than discussions of reproduction. They should cover other topics such as contraception, numerous sexual activities, the emotional and social aspects of sexual activity, values clarification, and decision making and communication skills. In addition to being concerned with the imparting of knowledge, they should also focus on the clarifying of values, the raising of self-esteem, and the developing of personal and social skills. These tasks clearly require that sex education topics be covered in many courses in many grades. (Kirby, Atter, and Scales 1979, 1)

When AIDS burst upon the scene in the 1980s, education with the goal of "social protection" from this deadly disease was targeted for inclusion in public-school curricula. In a relatively short time, most states came to require, or at least recommend, that AIDS education be included in school curricula. The number of states mandating or recommending AIDS education surpassed those mandating or recommending sexuality education. Money and other resources were being infused into AIDS-education initiatives. For example, in 1987-88, 80 percent of the $6.3 million spent nationwide on sexuality education went specifically to AIDS-education efforts. Today, policies and curricula addressing AIDS tend to be much more specific and detailed than those dealing with other aspects of sexuality education, including pregnancy prevention. This may lead to students receiving a narrow and negative view of human sexuality (e.g., "sex kills!").

Throughout this time, SIECUS remained committed to comprehensive sexuality education, as emphasized in its mission statement: "SIECUS affirms that sexuality is a natural and healthy part of living and advocates the right of individuals to make responsible sexual choices. SIECUS develops, collects, and disseminates information and promotes comprehensive education about sexuality" (Haffner 1989, 4). In 1989, SIECUS convened a national colloquium on the future of sexuality education, "Sex Education 2000," to which sixty-five national organizations sent representatives. The mission was to assure that all children and youth receive comprehensive sexuality education by the year 2000. Thirteen specific goals for the year 2000 were set forth as follows:

1. Sexuality education will be viewed as a community-wide responsibility.
2. All parents will receive assistance in providing sexuality education for their child(ren).
3. All schools will provide sexuality education for children and youth.
4. All religious institutions serving youth will provide sexuality education.
5. All national youth-serving agencies will implement sexuality education programs and policies.
6. The media will assume a more proactive role in sexuality education.
7. Federal policies and programs will support sexuality education.
8. Each state will have policies for school-based sexuality education and assure that mandates are implemented on a local level.
9. Guidelines, materials, strategies, and support for sexuality education will be available at the community level.
10. All teachers and group leaders providing sexuality education to youth will receive appropriate training.
11. Methodologies will be developed to evaluate sexuality education programs.
12. Broad support for sexuality education will be activated.
13. In order to realize the overall goal of comprehensive sexuality education for all children and youth, SIECUS calls upon national organizations to join together as a national coalition to support sexuality education (SIECUS 1990).

To aid in the attainment of the third goal of providing comprehensive sexuality education in the schools, a national Task Force with SIECUS's leadership published *Guidelines for Comprehensive Sexuality Education, Kindergarten Through 12th Grade* in 1991. These guidelines, based on six key concepts, provide a framework to create new sexuality-education programs or improve existing ones. The guidelines are based on values related to human sexuality that reflect the beliefs of most communities in a pluralistic society. They represent a starting point for curriculum development at the local level. Currently, another Task Force is working on ways to help providers of preschool education incorporate the beginnings of comprehensive sexuality education into their programs. In 1994, SIECUS also launched an international initiative in order to disseminate information on comprehensive sexuality education to the international community and to aid in the development of specific international efforts in this area.

Yet, in light of progress that has been made, challenges to sexuality programs from conservative organizations have become more frequent, more organized, and more successful than ever before (Sedway 1992). These nationally organized groups, including Eagle Forum, Focus on the Family, American Family Association, and Citizens for Excellence in Education, target local school programs that do not conform to their specific ideology. They attempt to control what others can read or learn, not just in sexuality education (which now is the major target), but in all areas of public education, including science (with the teaching of creationism), history, and literature (with censorship of many classics in children's literature). Although these groups represent a minority of parents in a school district, through well-organized national support, they often effectively use a variety of intimidating tactics to prevent the establishment of sexuality-education programs altogether or establish abstinence-only ones. Their tactics include personal attacks on persons supporting comprehensive sexuality education, threatening and sometimes pursuing costly litigation against school districts, and flooding school boards with misinformation, among other strategies. The greater impact of this anti-sexuality-education campaign on education, in general, and American society, overall, has been poignantly described:

> In another sense, the continuing series of attacks aimed at public education must be viewed in the context of the larger battle—what has come to be known as a "Cultural Civil War"—over free expression. Motion pictures, television programs, fine art, music lyrics, and even political speech have all come under assault in recent years from many of the same religious right leaders behind attacks on school programs. In the vast majority of cases, in the schools and out, challengers generally seek the same remedy, i.e., to restrict what others can see, hear, or read. At stake in attacks on schoolbooks and programs is students' exposure to a broad spectrum of ideas in the classroom—in essence, their freedom to learn. And when the freedom to learn is threatened in sexuality education, students are denied information that can save their lives. (Sedway 1992, 13-14)

B. Current Status of Sexuality Education

Youth-Serving Agencies

National youth-serving agencies (YSAs) in the United States provide sexuality education to over two million youths each year. Over the past two decades, YSAs began developing such programs, primarily in response to the problems of adolescent pregnancy and HIV/AIDS.

Second only to schools in the number of youth they serve, youth-serving agencies are excellent providers of sexuality education programs, both because they work with large numbers of youth, including many under-served youth, and because they provide an environment that is informal and conducive to creative and experiential learning. Some YSAs reach youth who have dropped out of school. Others reach youth who have not received sexuality education programs in their schools. The people who work at YSAs often build close relationships with the youth in their programs which allows for better communication and more effective educational efforts. (Dietz 1989/1990, 16)

For example, the American Red Cross reaches over 1 million youth each year in the U.S. with their "AIDS Prevention Program," "Black Youth Project," and "AIDS Prevention Program for Hispanic Youth and Families." The Boys Clubs of America has developed a substance abuse/pregnancy prevention program, called "Smart Moves." The Girls Clubs of America has a primary commitment to providing health promotion, sexuality education, and pregnancy-prevention services to its members and reaches over 200,000 youth each year. The Girl Scouts of the U.S.A. developed a curriculum, "Decision for Your Life: Preventing Teenage Pregnancy," that focuses on the consequences of teen parenthood and the development of communication, decision-making, assertiveness, and values-clarification skills. The March of Dimes Birth Defects Foundation developed the "Project Alpha" sexuality-education program that explores teenage pregnancy from the male perspective and helps young men learn how to take more responsibility. The National Network of Runaway and Youth Services has developed an HIV/AIDS education program for high-risk youth, called "Safe Choices." The program provides training for staff at runaway shelters, residential treatment facilities, detention facilities, group homes, street outreach programs, hot lines, foster-family programs, and other agencies that serve high-risk youth.

In addition to the national efforts of YSAs, many local affiliates have designed their own programs to meet the needs of their local communities in culturally sensitive ways. For example, the National 4-H Council estimates that most state extension offices have developed their own programs to reduce teenage pregnancy in their areas.

Schools

More than 85 percent of the American public approve of sexuality education being provided in the schools, compared with 76 percent in 1975 and 69 percent in 1965 (Kenney, Guardado, and Brown 1989). Today, roughly 60 percent of teenagers receive at least some sex education in their schools, although only a third receive a somewhat "comprehensive" program.

Each state can mandate or require that sexuality education and/or AIDS education be provided in the local school districts. Short of mandating such educational programs, states may simply recommend that the school districts within their boundaries offer education on sexuality, in general, and/or more-specific AIDS education. In 1992, seventeen states had mandated sexuality education and thirty more recommended it; see Table 3 (Haffner 1992). In addition, thirty-four states had mandated AIDS education, while fourteen more recommended it. Only four states (Massachusetts, Mississippi, South Dakota, and Wyoming) had no position on sexuality education within their schools; whereas Ohio, Wyoming, and Tennessee had no position on AIDS education. In 1995, the NARAL and NARAL Foundation (1995) issued a detailed state-by-state review of sexuality education in America with selected details of legislative action in 1994 and 1995.

Although the majority of states either mandate or recommend sexuality and AIDS education, this does not guarantee that local school districts are implementing the suggested curricula. Inconsistencies in and lack of implementation of these curricula result from: absence of provisions for mandate enforcement, lax regulations regarding compliance, diversity in program objectives, restrictions on course content, lack of provisions for teacher training, and insufficient evaluation.

In 1988, SIECUS conducted a project to examine and evaluate the recommended state sexuality and AIDS-education curricula (Di Mauro 1989-90). Of the twenty-three state curricula that they evaluated for sexuality education, only 22 percent were deemed to be accurate. Although most curricula stated that human sexuality is natural and positive, there was a lack of any content in the curricula to support this concept. Most focused on the negative consequences of sexual interaction, and little attention was paid to the psychosocial dimensions of sexuality, such as gender identification and roles, sexual functioning and satisfaction, or values and ethics. Only one half of the curricula provided thorough information about birth control.

In an evaluation of the thirty-four state-recommended AIDS-education curricula, 32 percent were found to be accurate in basic concepts and presentation. The majority (85 percent) emphasized abstinence and "just say no" skills, whereas only 9 percent covered safer sex as a preventive practice. Thorough information about condoms was provided in less than 10 percent of the curricula. There was no mention of homosexuality in over one third of the curricula. In 38 percent, homosexuals were identified as the "cause of AIDS." The Utah curriculum was especially negative and restrictive:

> Utah's teachers are not free to discuss the "intricacies of intercourse, sexual stimulation, erotic behavior"; the acceptance of or advocacy of homosexuality as a desirable or acceptable sexual adjustment or life-

Table 3

State Requirements for Sexuality, STD, and HIV/AIDS Education in Primary and Secondary Schools

Sexuality Education—Required from Kindergarten Through Senior High School

Alabama, Arkansas, Delaware, District of Columbia, Florida, Georgia, Illinois, Iowa, Kansas, Maryland, Minnesota, Nevada, New Jersey, New Mexico, North Carolina, Rhode Island, Tennessee, Vermont, Virginia, and West Virginia

Sexuality Education—Required for Grades Five or Six Through Senior High School

South Carolina, Texas, and Utah

Sexuality Education—Not Required

Alaska, Arizona, California, Colorado, Connecticut, Hawaii, Idaho, Indiana, Kentucky, Louisiana, Maine, Massachusetts, Michigan, Mississippi, Missouri, Montana, Nebraska, New Hampshire, New York, North Dakota, Ohio, Oklahoma, Oregon, Pennsylvania, South Dakota, Washington, Wisconsin, and Wyoming

STD/HIV/AIDS Education—Required from Kindergarten Through Senior High School

Alabama, Arizona, Arkansas, Connecticut, Delaware, District of Columbia, Florida, Georgia, Idaho, Indiana, Iowa, Kansas, Michigan, Minnesota, Missouri, Nevada, New Hampshire, New Jersey, New Mexico, New York, North Carolina, Ohio, Oregon, Pennsylvania, Rhode Island,[1] Tennessee,[2] Vermont, Virginia, Washington, and Wisconsin

STD/HIV/AIDS Education—Required Grades Five or Six Through Senior High School

California, Illinois, Maryland, Oklahoma, South Carolina, Texas, Utah,[3] and West Virginia

STD/HIV/AIDS Education—Not Required

Alaska, Colorado, Hawaii, Kentucky, Louisiana,[4] Maine, Massachusetts, Mississippi, Montana, Nebraska, North Dakota, South Dakota, and Wyoming

[1] Instruction in sexuality and HIV/AIDS is required at least once a year in all grades.

[2] Instruction in sexuality and HIV/AIDS is required only in counties with more than 19.5 pregnancies per 1,000 females aged 15 to 17. Only one county did not meet this standard.

[3] HIV/AIDS education is required from third to twelfth grades.

[4] Louisiana law prohibits sex education before the seventh grade, and in New Orleans, before the third grade.

Source: *Sexuality Education in America: A State-by-State Review.* NARAL/The NARAL Foundation, 1995.

style; the advocacy or encouragement of contraceptive methods or devices by unmarried minors; and the acceptance or advocacy of "free sex," promiscuity, or the so-called "new morality." This section of their curriculum is replete with warnings of legal violations for instructors crossing prohibition lines; their guidelines indicate that with parental consent it is possible to discuss condom use at any grade level, but without it, such discussions are Class B misdemeanors. (Di Mauro 1989-90, 6; see also the discussion of Mormon sexuality in Section 2A.)

Currently, a broad focus on sexuality education is being supplanted by a narrow focus on AIDS education. Sexuality and AIDS education are being treated independently with separate curricula and teacher training. The report concluded that: "What is needed [for each state] is a comprehensive sexuality education or family-life education curriculum with an extensive AIDS education component that contextualizes preventive information within a positive, life-affirming approach to human sexuality" (Di Mauro 1989-90, 6).

Yet, recommended curriculum content cannot automatically be equated with what is actually being taught in the classroom. To determine what is being taught, a study of public school teachers in five specialty areas (health education, biology, home economics, physical education, and school nursing) in grades seven through twelve was conducted (Forrest and Silverman 1989). It was estimated that nationwide 50,000 public school teachers were providing some type of sexuality education in grades seven through twelve in 1987-88; representing 45 percent of the teachers employed in those areas. Roughly 38.7 hours of sex education were being offered in grades seven through twelve; with 5.0 hours devoted to birth control and 5.9 hours covering STDs.

The teachers cited the encouragement of abstinence as one of their primary goals. The messages that they most want to give included: responsibility regarding sexual relationships and parenthood, the importance of abstinence and ways of resisting pressures to become sexually active, and information on AIDS and other STDs. The teachers agreed that sexuality education belongs in the schools and that students should be taught to examine and develop their own values about sexual behaviors. They reported that there is often a gap between what should be taught, and when and what actually is allowed to be taught. The largest gap concerned sources of birth-control methods; 97 percent of the teachers believed they should be allowed to provide information to students about where they could access birth control, but this was allowed in less than half of their schools. In fact, one quarter of the teachers were permitted to discuss birth control with students only when they are asked a student-initiated question. In addition, over 90 percent of the teachers believed that their students should be taught about homosexuality and abortion, topics that are often restricted by school districts. In addition, the teachers believed that the wide range of sexuality topics should be addressed with students no later than seventh or eighth grade; however, this is not usually done until tenth through twelfth grades, if at all.

The teachers described many barriers to implementing quality sexuality education in their classrooms. The major problem that they identified was opposition or lack of support from parents, the community, or school administrators. They also felt that they lacked appropriate materials because of the difficulties in getting current relevant materials approved for use. They also encountered student-related barriers, such as discomfort, lack of basic knowledge of anatomy and physiology, and misinformation, poor attitudes, and a lack of values and morals reflecting favorable attitudes toward teen pregnancy. Teachers also lacked enough time and training to teach the material effectively. Almost none of them were certified as sexuality or family-life educators by the American Association of Sex Educators, Counselors, and Therapists or the National Council on Family Relations. The level of the teachers' own knowledge on sexual topics was questionable, and some experienced personal conflicts in dealing with certain issues.

The authors concluded that:

> Perhaps the most important step toward improved sex education would be increased, clear support of the teachers. One form this support should take is the development of curricula that provide teachers with constructive, planned ways to raise and deal with the topics on their students' minds, since the data indicate that students will often raise topics even if they are not in the curriculum. Greater support should also help increase the availability of high-quality instructional materials and on-going education and information for teachers. Adequate teaching materials and support for teaching in earlier grades the topics students want to know about might help solve the problem of student inattention and negative reactions, to say nothing of helping with the problems of teenage pregnancy and the spread of AIDS and other STDs. (Forrest and Silverman 1989, 72)

Yet, in recent years, well-organized conservative organizations throughout the United States have been promoting the adoption of their own abstinence-only curricula in the public schools. Since 1985, the Illinois Committee on the Status of Women has received $1.7 million in state and federal funds to promote such a curriculum, called *Sex Respect*. They have been successful in having *Sex Respect* adopted in over 1,600 school systems, even though this curriculum is designed to proselytize a particular conservative sexual-value system. The *Sex Respect* curriculum has been criticized because it:

> (1) substitutes biased opinion for fact; (2) conveys insufficient and inaccurate information; (3) relies on scare tactics; (4) ignores realities of life for many students; (5) reinforces gender stereotypes; (6) lacks respect for cultural and economic differences; (7) presents one side of controversial issues; (8) fails to meaningfully involve parents; [and] (9) is marketed using inadequate evaluations. (Trudell and Whatley 1991, 125)

Careful scientific evaluation of over forty sexuality- and AIDS-education curricula commissioned separately by the Centers for Disease Control and the World Health Organization resulted in the following conclusions:

1. Comprehensive sexuality and HIV/AIDS-education programs do not hasten the onset of intercourse nor increase the number of partners or frequency of intercourse.
2. Skill-based programs can delay the onset of sexual intercourse and increase the use of contraception, condoms, and other safer-sex practices among sexually experienced youth.
3. Programs that promote both the postponement of sexual intercourse and safer-sex practices are more effective than abstinence-only programs, like *Sex Respect* (Haffner 1994).

C. Informal Sources of Sexual Knowledge

Researchers over the past fifty years have consistently found that adolescents identify peers, particularly of their same gender, as their primary source of sexuality education, followed by various types of media, including print and visual media. Parents and schools are usually identified as significantly less-influential sources.

Peers as a Sexual Information Source

Males seem to be more dependent on peers for their sexuality education than are females. One problematic aspect of receiving sexuality education informally from peers is that the information they provide is often inaccurate. However, when peers are formally trained to provide sexuality education, such as on the high school or college level, they are very effective in providing information and encouraging the development of positive attitudes towards responsible and healthy sexual expression. Thus, the peer model is being used more widely in school and community sexuality-education programs.

The Media

The various media are pervasive and influential sources of sexuality education in American culture. Media have been identified by adolescents and college students as being more influential than their families in the development of their sexual attitudes and behaviors. As to television, the radio, and movies, adolescents spend more time being entertained by the media than any other activity, perhaps with the exception of sleeping (Haffner and Kelly 1987).

Television, in particular, has been identified as the most influential source of sexual messages in American society, even though sexual behavior is not explicitly depicted. Yet, in an analysis of the sexual content of prime-time television programming, about 20,000 scenes of suggested sexual intercourse and other behaviors, and sexual comments and innuendos were documented in one year (Haffner and Kelly 1987). These portrayals of sexual interaction are six times more likely to happen in an extramarital, rather than a marital, relationship. In soap operas, 94 percent of the sexual encounters happen between people who are not married to one another. Minority groups are extremely underrepresented on TV, with gay and lesbian characters nearly nonexistent.

In the United States, by the time a child graduates from high school, she or he will have spent more time watching TV than being in a formal classroom setting. There is conflicting evidence as to the impact media portrayals have on youth's developing sexuality (Haffner and Kelly 1987). Gender-role stereotyping is a pervasive aspect of television programming, with children who watch more TV demonstrating more stereotypic gender-role behaviors than those who watch less. Some studies have linked young people's television-viewing habits, including the watching of music videos, to the likelihood that they would engage in sexual intercourse, while others have not supported this relationship. Yet, there is no denying that TV serves as a sexuality educator. Adolescents report that TV is equally or more encouraging about engaging in sexual intercourse than are their friends, and those that have high TV-viewing habits are likely to be dissatisfied about remaining virgins. In addition, those who believe that TV accurately portrays sexual experiences are more likely to be dissatisfied with their own.

Soap operas are one of the most popular television genres. Depictions of sexual behaviors are common. Yet, television censors still establish rules, such as not showing unbuttoning clothes or the characters at the moment of "penetration." Unfortunately, very few references to or depictions of safer sex are part of television programs. As the National Academy of Sciences concluded, the media provide "young people with lots of clues about how to be sexy, but . . . little information about how to be sexually responsible" (Haffner and Kelly 1987, 9).

Sexuality has become a focal point of some newer types of television programming. Sexual topics, such as teenage pregnancy, incest, or AIDS, are often the subject matter of made-for-TV movies and "after-school specials." In addition, the "sexually unconventional," such as transvestites, sex addicts, or bigamists, are often the guests of television talk shows, such as Donahue, Oprah, and Geraldo. Some critics believe that this diversity has encouraged viewers to become more tolerant and open, whereas others believe it has done the opposite, reinforcing negative and hostile attitudes. Among adolescents and young adults, music videos have become one of the most popular forms of television entertainment. Yet, context studies of these music videos indicate that women tend to be treated as "sex objects." Madonna is one exception, depicting a powerful image of female sexuality.

The motto that "Sex Sells" has been generously applied to television advertising. Television uses sexual innuendos and images to sell almost every product from toothpaste to automobiles. The most sexually explicit commercials are generally those for jeans, beer, and perfumes. Paradoxically, commercials and public service announcements for birth control methods are banned from television. Those for "feminine hygiene" products and the prevention of sexually transmissible diseases, including AIDS, are quite restricted.

Subscriber cable television offers more sexually oriented programming, such as the *Playboy Channel*, than does network TV. However, the *Exxxtacy Channel* was forced out of business because of numerous government obscenity prosecutions. Virtual-reality technology is being developed to allow cable subscribers to use goggles, gloves, and body sensors to enjoy their own virtual sexual reality.

Film making is a huge business and American films are marketed worldwide. Movies have been reported as one of the leading sources of sexual information for adolescent Anglo-American, Latino, and Native American males (Davis and Harris 1982). Films are given greater license to depict sexual behavior explicitly than on television; however, they are still censored. In fact, films, such as *Basic Instinct*, have more explicit sex in their uncut versions that are marketed abroad than the "cut" versions that are marketed domestically. Female nudity has become acceptable, whereas male frontal nudity is still censored. Sexual behaviors other than heterosexual intercourse tend to be missing from most films.

Video cassettes and videocassette recorders (VCRs) have revolutionized the viewing habits of Americans. Two hundred million X-rated video cassettes were rented in the U.S. in 1989. One study of college students determined that males viewed about six hours and females two hours of sexually explicit material on their VCRs a month (Strong and DeVault 1994).

Another very popular form of media, directed at females, is the romance novel, comprising 40 percent of all paperback book sales in the U.S. Romance novels are believed to both reflect and create the sexual fantasies and desires of their female American audience. The basic formula of this form of media is: "Female meets devastating man, sparks fly, lovers meld, lovers are torn apart, get back together, resolve their problems, and commit themselves, usually, to marriage" (Strong and DeVault 1994, 22).

Sexual language is disguised by euphemisms. For example, the male penis is referred to as a "love muscle" and the female vagina as a "temple of love." Yet, romance novels are filled with sensuality, sexuality, and passion, with some people considering them soft-core pornography.

Young males in the U.S. tend to learn about sexuality through more-explicit magazines, such as *Playboy* and *Penthouse*. *Playboy* is one of the most popular magazines worldwide, selling about 10 million issues monthly. Half of college men, but much fewer women, report that pornography has been a source of information for them regarding sexual behaviors (Duncan and Nicholson 1991).

Finally, with increased public access to computer technology, sexuality education is now being offered through the computer-based superhighway. This represents the "wave of the future" and is thoroughly discussed in a section at the end of this chapter.

Parents as a Source of Sexual Information

It is widely believed that parents should be the primary sexuality educators of their children. They certainly provide a great deal of indirect sexuality education to their children through the ways that they display affection, react to nudity and bodies, and interact with people of different genders and orientations—as well as the attitudes they express (or the lack of expression) towards a myriad of sexual topics.

However, most parents in the United States provide little direct sexuality education to their children, even though the majority of children express the desire to be able to talk to their parents about sexuality. Studies of American adolescents consistently find that up to three quarters state that they have not discussed sexuality with their parents (Hass 1979; Sorenson 1973). Parents have expressed the following as barriers to discussing sexuality with their children: anxiety over giving misinformation or inappropriate information for the developmental level of their children; lack of skills in communicating about sexuality, since very few parents ever had role models on how to handle such discussions; and fear that discussing sexuality with their children will actually encourage them to become involved in sexual relationships.

When sexuality education occurs in the home, the mother is generally the parent who handles such discussions with both daughters and sons. Studies do indicate that, when parents talk to their children about sexuality, the children are more likely to wait to become involved in sexual behaviors until they are older, than those children who have not talked with their parents (Shah and Zelnick 1981). Further, when parent-educated teens do engage in sexual intercourse, they are more likely to use an effective means of birth control consistently and to have fewer sexual partners. In addition, high family sexual communication seems to be related to similarity in sexual attitudes between parents and their children.

Recognizing the importance of having parents involved in their children's sexuality education, efforts are being made to prepare parents to become better sexuality educators. Sexuality-education programs for parents are offered separate from, and in conjunction with, children's programs in some schools, and through some community and religious organizations. The goals of these programs include developing parents' communication skills so that they can become more "askable," increasing their knowledge about various aspects of sexuality, and exploring their attitudes and values surrounding these issues. For example, the National Congress of Parents and Teachers' Associations (PTA) has created programs and publications on aspects of sexuality and HIV/AIDS prevention for use by local affiliates.

It is clear that we must continue to strive to reach all Americans with positive and comprehensive sexuality education through all of our available informal and formal channels. It is also imperative that sound qualitative and quantitative research methodologies be used to ascertain the impact of differing sexuality education strategies and sources on the diverse groups of people—e.g., gender, age, orientation, race and ethnicity—in the United States.

4. Autoerotic Behaviors and Patterns
ROBERT T. FRANCOEUR*

A. Research Weaknesses and Challenges

Five weaknesses or shortcomings and three challenges can be identified in the current research on autoerotic attitudes and behavior patterns in the U.S.A. The weaknesses are:

1. the virtual absence of recent data on noncollege men and women, especially married women and men;
2. the small sample sizes in available research;
3. a problem with the representativeness of the samples;
4. very limited or no data on African-Americans, Latinos, and other ethnic/racial groups; and
5. a limited use of theory as a driving force in the development of research questions.

The challenges include:

1. finding available research funds;
2. overcoming the negative views in academia toward sex research in general, and especially for research on masturbation; and
3. disseminating the findings to the "consumer" to relieve the guilt feelings that many persons experience as a result of their masturbation practices.

B. Children and Adolescents

In 1985, Mary Calderone, M.D., a pioneer of American sexology and co-founder of the Sex Information and Education Council of the United States, documented the presence of a functioning erectile reflex in a seventeen-week-old male fetus. Considering the homologies of the male and female genital systems, it is logical to assume that females also develop the capacity for cyclical vaginal lubrication while still in the womb. In a 1940 study of boys three to twenty weeks old, seven of nine infants had erections from five to forty times a day. Seven-month-old girls have been observed experiencing what to all appearances can only be judged to be

---

*With input from J. Kenneth Davidson, Sr.

a reflexive orgasm induced by rubbing or putting pressure on their genitals.

The natural reflexes that result in fetal and infant erections and vaginal lubrication are very much like the knee jerk and other reflexes, except that they are accompanied by smiles and cooing that clearly suggest the infant is enjoying something quite pleasurable (Martinson 1990, 1995). Sooner or later, most children learn the pleasures of stimulating their genitals. Once that connection is made, the threat of punishment and sin may not be enough to keep a child from masturbating. Generally, American adults are very uncomfortable with masturbation by infants and children. There are exceptions, of course, as for instance, the practice of indigenous Hawaiian adult caregivers masturbating or fellating infants to calm them at night.

Most children seem to forget their early masturbation experiences. Two thirds of the males in Kinsey's study reported hearing about masturbation from other boys in their prepubescent or early adolescent years before they tried it themselves. Fewer than one in three males reported they rediscovered masturbation entirely on their own. Two out of three females in Kinsey's sample learned about masturbation by accident, sometimes not until after they were married. Some women reported they had masturbated for some time before they realized what they were doing.

In the 1940s, Kinsey and his associates reported that close to 90 percent of males and about 50 percent of females masturbated by the midteens. Studies in the 1980s show an increase in these numbers, with a fair estimate that today nearly three quarters of girls masturbate by adolescence and another 10 percent or so wait until their 20s. About 80 percent of adolescent girls and 90 percent of adolescent boys masturbate with frequencies ranging from once a week to about daily (Hass and Hass 1993, 151, 285).

C. Adults

Race and ethnicity, religion, educational level, and sexual education appear to be important variables that affect the incidence of masturbation. African-Americans engage in masturbation less often than whites and are more negative about it. Very little is known about Latino masturbation attitudes and practices. We are not aware of any studies on masturbation among other major groups, such as Asians and Native Americans. Religion is a key variable, especially given the continuing condemnation of masturbation by the Roman Catholic Church. Granted many Catholics engage in masturbation, but on a continuum, they are more likely to experience guilt feelings than Protestants or Jews. Likewise, persons from fundamentalist-Protestant backgrounds are more likely to have negative attitudes toward masturbation than liberal Protestants. Kinsey and many subsequent researchers have found that, as education level increases, especially among women, the acceptance and approval of masturbation as a sexual outlet increases.

Finally, experience with sex education is an important variable (Heiby and Becker 1980). Persons who have had sex education appear to hold more-tolerant attitudes.

Data indicate that about 72 percent of young husbands masturbate an average of about twice a month. About 68 percent of young wives do so, with an average frequency of slightly less than once a month (Hunt 1974, 86). According to data reported by Edward Brecher in *Love, Sex and Aging* (1984), women in their 50s, 60s and 70s reported a consistent masturbation frequency of 0.6 to 0.7 times a week. In their 50s, men reported masturbating 1.2 times a week with a decline to 0.8 times a week in their 60s, and 0.7 times a week over age 70.

The incidence of masturbation has continued to increase in recent years among both college and postcollege women. During the 1980s, between 46 percent and 69 percent of college women in several surveys reported masturbating. In the 1990s, other surveys have found 45 percent to 78 percent. Postcollege women also became more accepting of masturbation as they received psychological permission, instruction, and support in learning about their own bodies. In fact, in self-reports of masturbation, a majority of postcollege-age, college-educated women indicated this was a sexual outlet. In a large-scale sample of college-educated women, without regard to marital status, frequency of masturbation was 7.1 times per month. By contrast, high-school-educated, married women engaged in masturbation only 3.7 times per month (Davidson and Darling 1993).

Not all women feel comfortable with masturbation. Among college women, 30 percent reported "shame" as a major reason for not engaging in this outlet. Other research indicates that only about half of college women believe that masturbation is a "healthy practice." Even with the apparent increasing incidence of masturbation, considerable data exist that suggest negative feelings toward the practice still deter many college women from choosing this source of sexual fulfillment. And, of those who do engage in masturbation, they do so much less frequently than men, 3.3 times a month for college women compared with 4.8 times for college men (Davidson and Darling 1993).

In general, women are more likely than men to report guilt feelings about their masturbation. Further, substantial evidence suggests that such guilt feelings may interfere with the physiological and/or psychological sexual satisfaction derived from masturbation. In fact, the presence of masturbatory guilt has various implications for female sexuality. Such guilt feelings have been found to inhibit the use of the diaphragm, which necessitates touching the genitals for insertion (Byrne and Fisher 1983). Presumably, this would also affect use of other vaginally inserted contraceptives. Women with high levels of masturbatory guilt experience more emotional trauma after contracting an STD, and exhibit greater fear about telling their sex partner about being infected, than women with low masturbatory guilt. Masturbatory guilt may also inhibit women from experiencing high levels of arousal during foreplay as a prelude to having vaginal intercourse.

One indication of changing attitudes of women toward self-loving is the publication of *Sex for One: The Joy of Selfloving*, by Betty Dodson (1988), and her subsequent appearance on television talk shows. At the same time, the swift dismissal of the U.S. Surgeon General for daring to suggest that masturbation might be mentioned as part of safer-sex education for children indicates that a prevailing negative societal attitude toward masturbation continues.

5. Interpersonal Heterosexual Behaviors

A. Childhood Sexuality

DAVID L. WEIS*

Within American culture, childhood sexuality remains an area that has been largely unexplored by researchers. Childhood is widely seen as a period of asexual innocence. Strong taboos continue concerning childhood eroticism, and childhood sexual expression and learning are still divisive social issues. This general ambience of anxiety associated with the sexuality of children is probably understandable, given the general history of sexuality in the U.S.A., with its focus on adult dyadic sex within committed intimate relationships and its opposition to other sexual expressions. This ambience remains, despite the fact that nearly a century has passed since Freud introduced his theory of psychosexual stages with an emphasis placed on the sexual character of childhood development. This reluctance to accept childhood sexuality is somewhat ironic, because Freudian theory, with its concepts of psychosexual stages (oral, anal, phallic, and latency), penis envy, the Oedipus/Electra complexes, repression, and the unconscious, has been immensely popular in the United States throughout much of the twentieth century. Yet, the general American public has been able to ignore the prominence given to childhood sexual development by Freudian theorists and to maintain its central belief that childhood is and ought to be devoid of sexuality.

Perhaps no area reviewed in this section has been the subject of less scientific research than this topic of childhood sexuality. To some extent, the paucity of research has been due to general social concerns about the ethical implications of studying children or assumptions about the possible harm to children that would result if they were to be included in sexuality research. Researchers have frequently had difficulty gaining the permission of legal guardians to ask children questions about their knowledge of sexuality. In this atmosphere, it would be exceedingly difficult to get permission to ask children about their sexual behavior. One consequence of this general social concern has been that most of the relevant research

---

*With input from Paul Okami.

has been confined to asking adults or college students to report retrospectively about events that occurred in their childhood. There are rather clear and obvious limitations to this approach.

On the other hand, we should recognize that many American scientists themselves have been unwilling to study the sexuality of children. A recent review, *Sexuality Research in the United States: An Assessment of the Social and Behavioral Sciences* (di Mauro 1995), is notable for the fact that it never mentions childhood sexuality. It might be interesting to determine the extent to which American researchers accept the premise that scientific explorations of sexuality might be harmful to children. For example, the field of child development, a sizable branch of American psychology, has largely ignored the issue of sexuality in their work (Maccoby and Martin 1983; Mussen 1983). An examination of standard developmental texts or reviews of the child development research literature is striking for its omission of sexuality. Significant bodies of child-development research in such important areas as language acquisition, cognition, communication, social behavior, parent-child interaction, attachment (Allgeier and Allgeier 1988), parenting styles, and child compliance have emerged with scant attention to the possible sexual elements of these areas, or to the ways in which these areas might be related to sexual development (Mussen 1983). As just one example, Piaget never investigated the issue of children's sexual cognition, and there has been little subsequent research exploring the application of his theoretical model to sexual development. Similarly, the emergence of family systems theory has also largely ignored the sexuality of children—except to explain the occurrence of incest.

At the same time, it is just as true that sexuality researchers have largely ignored the work of child developmentalists and other scientific disciplines in their own work. They have speculated about how theories of psychoanalysis, social learning, cognition, attribution, social exchange, and symbolic interactionism might be applied to the sexuality of children or to the process of sexual development, but they have rarely tested such assertions empirically (see Allgeier and Allgeier 1988 and Martinson 1976 for examples). Moreover, sex researchers have largely failed to examine how the various processes studied by developmentalists relate to sexuality.

A third domain of this fractured American approach to child development is the fairly recent emergence of professional fields devoted solely to the issue of child sexual abuse. We present a review of child sexual abuse itself later in this chapter (see Section 8A2). Here, we wish to make the point that professional groups—e.g., social workers and family therapists devoted to the treatment of victims of child sexual abuse—have emerged, largely since the 1970s, with a corresponding body of work devoted to that concern. After having been largely neglected for much of the twentieth century, the treatment of child sexual abuse has become a sizable "industry" in recent years. Unfortunately, much of the work that has been done within this perspective has failed to consider existing data on normative childhood sexuality (Okami 1992, 1995). For example, it is frequently asserted that child sexual abuse has the negative consequence of "sexualizing" the child's world. We do not mean to claim that child sexual abuse is either harmless or nonexistent. However, the notion that a "sexualized" childhood is a tragic outcome of sexual abuse rests on the American premise that childhood should be devoid of sexuality. It assumes that childhood should not be sexual. From this perspective, the concept of child sexual abuse has been extended to include family nudity—a point certain to shock naturists in many countries around the world—parents bathing with their children, "excessive" displays of physical affection (such as kissing and hugging), and even children of the same age engaging in sex play (Okami 1992, 1995). Thus, we seem to have come full circle. Many professionals have come to accept the premise that childhood ought to be an innocent period, free of sexuality. The fact that this view ignores much of the existing data seems to have had little impact on either the American public or many professionals working with children.

Childhood Sexual Development and Expression

In reviewing the process of child sexual development and the phenomenon of child eroticism, it is crucial to consider the meanings that children attach to their experience. There is a tendency to interpret childhood experiences in terms of the meanings that adults have learned to attach to similar events. This ignores the reality that young children almost certainly do not assign the same meanings to "sexual" events as adults. They have yet to conceptualize a system of experiences, attitudes, and motives that adults label as "sexual" (Allgeier and Allgeier 1988; Gagnon and Simon 1973; Martinson 1976). A good example is provided by the case of childhood "masturbation." Young children often discover that "playing" with their genitals is a pleasurable experience. However, this may well not be the same as "masturbating." Masturbation, as adults understand that term, is a set of behaviors defined as "sexual" because they are recognized as producing "sexual arousal" and typically having orgasm or "sexual climax" as a goal. Young children have yet to construct this complex set of meanings. They know little more than that the experience is pleasurable; it feels good. In fact, it would be useful to see research that examines the process by which children eventually learn to label such self-pleasuring as a specifically sexual behavior called masturbation.

From this perspective, sexual development is, to a considerable extent, a process characterized by the gradual construction of a system of sexual meanings. Gagnon and Simon (1973) have provided a theoretical model of sexual scripting that examines how these meanings are assembled in a series of stages through social interaction with various socialization agents. In their discussion of the model, Gagnon and Simon stressed their intention that it would serve as an organizing framework for future research on the process of sexual development. Although we believe that the model does provide a potentially fruitful framework for thinking about the process of sexual development, and despite the fact that more than twenty years have passed since its original presentation, there is nearly as great a need for research of this type today as when they formulated the model.

One component of the model proposed by Gagnon and Simon (1973) was the concept of assemblies, by which they meant to convey their view that sexual development is actively constructed by humans rather than merely being an organic process. Among the major assemblies they identified were:

1. the emergence of a specific gender identity,
2. the learning of a sense of modesty,
3. the acquisition of a sexual vocabulary,
4. the internalization of mass-media messages about sexuality,
5. the learning of specific acts defined as sexual,
6. the learning of gender, family, and sexual roles,
7. the learning of the mechanisms and process of sexual arousal,
8. the development of sexual fantasies and imagery,
9. the development of a sexual value system,
10. the emergence of a sexual orientation, and
11. the adoption of an adult sexual lifestyle.

Gagnon and Simon maintained that these assemblies were constructed through interactions with a variety of socialization agents, such as parents and family members, same-sex peers, cross-sex peers, and the mass media. To this list, we would suggest adding the church, the school, the neighborhood/community, and boyfriends/girlfriends as potentially important socialization agents. For Gagnon and Simon, the task for researchers was to examine and identify the associations between the activities of various socialization agents and the corresponding construction of specific sexual assemblies. Although a fair amount of research has been conducted on such associations among adolescents (see the following section), sadly there remains relatively little research along these lines for younger children. As such, we will not present a detailed discussion of the activities of each socialization agent here.

Lacking space to review each of the assemblies, we have had to be selective and have chosen to focus on the more explicitly erotic dimensions. However, we do wish to note that each is ultimately important to a full understanding of sexual development, and it is likely that each of these assemblies is related to the others. Although we do not have space to review the research on the development of gender roles and gender identity, it appears that most American children have formed a stable gender identity by the age of 2 or 3 (Maccoby and Martin 1983; Money and Ehrhardt 1972). It also seems likely that, as children acquire sexual information and experience, they filter what they learn in terms of what is appropriate for males and females. Since norms for male and female behavior, both sexual and nonsexual, tend to differ, this filtering process seems likely to lead to differences in the content of and processes of male and female sexual development.

On the other hand, we would caution the reader to resist the temptation to conclude that gender differences in sexuality are invariably large, or that they apply to all dimensions of sexuality. Recent reviews of existing research indicate that many aspects of sexuality are not characterized by male-female differences and that many differences are small in magnitude (Oliver and Hyde 1993). Ultimately, the issue is a matter for empirical investigation. Unfortunately, there has been relatively little empirical research attempting to link gender-role development (of which there has been a great deal of research in the last thirty years) with the processes of more overtly sexual development.

Childhood Sexual Eroticism and Expression. Martinson (1976) has drawn a distinction between what he calls reflexive and eroticized sexual experiences. Reflexive experience is pleasurable and may be a result of learning contingencies, but eroticized experience is characterized by self-conscious awareness and labeling of behavior as sexual. As a general guideline, younger and less-experienced children would seem more likely to react to sexual stimuli in a reflexive manner; older and more-experienced children are more likely to have learned erotic meanings and to define similar behaviors as "sexual." However, there has been virtually no research detailing the process in which this transition occurs or identifying the factors associated with it.

Sexual Capacity and Autoerotic Play. It has been clear for several decades that infants are capable of reflexive sexual responses from birth. Male infants are capable of erections, and female infants are capable of vaginal lubrication (Allgeier and Allgeier 1988; Halverson 1940). Lewis (1965) observed pelvic thrusting movements in infants as early as eight months of age. Generally, these events appear to be reactions to spontaneous stimuli, such as touching or brushing of the genitals. However, the Kinsey research group (1953) did report several cases of infants less than 1 year of age who had been observed purposely stimulating their own genitals. In their cross-cultural survey, Ford and Beach (1951) reported that, in cultures with a permissive norm, both boys and girls progress from absent-minded fingering of their genitals in the first year of life to systematic masturbation by the age of 6 to 8.

With few exceptions, most research on childhood sexual experiences has asked adolescents or adults to describe events in their past. Males participating in such studies commonly report memories of what they call "their first pleasurable erection" at such ages as 6 and 9 (Martinson 1976), although, as we have just seen, studies of infants themselves document the occurrence of erections from birth. Kinsey and his associates (1953) did report that almost all boys could have orgasms without ejaculation three to five years before puberty, and more than one half could reach orgasm by age 3 or 4. Comparable data for females have not been presented. In addition, both boys and girls between the ages of 6 and 10 have reported becoming sexually aroused by thinking about sexual events (Langfeldt 1979).

Much has been made in the U.S.A. of the fact that sexual arousal in boys is readily visible (erections). A number of authors have argued that this increases the probability that young boys will "discover" their penis and are, thus, more likely to stimulate their own genitals than are girls. This idea has become part of the folklore of American culture. We know of no evidence that substantiates this idea. In fact, Galenson and Roiphe (1980) report that there are no gender differences in autoerotic play during the first year of life.

American culture does not encourage such childhood sex play and actively seeks to restrict it. In a study in the 1950s, only 2 percent of mothers reported that they were "permissive" about their own children's sex play (Sears, Maccoby, and Levin 1957). It is also interesting to note that the researchers in this study did not provide a response category that allowed mothers to indicate they "supported" or "encouraged" sex play. Martinson (1973) found this pattern extended well into the 1970s. In a later investigation of parental views toward masturbation, Gagnon (1985) found that the majority (86 percent) of this sample believed that their preadolescent children had masturbated. However, only 60 percent of the parents thought that this was acceptable, and only one third wanted their children to have a positive attitude about masturbation.

Sex Play with Other Children. The capacity to interact with another person in an eroticized manner and to experience sexual feelings, either homosexual or heterosexual, is clearly present by the age of 5 to 6. Langfeldt (1979) did observe both mounting and presenting behaviors in boys and girls at 2 years of age. He also observed that prepubertal boys who engaged in sex play with other children typically displayed penile erections during sex play. Ford and Beach (1951) found that children in cultures, unlike the U.S.A., who are able to observe adult sexual relations will engage in copulatory behaviors as early as 6 or 7 years of age. Moreover, in some cultures, adults actively instruct children in the techniques or practice of sexual relations (Ford and Beach 1951; Reiss 1986). This cross-cultural evidence appears to have had little impact on the way in which most Americans, including many sexuality professionals, think about childhood sociosexual interactions.

Again, most of the research in the U.S.A. has been based on recall data from adolescents or adults. Our impressions of childhood sexual interactions are biased toward periods that such older respondents can remember. A number of studies have examined the frequency of childhood sexual behaviors (Broderick 1965, 1966; Broderick and Fowler 1961; Goldman and Goldman 1982; Kinsey et al. 1948, 1953; Martinson 1973, 1976; Ramsey 1943). Taken together, these studies demonstrate that many American children develop and maintain an erotic interest in the other or same sex, and begin experiencing a wide range of sexual behaviors as early as age 5 to 6. It is not uncommon for Americans to report that they remember "playing doctor" or similar games that provide opportunities for observing and touching the genitals of other children, undressing other children, or displaying their own genitals to others. Many American children also acquire experience with kissing and deep kissing (what Americans call French kissing). In fact, generations of American children have played institutionalized kissing games, such as "spin the bottle" and "post office." These studies also provide evidence that at least some American children experience sexual fondling, oral sex, anal sex, and intercourse prior to puberty. Many of these behaviors are experienced in either heterosexual or homosexual combinations or both.

We have purposely avoided reporting the specific frequencies of the childhood sociosexual experiences in these studies because each possesses severe limitations with respect to generalizability. Most have had small samples drawn from a narrow segment of the total population in a specific geographic region. As early as the 1960s, researchers found evidence of racial and community differences in the rate of such behaviors (Broderick 1965, 1966; Broderick and Fowler 1961). In addition, most have used volunteer samples, with respondents who were trying to recall events that had occurred ten or more years earlier. Moreover, these studies were conducted over a period of five decades, during which there would seem to be great potential for changes. Comparisons among these studies are virtually impossible. As a result, we would have little confidence in the specific accuracy of frequency estimates.

A review of a few of these studies illustrates this point. Interviewing a group of boys in a midwestern city in the early 1940s, Ramsey (1943) found that 85 percent had masturbated prior to age 13, one third had engaged in homosexual play, two thirds had engaged in heterosexual play, and one third had attempted or completed intercourse. The Kinsey group (1948), using a broader sample of adults, reported that 45 percent had masturbated by age 13, 30 percent had engaged in homosexual play, 40 percent had engaged in heterosexual play, and 20 percent had attempted intercourse. For girls, the Kinsey group (1953) reported that roughly 20 percent had masturbated prior to age 13, roughly one third had engaged in both heterosexual and homosexual play, and 17 percent had attempted inter-course. They also reported an actual decline in sexual behaviors after age 10 (Kinsey et al. 1948). The large differences between the Ramsey and Kinsey findings could be due to sample size, differences in geographic region or size of the city, differences in the time period of data collection, or differences in the age range of the samples. Here, it is interesting to note that the Kinsey group (1948) also interviewed a small sample of boys. Roughly 70 percent reported some form of child sex play, a figure that is much closer to Ramsey's findings. In the larger Kinsey sample, only 57 percent of adult males and 48 percent of adult females reported memories of childhood sex play, usually between the ages of 8 to 13 (Kinsey et al. 1948, 1953). It would seem possible, then, that studies with adult samples recalling their childhood experiences might well yield lower estimates than studies of children themselves.

John Money (1976) and Money and Ehrhardt (1972) argue that childhood sex play with other children is a necessary and valuable form of rehearsal and preparation for later adult sexual behavior. He has also suggested that such sex play may occur as part of a developmental stage in childhood. Certainly, this phenomenon has been observed in other primate species, such as the chimpanzee (DeWaal 1982). However, Kilpatrick (1986, 1987) found no differences in various ages of adult sexual functioning between persons who had childhood sexual experiences with other children and those who did not. Given the complexity of the model of sexual assemblies we have presented here, it is not surprising that the effects are not that simple.

Sibling Incest. We discuss incest and child sexual abuse more fully later in Section 8A on coercive sex. Here, we merely wish to note that, in one of the few studies of sibling incest with a nonclinical sample, Finkelhor (1980) found that 15 percent of female and 10 percent of male college students reported having a sexual experience with a brother or sister. Approximately 40 percent of these students had been under the age of 8 at the time of the sexual activity, and roughly 50 percent had been between the ages of 8 and 12. Three quarters of the experiences had been heterosexual. Some type of force had been used in one quarter of the experiences. The most common sexual activities were touching and fondling of the genitals. Only 12 percent of the students had ever told anyone about these sexual activities with a brother or a sister. Interestingly, most of the students reported that they did not have either strong positive or negative feelings about these experiences. Positive reactions were reported by 30 percent, and another 30 percent reported negative reactions. Positive reactions were associated with consensual activities (no force had been used) and an age difference of four or fewer years. For males, there were no correlations between prior sibling experiences and current sexual activity. Among females, those who had had sibling sexual experiences were more likely to be currently sexually active. Those women who had positive sibling experiences after age 9 had significantly higher sexual self-esteem, whereas those who had sexual experiences before age 9 with a sibling more than four years older had lower self-esteem.

Sexual Contacts with Adults. A recent national survey (Laumann et al. 1994) found that 12 percent of men and 17 percent of women reported they had been sexually touched by an older person while they were children. The offender was typically not a stranger, but a family friend or a relative, a finding that is comparable to more-limited samples. We present a more complete review of sexual contacts with adults later in Section 8A2 on child sexual abuse and incest. Relatively few studies of adult-child sexual contacts have been conducted with nonclinical samples. In general, they indicate that children experience a wide range of reactions, from highly negative or traumatic to highly positive, to such contacts in both the short term and long term (Kilpatrick 1986, 1987; Nelson 1986; Farrell 1990). Moreover, there do not appear to be any simple or direct correlations between such childhood experiences and later measures of adult sexual functioning. In her study of incest, Nelson (1986) found no correlation between affective outcomes and type of erotic activity, sexual orientation, or consanguinity. Kilpatrick (1986) did find that the use of force or abuse was significantly related to impaired adult sexual functioning in several areas.

Same-Sex Childhood Experiences. Our discussion to this point has not focused exclusively on heterosexual experience, but it is certainly fair to say that investigations of heterosexual child sex play have dominated existing research. One study of 4- to 14-year-old children found that more than one half of boys and one third of girls reported at least one homosexual experience (Elias and Gebhard 1969). Masturbation, touching of the genitals, and exhibition were the most common activities, although there were also some reports of oral and anal contacts. The fact that children have had such a homosexual experience does not appear to be related to adult sexual orientation (Bell, Weinberg, and Hammersmith 1981; Van Wyk and Geist 1984).

Storms (1981) has hypothesized that such experiences may be related to adult sexual orientation as a function of sexual maturation. He suggests that persons who become sexually mature during the period of homosocial networks (discussed below) may be more likely to romanticize and eroticize these childhood homosexual experiences and, thus, develop a later preference for sexual partners of the same gender. In effect, when sexual maturation, goal-directed masturbation, homosexual explorations, and eroticized fantasies are paired before heterosexual socialization occurs (typically at about age 13), they are more likely to lead to a homosexual orientation later. As far as we know, Storms's ideas have never been directly tested through research.

Childhood Social Networks. During middle childhood (roughly ages 6 to 12), both boys and girls in the U.S.A. tend to form networks of same-sex friends. A pattern of gender segregation, where boys and girls have separate friends and play groups, is central to the daily life of middle childhood. This pattern of homosocial networks is readily observable at elementary schools across the U.S.A. Girls and boys tend to cluster at school into separated, same-sex groups. At lunchtime, they frequently sit at separate "girl's tables" and "boy's tables." On the playground, space and activities tend to be gendered. After school, children tend to associate and play in gender-segregated groupings. In fact, this pattern of gender separation may be more pronounced in middle childhood in the U.S.A. than the more-publicized racial segregation.

It should be acknowledged that these homosocial networks are not characterized by a total separation of the genders. There are some opportunities for heterosocial interactions and play, and children do vary with respect to the extent in which they associate with the other sex. As just one obvious example, some girls, who are known as "tomboys," spend considerable time associating with boys. Still, to a large extent, the worlds of boys and girls in middle childhood in the U.S.A. are separated.

Maltz and Borker (1983) have suggested that these homosocial networks can be viewed as distinct male and female cultures. As cultures, each has its own set of patterns, norms, and rules of discourse. Boys tend to play in groups that are arranged in a hierarchy. They stress a norm of achievement ("doing") and emphasize competitive, physical activities. Conflict is overt and is often resolved directly through physical fighting. Differentiation between boys is made directly in terms of power and status within the group. Since boys belong to more than one such group, and because group memberships do change over time, each boy has an opportunity to occupy a range of positions within these hierarchies. Boys' groups also tend to be inclusive. New members are easily accommodated, even if they must begin their membership in a lower-status position. Courage and testing limits are prime values of boys' groups, and breaking rules is a valued form of bonding. In examining how these patterns influence male communication, Maltz and Borker (1983) report that males are more likely to interrupt others, they are more likely to ignore the previous statement made by another speaker, they are more likely to resist an interruption, and they are more likely to directly challenge statements by others.

Girls tend to associate in smaller groups or friendship pairs. Girls, for example, tend to be highly invested in establishing and maintaining a "best friend" relationship. They stress a norm of cooperation ("sharing") and pursue activities that emphasize "working together" and "being nice." They frequently play games that involve "taking turns." Friendship is seen as requiring intimacy, equality, mutual commitment, and cooperation. However, girls' groups also tend to be exclusive. Membership is carefully reserved for those who have demonstrated they are good friends. Conflict tends to be covert, and it is highly disruptive, leading to a pattern of shifting alliances among associates. Differentiation between girls is not made in terms of power, but rather in relative closeness. Girls are more likely to affirm the value of rules, especially if they are seen as serving group cohesion or making things fair. Girls may break rules, but their gender group does not provide the intense encouragement and support for this behavior seen among boys. Maltz and Borker (1983) note that girls are more likely to ask questions to facilitate conversation, they are more likely to take turns talking, they are more likely to encourage others to speak, and they are more likely to feel quietly victimized when they have been interrupted.

These largely segregated gender networks in middle childhood serve as the contexts for learning about adolescent and adult sexual patterns, as well as for other areas of social life. There is, of course, a certain irony to the fact that homosocial networks serve as a principal learning context for heterosexuality in a culture with such strong taboos against homosexuality as the U.S.A. In fact, Martinson (1973) has argued that these gender networks and this period serve as the settings for a fair amount of homo-sexual exploration and activity. In one sense, it is almost certainly true that some homosexual activity results from these patterns of social organization. However, this assertion is largely undocumented, and we are not aware of any studies that compare the level of homosexual activity in cultures with homosocial networks with cultures having some other form of childhood networks.

Thorne and Luria (1986) have used this concept of gendered cultures to examine the process of sexual learning in middle childhood. They found that "talking dirty" is a common format for the rule-breaking that charac-terizes boys' groups. They noted that talking dirty serves to define boys as apart from adults, and that boys get visibly excited while engaging in such talk. Boys also often share pornography with each other and take great care to avoid detection and confiscation by adults. These processes provide knowledge about what is sexually arousing, and they also create a hidden, forbidden, and arousing world shared with other boys, apart from adults and girls. Miller and Simon (1981) have argued that the importance attached to rule violations creates a sense of excitement and fervor about sexual activity and accomplishment.

One other feature of boys' groups is that they serve as a setting for learning both homoeroticism and homophobia. Boys learn to engage in what Thorne and Luria call "fag talk." That is, they learn to insult other boys by calling them names, like "faggot" and "queer." Eventually, they learn that homosexuality is disapproved by the male peer group. Boys at age 5 to 6 can be observed touching each other frequently. By age 11 to 12, touching is less frequent and reduced to ritual gestures like poking each other. On the other hand, much of the time spent with other boys is spent talking about sex. This serves to maintain a high level of arousal within the group. Moreover, the sanctioning of rule-breaking leads to some homosex-ual experimentation that is kept hidden from the group. Homosexual experiences may become one more form of breaking the rules and one more feature of the secret, forbidden world of sexuality.

In contrast, girls are more likely to focus on their own and their friends' physical appearance. They monitor one another's emotions. They share secrets and become mutually vulnerable through self-disclosure. They have giggling sessions with their friends, with sex often being the source of amusement. Their talks with other girls tend to focus less on physical activities and more on relationships and romance. They also plot together how to get particular boys and girls together in a relationship.

These sexual patterns are largely consistent with the norms of the respective gender cultures. Males tend to focus on physical activities; females on cooperation and sharing. They are also quite consistent with patterns that will become firmly established in adolescent sociosexual patterns. Thus, male and female peer groups become the launching pads for heterosexual coupling as boys and girls begin to "go together." Finally, they serve to heighten the romantic/erotic component of interactions with the other gender.

Professional and Social Issues of Childhood Sexuality

As we stated at the beginning of this section and as should be apparent from the review of sex education in the U.S.A., there are a number of issues concerning childhood sexuality that have been controversial for decades. Moreover, several new issues have become points of social conflict in recent years. We can only briefly mention four here.

The Oedipus and Electra Complexes. The Goldmans' (1982) multinational study of children and sexual learning, including a sizable American sample, raises questions about these complexes. Freud's thesis about castration anxiety and its resolution (typically by the age of 5) would presumably require some awareness of genital differences between males and females, unless one wishes to interpret Freud's terminology strictly as metaphorical. In the Goldman study, the majority of English-speaking children did not understand these differences until they were 7 to 9 years old. Interestingly, a majority of the Swedish children could accurately describe these differences by the age of 5.

Is There a Latency Period? The notion of a latency period, roughly from ages 6 to 11, has had great appeal in American culture. This may be due to the impression that the homosocial networks of middle childhood reflect a lack of sexual interest, and to the fact that many Americans prefer to believe that childhood is a period of sexual innocence. Freud (1938) originally proposed in 1905 that middle childhood is characterized by relative sexual disinterest and inactivity, something like a dormant period. Freud also maintained that latency was more pronounced among boys than girls. The review above should certainly dispel the notion that childhood, at any point, is essentially characterized by sexual disinterest.

In addition, Broderick (1965, 1966) not only provided evidence of active sex play during middle childhood, but also demonstrated that most children indicate they wish to marry as an adult, and that most of these children are actively involved in a process of increasing heterosocial interaction and love involvements during childhood. A majority said they had had a boyfriend or girlfriend and had been in love, and 32 percent had dated by age 13. If anything, we would expect that the age norms for many of these behaviors have actually decreased since that time. Interestingly, those children who indicated that they did not wish to marry eventually were substantially less likely to report any of these activities.

Parental Nudity. Experts have disagreed over the years as to the impact of parental nudity on children (Okami 1995). Some have argued that childhood exposure to parental/adult nudity is potentially traumatic—largely because of the large size of adult organs. Others have insisted that strong taboos on family nudity may lead to a view that the body is unacceptable or shameful. This group has argued that a relaxed attitude toward nudity can help children develop positive feelings about sexuality. Similar concerns have been expressed about the primal scene and sleeping in the parental bed. In a survey of 500 psychiatrists, 48 percent indicated that they believe that children who witness their parents engaging in intercourse do suffer psychological effects (Pankhurst 1979). American experts appear to overlook the fact that most families throughout the world sleep in one-room dwellings. In one study of these issues, Lewis and Janda (1988) asked 200 college students to report their childhood experiences. Exposure to parental nudity for ages zero to 5 and 6 to 11 was generally unrelated to a series of measures of adult sexual adjustment. Sleeping in the parental bed yielded several small, but significant correlations. Persons who had slept in their parents' bed as children had higher self-esteem, greater comfort about sexuality, reduced sexual guilt and anxiety, greater frequency of sex, greater comfort with affection, and a higher acceptance of casual sex as college students.

Okami (1995) reviewed the literature in these same three areas. His review provides a thorough summary of clinical opinions in each area, as well as an assessment of the empirical evidence. Despite the growing number of clinical professionals who label such acts as sexual abuse, there is virtually no empirical evidence of harm. In fact, the only variable found to be associated with harm is cosleeping, which has been found to be associated with sleep disturbances. However, Okami notes that these sleep disturbances may well have preceded and precipitated the cosleeping, rather than vice versa.

Female Genital Cutting. In December 1996, the Centers for Disease Control and Prevention (CDC) estimated that more than 150,000 women and girls of African origin or ancestry in the United States were at risk in 1995 of being subjected to genital cutting or had already been cut. This estimate was based on 1990 Census Bureau data gathered before the recent increase in refugees and immigrants from the 28 countries that span Africa's midsection where female genital cutting varies widely in prevalence and severity (Dugger 1996ab). A second source cites a different estimate from the CDC using data on how much circumcision is practiced in immigrants' homelands and, making assumptions about sex and age, that about 270,00 African females in the United States were circumcised in their home country or are at risk here (Hamm 1996)

In 1996, Congress adopted a dual strategy to combat the practice here. In April 1996, Congress passed a bill requiring the Immigration and Naturalization Service to inform new arrivals of U.S. laws against genital cutting. It also mandated the Department of Health and Human Services to educate immigrants about the harm of genital cutting and to educate medical professionals about treating circumcised women. A law, which went into effect March 29, 1997, also criminalizes the practice, making it punishable by up to five years in prison and a fine of up to $250,000 for individuals and $500,000 for organizations such as hospitals. Enforcement of the law, however, is problematic for several reasons. First, no one is sure how the law will apply to those immigrants who take their daughters out of the country for the rite. Second, doctors who spot cases of genital mutilation are reluctant to report it for fear of breaking up tight-knit families. Also, when the wounds are healed, it is impossible to ascertain whether the rite was performed here or before arrival in the United States. Finally, there is the secretiveness surrounding this rite of passage, which many African cultures consider essential, and also the hidden nature of the wounds and scars. Sierra Leoneans, for instance, who consider genital cutting part of an elaborate, highly secret initiation rite, view questions about it as a profound invasion of their privacy (Dugger 1996ab).

A government's prevention program focuses on educating both old and recent immigrants in how to survive and assimilate in American society while maintaining their own culture and religion. To this purpose, the U.S. Department of Health and Human Services has organized meetings with advocates for refugees and nonprofit groups that work closely with Africans to develop strategies for combating this practice. Muslim religious leaders, for instance, are invited to explain that the Koran does not require this practice. However, lack of a specific budget hampers this effort.

In one attempt to ameliorate this clash of cultural values, doctors at Harborview Medical Center in Seattle, Washington, persuaded Somali mothers to be satisfied with nicking the clitoral hood without removing any tissue. The ritual usually involves removing the clitoris and sewing the labia closed. The compromise was abandoned in December of 1996 when the hospital was inundated with hundreds of complaints, led by a group of feminists, protesting even this compromise, even though the nicking of the clitoral hood has no short- or long-term negative consequences. The massive objection to this compromise raises serious questions of ethnocentrism on the part of the Americans who protested it. It seems somewhat ironic that such complaints would be made in a culture where we routinely circumcise penises. Although some maintained that the compromise of nicking may violate the letter of the law, it remains to be seen what kind of solution will be achieved in this matter (Dugger 1996b).

Child Pornography. It is widely believed, and the Federal Bureau of Investigation (FBI) perpetuates the notion, that child pornography is pervasive and increasing. Several state and federal laws have been enacted in the last twenty years to combat this perceived social problem. The mere possession of a photograph of a naked child has been criminalized in some states. Yet, it is virtually impossible to find any commercial child pornography in the U.S.A. In fact, most of the materials seized by the FBI are private photographs of naked children—with no adults appearing in the photos and no sexual behaviors depicted (Klein 1994; Stanley 1989). Efforts to raid child-pornography businesses have routinely failed to seize any child pornography. FBI sting operations may well have arisen from the corresponding frustrations of government agencies to find any child pornography. One recent legend now circulating is the claim that the U.S. government is now the largest producer of child pornography in the world. This claim is unsubstantiated as far as we know, but, again, it reflects the anxiety of American culture over the sexuality of its children.

B. Adolescent Sexuality

DAVID L. WEIS

Courtship, Dating, and Premarital Sex

In stark contrast to the relative inattention given to childhood sexuality in the U.S.A., Americans have been fascinated by the sexual behavior of adolescents throughout the twentieth century. One is tempted to describe the interest as an obsession. Perhaps no area of sexuality has received as much scrutiny, by both the general public and professionals, as the sexual practices of American teenagers. There have been literally hundreds of scientific studies attempting to determine the rate of adolescent premarital coitus, as well as other aspects of adolescent sexuality. The easy availability of populations to study is only one of the more-obvious reasons for this extensive research.

Since more than 90 percent of Americans ultimately do marry, investigations of adolescent sexual development and premarital sexual practices largely overlap. General trends have been well documented, compared to other areas of sexuality. Given the vast scope of this research, we can review only the highlights here. (For more extensive reviews of research on adolescent and premarital sexuality, see Cannon and Long 1971; Clayton and Bokemeier 1980; and Miller and Moore 1990.)

The issue of premarital sexuality (hereafter PS) and virginity has been a focus of considerable social conflict and concern throughout this century, and remains so to this day. Beginning in the early years of this century, a large literature documents the continuing concern of American adults about the increasing number of teenagers who have experienced sexual intercourse prior to marriage. Interestingly, each successive birth cohort of American adults in this century has been concerned about the tendency of their offspring to exceed their own rate of premarital coitus.

Much of the professional literature has reflected these same concerns. Through much of the twentieth century, the tone of most professional writings has been moralistic. Adults in the U.S.A., including most sexuality researchers, have tended to view adolescent premarital sexual intercourse, PS, as a deviant behavior, as a violation of existing social norms, and as a growing social problem (Spanier 1975). Research has tended to parallel this perspective by emphasizing the costs or negative consequences of adolescent sexuality, such as sexually transmitted disease (venereal disease), "illegitimate" pregnancy, and loss of reputation (Reiss 1960). This tone may have shifted to a less-judgmental, more-analytic perspective in the 1960s and 1970s (Clayton and Bokemeier 1980). However, with the emergence of AIDS and the rise of out-of-wedlock pregnancies in the early 1980s, the general tone has reverted in recent years, with studies of "risk-taking" behavior, "at-risk" youth, and portrayals of adolescent sexuality as a form of delinquency (Miller and Moore 1990).

Trends in Adolescent Sexuality

Despite these adult concerns, it would be fair to suggest that premarital virginity has largely disappeared in the U.S.A., both as a reality and as a social ideal. As we approach the end of the century, the overwhelming majority of Americans now have sexual intercourse prior to marriage, and they begin at younger ages than in the past. "Love" has largely replaced marital status as the most valued criteria for evaluating sexual experience (Reiss 1960, 1967, 1980). Virtually all Americans believe that intimate relationships (like marriage) should be based on love, that love justifies sexual activity, and that sex with love is a more-fulfilling human experience. This view has not only been used to justify PS activity between loving partners, but has also become a criteria for evaluating marital sexuality itself and justifying a pattern of divorce and remarriage.

Premarital Sexual Behavior. These trends may not be quite as dramatic as most Americans imagine. A study of marriages in Groton, Massachusetts, from 1761 to 1775 found that one third of the women were pregnant at the time of their weddings (cited in Reiss 1980), demonstrating that PS was already fairly common in the colonial period (see discussion of bundling in Section 1A). Several early sexuality surveys also document that PS occurred among some groups prior to the twentieth century. Terman (1938) compared groups who were born in different cohorts around the beginning of the century. Of those born before 1890, 50 percent of the men and only 13 percent of the women had premarital coitus. Two thirds of the men who had PS did so with someone other than their future spouse, whereas two thirds of the women who had PS did so only with their future spouse. For those born after 1900, two thirds of the men and nearly half of the women had PS. The relative percentage having PS with their fiance also increased. Fully half of the men and 47 percent of the women had sexual relations with their fiance prior to marriage.

The Kinsey team (1953) found that one quarter of the women born before 1900 reported they had PS, whereas one half of those born after 1900 said they had PS. Like the Terman study, the major change was an increase in the percentage of women born after 1900 who had PS with their fiance. The Kinsey study also indicated that the period of most-rapid change was from 1918 to 1930—the "Roaring Twenties." Burgess and Wallin (1953) reported similar findings for a birth cohort born between 1910 and 1919. These studies indicated that roughly two thirds of the men born after 1900 had PS. The Kinsey studies also found that there had been comparable increases in female masturbation and petting behavior as well.

It is important to note that the growth of PS in the first half of the century occurred primarily within the context of ongoing, intimate relationships. It appears that the percentage of males and females having PS remained fairly stable through the 1950s and early 1960s. In a study of college students during the 1950s, Ehrmann (1959) found rates similar to the Kinsey figures cited above. Ehrmann found that males tended to have greater sexual experience with females from a social class lower than their own, but they tended to marry women from their own social class. Males who were "going steady" were the least likely to be having intercourse. In contrast, females who were "going steady" were the most likely to be having intercourse. In a study comparing college students in Scandinavia, Indiana, and Utah (predominantly Mormon), Christensen (1962) and Christensen and Carpenter (1962) found that rates of PS vary by the norms of the culture and that guilt is most likely to occur when PS is discrepant with those norms.

A second wave of increases in PS seems to have occurred in the period from 1965 to 1980. A number of studies of college students through this period indicated increasing percentages of males and females having premarital coitus (Bauman and Wilson 1974; Bell and Chaskes 1968; Christensen and Gregg 1970; Robinson, King, and Balswick 1972; Simon, Berger, and Gagnon 1972; Vener and Stewart 1974). For example, Bauman and Wilson (1974) found that, for men, the rate having PS increased from 56 percent in 1968 to 73 percent in 1972. For women, the increase was from 46 percent to 73 percent. There was no significant change in the number of sexual partners for either gender. Several of these studies indicate that the increases were still moderate by 1970 (Bell and Chaskes 1968; Simon et al. 1972). In an unusual study of male college students attending an eastern university in the 1940s, 1960s, and 1970s, Finger (1975) found that

45 percent had PS in 1943-44, 62 percent in 1967-68, and 75 percent in 1969-73.

Subsequent studies have indicated that this pattern of increasing PS characterized American youth in general. In a study of urban samples in the mid-1970s, Udry, Bauman, and Morris (1975) found that 45 percent of white teenage women had intercourse by age 20, and 80 percent of black women did. Roughly 10 percent of whites had PS by age 15 and 20 percent of blacks did. Zelnik and Kantner found similar percentages in their studies in 1971 and 1976 (Udry, Bauman, and Morris 1975; Zelnik, Kantner, and Ford 1981).

Reports of increasing sexual activity among adolescents have not been limited to coitus. A number of researchers have reported similar increases in the rate of heavy petting (manual caressing of the genitals) through the late 1960s and 1970s (Clayton and Bokemeier 1980; Vener and Stewart 1974). There have also been reports of increasing levels of oral sex among adolescents (Haas 1979; Newcomer and Udry 1985). In some studies, teenage girls have been more likely to have participated in oral sex than intercourse, and between 16 percent to 25 percent of teens who have never had intercourse have had oral sex (Newcomer and Udry 1985). Weis (1983) has noted that this group may be involved in a transition from virginity to nonvirginity, at least among whites.

Perhaps the single best indicator of the trends occurring from 1965 to 1980 is the series of studies by Zelnik and Kantner in 1971, 1976, and 1979 (Zelnik et al. 1981). These studies, known as the *National Surveys of Young Women*, investigated the sexual histories of 15- to 19-year-old women. The 1971 and 1976 studies were full national probability studies while the 1979 study focused on women living in metropolitan areas. The Zelnik and Kantner research shows a dramatic rise in sexual activity for both black and white women from 1971 to 1976. The pattern of increases continued for white women through 1979, but PS rates for black women remained stable from 1976 to 1979. Among metropolitan women, PS rose from 30.4 percent in 1971 to 49.8 percent in 1979. For blacks, the rate moved from 53.7 percent in 1971 to 66.3 percent in 1976, and was 66.2 percent in 1979. The 1979 study also showed that 70 percent of males had PS intercourse; the figure for black men was 75 percent (Zelnik and Shah 1983; Zelnik et al. 1983).

In a review of these trends, Hofferth, Kahn, and Baldwin (1987) noted that females in the 1980s became sexually active at younger ages and that fewer teenagers married. As a result, the rate of PS increased. The proportion of women at risk of premarital pregnancy increased dramatically from 1965 to the 1980s. The out-of-wedlock pregnancy rate among teenagers increased for both blacks and whites from 1971 to 1976. This trend continued for whites through 1982, but remained level for blacks after 1976. Finally, they noted that, for women born between 1938 and 1940, 33.3 percent had PS by age 20. For women born between 1953 and 1955, the figure was 65.5 percent.

Despite recent claims in some quarters of a return to chastity and abstinence in the late 1980s and 1990s (McCleary 1992), there is no evidence of a decline in PS behavior. National data from 1988 indicate that one quarter of females have PS intercourse by age 15; 60 percent do so by age 19. About one third of United States males have PS intercourse by age 15, and 86 percent by age 19 (Miller and Moore 1990). In fact, a random telephone survey of 100 students attending a midwestern state university in 1994 found that 92 percent had had sexual intercourse; only 8 percent said they were still virgins. Nearly two thirds (63 percent) said that they had participated in what the survey described as a "one-night stand." With respect to their most recent sexual intercourse, 42 percent reported using something to "protect" themselves. Of these, 84 percent reported using condoms; 16 percent said they used the pill (Turco 1994). If anything, the trends that have been well established throughout this century appear to be continuing. Given the continuation of patterns that have been frequently cited as leading to increasing rates of PS, such as industrialization, rapid transportation, dating, and "going steady," we would not expect a reversal in what is now a century-long trend.

Premarital Sexual Attitudes (Permissiveness). There has also been a substantial number of studies examining the attitudes of Americans toward PS, although systematic research in this area began later than research on PS behavior. Reiss (1960) used the term "permissiveness" to describe the extent to which the attitudes of an individual or a social group approved PS in various circumstances. In general, research has found that PS attitudes have become progressively more permissive throughout this century, roughly parallel to the increases in PS behavior (Bell and Chaskes 1970; Cannon and Long 1971; Christensen and Gregg 1970; Clayton and Bokemeier 1980; Glenn and Weaver 1979; Vener and Stewart 1974). Reiss (1967) developed what has come to be called Autonomy Theory to explain this process. According to Reiss, PS permissiveness will increase in cultures where the adolescent system of courtship becomes autonomous with respect to adult institutions of social control, such as the church, parents, and the school. This appears to have happened in the U.S.A. and most other industrialized nations in the twentieth century.

By far, the biggest change has been the growth of a standard that Reiss (1960, 1967, 1980) called "permissiveness with affection," in which PS is seen as acceptable for couples who have mutually affectionate relationships. This standard has grown in popularity in the U.S.A. as the double standard—the view that PS is acceptable for males but not females—has declined (Clayton and Bokemeier 1980; Reiss 1967, 1980). By 1980, a majority of adults as well as young people in the U.S.A. believed that PS is appropriate for couples involved together in a serious relationship (Glenn and Weaver 1979). Moreover, although there has been a historical tendency for males to be more permissive about PS than females, these gender differences have been diminishing in recent decades (Clayton and Bokemeier 1980).

Circumstances of Adolescent Sexual Experiences

Most research on adolescent sexuality has tended to focus on whether or not teenagers or college students have had PS intercourse. Although this allows us to provide reasonable estimates of the percentages of Americans who have had PS in various time periods and to track trends in the rate of virginity and nonvirginity, this same focus has frequently led researchers to ignore the circumstances in which adolescent sexuality occurs (Miller and Moore 1990). As a consequence, we cannot be as confident about the trends in several related areas, and many questions about the specific nature of adolescent sexual experiences and relationships remain to be explored.

First Intercourse. A good example of this lack of perspective is provided by the evidence concerning age at first intercourse. The available research indicates that the average age of first intercourse has been declining since 1970. It seems likely that this trend extends back prior to 1970, but the paucity of relevant data from earlier time periods makes such a conclusion highly tentative. As late as that year, only about one quarter of the males and 7 percent of the females who attended college had intercourse prior to age 18 (Simon et al. 1972). In the Zelnik and Kantner studies, the average age for females dropped from 16.5 in 1971 to 16.2 in 1976 (Zelnik et al. 1981). By 1979, the average age of first intercourse for women was 16.2; for males, it was 15.7. Blacks of both genders tended to experience sexarche at slightly younger ages than whites. Females had first partners who were nearly three years older; whereas males had first partners who were about one year older than they (Zelnik and Shah 1983).

In a study of college females in the 1980s, Weis (1983) found the average age of sexarche to be 16.2. A later study of college students found that the average age was 16.5 (Sprecher, Barbee, and Schwartz 1995). It should be noted, however, that persons who attend college may well be more likely to postpone sexual activity. It is conceivable that a trend of declining age at first intercourse is still occurring among populations that do not attend college, and it is possible that teenagers in the 1990s (who have yet to reach the age of college) may also be having intercourse at younger ages.

Intercourse appears to be, at least among whites, the culmination of a sequence of increasing and expanding experiences with kissing, petting, and possibly oral sex (Spanier 1975; Weis 1983). There is some evidence that women who have rehearsed these noncoital activities extensively, and thus gradually learned the processes of sexual interaction, are more likely to report positive reactions to their first intercourse (Weis 1983). Weis (1983) found that there is great variation as to when people go through these stages and how quickly.

Most authors have stressed the negative aspects of first intercourse for females by citing the finding that females are significantly more likely to report negative affective reactions to their first intercourse than males (Koch 1988; Sprecher et al. 1995). However, the available data strongly suggest that the differences between males and females may not be large in magnitude. It is clear that females report a wide range of affect, from strongly positive to strongly negative (Koch 1988; Schwartz 1993; Weis 1983), but it is also clear that many males report experiencing negative reactions as well. In a study of college students, the males were more likely to report experiencing high levels of anxiety, the females were less likely to report experiencing high levels of subjective pleasure, while sizable numbers of both genders reported experiencing guilt (Sprecher et al. 1995). Positive reactions to first intercourse have been found to be related to prior experience with noncoital sexual activities, having an orgasm in that first intercourse encounter, descriptions of the partner as gentle and caring (for females), involvement with the first partner for more than one month prior to first intercourse, continued involvement with the partner following the first intercourse, and situational factors, such as the consumption of alcohol (Schwartz 1993; Sprecher et al. 1995; Weis 1983). Several researchers have reported that age is associated with affective reactions, but Weis (1983) found that age was not as strongly or directly related as the level of prior noncoital experience. Schwartz (1993) also reported that Scandinavian teenagers were more likely to report positive reactions than a group of American adolescents.

Over the past three decades, a convergence of male and female PS behavior has been identified, with females reporting less emotional attachment to their first coital partners than in the past (Hopkins 1977; Kallen and Stephenson 1982; Koch 1988). Yet, there is still a significant difference between the genders, with males reporting more casual relationships and females more intimate relationships with their first partners (Koch 1988).

In the only national study of first intercourse, Zelnik and Shah (1983) found that more than 60 percent of the females were "going with" or engaged to their first partner. Another third described their first partner as a friend. Roughly a third of the males described their first partner as a friend, and 40 percent were "going with" or engaged to their first partner. The males were twice as likely to have their first intercourse with someone they had just met, although few males or females did this (Zelnik and Shah 1983).

Relationship factors have been reported to be associated with affective reactions to the first intercourse. However, the precise nature of this association remains unclear. There is some evidence that involvement with a partner for longer than one month, and continuing involvement following the first intercourse, are associated with positive affective reactions (Sprecher et al. 1995). There is some evidence that females who are "going with" or engaged to their first partner are more likely to experience positive affect (Weis 1983). However, Weis (1983) also found that attributions that the first partner was caring, considerate, and gentle were more strongly related to affective reactions. Moreover, many women who were "going with" or engaged to their first partner, nonetheless, described their partners as uncaring and inconsiderate. It should be noted that each of these studies found so few participants who were married at the time of their first intercourse that no analyses could be done for that relationship category. For example, not one woman in the Weis (1983) study was married at the time of her first intercourse.

Adolescents appear to have many reasons for becoming involved in PS behavior. Motivations most frequently mentioned by a group of college women for becoming involved in their first intercourse experience included (rank-ordered by declining frequency): love-caring, partner pressure, curiosity, both wanted to, alcohol or other drugs, and sexual arousal (Koch 1988). The comparable rank-ordering of motivations by a group of college men included: both wanted to, curiosity, love-caring, sexual arousal, to "get laid," and alcohol/drug use. Women were four times more likely to report partner pressure than men, whereas men were seven times as likely to say they were looking to "get laid" and twice as likely to report sexual arousal as a motivation for sexarche (Koch 1988).

Most American teenagers describe their first intercourse as an "unplanned, spontaneous" event. Only 17 percent of the females and one quarter of the males in a national study said they had planned their first intercourse (Zelnik and Shah 1983). In the same study, less than one half of the males and females used a contraceptive. Those who had their first intercourse at age 18 or older were more likely to use a contraceptive. White women were more likely to have used some form of contraception, but black women were more likely to use a medically prescribed method. Women who described their first intercourse as planned were more likely to have used a contraceptive—fully three quarters of these women did. However, more than two thirds of these women relied on their partners to use a condom or withdrawal. Black women were more likely to use a contraceptive themselves, rather than rely on their partner.

Finally, various aspects of sexarche have been found to be significantly related to later sexual functioning among college students (Koch 1988). Women who had experienced first coitus at an earlier age had less difficulty reaching orgasm during later sexual interactions than did women who had sexarche at a later age. Men with earlier sexarche had less difficulty in keeping an erection during later sexual interactions than men who had been older at sexarche. Also, women who had reported negative reactions to their first intercourse were subsequently more likely than those who felt more positively to experience: lack of sexual interest, sexual repulsion, inability to reach orgasm, or genital discomfort, pain, or vaginal spasms. Men who reacted negatively to their first intercourse were more likely to ejaculate too quickly during later sexual experiences than men who had positive reactions. Both men and women were more likely to experience subsequent sexual functioning concerns when they were pressured by a close partner to engage in intercourse for the first time.

Number of Premarital Sexual Partners. It is difficult to provide good estimates on the number of PS partners prior to 1950, simply because researchers failed to ask such a question. On the other hand, it does seem clear that the increase in the percentage of American women who reported they had ever had PS after 1900 was due primarily to an increase in the percentage of women who reported they had PS only with their fiance (Kinsey et al. 1953; Terman 1938). In contrast, there is abundant evidence of a significant increase in the number of PS coital partners for females from the late 1960s through the late 1980s (Cannon and Long 1971; Clayton and Bokemeier 1980; Miller and Moore 1990; Vener and Stewart 1974; Zelnik et al. 1983). This finding is, however, potentially misleading. A close inspection of the results of pertinent studies reveals that most of the increase is explained by a shift from zero to one partner and from one to two partners. There were no increases in the percentage with seven or more partners.

Among males, there is some evidence that adolescent boys of recent decades are less likely to use the services of a prostitute than in the past (Cannon and Long 1971). In a unique study of males attending the same eastern university from the 1940s through the 1970s, Finger (1975) actually reported a decline in the number of PS partners with a corresponding increase in the frequency of sexual relations. This was primarily due to an increase in the percentage of men who had PS only with their girlfriends. Finger also reported a decline in the percentage of males reporting they ever had a homosexual experience. However, among those who had a homosexual experience, the frequency of such encounters had increased.

Although there appears to be consistent evidence that there have been significant increases in the number of PS partners throughout this century, at least for females, it should be stressed that, as late as 1990, the majority of American teens had had zero or one PS partner. Only 4 percent of white females, 6 percent of black females, 11 percent of white males, and 23 percent of black males reported six or more partners (Miller and Moore 1990). Thus, the widely held idea that large percentages of American adolescents are now "promiscuous" is greatly exaggerated.

Rates of Teen Pregnancy and Birth. In an examination of how the trends we have been reviewing are related to trends in adolescent pregnancy and birth, it is important to bear in mind that, as late as 1965, several states in the U.S.A. prohibited the sale of contraceptives to married couples. Such laws banning the sale of contraceptives to teenagers and/or single persons were common until 1977 (see Section 9A). Details on out-of-wedlock births, contraception, and abortion are presented later. Here, we want to note that the birthrate among unmarried women has been increasing since 1965, with a notable surge in the rate during the 1980s (Baldwin 1980; Forrest and Fordyce 1988; Miller and Moore 1990). Throughout this period, the percentage of unmarried, adolescent women exposed to the risk of pregnancy has been increasing. One principal reason for this is, of course, the increasing percentage of unmarried persons having PS in the U.S.A. (Forrest and Fordyce 1988).

However, there are several interesting twists among these trends, many of which do not fit with the conventional wisdom in the U.S.A. First, much of the increase since 1980 is attributable to women 20 years of age or older. In fact, the adolescent birthrate has actually been declining since the early 1970s (Baldwin 1980; Forrest and Fordyce 1988). Second, the overall birthrate for adolescent women increased through the late 1940s and 1950s, remained stable in the 1960s, increased in the early 1970s, and has been declining since (Baldwin 1980). The misperception, widespread through the U.S.A., that teen-pregnancy rates have been rising is largely due to two factors: (1) the increasing number of such pregnancies, but not the rate, when the children of the baby-boomer generation began having children, and (2) the fact that, as the average age at first marriage has been increasing, adolescent pregnancies are more likely to occur with unmarried women (Baldwin 1980; Miller and Moore 1990). Finally, the perception that adolescent pregnancy has become a recent social problem has emerged as the out-of-wedlock birthrate has increased more dramatically among white women in the last two decades (Baldwin 1980; Miller and Moore 1990).

Contraceptive Use. To most Americans, an increase in the rate of adolescent pregnancy (widely assumed, though not true) would seem to be an inevitable result of increases in PS activity. However, research in many European countries demonstrates that high rates of adolescent sexual activity can be associated with low rates of adolescent pregnancy, when contraceptives are used widely, consistently, and effectively (Jones et al. 1985). There seems little doubt that the U.S.A. has one of the highest adolescent-pregnancy rates among developed nations, largely because of inconsistent contraceptive use (Forrest and Fordyce 1988; Miller and Moore 1990).

It appears that roughly one half of adolescent women use no contraceptive during their first intercourse (Miller and Moore 1990), and most of the women reporting the use of some contraceptive during their first intercourse note that their partner used a condom (Weis 1983). Moreover, most adolescent girls who seek contraceptive services have been having sexual intercourse for some time, many for more than a year before they seek services (Miller and Moore 1990; Settlage, Baroff, and Cooper 1973). After this delay, it appears that roughly two thirds of American teenagers now use some form of contraceptive (Miller and Moore 1990).

Although these figures certainly indicate that large numbers of American youths continue to experience sexual intercourse with no contraceptive protection, they nonetheless represent an increase in contraceptive use over the last several decades. Research in the early 1970s indicated that two thirds to three quarters of American teens rarely or never used contraceptives (Sorensen 1973; Zelnik et al. 1981). Forrest and Fordyce (1988) report that overall use of medically sound contraceptives remained stable through the 1980s. Of those women age 20 or less who sought family-planning services in 1980, nearly three quarters used the pill. By 1990, this had dropped to 52 percent. In 1980, 14 percent had used no contraceptive at all (Eckard 1982).

By 1990, Peterson (1995) reported that 31.5 percent of 15- to 19-year-old women consistently used some form of contraceptive; 24.3 percent of 15- to 17-year-olds did so, as did 41.2 percent of 18- and 19-year-olds. This behavior appears to be unrelated to social class (Settlage et al. 1973). Among women of childbearing age (15 to 44), Peterson (1995) found that 52.2 percent of Hispanic, 60.5 percent of white non-Hispanic, and 58.7 percent of black non-Hispanic women reported using some form of contraceptive (see Table 6 in Section 9A under current contraceptive behavior).

Despite the popularity of the idea that adolescent pregnancy is a result of poor sexual knowledge, knowledge of one's sexuality or birth control has not been shown to be a strong predictor of contraceptive behavior among teenagers (Byrne and Fisher 1983). No relationship was found between contraceptive use and early sex education by family, or a congruence between attitudes and behavior. Reiss, Banwart, and Foreman (1975), however, reported that contraceptive use among teenagers is correlated with endorsement of sexual choice (permissiveness), self-confidence about desirability, and involvement in an intimate relationship.

Explanations of Adolescent Sexuality

Of course, researchers are not content to provide descriptions of social trends. Instead, they seek to provide theoretically useful explanations of the factors underlying those trends. The essence of scientific analysis is the identification and testing of potential correlates of those trends. There have been thousands of studies of adolescent sexuality testing possible correlates. We cannot review them all here. We will, however, briefly identify several different approaches that have been used to explain the trends we have described above. We have tried to select perspectives that have enjoyed some popularity among sexuality professionals at some point. We have also tried to include explanatory models that represent the diversity of professional opinions about adolescent sexuality.

Changes in Social Institutions. By far, the most common approach to explaining the growing acceptance of PS within American culture and the increasing tendency of adolescents to have PS has been a sociological perspective that locates these trends as part of a series of social changes occurring in response to industrialization and urbanization. (Much of this explanation was presented in Section 1, where we reviewed the sexual history of the U.S.A.) As patterns of residence and community relations changed in the late nineteenth and early twentieth centuries, changes began to occur in most social institutions. These included changes in male-female roles, a lengthening of the period of formal education, and the emergence of new forms of heterosexual courtship (Ehrmann 1964; Reiss 1967, 1976). One example of the complex web of social changes that have occurred in the last century is the increasing average age of first marriage (Surra 1990). In one century, the average age at first marriage has shifted from the late teens to the mid-20s. Combined with the earlier age at which American adolescents reach puberty, this has led to a much longer period between physical maturation and marriage, thus, greatly expanding the probability that sexual activity will occur prior to marriage.

As social institutions changed in response to the growing industrial character of American society and the increasingly urban pattern of residence, new forms of adolescent courtship emerged. The custom of dating appeared in the 1920s following World War I, and the practice of "going steady" emerged in the 1940s following World War II (Reiss 1980). By the 1990s, the practice of "going together" has become so universally common that few American young people can conceive of other courtship forms. Dating provided a forum for adolescents to pursue male-female relationships independent of adult supervision and control. The appearance of modern transportation, such as the automobile, and the development of urban recreational businesses allowed adolescents to interact with each other away from home. Increasingly, decisions about appropriate sexual behavior were made by adolescents themselves. The practice of "going steady" placed adolescents into a relationship with many of the features of marriage. Steady relationships were defined as monogamous and exclusive with respect to sexuality and intimacy. As such, they carried high potential for intimacy, commitment, and feelings of love. Together, the increased independence and greater potential for intimacy led to increased rates of PS behavior (D'Emilio and Freedman 1988; Kinsey et al. 1948, 1953; Seidman 1991). There is evidence that this general pattern has occurred in other countries as a consequence of industrialization as well (Jones et al. 1985).

Reiss (1960, 1967) developed the Autonomy Theory of Premarital Permissiveness, mentioned earlier, to explain the association between social institutions and premarital sexual permissiveness. Essentially, Reiss maintained that, as adolescent courtship institutions (dating and going steady) become independent of adult institutions of social control (parental supervision, the schools, and the church), the level of premarital permissiveness in a culture increases. There has been considerable research testing the specific propositions of the theory since Reiss proposed it (Cannon and Long 1971; Clayton and Bokemeier 1980; Miller and Moore 1990).

Generally, research from this perspective has tended to presume that PS has become normative within American culture.

Sources of Sexual Information and Sexual Knowledge. Several other explanations of PS behavior have been more likely to view it as a social problem and more likely to focus on the individual character of PS attitudes and behavior. One of the more popular and enduring ideas within American culture about adolescent sexual activity is the belief that sexual behavior and pregnancy risk are influenced by knowledge about sexuality and its consequences. In fact, advocates of sex education in the schools have argued for more than a century that American teens typically possess inadequate and inaccurate sexual knowledge. Some have maintained that sex education could solve such social problems as out-of-wedlock pregnancy and sexually transmitted disease by providing thorough and accurate information about sexuality. Embedded in these assertions is an underlying presumption that sexual decision making and behavior are primarily cognitive processes. Operating from this perspective, there have been dozens of studies of the sources of sexual information for children and adolescents in the U.S.A. Generally, these studies have found that young people in the U.S.A. are more likely to receive sexual information from their peers or the mass media than from adult sources, such as parents or the school (Spanier 1975; Wilson 1994). These studies have been used to conclude that peers are a poor source of sexual information, and that such inaccurate information leads directly to unwanted pregnancies and disease. We should note here that few studies of sexual information have sought to demonstrate a correlation between source of information and sexual decisions or outcomes. That connection has typically been assumed. (See also Section 3, which deals with formal and informal sources of sexual knowledge and education.)

However, in a national probability study of American college students, Spanier (1975; 1978) found no differences in premarital sexual behavior between those students who had ever had a sex-education course and those who had not—regardless of who taught the course, when it was offered, or what material was included. Moreover, a number of studies have found a weak correlation between sexual knowledge and sexual behavior or contraceptive use (Byrne and Fisher 1983). More generally, researchers have consistently found a low correlation between knowledge level and a variety of health-related behaviors, such as smoking, drug use, and eating patterns (Kirby 1985).

Cognitive Development. A somewhat similar focus on cognitive processes has been the basis for an argument that adolescents typically lack a sufficient level of cognitive development required for effective sexual decisions. A number of authors have argued that adolescence is characterized by a cognitive level that is inconsistent with sound sexual decision-making and contraceptive use (Cobliner 1974; Cvetkovich, Grote, Bjorseth, and Sarkissian 1975). Within this perspective, it has become common to describe adolescents as having an unreal sense of infallibility that leads them to underestimate the actual risks of sexual experience (Miller and Moore 1990).

Although references to the works of Jean Piaget have been common in this realm, actual empirical tests of a correlation between Piaget's stages of cognitive development and sexual decisions remain to be conducted. Moreover, this explanation has failed to incorporate the cross-cultural evidence that adolescents in many other nations establish high rates of sexual frequency, maintain consistent contraceptive use, and experience low rates of adolescent pregnancy (Jones et al. 1985).

Interaction of Hormonal and Social Determinants. Udry (1990) has attempted to examine how pubertal development, hormones, and social processes may interact to affect the sexual behavior of adolescents. Hormonal studies seem to indicate that androgenic hormones at puberty directly contribute to explaining sexual motivation and noncoital sexual behaviors in Caucasian male and female adolescents (Udry and Billy 1987; Udry et al. 1985, 1986). Because of the differing social encouragement versus constraints for young white males and females, initiation of coitus seems to be strongly hormone dependent for males, whereas for females it seems to be strongly influenced by a wide variety of social sources with no identifiable hormone predictors. The interaction of hormonal and social determinants is unclear for African-American youth and does not fit the models for white youth that emphasize the importance of sociocultural context on sexual behavior.

Delinquency Models. Perhaps the zenith of models which regard adolescent sexuality as a social problem is the emergence of frameworks that explicitly define adolescent sexual behavior as a form of juvenile delinquency (Jessor and Jessor 1977; Miller and Moore 1990). Vener and Stewart (1974) reported that sexual behavior by 15- and 16-year-olds was correlated with the use of cigarettes, alcohol, and illicit drugs, and with less approval for traditional institutions like the police, the school, and religion.

In a subsequent study using this perspective, Jessor and Jessor (1977) conceptualized sexual behavior as a "problem behavior" if it occurred prior to age-appropriate norms. In other words, intercourse was characterized as deviant and delinquent if it occurred prior to the mean age (roughly 17 years of age at the time of the study). Jessor and Jessor found that such early sexual behavior was correlated with other "problem behaviors" such as alcohol use, illicit-drug consumption, and political protest. They concluded that these associations demonstrated that adolescents tend to exhibit multiple forms of delinquency.

By the 1990s, Miller and Moore (1990) reported that a number of studies have found that "early" sexual behavior is associated with a variety of "criminal" behaviors such as those described above. Some authors have overlooked the fact that these studies have found this association with delinquent behaviors only for early sexual behavior and have tended to characterize all adolescent sexual behavior as delinquent. These studies do suggest the possibility that developmental issues may be relevant to these findings.

Sexual Affect. A different approach has been taken by a group of researchers interested in examining the role of affective reactions to sexual stimulation, both as a factor that may influence sexual decisions and behavior and as an outcome of sexual experience. Sorensen (1973) reported that 71 percent of teenagers agreed with the view that using the birth-control pill indicates that a girl is planning to have sex. This has been offered as evidence that adolescents are unwilling or unable to accept responsibility for contraceptive use, and thus lack cognitive development. However, affective theorists would argue that it is just as likely that sexual guilt, fear, or embarrassment prevent such a decision.

In the early 1960s, Christensen (1962) conceptualized sexual guilt as a variable response to sexual experience. He found that adolescents are more likely to report experiencing guilt in cultures with restrictive PS norms. He called this a value-behavior discrepancy. Schwartz (1973) found that persons with high sex guilt retain less information in a birth-control lecture, especially when aroused by a sexually stimulating condition. In the Schwartz study, females retained more information than males across all conditions.

Donn Byrne and his associates have maintained that individuals can be placed on a continuum ranging from erotophilic, reacting to sexual stimuli with strongly positive emotions, to erotophobic, reacting to sexual stimuli with strongly negative emotions. Erotophobic persons have been shown to be less likely to seek contraceptive information, to have lower levels of contraceptive knowledge, and to be less likely to purchase contraceptives or use those contraceptive methods that require them to touch themselves (Byrne and Fisher 1983; Goldfarb, Gerrard, Gibbons, and Plante 1988). However, they are no less likely to retain information about contraceptives, even though they become more sexually aroused by a lecture (Goldfarb et al. 1988).

There is a need for much future research on the association between adolescent sexuality and affective variables. However, the studies just mentioned suggest that affective variables may prove to be a fruitful way of explaining adolescent sexual behavior and its consequences. This approach seems particularly suited to examining the variety of ways that adolescents behave and the diverse consequences of such behavior.

Reference Group. Yet another approach to explaining adolescent sexuality has been the attempt to identify persons or groups who have influenced teenagers. Perhaps the most developed theoretical perspective of this type is known as Reference Group Theory. There is some evidence that, as adolescents progress from age 12 to 16, they shift their primary reference-group identification from their parents to their peers. Peer orientation has been shown to be related to sexual intercourse. Moreover, association with peers who are seen as approving PS is correlated with PS permissiveness and PS behavior (Cannon and Long 1971; Clayton and Bokemeier 1980; Floyd and South 1972; Reiss 1967; Teevan 1972). Similarly, Fisher (1986) found that the correlation between the attitudes of teenagers and their parents decreased as adolescence progressed. However, females who cited their mothers as their major source of sexual information were less likely to engage in intercourse and more likely to use contraceptives when they did.

These results should not be interpreted to mean that parents or families do not or cannot exert influence on the sexuality of adolescents. There have been relatively few scientific studies of the influence of differing parental styles and the PS behavior of children. One study (Miller, McCoy, Olson, and Wallace 1986) found that adolescents were least likely to have PS or to approve of PS when their parents were moderately strict. Teenagers who described their parents as very strict or not at all strict were more likely to have had PS. This correlation also held when parents were asked to describe the rules they set for their children. There is some evidence that the age of a mother's first intercourse is related to the age of her daughter's first intercourse (Miller and Moore 1990). Miller and Moore (1990) also showed that girls from single-parent families tend to have sex at younger ages.

Thus, there appears to be two conflicting sets of empirical findings. One set of studies finds evidence that adolescent sexuality is most strongly related to peer influences, especially as age increases. Another set of studies provides evidence that families and parents can exert influence in various ways. Obviously, important questions remain to be resolved.

Rehearsal. A more direct perspective views adolescent sexuality as a developmental process, in which intercourse is seen as the culmination of a sequence of progressively sexual behaviors (Miller and Moore 1990; Simon et al. 1972; Weis 1983). Adolescents appear to move through a series of stages, from kissing to petting of the female's breasts to genital petting to intercourse. There is evidence that, among white adolescents, this pattern is strongly consistent. White adolescents appear to take an average of two years to move through this sequence (Miller and Moore 1990; Weis 1983). In contrast, blacks appear to move through the stages more quickly, and there is greater variability in the actual sequence of behaviors (Miller and Moore 1990). Within this perspective, each subsequent sexual behavior can be viewed as a rehearsal for the next behavior in the sequence.

Not only is there evidence that adolescent sexual experience is acquired in a process that produces an escalating and expanding repertoire of sexual behaviors, but dating and "going steady" appear to serve as the key social contexts in which this process occurs (Clayton and Bokemeier 1980; Reiss 1967; Spanier 1975). The age of onset of dating and the frequency of dating appear to be major factors in the emergence of sexual behavior (Spanier 1975). In fact, adolescent experiences with intimate relationships (dating and "going steady") and the sequencing of sexual behaviors have been shown to be more influential in predicting PS intercourse than general social background variables, parental conservatism or liberalism, or religiosity (Herold and Goodwin 1981; Spanier 1975).

As dating frequency and noncoital experiences increase, exposure to eroticism, sexual knowledge, and interest in sex are all likely to increase concomitantly. Male behavior appears to be more strongly related to the sequencing of behaviors. In contrast, female behavior seems to be more a result of involvement in affectionate relationships. Increased dating interaction and frequency increase sexual intimacy, since opportunities and desire increase. This process is likely to overshadow the influence of prior religious, parental, or peer influences. Thus, adolescent courtship provides the context for the general process of sexual interaction. As Reiss (1967, 1980) has noted, such adolescent courtship also serves as a rehearsal experience for adult patterns of intimate involvement. It is also possible that such adolescent rehearsal experiences are a more powerful and direct explanation of adolescent sexual behavior (Spanier 1975; Weis 1983).

Multivariate Causal Models. An important trend in American research on adolescent sexuality has been the growing recognition that several of the factors reviewed here will eventually need to be included in a sound theory of adolescent sexual development and expression. Reiss (1967) was one of the first to test competing hypotheses in an attempt to identify the strongest predictors of PS permissiveness. Since then, a number of researchers have used multivariate techniques to examine the relative strength of PS correlates (Byrne and Fisher 1983; Christopher and Cate 1988; DeLamater and MacCorquodale 1979; Herold and Goodwin 1981; Reiss et al. 1975; Udry 1990; Udry, Tolbert, and Morris 1986; Weis 1983).

A few examples should illustrate the potential usefulness of this multivariate approach. Herold and Goodwin (1981) found that the best predictors of the transition from virginity to nonvirginity for females were perceived peer experience with PS, involvement in a steady, "committed" relationship, and religiosity. In contrast, parental education, grade-point average, sex education, and dating frequency failed to enter the multivariate equation.

Udry and his associates (1990; Udry et al. 1986) have investigated the relative influence of hormonal and social variables in explaining adolescent sexual behavior. Several studies demonstrate that androgenic hormones present at puberty directly contribute to the sexual motivation and precoital sexual behavior of white males. For white males, the initiation of coitus seems to be strongly related to androgen levels. Female initiation of coitus seems, on the other hand, to be strongly related to a series of social variables, but not to any hormonal predictors. Udry has argued that these results reflect the differing social encouragement versus constraints placed on males and females respectively. Interestingly, the behavior of African-American youth does not appear to fit with these same explanations, so that the exact interaction between social factors and hormonal variables remains unclear.

Adolescent Sexual Relationships: The Neglected Research

Before moving to the issue of adult heterosexuality, we wish to make a few comments about the nature of intimacy in adolescent sexual relationships and the process of relationship formation. Most of the research on adolescent sexuality reviewed here has tended to focus on the specifically and explicitly sexual elements of such experiences and to ignore the broader relational aspects. In one sense, this is understandable, given the fact that Americans have generally viewed adolescent sexuality, especially its premarital forms, as a social problem. Consistent with this perspective, Americans have tended to deny the possibility that any genuine intimacy occurs in sexual experiences involving adolescents. This is unfortunate in at least two respects. First, it tends to ignore the fact that most adolescent sexual encounters in the U.S.A. occur within the context of what the participants define as a meaningful, intimate relationship. It also ignores the reality that sexual expression within loving, intimate relationships (rather than marital status) has become the dominant attitudinal standard for Americans of all ages. Second, the tendency to ignore the relational character of adolescent sexuality means that researchers have tended to overlook the reality that patterns of sexual and intimate interactions are largely learned within the context of adolescent experiences, and these are likely to be extended well into adulthood. Thus, the failure to investigate these larger relational questions probably impairs our ability to fully understand adult intimate relationships as well. This is not meant to denigrate other forms of sexual expression or to deny that other forms of expression do occur, both in adolescence and later. Rather, it is to suggest that one strong characteristic of American sexuality is the tendency to associate love and sexuality. Any attempt to understand or explain American sexual expression must acknowledge that it generally occurs within the context of ongoing, intimate relationships. This is as true for adolescents as for adults.

The separation of sexuality and relational concerns is well reflected by the emergence of two independent bodies of research within the American academy. On the one hand, there is a well-established field of research on the formation of adolescent intimate relationships, dating and courtship, and mate selection. This tradition extends back to the 1920s and has largely been explored by family sociologists. Social exchange theory has become the dominant perspective in this tradition in recent decades. Surra (1990) provides an excellent review of such research through the 1980s. However, this tradition has largely failed to consider sexuality as an issue in courtship and mate selection, although it ought to be apparent that sexual dynamics and processes are key components of adolescent attraction, dating, court-ship, and mate selection. Sexuality carries the potential both for increasing intimacy between teenagers or young adults and for creating intense relationship conflict and, possibly, termination. Yet, Surra's (1990) review is notable precisely for the fact that there is not one single citation of a study including sexuality variables. This is not an indictment of Surra per se. Her goal was to review the field of mate selection as it stood at the beginning of the 1990s. Her assessment serves to document that researchers in this area continue to ignore the role of sexuality in adolescent relation-ship processes after seven decades of empirical research.

This tendency to ignore sexuality within the courtship process is unfor-tunate, because of the growing evidence that one of the major influences on PS behavior is the intimate relationship in which most adolescent sexual activity occurs. Being involved in a loving and caring relationship increases the probability of a decision to engage in intercourse (Christopher and Cate 1985) and contributes to sustained activity once it begins (DeLamater and MasCorquodale 1979; Peplau, Rubin, and Hill 1977). In fact, most adolescent sexual experiences in the U.S.A., especially for females, occur within the context of an ongoing intimate relationship. It does appear, however, that as the general rates of PS have increased and as the average age of first intercourse have declined throughout this century, intercourse has tended to occur at earlier stages in a relationship (Bell and Chaskes 1970; Christensen and Carpenter 1962; Christensen and Gregg 1970). With respect to attitudes, Americans are more likely to approve of PS in the context of a relationship. This permissiveness-with-affection-and/or-com-mitment standard has increasingly become the norm for both adults and young people (Christensen and Carpenter 1962; Christensen and Gregg 1970; Reiss 1960, 1967).

A second body of research examining the formation of sexual relation-ships has begun to emerge in recent decades. Much of this work has been done by biologists or evolutionary social psychologists and extends a model of mammalian mating first presented by Beach (1976). We discuss it here because it also reflects the separation of the sexual and intimate domains of relationships, and because much of the pertinent human research has been done with samples of college students. Essentially, this body of work forms the foundation for what might be called female selection theory.

The traditional view had always been that males are the aggressors and initiators of sexual involvement. From this perspective, females were seen as sexual "gatekeepers." Their role supposedly was to regulate male access by accepting or rejecting male advances (Perper 1985; Perper and Weis 1987). Beginning with Beach (1976), a growing number of researchers have provided evidence that this traditional view is highly flawed. Instead, females select desirable partners and initiate sexual interaction by proceptively signaling selected males (Fisher 1992; Givens 1978; Moore 1985; Moore and Butler 1989; Perper 1985; Perper and Weis 1987). Males, in turn, respond to these proceptive signals. Moore (1985; Moore and Butler 1989) has demonstrated that, not only do women use such signaling, but that men are more likely to "approach" women who do. Perper (1985; Perper and Weis 1987) has provided evidence that American women employ a variety of complex strategies to arouse male interest and response. Finally, Jesser (1978) has provided some evidence that males are just as likely to accept direct initiations from women as they are to respond to more covert strategies, although females tend to believe that men are "turned off" by female sexual assertiveness.

This new line of research raises fundamental questions about the roles of males and females in the formation and maintenance of sexual relationships—for both adolescents and adults. It indicates a need for research that is focused on the dynamics within and the processes of sexual relationships themselves. As just one example, Christopher and Cate (1988) found that, early in a relationship, the level of conflict was positively related to a greater likelihood of intercourse. As the relationship progressed, love and relationship satisfaction eventually became significant predictors of sexual involvement. In the case of adolescence, we need to move beyond "social bookkeeping," counting the number of American teenagers who have PS, to examine what actually happens in their relationships with each other.

C. Adult Heterosexuality

DAVID L. WEIS

The National Health and Social Life Survey

Strangely, there has been considerably more research on the sexual conduct of American adolescents than of adults, and much of the existing research on adults has tended to focus on sexual "problems" such as extramarital sex (ES) and sexual dysfunction (see Section 12 on sex dysfunctions and therapies). There has been little research on the patterns of sexual interactions within nonclinical marital relationships. This is striking, precisely because of the fact that marriage is the most widely accepted setting for sexual relations in the U.S.A. and because more than 90 percent of Americans do marry. Taken together, the preponderance of research on adolescent sexuality, ES, and dysfunction indicates the tendency of American sexuality professionals to focus on sexual behaviors that have been defined as social problems, rather than on "normal" sexuality.

In October 1994, a national survey of adult sexual practices was released with great media fanfare (Laumann, Gagnon, Michael, and Michaels 1994). The survey, titled the *National Health and Social Life Survey* (NHSLS), randomly sampled 3,432 persons, aged 18 to 50. It was touted as the most comprehensive American sex survey ever, and the first national study of adult sexuality. However, Reiss (1995) has noted that this claim is misleading, as there have been more than a dozen national surveys of a more-limited scope. Given our interest in reviewing the nature of American sexuality research, it is interesting to note that the survey was originally planned and approved as a government-sponsored project. Funding was denied for this project and a similar study of teens (the Udry study) when conservatives in the U.S. Congress objected to the studies. Conservatives argued that the government should not use taxpayer money to study private matters like oral sex—clearly rejecting the significance of the health concerns involved. The researchers found private funding instead. Also interesting is the fact that conservatives hailed the findings when the study was released (Peterson 1994).

There is little doubt that the NHSLS is the most comprehensive study of adult sexuality to date, with literally hundreds of variables assessed. Among the key findings are the following:

- Most Americans report that they are satisfied with their sex life—even those who rarely have sex. Among married persons, 87 percent reported they were satisfied with their sex life.
- For the entire sample, 30 percent of men and 26 percent of women have sex two or three times a week; 36 percent of men and 37 percent of women have sex a few times a month; and 27 percent of men and 30 percent of women have sex a few times a year. Married persons have sex more often than single people, and persons who are cohabiting have sex more often than marrieds.
- Approximately 80 percent of married women and 65 percent of married men have never had ES. The majority of those who are cohabiting also have never "cheated." The group most likely to have extradyadic sex is unmarried men, aged 42 to 51, who have lived with a woman for three years or less (32 percent).
- There has been a slight increase in the number of lifetime sexual partners, largely because people now have intercourse earlier, marry later, and are more likely to get divorced.
- Among marrieds, 94 percent had sex only with their spouse in the last year; 75 percent of cohabiting persons had sex only with their partner in the last year. About 80 percent of American adults have had either one or no sexual partners in the last year. Only 3 percent have had five or more partners in the last year. About 50 percent of men and 30 percent of women have had 5 or more partners since age 18.
- Most Americans have a fairly limited sexual "menu" of activities. Roughly 80 percent of both men and women reported that sexual intercourse is very appealing; only 50 percent of men and 33 percent of women find receiving oral sex appealing; 37 percent of men and 19

percent of women describe giving oral sex as appealing. About 25 percent of both men and women have tried anal sex at least once.

- People who already have an active sex life with a current sexual partner are more likely to masturbate. Among married people, 57 percent of husbands and 37 percent of wives have masturbated in the last year.
- About 2.8 percent of men and 1.4 percent of women identified themselves as homosexual or bisexual. Only 9 percent of men and 4 percent of women reported ever having a homosexual experience. These rates are considerably higher in the twelve largest U.S. cities.
- Most heterosexuals are not at risk of contracting AIDS, because they are not part of social networks with high risk.

The NHSLS has sparked considerable controversy among sexuality professionals. Questions have been raised, primarily about the legitimacy of the prevalence estimates for such behaviors as number of sexual partners, homosexual experience, and ES. In general, the NHSLS estimates tend to be lower than those found in most prior sex research—including prior national studies (Billy, Tanfer, Grady, and Klepinger 1993). It should be noted that the NHSLS estimates are remarkably similar to findings in a series of studies conducted by the National Opinion Research Center using similar national probability samples (Davis and Smith 1994; Greeley et al., 1990; Smith 1990, 1991). These national samples have been carefully constructed to be representative of gender, age, race, education, marital status, size of city of residence, and religion in the U.S.A. The NHSLS did obtain a 79 percent response rate, probably because participants were financially reimbursed. Few prior studies have had comparable response rates, and few have reimbursed participants. Questions about how this impacted the results are a legitimate matter for future research.

In a review of the NHSLS, Reiss (1995) credits the study for its comprehensiveness, the richness of the data generated, the theoretical nature of the investigation, and the high quality of the sampling techniques. However, he also raises several questions that may influence the validity of the findings. Here, we will focus on a few of the more serious. One concerns the fact that 21 percent of the respondents were interviewed with someone else present during the interview. As Reiss notes, a person with an intimate partner or a family member present may well have answered questions differently for obvious reasons. For example, only 5 percent of persons interviewed with another person present reported that they had two or more sexual partners in the last year. In contrast, 17 percent of those interviewed with no one else present reported two or more partners in the last year. This is a sizable difference, and it raises questions about the validity of responses to many questions in the survey. Similarly, the NHSLS asked respondents to report the number of sexual partners they have had since age 18. Most previous studies asked respondents to report their lifetime number of sexual partners. Here, one half of the sample did have sexual relations prior to age 18. This reduced estimates for lifetime number of partners. The NHSLS reported a median number of six sexual partners for men and and two for women. Reiss notes that these estimates are lower than comparable studies (Billy et al., 1993), and that this reported gender difference cannot possibly be true in the real world.

To this critique, we can add that it is possible that prevalence estimates have been inflated by the volunteer bias of most sex research. There are unexamined questions about the effects of volunteer bias and response rates. Paul Gebhard (1993), a member of the original Kinsey research team, has argued that estimates of lifetime prevalence rates for homosexual behavior have been remarkably similar when adjusted for sampling weaknesses. Gebhard also criticized the NORC and NHSLS studies for failing to use trained sex researchers to conduct their interviews, and for their own sampling flaws that overrepresented rural populations. In fairness, it is appropriate to note that several of the volunteer samples overrepresent urban populations, and there is evidence that urban-rural differences in sexual attitudes remain substantial (Weis and Jurich 1985). Finally, although there is a general consensus that persons who agree to participate in sex research are more permissive and more sexually experienced, two recent studies strongly suggest that persons who decline to answer particular items in a sex survey are attempting to hide behavior in which they have engaged (Wiederman 1993; Wiederman, Weis, and Allgeier 1994).

Although these questions will require considerable future research to resolve, it should be acknowledged that the NHSLS is a major contribution to the field of sex research in the U.S.A. It is a landmark study with important new information about the sexual practices of the vast and diverse American adult population, and it will set the parameters for questions yet to be explored. Finally, it provides important data on each of the topics we will explore further in this section.

Sexuality and Single Adults

Practically every American spends at least a portion of his or her adult life unmarried. At any one point in time, more than 20 percent of the U.S. population is single, and this percentage has been increasing for several decades (Francoeur 1991; Shostak 1987). The chief reasons for this are the greater tendency to postpone marriage (median age is now in the late 20s), the increasing divorce rate (5 per 1,000 by the 1980s and fairly stable thereafter), and the increasing rate of cohabitation (which tripled since 1960), both as an alternative to marriage and as a form of courtship prior to marriage (Glick 1984; Norton and Moorman 1987; Shostak 1987). Glick (1984) has speculated that the prolongation of formal education, the increasing acceptability of premarital sexuality, the growing independence of women, and the earlier mortality of males may also be factors promoting the growth of singlehood.

Actually, the single adult population contains three groups who may share little in common: Those who have never married, those who have divorced, and those who are widowed. Persons within each group may or may not have chosen to be single, and they may or may not intend to remain single. Also, persons in each group may be living alone, may be living with roommates who are not intimate or sexual partners, or may be cohabiting with an intimate partner. By 1980, it was estimated that close to 2 percent of the adult U.S. population was cohabiting (Glick and Norton 1977; Yllo 1978). Of course, some single persons are gay or lesbian, although they are not typically included in estimates of cohabitation, even when they live with their partners.

It should be stressed that the population of single adults is a fluid one. The U.S.A. has high rates of marriage, divorce, and remarriage (Glick 1984; Norton and Moorman 1987). Most of those who are classified as having never married at any one point will eventually marry. This is especially true for the growing group who have remained unmarried well past the age of 20. Approximately three quarters of women who get divorced, and more men, eventually remarry (Glick 1984; Norton and Moorman 1987). Thus, the composition of the single population is always shifting as some marry and others divorce or are widowed. We are not aware of any research examining the impact of this shifting character on the sexual lifestyles of single persons. Some singles become involved in intimate relationships that lead to cohabitation or marriage, although we know little about whether these processes are similar to adolescent courtship. For those singles who are not involved in an ongoing intimate relationship, it is possible that finding sexual partners can be problematic.

It is popularly believed that being single in adulthood has become more acceptable in the U.S.A. today. There is, however, some evidence that married couples continue to associate primarily with other couples. Certainly, it is more acceptable to be sexually active while single today. Singles have greater social and sexual freedom than ever before to pursue a variety of lifestyles. In fact, the labeling of a category of "single adults" may serve to obscure the fact that the range of sexual and intimate lifestyle options is just as wide as for married persons.

Despite the large number of single adults in the U.S.A., there has been virtually no research on the sexual practices or attitudes of these groups. The NHSLS (Laumann et al. 1994) did distinguish between "single" and cohabiting respondents, an important distinction. As we discussed earlier, the NHSLS did find that "single" persons had sex less frequently than married persons, and that cohabiting persons had sex more often than married persons.

The Never Married. We know of no research that has focused on the population of never-married adults who are not cohabiting. Of course, this group does include persons in their early 20s who have yet to marry. A portion of that group is included in many of the studies of premarital sexuality, although that group is not isolated for separate analysis. There is virtually no scientific information on how never-married persons find or meet sexual partners, establish sexual encounters, or maintain sexual relationships.

Divorced (Postmarital Sex). Divorce has increased in the U.S.A. dramatically throughout the twentieth century (Berscheid 1983). The rate has leveled since 1980 (*Current Population Reports* 1985; Glick 1984; Norton and Moorman 1987; Shostak 1987). Of the roughly 40 percent of the American population that gets divorced, about 70 percent eventually remarry, often within a few years (Glick 1984; Norton and Moorman 1987).

Again, there has been little research on this group. It appears that about 80 percent of women, and nearly all men, remain sexually active following a divorce (Gebhard 1968; Hunt 1974). Most persons have sex with a new partner within the first year following a divorce (Hunt, 1974). In the 1970s, Hunt (1974) reported that divorced women averaged four sexual partners a year, and had a higher frequency of orgasm in their postmarital sex than they had had in their marriage. Men averaged nearly eight partners a year.

Again, there has been little research on the process by which divorced persons form or maintain sexual relationships. However, it is fair to suggest that, as the title of an American novel and corresponding movie implies, most divorced persons find that they must "start over." After a period of marriage, they find themselves in the position of dating and courting again. Some have anecdotally reported that they find this anxiety-provoking, whereas others find it exhilarating.

Widowed. This process of "starting over" may be relevant to those persons who are widowed as well. Our review of the research literature identified only one study of the sexual practices of widowed persons. Nearly three decades ago, Gebhard (1968) reported that widowed persons were less likely to have sexual experiences than divorced persons. Francoeur (1991) has suggested that this may be due, in part, to a sense of loyalty to the former spouse or to perceived and real pressure from kin members.

Marital Sex

By far, the most common adult sexual lifestyle in the U.S.A. is legal marriage, and marriage is the context for the overwhelming majority of sexual experiences in the U.S.A. In fact, marriage is the only context in which sexuality is universally approved. Despite this, researchers have investigated marital sexuality less than nonmarital forms of sexual expression. Greenblat (1983) has suggested that sex within marriage is more likely to be the object of jokes than of scientific investigation. Strong and DeVault (1994) report that only nine of 553 articles on sexuality that appeared in scholarly journals between 1987 and 1992 were devoted to marital sexuality.

This pattern of research is somewhat odd in light of the widespread belief that effective sexual functioning is indispensable to a good marriage (Frank and Anderson 1979). In this regard, it is striking that much of the research conducted on couples has utilized clients in sex therapy. Here we review works on nonclinical samples.

Sexual Frequency and Practices. Most of the research on sexual relations within marriage has assessed the frequency of sexual relations. Many of these studies have also examined how that frequency is related to marital satisfaction. Americans seem to be fascinated with comparing their own frequency to other couples. Until recently, this research was based on volunteer samples, which typically were also quite small.

Perhaps the first sex survey ever conducted in the U.S.A. was done by Clelia Duel Mosher (1980), who investigated the sexual practices and attitudes of forty-five women between 1890 and 1920. Most of these women reported that they found sex to be pleasurable and believed that it was "necessary" for both men and women. The women who were interviewed before 1900 were less likely to describe sex as important or enjoyable, and they were less likely to associate sex with the expression of love. The Mosher survey documents the first signs of a shift to a post-Victorian culture.

In a study of more than 1,000 men and women, Dickinson and Bean (1932) reported that sexual dissatisfaction was more important in explaining marital difficulties than disputes over work, money, and children. Davis (1929) drew similar conclusions in her study of 2,200 women. Sexual satisfaction within marriage had clearly become a norm in the U.S.A. by the early twentieth century. Somewhat later, Hamilton (1948) interviewed a hundred married men and women and concluded that an unsatisfactory sex life is the principal cause of marital dysfunction. Without addressing the validity of that particular claim, the Hamilton data do demonstrate that, in the small sample surveyed in the 1930s and 1940s, sex was considered to be an important part of a marriage.

The Kinsey group (1953) reported that married couples in the 1940s had sex an average of two times a week in the early years of marriage, declining to about once a week after ten years of marriage. By comparing those born before 1900 and those born after 1900, they found that the frequency of marital coitus had remained the same. However, virtually every other aspect of marital sex had changed. Couples born after 1900 engaged in more and longer foreplay, used more coital positions, were more likely to have oral sex, were more likely to use French (deep) kissing and manual caressing of genitals, and had sex more often naked.

More-recent studies have tended to fit two patterns. Small samples with volunteers have found a general average of three to four times a week in early marriage with a decline to twice a week in later years. However, studies with national samples have tended to get lower figures more like Kinsey's (Bell and Bell 1972; Blumstein and Schwartz, 1983; Call, Sprecher, and

Schwartz 1995; Hite 1976; 1983; Hunt 1974; Sarrel and Sarrel 1980; Tavris and Sadd 1974; Trussell and Westoff 1980; Udry 1980; Westoff 1974). Interestingly, married women tend to report lower frequencies than married men (Call et al. 1996).

A few researchers have asked respondents to report their ideal or preferred frequency. Hite (1976) found that one third of married women would like to have sex at least daily, another third wanted it two to five times a week, and a final third less often.

(1) Changes Throughout Marriage. The evidence of a decrease over time or length of marriage is strong and consistent (Blumstein and Schwartz 1983; Edwards and Booth 1976; Greeley 1991; Hunt 1974; Kinsey et al. 1953; Michael et al. 1994; Trussell and Westoff 1980; Westoff 1980). Longitudinal studies of the same couples over time have also documented this pattern (James 1981; Udry 1980), as have retrospective studies of couples looking back over the course of their marriage (Greenblat 1983).

In a national study of the 1988 *National Survey of Families and Households* (Call et al. 1995), frequency decreases over the length of marriage were correlated with biological aging, diminished health, and habituation. In a multivariate analysis, age was most strongly related to frequency, followed by marital happiness, and factors that reduce the opportunity for sex (such as pregnancy and small children). Couples who had not cohabited prior to marriage and who were still in their first marriage had less-frequent sex than cohabitors, married persons who had cohabited prior to marriage, and those who were in their second or later marriage.

These findings are largely consistent with prior research. Decreasing frequency of marital sex has been found to relate to age-related reductions in the biological capacity for sex, including declines in male motivation and physical ability, declines in women's testosterone levels, and increases in illness (Greenblat 1983; Hengeveld 1991; James 1983; Udry, Deven, and Coleman 1982). Negative social attitudes about sex and the elderly may also lead some to believe that their interest and capacity should decline (Masters and Johnson 1970; Riportella-Muller 1989). However, these aging factors do not explain the decline in frequency that occurs within the first several years of marriage (Jasso 1985; Kahn and Udry 1986). James (1981) found that the coital rate dropped by one half during the first year of marriage. Some have suggested that there is a honeymoon effect early in the marriage. As the honeymoon period ends, habituation occurs and frequency declines (Blumstein and Schwartz 1983; Doddridge, Schumm, and Berger 1987). Habituation may be seen as a decreased interest in sex that occurs with the increased accessibility of a regular sexual partner and the routine predictability of behavior with that partner over time (Call et al. 1995).

Other reasons that have been cited as influencing a decrease in frequency include fatigue, work demands, child care, and management of complex schedules (Michael et al. 1994).

(2) Effects of Children. A few comments on the effects of children are worth special note. There is some evidence that sexual frequency declines by the third trimester of pregnancy—prior to the actual birth of a child (Kumar, Brant, and Robson 1981). The birth of a child introduces parental roles into the marital relationship. The child increases fatigue, reduces time alone together for the couple, and decreases time in situations that are conducive to sexual encounters (Blumstein and Schwartz, 1983; Doddridge, et al. 1987; Greenblat 1983).

(3) Association with Sexual and Marital Satisfaction. A majority of Americans report that they are satisfied with their marital sex life (Hunt 1974; Lauman et al. 1994). In general, researchers have not found frequency to be related to sexual or marital satisfaction (Blumstein and Schwartz 1983; Frank, Anderson, and Rubinstein 1978). However, there is evidence that the congruence between ideal and actual frequency is related (Frank and Anderson 1979). There is some evidence that sexual problems are likely to occur fairly early in a marriage (Brayshaw 1962; Murphy et al. 1980).

Some studies have found social factors associated with relationship satisfaction. Rainwater (1964) found, in a study of couples in poverty in four different cultures, that lower-class couples were more likely to have highly gender-segregated role relationships (traditional gender roles); they were less likely to have close sexual relationships, and the wife was not likely to view sex with her husband as gratifying.

Several studies have found that sexual satisfaction is related to both sexual and nonsexual aspects of the marriage. The Kinsey group (1953) found that divorce was related to decreases in the wife's orgasm rate. Hunt (1974) reported a strong correlation between marital closeness and sexual satisfaction. He found that the most important predictor was the extent to which couples share similar sexual desire. Thornton (1977) found that couples who spend more time having sex than they do fighting tend to have happier marriages. Sarrel and Sarrel (1980) found that couples who talk with each other about sex often, who rate their communication about sex as good, where the wife likes oral sex, and where the man believes the women's movement has been good for women tend to have more satisfying sexual relationships.

Hite (1976) asked women to identify what aspect of their marital sex gave them the greatest satisfaction. Responses given by 20 percent or more included closeness, orgasm, coitus, and foreplay. In response to what they liked least, more than 10 percent said oral or anal sex, lack of orgasm, the "messiness" following sex, excessive or rough foreplay, and the routine nature of their activities.

In the *Redbook* magazine surveys (Tavris and Sadd 1975; Tavris 1978), marital satisfaction did not decline with length of marriage or age. The majority reported enjoying oral sex. Most respondents believed that good communication is an important ingredient of marital and sexual happiness. The most common complaint was that they had sex too infrequently. For women, religiosity was related to a happier sex life and marital satisfaction.

In an unusual study of a hundred mostly white and well-educated couples who were happily married (selected because none had ever had ES or been in therapy), Frank and Anderson (1979) found that 85 percent described themselves as sexually satisfied. One half of the wives reported they had difficulty becoming aroused or reaching orgasm. Roughly 10 percent of the husbands reported they had experienced erectile difficulties. One third of the couples expressed complaints about such things as anxiety, too little foreplay, and low sexual desire. There was no correlation between sexual dysfunctions and marital satisfaction, but complaints by the wife were associated with reduced marital happiness.

(4) Unexplored Issues. This review of research on marital sexuality serves to confirm the narrow range of the questions researchers have investigated. We know little about the dynamics of sexual relationships in marriage— about the ways couples interact sexually, about how they transact or negotiate sexual encounters, or about how they initiate and terminate encounters. Little is known about how sexuality in marriage is affected by power dynamics between the couple. There has been little study of sexual coercion in marriage. Perhaps it is time to end the focus on counting episodes and begin to examine what happens within marital sexual relationships.

Extramarital Sexual Relationships. Researchers have been studying ES for decades, although the range of the questions they have examined has been fairly narrow (For more-thorough reviews of ES research and nonexclusive lifestyles, see Macklin 1980; Thompson 1983; Weis 1983).

(1) ES Attitudes. One focus of concern has been the degree of normative consensus reflected by ES attitudes. A series of national surveys indicate that ES has consistently been disapproved by 75-85 percent of the adult American population (Glenn and Weaver 1979; Greeley, Michael, and Smith 1990; Reiss, Anderson, and Sponaugle 1980; Weis and Jurich 1985). Weis and Jurich (1985) found that nearly one third of residents in the twelve largest cities found ES acceptable, the only locations in the U.S.A. where as many as 20 percent approved. In small towns and rural areas, fewer than 10 percent approved. The norm of sexual exclusivity within marriage is so widespread in American culture that few question it.

Approval of ES has been found to be related to (1) being male, (2) young age, (3) being nonwhite, (4) living in a large city, (5) high levels of education, (6) low religiosity, and (7) being unmarried (Glenn and Weaver 1979; Reiss et al. 1980; Weis and Jurich 1985; Weis and Slosnerick 1981). Although a number of researchers have reported that approval of ES is related to lower levels of marital happiness, Weis and Jurich (1985) found that marital happiness was less strongly related to ES attitudes than several of these other variables.

(2) ES Incidence/Prevalence. A second major concern of researchers has been the attempt to establish estimates of the prevalence and/or incidence of ES behavior. Generally, this has taken the form of asking respondents to indicate whether or not they have ever had ES. Authors have regularly claimed that roughly one half of married persons in the U.S.A. have had at least one ES experience, citing the Kinsey research (1948, 1953) as the basis for this claim. Although the point is often ignored, the Kinsey team actually found that 33 percent of husbands and 26 percent of wives reported having ES. Because of suspicions of underreporting, they raised the estimate for male—but not female—ES to 50 percent. Several researchers have reported that the figures for husbands have remained "fairly stable" since then, but that the rate for wives has increased to approximately that of husbands (Blumstein and Schwartz 1983; Hunt 1974; Levin 1975). Researchers have reported lifetime prevalence rates from as low as 20 percent (Johnson 1970) to nearly 75 percent (Hite 1981).

Several recent studies by the National Opinion Research Center (Smith 1990; 1991; Greeley et al. 1990) have found that only 2 to 3 percent of American married men and women have ES each year. Further, they reported that 65 percent of wives and 30 percent of husbands have the same number of lifetime sexual partners as spouses. According to these researchers, the increases in premarital sex and cohabitation, the rising rate of divorce, and the later age at first marriage that have characterized the last forty years have resulted in less sexual exclusivity among the unmarried, but no such trend has occurred among married persons in the U.S.A. The Greeley group concluded that Americans are overwhelmingly "monogamous" [sic] and that rates of ES have been overestimated by previous researchers. *The National Health and Social Life Survey* (Laumann et al. 1994), also conducted by the NORC, found that only 35 percent of men and 20 percent of women reported ever having ES, and 94 percent had sex only with their spouse in the last year.

As we have already discussed, making comparisons between the results of the NORC national probability samples and previous studies is most difficult. Most previous studies have reported lifetime prevalence rates. The NORC studies have generally reported annual incidence rates. It seems likely that the conditions surrounding the collection of data and the greater representation of rural respondents in the NORC studies led to low estimates. On the other hand, the volunteer nature of most previous studies and their greater inclusion of urban respondents may well have led to high estimates. For the time being, we must conclude that questions about the incidence and prevalence of ES in the U.S.A. remain largely unanswered.

(3) Marital Happiness. The third major focus of ES research has been the attempt to demonstrate an association between ES behavior and marital happiness/satisfaction. By far, this has been the most frequently tested hypothesis. As a consequence, there has been little research exploring the circumstances or conditions surrounding ES behavior itself or testing alternative hypotheses. A number of researchers have found that ES behavior is significantly related to lower levels of marital happiness (Bell et al. 1975; Edwards and Booth 1976; Glass and Wright 1977; 1985; Prins, Buunk, and Van Yperen 1993; Saunders and Edwards 1984). Lower marital happiness has also been found to be related to ES attitudes (Reiss et al. 1980; Weis and Jurich 1985).

However, the association may not be as strong as these findings imply. The research by Glass and Wright (1977, 1985) suggests that the actual association between ES and marital happiness may be quite complex. In their earlier study, Glass and Wright (1977) found that husbands who had ES in the early years of marriage did have lower marital satisfaction. However, there were no differences in marital satisfaction between husbands who had never had ES and those who began ES later in their marriages. Interestingly, exactly the reverse was true for wives. There were no differences in marital satisfaction between wives who had never had ES and those who began it early in their marriages. Yet, wives who began their ES experiences later in marriage did have significantly lower marital satisfaction. In their later study, Glass and Wright (1985) found that ES was related to lower marital happiness only for wives. They concluded that male ES is likely to be more strongly associated with individual factors, rather than marital issues.

The Glass and Wright studies represent a level of complexity that has rarely been seen in ES research. Few studies have examined the possibility that marital happiness might relate to different types of ES experiences. As just one example, we can take the case of consensual ES. In one of the few comparisons of couples who had made an agreement to include ES in their marriage with couples who did not have this agreement and had a sexually exclusive relationship, there were no significant differences in marital stability, marital happiness, or level of jealousy (Rubin and Adams 1986). Similarly, Gilmartin (1978) found no differences in marital happiness between a group of couples who participated in swinging and a control group of nonswinging couples.

Moreover, Ellis (1969) has made the obvious point, substantiated by all the studies cited here, that some people who have ES also report high marital satisfaction. In fact, although the two variables have been consistently found to be significantly related, the proportion of ES variance explained by marital quality variables has tended to be rather small. This may be due, in part, to the tendency to dichotomize ES into "ever versus never" categories, thus ignoring the diversity of ES types. This treatment of ES as a simplistic construct that uniformly reflects poor marital dynamics may reduce our ability to establish better explanations of ES. For example, Weis and Jurich (1985) did report that ES attitudes and marital happiness were significantly related in a series of national probability samples, but they also found that marital happiness was more weakly related to ES attitudes than several background variables.

(4) Exploring the Diversity of ES Experience. This failure to recognize the diversity of ES experience may be the single greatest obstacle to the development of sound research and theory. ES experiences are, in fact, a class of relationship types, every bit as complex as other relationship forms. With few exceptions, American researchers have failed to recognize the historical and cross-cultural evidence that male and female ES behavior is universal, despite the strong normative traditions and sanctions against it. They have also largely ignored the cross-cultural evidence that amply demonstrates a wide variety of ES patterns and normative responses to it (Buss 1994; Fisher 1992; Ford and Beach 1951; Frayser 1985; Murdock 1949).

(5) Specific Aspects of ES. Ultimately, a full understanding of ES will require more-thorough investigation of the myriad ways in which ES experiences vary. Several factors require additional research. These include:

- *Specific Sexual Behaviors Involved.* ES can range from flirting,kissing, and petting to intercourse (Glass and Wright 1985; Hurlbert 1992; Kinsey et al. 1948; 1953).
- *Specific Relationship Behaviors Involved.* ES relationships vary from those in which sexual interaction is nearly the sum total of the relationship to those where sexuality is a minimal component (Hurlbert 1992; Richardson 1985; Thompson 1983, 1984).
- *Number of ES Partners.* In general, the scant evidence available suggests that most Americans have a small number of ES partners (Bell et al. 1975; Greeley et al. 1990; Kinsey et al. 1953; Pietropinto and Simenauer 1977).
- *Length of ES Relationship.* It appears that most, but certainly not all, ES relationships are of relatively short duration and entail less than ten actual sexual encounters, with some evidence that females tend to be involved for longer periods (Bell et al. 1975; Gagnon 1977; Hall 1987; Hunt 1974; Hurlbert 1992; Kinsey et al. 1953; Pietropinto and Simenauer 1977).
- *Level of Involvement.* ES ranges from single sexual encounters in which partners know little of each other to highly intimate affairs with characteristics that are quite similar to intimate marriages.
- *Consensual Versus Secretive.* Although most ES is secretive or clandestine (Gagnon 1977; Hunt 1974), it is important to recognize that some spouses do know about their partner's ES activities and expressly agree

to permit ES (see section below on alternatives to traditional marriage) (Blumstein and Schwartz 1983; Thompson 1983; Weis 1983).

- *Motives and Meanings.* There are dozens of motives for ES. Weis and Slosnerick (1981) demonstrated that a distinction between individual motives (such as adventure, variety, romance, or pleasure) and marital motives (such as revenge against a spouse, marital hostility, marital sex problems, or as an alternative marriage form) was useful in explaining differences in ES attitudes.
- *Bisexual/ Homosexual.* ES has usually been assumed to be heterosexual, but there is evidence that, at least some ES is homosexual (D. Dixon 1985; J. K. Dixon 1984).

(6) Gender Issues. Before discussing theoretical factors for ES, we want to note that the available evidence strongly suggests that researchers explore the possibility of separate predictive models for men and women. There is evidence that men are more likely to have ES than women and to have more numerous ES encounters (Buss 1994; Glass and Wright 1985), more likely to report ES relationships with limited involvement (Glass and Wright 1985; Spanier and Margolis 1983), and tend to have more partners (Buss 1994; Thompson 1983). Men and women may also experience different outcomes. There is some evidence that women are more likely to report experiencing guilt as a result of ES (Spanier and Margolis 1983). It is possible that women, as a group, are more likely to be motivated to engage in ES activities by marital factors and may be more likely to seek intimacy as a primary goal in ES (Reibstein and Richards 1993). Several studies have found that marital variables are more strongly related to ES for women than for men (Glass and Wright 1985; Saunders and Edwards 1984). All of these findings indicate that the ES experiences of men and women may differ substantially.

(7) Building Theoretical Models. Edwards and Booth (1976) have argued that the context of marital interaction is more important than background factors in explaining the process leading to ES involvement. However, Weis and Slosnerick (1981) have maintained that individuals enter marriage with internalized scripts for sex, love, and marriage. Ultimately, the scripts of married persons stem from an interaction of marital dynamics and background factors. Each of these, in turn, is likely to be influenced by one's position within the social structure.

As just noted, there is evidence of a significant correlation between marital happiness and both dichotomous measures of ES experience and ES attitudes, although this association has not always been a strong or robust one. In a study of ES attitudes (approval), Weis and Slosnerick (1981) isolated two orthogonal factors of justifications for ES. One was a set of motivations for ES that mentioned aspects of the marital relationship. The other was a set of individual motives for ES. Both factors were significantly related to approval of ES, but the individual motivations were more strongly related than the marital motivations.

These findings suggest two possible paths for future research that seeks to elaborate the complex nature of the association between ES and marital satisfaction. One is to contrast the types of ES experiences that persons with individual versus marital motivations tend to have and to explore how these relate to marital satisfaction and, perhaps, to outcomes of ES relationships. The other is to separate happily and unhappily married persons and to investigate the types of ES experiences and outcomes for each group. It seems reasonable to expect that the two groups might well pursue different kinds of ES experiences under different circumstances, with different outcomes.

A second theoretical factor may be background variables. A number of researchers have reported that premarital sexual attitudes and behavior are related to ES attitudes and behavior, several arguing that it is the best predictor of ES involvement (Bukstel et al. 1978; Christensen 1962, 1973; Glenn and Weaver 1979; Medora and Burton 1981; Reiss et al. 1980; Singh et al. 1976; Thompson 1983; Weis and Jurich 1985; Weis and Slosnerick 1981). ES variables have been found to correlate with premarital sexual permissiveness, number of premarital sexual partners, and early premarital sexual experience (low age). Weis and Jurich (1985) found premarital sexual permissiveness was the strongest and most consistent predictor of ES attitudes in a series of regression analyses with national probability samples throughout the 1970s.

Several questions remain to be explored. Do these findings suggest that there is something particular about premarital sexual interactions with partners that is associated with ES, or are measures of premarital sex merely indicative of a broader interest in and history of sexual pleasure in various forms? Which of these will prove to be more useful in explaining various types of ES activities? For example, Joan Dixon (1984) found that female swingers tend to have early and continuing histories of heterosexual involvement, but that they also tend to have early and continuing histories of masturbation and high current sexual frequencies with partners. Gilmartin (1978) also found that swingers tend to have early heterosexual experiences and high sexual frequencies with their spouses. One might conceivably argue that such persons like sex, and ES is an extension of a broader orientation to pleasure.

A third factor has been suggested by Cazenave (1979), who has criticized work in the area of alternative lifestyles for its emphasis on ideological preference and its failure to explore how structural variables (such as age, gender, and race) may impose external constraints. In fact, there is evidence that ES behavior and ES permissiveness (attitudes) are related to (1) young age, (2) being nonwhite, (3) low education for behavior and high education for attitudes, (4) low religiosity, and (5) residence in a large city (Fisher 1992; Greeley et al. 1990; Smith 1990, 1991). Several of these associations may, in fact, be quite complex. For example, the Kinsey group (1948, 1953) found that blue-collar males tend to have ES in their 20s and their behavior diminishes by their 40s. White-collar males with college educations tended to have little ES in their 20s. This rate gradually increased to an average of once a week by age 50. In contrast, female ES peaked in the late 30s and early 40s. Finally, there is a need for research that explores the role of such American social trends as the increasing age at first marriage, the growing divorce rate, the unbalanced gender ratio, and greater mobility and travel in ES behavior.

(8) Unexplored Issues. There has been little research to this point on the process of ES relationships. For example, there has been little investigation of how opportunities for ES involvement occur in a culture with strong prohibitions against ES. Cross-sex friendships and interactions have been frequently cited as creating the opportunity for ES (Johnson 1970; Saunders and Edwards 1984; Weis and Slosnerick 1981), although this has not been empirically tested. The matter is somewhat complicated by the evidence that friendships outside of marriage are associated with higher levels of marital satisfaction (Weis and Slosnerick 1981). Wellman (1985, 1992) has documented how the friendship networks of men have shifted from public spaces (bars, cafés, and clubs) to private homes. This has led to a narrowing of the concept of friendship to emotional support and companionship. Husbands' and wives' networks are now both based in private, domestic space, and many wives actively maintain their husbands' ties to friends and kin. Men get much of their emotional support from women, as well as men, and women get almost all of their support from women. Wellman argues that marriage may impose constraints on men's ability to spend time and be intimate with other men or women. Whether this is related to ES remains to be explored.

Similarly, little is known about the outcomes of ES involvement. Generally, it is assumed that ES relationships are short in duration, exploitive in character, and tragic in outcome. For example, it is generally assumed that ES and cross-sex friendships will be a source of jealousy in a marriage. Although there is a growing body of evidence about jealousy, little research has specifically investigated jealousy in the context of ES (Bringle, 1991; Bringle & Boebinger, 1990; Buunk, 1981; 1982; Denfeld, 1974; Jenks, 1985).

Alternatives to Traditional Marriage. Although most ES is secretive, some couples do pursue lifestyles that permit ES (Blumstein and Schwartz 1983; Thompson 1983; Weis 1983). There is some evidence that consensual ES is unrelated to marital satisfaction (Gilmartin 1978; Ramey 1976; Rubin and Adams 1986; Wachowiak and Bragg 1980), suggesting there might be different outcomes for the consensual and nonconsensual forms of ES.

A number of models for consensual ES have been proposed, particularly during the 1970s. These include swinging (recreational and shared ES)

(Bartell 1971; Gilmartin 1978; Jenks 1985), comarital sex (Smith and Smith 1974), open marriage (O'Neill and O'Neill 1972), intimate friendship networks (ES within context of friendship) (Francoeur and Francoeur 1974; Ramey 1976), and group marriage (Constantine and Constantine 1973; Rimmer 1966). Certainly, there are differences among these various nonexclusive lifestyles. We do not have the space to review fully the distinctions among them here (see Libby and Whitehurst 1977; Weis 1983). What unites them for the discussion here is that they all represent a consensual agreement to allow multilateral sexual involvement. As such, ES is assigned a different set of meanings from betrayal.

Consensual agreements can vary in terms of the degree of sexual involvement desired, the degree of intimate involvement desired, the degree of openness with the spouse, and the amount of time spent with the ES partner (Sprenkle and Weis 1978). Buunk (1980) studied the strategies couples employ in establishing ground rules for sexually open marriages. The five most common were: (1) primary value placed on maintaining the marriage, (2) limiting the intensity of ES involvements, (3) keeping the spouse fully informed of ES relationships, (4) approving ES only if it involves mate exchange, and (5) tolerating ES if it is invisible to the spouse. It would be useful to see research on the association between the types of strategies employed and outcomes of ES.

Interestingly, husbands tend to initiate swinging (Bartell 1971; Weis 1983). There is some evidence that most couples swing for a few years, rather than pursuing it for a lifetime (Weis 1983). Dropouts from swinging report problems with jealousy, guilt, emotional attachment, and perceived threat to the marriage (Denfeld 1974). As far as we know, there have been no studies comparing dropouts and those who enjoy and continue swinging.

The Constantine study (1973) is virtually the only source of data on group marriage in contemporary America. They report that the typical relationship includes four adults. Most enter a group with their spouses, and if the group dissolves, most of the original pair bonds survive. In fact, the original pair bonds retain some primacy after the formation of the group, and this may be a factor working against the success of the group. Jealousy between male partners appears to be a common problem.

Studies of marital models that permit ES have tended to employ small, volunteer samples with no control or contrast groups for comparison. There is no basis for a firm estimate of the incidence or prevalence of such alternative lifestyles, although Blumstein and Schwartz (1983) suggested that as many as one of seven marriages in the U.S.A. may have some agreement allowing ES. Despite the vast attention given to these alternative lifestyles in the 1970s, and despite the more recent claims that Americans are "returning to traditional models of monogamous marriage," there is no scientific basis for concluding that these patterns increased in popularity earlier or that they have become less common in the 1980s and 1990s.

Sexuality and People with Physical and   MITCHELL S. TEPPER
Developmental Disabilities

Government Policies Affecting Sexuality and Disability. Over the past twenty years, pivotal legislation has been enacted in the United States that enables people with disabilities to gain their rightful place as equal members of American society. These changes have been led by spirited people with disabilities and their advocates. The Rehabilitation Act of 1973, the 1975 Education for All Handicapped Children Act (Public Law 94-142), and the Americans with Disabilities Act passed in 1990 have all added opportunities for inclusion and integration into the community for people of all abilities. With inclusion and integration have come greater opportunities for social interaction and sexual expression. The same spirit that has raised disability-rights issues to a national priority is now demanding that people with disabilities be recognized as sexual beings with a right to sexual education, sexual health care, and sexual expression afforded under the law.

Demands for the sexual rights of people with disabilities have resulted in a resurgence of research interest in the area of sexuality and disability in the 1990s. Notably, the National Center for Medical Rehabilitation Research (NCMRR) of the National Institute of Child Health and Human Development under the National Institutes of Health has identified sexuality as a priority issue that impacts the quality of life of people with disabilities. It subsequently issued a Request for Applications on Reproductive Function in People with Physical Disabilities in February of 1992. The purpose of the request was to develop new knowledge in the areas of reproductive physiology, anatomy, and behavior that are common to people with disabilities with the goal of restoring, improving, or enhancing reproductive function lost as a consequence of injury, disease, or congenital disorder. The request for applications included a specific objective to characterize the effect of impairments of sexual function on psychosocial adaptation, emotional state, and establishment of intimate relationships. Special focus was placed on research with women and minorities who have disabilities. NCMRR has funded six studies on sexuality and disability over the last three years. Two of the studies were with women who have spinal cord injury, and a third was a study of women with a variety of disabilities.

Consumers with Disabilities Leading the Way. Research, education, and advocacy efforts in the area of sexuality and disability are being led by people with disabilities (consumers). A review of the most recent annotated bibliography on sexuality and disability published by the Sexuality Information and Education Council of the United States (SIECUS, 1995) reveals a growing number of books, newsletters, special issues of publications, and curricula on sexuality and disability written by people with disabilities. In addition, national consumer-based organizations like the National Spinal Cord Injury Association, the National Multiple Sclerosis Foundation, and the Arthritis Foundation are beginning to publish self-help brochures on the specific effects of particular disabilities on sexuality. Most recently, self-help groups have been appearing on the Internet, computer bulletin-board services, and commercial computer services like American Online.

Health-Care Professionals Involved in Sexuality and Disability. In addition to the work by people with disabilities and nonprofessional advocates, health-care professionals are also taking an increased interest in sexuality and disability. The American Association of Physical Medicine and Rehabilitation has a Sexuality Task Force; the American Association of Sexuality Educators, Counselors, and Therapists has a special-interest group that focuses on educating medical and allied help professionals in the area of sexuality and disability; the Society for the Scientific Study of Sexuality includes presentations and workshops in the area of sexuality and disability for its members; and Planned Parenthood agencies around the country have increased education and services in the area of sexual health care to people with disabilities. More rehabilitation hospitals are including "privacy" rooms to give patients an opportunity to experiment sexually while still in the hospital, and many are adding specialty programs in the area of fertility and erectile function for men, obstetric and gynecological care for women, and parenting for both men and women with disabilities.

Portrayals of Sexuality and Disability in the Popular Media. The portrayal of people with disabilities as sexual beings has improved over time in the popular media. Movies that include a focus on the sexuality and relationships of people with disabilities, such as *Forest Gump, Passion Fish, Water Dance, Regarding Henry, My Left Foot, Children of a Lesser God,* and *Born on the Fourth of July* have dealt with the issue of sexuality and disability with varying degrees of sensitivity, and have enjoyed success at both the box office and in video stores. TV shows have also included people with disabilities and sexuality themes. One show, *LA Law,* where one of the stars portrayed a person with a developmental disability who had a sexual relationship with another person with a developmental disability, was honored by the Coalition of Sexuality and Disability for the positive portrayal of sexuality and disability in the media. There has also been an increase in TV commercials that include people with disabilities in relationships or with children. Popular magazines ranging from *Bride* to *Penthouse* and *Playboy* are also beginning to include feature articles on sexuality and disability. Efforts to portray people with disabilities as part of everyday life in the media are slowly helping to explode the myth that people with disabilities are asexual.

Problems, Controversies, and Hurdles. Two of the most serious sexual problems facing people with disabilities are (1) the high rate of sexual abuse, exploitation, and unwanted sexual activity, especially among women with physical disabilities and all people with developmental disabilities, and (2) the risk of STDs, including HIV, among people with cognitive impairments who are sexually active. Two leading areas of controversy are (1) the issue of what constitutes informed consent for sexual activity in people with serious cognitive impairments, and (2) the area of reproductive rights, eugenics, abortion, and prenatal testing for disabilities. As far as hurdles, there is still a need for greater access to information and educational material that affirms the sexuality of people of all abilities, including people with early- and late-onset disabilities, physical, sensory, and mental disabilities, and disabilities that hinder learning. Despite the positive current trends in sexuality and disability, we still have a long way to go in increasing the number of sexuality education and training programs for teachers, health-care workers, and family members to help them understand and support the normal sexual development and behavior of persons with disabilities. A goal is that all social agencies and health-care delivery systems develop policies and procedures that will insure sexual-health services and benefits are provided on an equal basis to all persons without discrimination because of disability.

Sexuality and Older Persons   ROBERT T. FRANCOEUR

In 1860, over half of the American population was under 20 years of age and only 13 percent over age 45. In 1990, less than a third were under age 20 and 21 percent were over age 45. The so-called Baby Boomers born between 1945 and 1965 are now in their middle years. With the birthrate less than 15 per 1,000, America has become a graying society.

Although Americans over age 50 are the fastest-growing segment of our population, research on their lifestyles and patterns of intimacy has been almost exclusively limited to studies of the chronically ill, the socially isolated, and the poor. Edward Brecher (1984) was one of the first to study older healthy Americans. His sample of 4,246 persons between ages 40 and 92 was largely white and affluent, although he did include a low-income group. His overall conclusion was that the sexual interests and activities of older persons are the best-kept secrets in America. Although there is a common belief that the elderly are no longer interested in sexual intimacy, older persons were just as affected as young people by the social turmoil and changing attitudes of the 1960s and 1970s.

Brecher found that healthy, older person today are "enormously different from the older person of forty or fifty years ago," and very much interested in intimacy and sexual relations. Not one of Brecher's 4,246 respondents was sexually inactive, although masturbation was the most common sexual outlet. Forty-four percent rated their sexual satisfaction as most enjoyable; less than 1 percent rated their sexual activity as not enjoyable (Table 4). Poor health was a major determinant in hindering older persons from maintaining an active sexual life.

Table 4

**Sexual Activity Among 4,246 Americans, Ages 45 to 92,
in the Brecher 1984 Survey**

	Age Group		
	50s	**60s**	**70+**
Women			
Orgasms while asleep or awakening	26%	24%	17%
Women who masturbate	47%	37%	33%
Masturbation frequency for women who masturbate	0.7/week	0.6/week	0.7/week
Wives having sex with husband	88%	76%	65%
Frequency of marital sex	1.3/week	1.0/week	0.7/week
Men			
Orgasms while asleep or awakening	25%	21%	17%
Men who masturbate	66%	50%	43%
Masturbation frequency for men who masturbate	1.2/week	0.8/week	0.7/week
Men having sex with wife	87%	78%	59%
Frequency of marital sex	1.3/week	1.0/week	0.6/week

About half of these couples reported engaging in oral-genital sex and did not limit their sexual activities to nighttime. Most of the men and women were usually orgasmic. About one in fifteen had participated in group sex after age 50. One in five couples had engaged in extramarital sex; 1 percent of couples had a mutually accepted "open marriage." Forty percent of older single women reported a relationship with a married man. A third thought it was acceptable for an older man or woman to have a much younger lover.

In another study of healthy, upper-middle-class men and women, ages 80 to 102 living in residential retirement communities, 14 percent of the men and 29 percent of the women were still married. Sexual touching and caressing, followed by masturbation and then intercourse were the most common sexual activities. Of these outlets, only touching and caressing declined with age, a decline more evident in men than in women. Those who had been sexually active earlier in life tended to remain sexually active in their 80s and 90s, although the frequency of sexual intercourse was sometimes limited by their current physical health and by social circumstances including the lack of an available partner (Bretschneider and McCoy 1988).

The Starr-Weiner Report on Sex and Sexuality in the Mature Years (1981) examined the sexual lives and attitudes of 800 persons, aged 60 to 91, from four regions of the country. When the sexual activities of these 60- to 90-year-olds were compared with the 40-year-olds Kinsey studied thirty-five years earlier, there was no significant decline when opportunities for sexual activity existed. "Sex remains pretty much the same unless some outside event intrudes, such as a health problem, the loss of a spouse, impotence, or boredom." A reliable predictor of the sexually active life of older persons is their acceptance or rejection of the social stereotype of the dependent, sickly older person. Older persons who maintain an active participation in life in general tend to be more sexually active in their later years.

Starr and Weiner also identified two major problems with no easy remedy. First is the tendency for older men to become asexual when they encounter an occasional erection or orgasmic problem. Instead of exploring noncoital pleasuring, many older men simply give up all interest in sex. The second problem is the ever-growing number of older women who are without sexual partners and, thus, deprived, against their will, of sexual intimacy and pleasure. (See Section 6B below on sexuality among older homosexual men and women.)

A Closing Comment

Throughout this section, we have noted the tendency of sexuality researchers in the U.S.A. to focus on the incidence and/or frequency of sexual behaviors in various lifestyles. There has been little corresponding research on the process of sexual relationships or the dynamics within them. This is precisely the same point we made in summarizing the section on adolescent sexuality. Suffice it to say that American researchers need to move beyond asking how many people "do it" and how often they "do it" to more fully investigate the contexts surrounding adult sexual lifestyles, and to identify the social, psychological, and biological factors associated with sexual practice.

6. Homoerotic, Homosexual, and Ambisexual Behaviors

To this point, we have examined the general socio-historical context of sexuality in the U.S.A. and reviewed evidence concerning what may be called mainstream sexual behaviors, in the sense that a majority of Americans engage in these activities. Our review of autoerotic behaviors and the development of heterosexual patterns throughout the life cycle may be seen in this light. We did occasionally mention less-common patterns. For example, the review of childhood sexuality did note that homosexual activities do occur in childhood, and research that examined the development of homosexual behavior was briefly discussed. However, the focus of the chapter so far has clearly been on mainstream, and essentially heterosexual, patterns.

Our review will now shift to an examination of a variety of sexual patterns that are less common, as this has also been a prime concern of sexuality professionals in the U.S.A. We hope that the reader will note that many of the general themes we have stressed so far—change and diversity, for example—are applicable to these patterns as well. In reviewing heterosexual lifestyle patterns, we stressed that researchers have tended to focus on the incidence or frequency of sexual behaviors and less likely to investigate relationship dynamics or theoretical explanations of behavior. These same trends also tend to characterize the study of less-conventional sexual behavior.

A. Children and Adolescents   ROBERT HAWKINS AND WILLIAM STACKHOUSE

Although research on childhood sexual activity in the United States is limited, what little we know (and can remember on a personal level) indicates that a great deal of same-gender sex play takes place among children, usually of an exploratory nature. Occasionally a lesbian, gay, or bisexual adult will recall such childhood activity as being different from exploratory activity with someone of the other gender, and therefore indicative of an early awareness of orientation. But it appears that, for the majority of people, childhood sexual play, while it includes same-gender activity, has little implication for adult orientation.

Some research shows a relationship for males between cross-gender behavior as a child (known as "sissy" behavior) and homoeroticism as an adult, but that relationship has not been shown to be causal and may be more a result of the patriarchal homophobic character of the culture than any innate biological characteristic of the child. This is more apparent when one compares the research on females who engage in cross-gender role behavior as a child (known as "tomboy" behavior), wherein the same relationship is not present. Even the labels for the person engaging in cross-gender role behavior carry different connotations in the culture. For a boy, being called "sissy" is considerably more detrimental to healthy development than is being called "tomboy" for a girl (Green 1987).

When the American child is developing a lesbian, gay, or bisexual identity, the heterosexism and homophobia of the culture dictates that this is not an acceptable orientation, and it becomes difficult at best for the child to develop into an adolescent or adult with a positive self-image. Lesbian and gay youth, particularly those from small communities, seldom receive support from their peers or from the sex education and family life courses in their school. Books that could be supportive, such as Leslea Newman's *Heather Has Two Mommies* (1989), or *Gloria Goes to Gay Pride* (1991), are usually banned from school curricula or simply not considered appropriate for children, even though they were written specifically for all children to read. Counselors and teachers generally assume that all of their students are heterosexually oriented, even though some students in any school will have a same-gender orientation.

As children grow into adolescents and attempt to deal constructively with the tensions and uncertainties of adolescence, gay, lesbian, and bisexual teenagers have to confront the question of the gender of the person to whom they find themselves sexually attracted. Do they surrender to peer and cultural pressure and date only members of the other gender? Do they tell a best friend of their orientation and risk losing that friend or being ostracized or physically attacked? Should they get sexually involved with someone of the other gender to attempt to prove that they really are "straight"? Just what do they do when they find themselves sexually attracted to someone of the same gender? Fortunately, the number and quality of resources that lesbian and gay teens can use are increasing, both on national and local levels. During the late 1980s and early 1990s, many books, pamphlets, and other resources have been published, providing practical guidelines and insights into what lesbian and gay youth should know about dating, living together, and coping in a hostile world.

However, the resources that are available for them are usually available only through homophile groups and a few commercial bookstores, and are generally not available through school libraries or other youth agencies. For example, the Boy Scouts organization has been explicitly noninclusive for both homosexual youth members and adult leaders. In rare cases, such as in New York City, a special high school has been established for gay and lesbian youth who are unable to cope with the discrimination that they face in a regular school setting. This discrimination comes from other students, as well as teachers, administrators, and counselors, making it difficult for these students to obtain an education.

Although this discrimination is still rampant in elementary and secondary schools, it is lessening somewhat in colleges and universities. Most American public and large private colleges and universities recognize and fund student organizations such as a Gay and Lesbian Alliance (GALA) or a Lesbian and Gay Organization (LAGO). Several chapters of gay fraternities and lesbian sororities have been organized. However, even where such organizations exist, many lesbian and gay collegians avoid them or keep their membership quiet. Even at religiously based institutions of higher education, there are differences with respect to the acceptance of these organizations. As late as 1995, one university, the Roman Catholic-affiliated Notre Dame, refused to allow any homophile organizations, and even denied the availability of counseling-center-sponsored group-support activities for lesbians, gays, and bisexuals. At the same time, a large Jewish orthodox-affiliated university, Yeshiva, provides numerous opportunities and funding for gay and lesbian organizations at both the graduate and undergraduate levels.

Even though information on issues confronting lesbian, gay, and bisexual adolescents may be available in printed form, the difficulty in gaining access to such materials, the anti-homoeroticism that is rampant in the media, the negative stereotypes that are still being touted as representative of all who are homoerotic, and the silence on ambieroticism or bisexuality all combine to make life unnecessarily difficult for the adolescent lesbian, gay, or bisexual person in this country. One result is that almost one third of adolescent suicides are related to the issue of homoeroticism. The data on attempted suicide among adolescents are also informative. About 10 percent of heterosexual male and female adolescents attempt suicide, while twice as many lesbian adolescents and three to four times as many gay adolescents attempt suicide (Youth Suicide National Center Report, 1989). The lack of support and acceptance of these young people is undoubtedly a factor in this difference.

B. Adults   ROBERT HAWKINS AND WILLIAM STACKHOUSE

Research on Gender Orientation

The question of gender orientation and the definition of orientation is complex and confusing for both sexuality researchers and the layperson alike. Several researchers have concluded, after extensive study, that there is no clinical description that can be applied to the label "homosexual"— that there is virtually no single phenomenon that can be labeled "homosexuality" and then described in clinical terms. Yet, some theorists have suggested models to define and categorize. When researchers then indicate that they are using a specific model, usually there is no internal consistency. Take, for example, the Kinsey continuum of orientation. After interviewing 5,300 men and 5,940 women in the 1940s, Kinsey and associates developed a continuous scale based on the ratio of sexual fantasies and physical contacts with one's own gender and with the other gender. Along this continuum are seven points, labeled from 0 to 6, with a "Kinsey 0" being a person whose behavior and fantasies have always involved persons of the other gender, and a "Kinsey 6" being a person whose behavior and fantasies have always involved persons of their own gender.

Even where researchers have indicated their use of the Kinsey scale, the actual definitions of research subjects have varied significantly from the original and also varied from study to study. In some instances, fantasy data are not available and consequently not considered; in other instances, behavior alone is the criteria for being placed in a "Kinsey" category, with no recognition of the difference in subjective experience of the sexual activity. In other studies, subjects are placed on the continuum solely according to the gender of the partner with whom they are living.

There are other models available that begin to reflect some of the complexities of gender orientation. Moses and Hawkins (1982; 1986) indicated that the minimum data necessary for identifying orientation in subjects were an assessment of the gender of emotional relationship partners, the gender of sexual attraction partners, and the gender of partners in sexual fantasy content, and that all three of these should be considered from a past and a present perspective, implying that although orientation may be consistent throughout one's life, it is not necessarily so. It is seen as a potentially dynamic characteristic.

An even more complex model was developed by Fred Klein, a physician and gender-orientation researcher. Klein indicated that an assessment of orientation needed to consider seven criteria over three time periods, resulting in a Sexual Orientations Grid of 21 cells. The criteria are: (1) sexual attraction; (2) sexual behavior; (3) sexual fantasies; (4) emotional/affectional relationship preference; (5) social relationship preference; (6) lifestyle; and (7) self-identification, with each of these criteria being assessed over three time periods: the past, the present, and the future ideal. This was the first model to present the notion that one's self-label might be an important facet of one's orientation, and the time factor was an acknowledgment of the potentially dynamic character of orientation. Research subjects can rate themselves on these criteria using a three-by-seven grid and the Kinsey ratings, summing the ratings, and then dividing by 21 to produce a position on a scale identified popularly as "The Kinsey Scale" (Klein 1978; Klein, Sepekoff, and Wolf, 1985). Although the initial response to Klein's model was that it was more comprehensive and realistic, its complexities have kept most researchers from using or disseminating it widely. It has thus remained unfamiliar to many.

Developmental Biological Insights

Several studies in the past decade have attempted to identify biological determinants for adult homoeroticism from a heterosexist theoretical base, in which heterosexual behavior is viewed as the basic, natural human behavior, and anything else is deviant. There is usually little recognition of definitional complexity or the possibility of precursors rather than determinants. Subjects are typically placed in the dichotomous classification so prevalent in the culture—that one is either gay or straight, homosexual or heterosexual—with no recognition of the Kinsey continuum, and especially no recognition of Klein's model. Researchers have purported to examine twins, siblings, adopted children, and brains of people who are homosexual and those who are not.

For example, Simon LeVay (1991) reported finding a portion of the hypothalamus that was smaller in homosexual men than in heterosexual men and was equal in size to that portion in heterosexual women. There were no lesbian brains identified as such in this study. The "finding" was quickly seized by the popular media and soon became what is called "common knowledge." There were many problems with the study, but these were generally ignored, even in the scientific press. The definitional problem, whereby subjects were classified according to whether they were known to be gay or not (obviously all subjects were no longer living, so no information could be garnered from the subjects), has been ignored. The size of the sample (nineteen men previously identified as gay, sixteen men identified as not known to be gay and, therefore, heterosexual; one man known to be identified as bisexual and included in the study as such; and six women, all classified as heterosexual) has also generally been ignored. The fact that the size of another part of the hypothalamus in the women's brains did not coincide with other research on women's brains was ignored in discussions, and the possibility that what was found may have had something to do with body build and general physical characteristics rather than directly with sexual orientation was also never discussed. The overly simplistic design was convenient, because including even a few of the other variables, such as body build or sexual history, would mean that the sample size would have to be considerably larger to enable any conclusions to be drawn.

Dean Hamer and his research team (1993) have reported the discovery of a genetic region, the Xq28 region on the X chromosome, that is claimed to be associated with male homosexuality in about three quarters of gay men and inherited on the maternal side of the family. Similar research on lesbian women does not show similar findings. There is also no attempt in all of this research to explain the "exceptions" that are reported. If there is a "gay" gene, then why is it that all men who are gay do not show it? Most biologically focused studies suffer from similar problems, first with the issue of definition, then with the exclusion or nonsimilarity of research on women who are attracted to women, and finally with assumptions, conclusions, and discussions of results that assume the "natural" state of the human being is exclusively heterosexual.

Although the question of a biological basis for homoeroticism has, in recent years, seen increased interest and attention, such research consistently does not consider the complexities of orientation, such as emotional attraction, behavior, and other criteria that constitute sexual orientation in Klein's model. Most of the classification methods for identifying orientation of subjects in these studies are overly simplified. Although there may be biological precursors to orientation, no well-designed, appropriately controlled study has been done to support that conclusion.

One positive side effect of the popular interpretation of research into possible biological roots of homoerotic orientation has been in easing the acceptance of gay and lesbian persons by some churches. One can paraphrase a common response among some mainstream Protestant church people and leaders: "If homosexual orientations are not a freely chosen preference but in some way rooted in prenatal genetic, hormonal, and/or neural templates, then God and nature made them this way, and we and the church must accept that reality."

Bisexuality Research

The research on bisexuality or ambieroticism is even more scant. It is very difficult to do research on bisexuality if one cannot define it, and there is no simple, dichotomous cultural model as is available with research on homosexuality. In a 1994 book, *Dual Attraction*, Weinberg, Williams, and Pryor report that using the Kinsey scale with sexual behaviors, sexual feeling, and romantic feelings, they identified five different types of bisexuals in their study of 435 men and 338 women:

1. The Pure Type, scoring at least 3 on all criteria;
2. The Mid Type, scoring 3 on one criteria and 2 to 4 on the other two;
3. The Heterosexual-Leaning Type, scoring 0-2 on each of the three criteria;
4. The Homosexual-Leaning Type, scoring 4 to 6 on each dimension; and
5. The Varied Type, whose scores did not fit any of the first four categories or types.

Additionally, it is only in the recent past that models for development of a bisexual identity have been proposed, and further research into ambieroticism, such as was begun by Fred Klein, has moved very slowly. The heterosexist nature of the culture, combined with the indigenous psychological and sociological perspectives of many researchers, has precluded the acceptance of a somewhat radical notion that the basic state of the human sexual orientation is ambierotic and mutable, with exclusive heterosexual or exclusive homosexual behavior being equally deviant from the biological norm. Further research on bisexuality appears to be moving in that direction. (See Section C below for more on bisexuality.)

Incidence

In much of the public discussion of homoeroticism, there is a preoccupation with the general question, "How many are there?" The answer to this question carries political and economic implications, and there is a need to understand the extent of the economic power and political power that this group wields. For example, is the culture required, in policy decisions, to provide for this group, or is it such a small number that policymakers are not required to respond to identified needs of this population? Commerce is in a strategic position to profit from this population, and economically driven decisions in the marketplace are taking these numbers into serious account. For example, in 1994, advertisements focusing directly on lesbian women and gay men as consumers were introduced in popular television and print media, and more mainstream commercial advertisements were being placed in homoerotically focused magazines, such as *The Advocate*, and in programs for fund-raising benefits for homoerotic communities.

Another area where numbers are considered in policy decisions is the increasing recognition and development of domestic-partner benefits, such as health insurance and death benefits. This began in the early 1990s when some employers became aware that lesbians, gay men, and bisexuals comprise enough of the work force to have an effect on productivity and efficiency, and that accommodating their needs is beneficial to the company so that it can have and keep well-qualified people.

Ignoring the basic fact that there is no definition of what "a homosexual" or "a bisexual" person is, until the mid-1990s the most-often cited figure for incidence of homosexuality came from the research of Kinsey and associates carried out in the 1940s. These data have been used to estimate the number of homoerotic people in the population without any indication of the simplistic nature of the definition. The commonly cited figure that 10 percent of American men are homosexual is a combination of Kinsey's finding that 4 percent of his sample were exclusively homosexual (Kinsey 6) and 6 percent were predominantly homosexual (Kinsey 5) (Kinsey et al. 1948). His data on homosexual activity in women indicated approximately 9 percent were either exclusively or predominantly homosexual (Kinsey 5 or 6) (Kinsey et al. 1953).

Laumann et al. (1994) found that almost 3 percent of their subjects were homosexual. Although these two sets of figures may, at first, seem at odds, the 1994 figure had a 1 percent error rate, and the Kinsey figure for exclusive homosexuality was 4 percent, so the two major studies do not differ greatly. There were some other problems with the 1994 study, such as the use of females as interviewers and the tendency of males in this culture to deny homosexual activity, even in anonymous questionnaires, but especially in face-to-face contact with anyone else; however, even with those design problems, the numbers are similar (Schmalz 1993).

Clinical View

In 1973, the American Psychiatric Association removed homosexuality from the *Diagnostic and Statistical Manual of Mental Disorders*. This was a major turning point, both in the United States and worldwide, in the clinical acceptance of homosexuality. Homosexuality was no longer to be viewed as an illness. The impact within psychology and psychiatry was profound, and has influenced many aspects of society. The basis for this change was the scientific conclusion that, among individuals who were not in clinical treatment, it was impossible to distinguish heterosexual and homosexual persons. Evelyn Hooker first arrived at this conclusion in 1957 with the first controlled study to include a comparison on a non-clinical sample of heterosexual and homosexual men.

Since then, research designs employing the principle that such non-clinical participants exist have resulted in many studies confirming that, in itself, homosexuality is not an illness. The illness model of homosexuality that had existed as the basis for so much discrimination is no longer supported by the psychiatric and psychological establishments. In 1973, the *Compre-*

hensive Textbook of Psychiatry was revised to state: "many homosexuals, both male and female, function responsibly and honorably, often in positions of high trust, and live emotionally stable, mature, and well adjusted lives, psychodynamically indistinguishable from well-adjusted heterosexuals, except for their alternative sexual preferences."

This has led clinicians to change their point of reference regarding homosexuals, from a pathological frame to a counseling frame, from looking at persons as sick to looking at how persons may maximize their human potential in society. Since then, many studies and books have examined aspects of the development of gay men and lesbian women, looking at identity development (social, sexual, and psychological), family issues, relationship issues, work and career development, and other dimensions of identity and lifestyle. There now exists a large body of American literature, in both the professional and general press aimed at maximizing the health and wholeness of gay men and lesbians.

Still, gay and lesbian individuals often have difficulty with their own self-acceptance and the process of deciding just how to live as gay or lesbian persons. Mental-health professionals who specialize in working with gay and lesbian clients offer individual and group counseling throughout the U.S.A. Various organizations also routinely offer support groups for a wide range of concerns. In addition, counseling is now available to the family members and friends of gay and lesbian persons who have difficulty in accepting the homosexuality of their loved ones.

Legal Perspectives

In examining the legal status of lesbians, gays, and bisexuals, one needs a rudimentary understanding of the legal system in the United States. There are levels of jurisdiction throughout the country; each jurisdiction, from local villages, to city, county, state, and the federal governments, has its own legal codes. In addition, the military has its own legal code. The issue of rights for lesbians and gays has been raised at all levels of jurisdiction. Supposedly, all of these laws are subject to the provisions of the Constitution of the United States, which provides consistency. Each state has its own state constitution, which is also to be consistent with the federal Constitution, as are the governing documents of cities and local communities.

Generally, lesbian women and gay men have no protection against discrimination based on orientation or the perception of orientation, and in 1995, only nine states had laws including sexual orientation as a minority protected from discrimination. Historically, attempts to obtain protection have followed the patterns of other oppressed groups in the United States. First, there were attempts to gain protection against discrimination in public accommodations and employment. More recently, this has expanded to include equal treatment with regard to employment-related benefits accorded to married heterosexual relationships. Examples include the benefits accrued to persons by their legally married status (as of 1995 same-gender partners are not allowed to marry legally in any state in the U.S.), as well as benefits in relation to parental status (such as adoption or custody issues), and bereavement leave with respect to family members.

Opposition to these attempts to expand discrimination protection either takes the stance that homosexual activity is immoral and, therefore, not deserving of consideration for equal protection, or suggests that lesbian women and gay men are seeking "special treatment." There is even an argument put forth that suggests that lesbian women and gay men are not an oppressed minority and should not be treated as such. Where legal protections have been instituted, it has usually been based on the need for equal treatment.

In the past decade, some local jurisdictions have passed laws recognizing the civil rights of same-gender couple relationships and of homoerotic individuals. Similarly, many corporations, of all sizes, have granted gay and lesbian couples the same benefits as heterosexual couples. For example, in Dallas, Texas, a major corporation threatened not to locate a new corporate facility in that city if the corporation's policy on domestic partnership benefits for same-gendered couples was declared illegal by virtue of the city's discriminatory laws. The economic impact of this decision caused the city government to rescind the law.

In May 1993, a court case highlighted a conflict between the antidiscrimination clause in the Constitution of the State of Hawaii and that state's ban on the recognition of same-gender unions. The state's Supreme Court asked the state to prove its "compelling interest" for continuing the discrimination or to end it. Lawyers generally admit that it will be very difficult to prove a "compelling interest," and if it cannot be done, the state will be forced to grant legal recognition of same-gender partnerships. Currently, all fifty states grant reciprocal recognition of the legality of heterosexual marriage, but if Hawaii legalizes homosexual marriages, the other forty-nine states will have to decide whether to continue that reciprocity. In early 1995, several states sought to pass legislation that would limit their reciprocity to heterosexual marriage, in the event that Hawaii recognized same-gender marriages (Rotello 1996; Eskridge 1996; Sullivan 1996).

Lesbians and gays are also treated differently with respect to serving in the United States armed forces. For many years, they were specifically excluded in official policy, yet were differentially managed in individual cases. For example, when the war in Kuwait broke out, some lesbians and gays who were scheduled for separation from the service were required to serve until the end of the conflict. In another instance, an enlisted man, Perry Watkins, repeatedly told the military that he was gay, but they kept reenlisting him until someone finally decided that he should be separated from the service, and the legal process to do so was instituted (Shilts, 1993).

In 1994, the military instituted a policy called "Don't ask, Don't tell," in which recruits were no longer to be asked if they had "homosexual tendencies," but were also forbidden from telling anyone if they were homoerotic. Prior to this, the official policy being enforced was one in which activity was not a requirement for dismissal; simply acknowledging one's homoerotic orientation was enough to cause separation from the service. For example, Joseph Stephan, a midshipman at the United States Naval Academy, was only three months from graduation when he was asked if he was a homosexual. He indicated that he was, but never was asked, nor did he ever acknowledge any homosexual activity. He was separated from the navy and was denied his bachelor's degree from the Naval Academy (Rotello 1996; Eskridge 1996; Shilts 1993; Sullivan 1996).

Lesbians and gays have to pay special attention to wills, as biological families have successfully contested wills that left nothing to the blood relatives and everything to the person's life partner. This situation has led to the development of agencies and books focusing specifically on estate planning for lesbian and gay couples and individuals.

The legal issues for bisexuals generally focus on that part of their lives that includes someone of the same gender, so it is the homoerotic aspect of their ambieroticism that suffers from the lack of legal protection. Additionally, there is no legal option for triangular relationships that provides legitimacy, so if a bisexual person has a primary relationship simultaneously with a man and a woman, that relationship cannot be legitimized as a marriage.

Religious Issues

With the removal of homosexuality from the category of mental illness in 1973, the major foundation for legal discrimination against homosexuality was removed. As a result, religious intolerance of homosexuality, which had always been present, took on a more significant role in the debate on homosexuality within American social and political dialogue. Those who believe homosexuality to be immoral on religious grounds have since become more vocal in their quest to have their particular moral positions on homosexuality and other religious and moral issues inserted into the nation's laws (see also Section 2 of this chapter).

At the same time as Americans witnessed the radical change in the clinical view of homosexuality and the emergence of the gay-liberation movement, religious bodies in the U.S. were challenged on their stances with regard to homosexuality. Within Christian and Jewish sects, the debate generally has centered on the interpretation of sacred Biblical texts (Boswell 1980; Countryman 1988; Curran 1993; Francoeur in Gramick and Furey 1988; Gold 1992; Kosnick et al. 1977; Helminiak 1994; McNeill 1976; Presbyterian Church 1991; Thayer et al. 1987). The central locus of the debate is concerned with certain Old Testament texts, particularly the story of Sodom and Gomorrah, and the New Testament comments of the Apostle Paul in 1 Corinthians 6:9 and I Timothy 1:9-10 (Helminiak 1994), which appear to condemn homosexuality. In actuality, the debate is waged on the basis of how ancient texts are interpreted and used for modern guidance. Many "fundamentalist" and traditional sects accept the ancient texts for their literal meaning and condemn all homosexual expression (Presbyterian Church, Part 2, 1991). These sects, however, generally do not address the extent to which they completely ignore many other Biblical texts and do not use them for modern guidance. Other, liberal, bodies interpret the ancient texts in their historical context in the light of current biological and psychological knowledge about the origins and nature of homosexual and other orientations. These bodies, particularly liberal reformed—and to some extent conservative—Judaism, the Episcopal Church, and the United Church of Christ, frequently welcome homosexual men and women to membership, and even to the ministry (Heyward 1989; Presbyterian Church 1991; Thayer 1987). Within the Catholic Church in America, there is a quite-visible split that, on the grassroots level, constitutes a silent schism on the issue of homosexuality. On the pastoral level, many, perhaps a majority of the clergy, accept the tolerant and liberal position expressed by the Catholic Theological Society of America (Kosnick et al. 1977), and quietly ignore the dogmatic condemnation of homosexuality by the Vatican (Curran 1993; Francoeur in Gramick and Furey 1988; McNeill 1976).

Among American religious bodies, the major continuing issues regarding homosexuality center on welcome, support, and affirmation of members within congregations and on the presence of openly gay and lesbian persons in religious leadership. Recently, support for gay and lesbian members has often led to performing "holy unions" for gay and lesbian partners. Given that the legal option of marriage has not been available, religious bodies have been the logical place for couples to seek such recognition and support. Many congregations have offered these services to both their members and to gay and lesbian persons in their communities. Although there are gays and lesbians in leadership in some religious bodies, they are few and often do not receive the support of predominantly heterosexual congregations. The one religious place where gay and lesbian persons have found a guaranteed welcome has been in the special ministries that exist for gay and lesbian persons. This includes a variety of individual denominations and individual congregations with a special outreach to gay and lesbian persons.

Social Issues

The growing visibility of homosexuals in American society and the scrutiny of the press probing the private lives of public figures have led some politicians to acknowledge publicly their homoerotic orientation. In 1980, Robert E. Bauman, a leading conservative Republican Congressman from Maryland, lost his bid for reelection after revealing his homoerotic orientation. About the same time, Congressman Gerry E. Studds from Massachusetts revealed his homoeroticism and he served in the House of Representatives until 1996. Elaine Noble was the first openly lesbian legislator in the state of Massachusetts. On the federal level, Representative Barney Frank, also from Massachusetts, disclosed his homoerotic orientation in 1987, and also continues to serve. In 1994, President Bill Clinton named Roberta Achtenberg as his highest-ranking lesbian appointee, and she was confirmed by the Congress as assistant secretary for fair housing and equal opportunity in the Department of Housing and Urban Development. In 1995, she announced that she was leaving that post to run for mayor of San Francisco.

Thanks to the political and educational activism of a wide variety of gay and lesbian individuals and groups, American society is becoming increasingly sensitized to the prevailing discrimination of heterosexism and homophobia. On the negative side, there has been an apparent increase in violence against people perceived to be homosexual. Studies have indicated increases in the reporting of violent crimes that are based on the perceived homosexuality of the victim, and students have reported witnessing harassment of students and teachers thought to be homosexual. In some instances, the growing hostility is purported to be linked with fear and anxiety about AIDS, but lesbian and gay leaders suggest that this is simply a convenient new excuse to further hate and discrimination. Lesbians, gays, and bisexuals see themselves as the last large minority that is not legally protected from discrimination, and thus, as a group, they fulfill the need of some people to find scapegoats for whatever social ills occur. The other negative aspect of this increased visibility is that it causes the opposition to become aggressive. Observing the progress made by lesbians and gays in attempting to obtain equal rights, those opposed have taken a proactive approach in attempting to limit the rights and opportunities for lesbians and gays to enjoy a full and unrestricted life. This has taken many forms, including the development and dissemination of a video filled with partial truths and false information designed to arouse fear of and hatred toward homoerotic individuals and groups. There have also been referendums on ballots to deny homosexuals equal protection. While some of these have been passed in several jurisdictions, some of them have subsequently been declared unconstitutional by state and federal courts. That has not deterred others from developing similar referendums. In September 1996, Congress voted to deny Federal benefits to married people of the same sex and to permit states to ignore such marriages sanctioned in other states. A separate bill that would have banned for the first time discrimination against homosexuals in the workplace was defeated by a single vote.

On the positive side, openly gay or lesbian people have been elected to almost every level of government, with the exception of the executive branch of the state and federal governments (governors and the president and vice president). Voters in several jurisdictions have enacted legislation to protect the civil rights of lesbians and gays. The amount of literature and published research on lesbian and gay issues has increased exponentially in recent years, and the arts have moved to include lesbian, gay, and bisexual subjects in other than classically stereotypic and tragic roles. Research and commentary regarding gay, lesbian, and bisexual issues in the academic disciplines has become acceptable, and the result has been a concomitant exponential increase in published works in all the academic disciplines. There are even a few departments in universities specifically devoted to studies of lesbian, gay, and bisexual issues. In all the arts and literature, there are more and more instances of openly lesbian and gay themes, stories, and characters. And there are more openly gay, lesbian, and bisexual people in professional and amateur sports (such as Martina Navratalova in tennis, and Greg Louganis, the Olympic multiple-gold-medal diver), and in commerce (billionaire David Geffan).

Some people who are known privately but widely to be lesbian or gay are challenged by the gay and lesbian communities to be open. On occasion they are "outed," that is, they are publicly announced to be lesbian or gay. Whether this is appropriate and ethical, given the extent of the homophobia in the culture, is a question. Originally, this practice was instituted only in cases where a person was widely known to be homoerotic and was not only keeping that information secret, but also was engaging in antihomosexual activity, such as gay public officials supporting antigay, antilesbian legislation. It later developed into a more-general application of "outing," which many have questioned and challenged.

One of the major problems for lesbian, gay, and bisexual adolescents is the lack of positive role models available in the homophobic, heterosexist culture. This lack contributes to the lowered self-esteem of lesbian and gay youth. The increased visibility of lesbian women and gay men throughout all levels of the society means that younger lesbians and gays are able to see others of identical orientation who have succeeded in whatever their chosen career. This has a positive effect on ego and the development of self-image.

Family Issues

Gay and lesbian people have been at the forefront of defining operative, nontraditional, nonbiological family concepts. Although this may have grown from the difficulties of association with biological families and the impracticality of the "heterosexual husband-wife with children" relationship model, it has resulted in the active development and maintenance of alternative family structures of great depth and commitment that have subsequently provided an alternative model for the heterosexual society. This includes not only nonmarital couples and their children, but also committed long-standing friendship circles that constitute a chosen extended family, a set of associations often with stronger bonds than those that may exist through the unchosen avenue of blood relatives.

The depth and extent of these intentional relationships have become dramatically evident in the caring provided to those within such networks in the HIV/AIDS epidemic. The depth and extent of this caring has provided incontrovertible evidence of the wholesomeness and loving nature of these associations, and has significantly challenged the remainder of society.

The social, familial, and internalized heterosexist homophobia sometimes creates a situation in which the lesbian or gay man sees heterosexual marriage as the only public option for life. They may or may not include secret homosexual activity while married. With the increased visibility of lesbians, gays, and bisexuals, this pattern of behavior is less likely to occur without conscious awareness and dissonance on the part of both marital partners. Sometimes, but rarely, the only way a gay man or lesbian can cope successfully with the social pressures is to find a homoerotic person of the other gender to agree to a "marriage of convenience," in which they might live as roommates and have separate sexual lives.

Some lesbians and gay men choose to have children. Women have the option of childbearing through the medically established procedure of donor insemination available in this country, or they can, and sometimes do, seek and find a man who will biologically impregnate them. Men obviously do not have this option. Therefore, the issues for lesbians who want a child are different from those for a gay man who wants one. In keeping with the resourcefulness and creativity of many lesbians and gay men, there are many patterns that have been developed to achieve biological parenthood.

Support organizations for the heterosexual relatives of homoerotic individuals have formed and become available. Most notable is the organization Parents and Friends of Lesbians and Gays, (PFLAG), with headquarters in Washington, D.C. and groups throughout the United States. Where there are lesbian and gay community centers, usually one finds programs for children of lesbian and gay parents, such as The Center Kids, a program at the Lesbian and Gay Community Center in New York City. These centers also usually have support groups and education sessions for the biological families of lesbians and gays, as well as for the chosen families.

Health Issues

American lesbian women and gay men have many of the same health issues as their heteroerotic counterparts, but there are some issues that are unique, including the fact that the assumption of heterosexuality for individuals in the culture in general continues into the sphere of the health-care consumer. When the health-care professional is taking a history and asks, "Are you married or single or divorced?" there is little room for the lesbian or gay individual to indicate that she or he is in a long-term relationship with another person. And if the person is bisexually active, the answer to that question could be very misleading to the professional who should be concerned with whatever may impact the patient's health.

Lesbian women and gay men also have to interact with hospitals and other health-care facilities that often do not recognize the rights of a nonmarital partner to determine the course of treatment or to visit in an intensive-care unit unless they have obtained either a power of attorney or have officially been designated as a "health-care proxy."

Although lesbians have the lowest rates of sexually transmitted diseases of any orientation group, they also have some special concerns that would not apply to heteroerotic women, but would apply to bisexual women. Those issues are related to the fact that this person is sexually active with another woman. There is some debate concerning whether lesbians who are not sexually active with a man should have a Pap smear as often as a woman who is sexually active with a man. Additionally, if a patient tells the health-care professional that she is a lesbian, the assumption is then made that she is not being sexually active with a man. This assumption should always be checked, because it is not necessarily true. A comprehensive sex history is needed to avoid incorrect assumptions, but is seldom done.

Gay men, on the other hand, have a high rate of sexually transmitted diseases. Prior to the 1980s, there was no major push for these men to wear condoms to prevent STDs, because most of the diseases could be cured by medical intervention. However, with the advent of HIV/AIDS, that situation changed, and the increased use of condoms in this population has significantly decreased the incidence of other STDs. The high frequency of sexual activity in many gay men means that their health care needs include concerns for the many diseases that can be transmitted sexually—and a comprehensive sex history is mandatory if the professional is to provide appropriate health care.

In the early 1980s, what we now know as AIDS was called GRID, Gay Related Immunodeficiency Disease, and it was believed that gay men were the only people who had it. While that has changed, the largest percentage of cases of AIDS in the United States continues to be among gay men, and part of gay-male identity is now referenced to HIV status, i.e., whether he is HIV-positive or HIV-negative. There is some concern about the effect that this has on one's psychological health, with some people questioning the acceptance of that reference to "Gay Related" when the infectious potential of HIV is not influenced by a person's sexual orientation.

Additionally, gay men have been likened in a psychological manner to Vietnam veterans in that both have experienced the death of many people with whom close bonds had been established. There has been a suggestion that many gay men, particularly in the regions of the country that are hardest hit by the HIV/AIDS epidemic, are suffering from post-traumatic stress disorder, and are in need of psychological treatment. Those lesbians who are very involved in the care of and are friends of HIV-positive gay men, are also experiencing trauma associated with multiple bereavement.

Another group that is receiving little attention in this epidemic are those gay men who are HIV-negative, who have lost partners to AIDS, and who are having to deal with survivor guilt and associated issues. Many of these men must also cope with the very strong feelings of pleasure that were associated with sexual activity before HIV became a threat. These men are at great risk for HIV infection; yet in the mid-1990s, the public-health focus has turned to women and children at risk, generally ignoring gay men.

Homosexuality in the Later Years

Very little is known about sexuality and aging among the estimated 3.5 million American men and women over age 60 who are homosexual. For gay men and lesbians, aging can create unique conflicts and problems. The death of a partner in a long-term relationship may bring out homophobic reactions among family members that lead these relatives to ignore the bereaved partner or contest a will and estate. Gay men and lesbians who decide to acknowledge their orientation after years of passing as heterosexual face the possibility of quite different outcomes when loved ones, children, and grandchildren, learn of their relative's sexual orientation. Gay men, who are fearful that their orientation will be discovered as it becomes evident they are not going to marry, may adopt a loner life with relatively little sexual and social intimacy. Lesbian couples have to cope with two female incomes, which would usually be lower than most dual-career gay male or heterosexual couples (Friend 1987).

By necessity, gay men and lesbians develop skills in coping and crisis management, which give them an advantage in the aging process. More-flexible gender roles may allow older homosexuals to take aging more in stride and develop ways of taking care of themselves that seem comfortable and appropriate. "These skills may not be developed to the same degree among heterosexual men or women, who may be used to having or expecting a wife or husband to look after them" (Friend 1987, 311). Gay people tend to plan ahead for their own independence and security, whereas heterosexuals are more likely to assume that their children will take care of them in their old age. Homosexual men and women have significantly more close friends who serve as a "surrogate family" than do heterosexuals. In larger urban areas, organizations like Senior Action in a Gay Environment (SAGE) provide a variety of social and support services for older homosexuals.

Gay Men, Lesbian Women, and Bisexuals—Comparisons

Because gay men are socialized as males and generally perceive themselves as males, their socialization process is somewhat different from that of lesbian women, who are socialized as females and generally perceive themselves as being female. This means that, from a general perspective, just as there are differences in male and female socialization, there are differences between lesbians and gay men, as well as differences among them. For example, in general analyses of gay and lesbian relationships, one difference often noted between the two is the role of sexual activity and sexual exclusivity. Generally, lesbian relationships are sexually exclusive and gay male relationships are not. This appears to be especially true of long-term relationships, and can be explained by the differences in socialization of women and men around sexual activity issues.

When gay men and lesbian women join together to form groups working toward a common goal, sometimes there are issues of power differentials and attitudes toward sexual activity that prevent the original goals from being reached by dividing the group along gender lines. Again, this can be explained by the differential socialization process.

It was not until the late 1980s that people identified as bisexual were welcomed into what were previously lesbian and gay organizations, and they are still viewed with caution in many circles. Bisexuals are sometimes accused by heterosexual people of being gay or lesbian and are labeled homophobic and fake by some homoerotic people. There are few bisexual support groups, most of them in large cities. The United States is only just beginning to attempt to understand the bisexual phenomenon.

C. Bisexuality   CAROL QUEEN WITH ROBERT MORGAN LAWRENCE

The ambivalence about bisexuality is reflected in the history of the concept. For several years after the terms homosexuality and heterosexuality were coined in the late 1800s, bisexuality was largely ignored by the physicians and sex researchers who had newly medicalized sex. Sigmund Freud, with his theory of sexual development borrowed from Darwinian evolutionary models, helped to change that. By the 1920s, when Wilhelm Stekel wrote *Bi-Sexual Love*, the erotic capacity to desire both males and females could be envisioned as universal, if likely to be outgrown by adulthood. Havelock Ellis, by contrast, viewed bisexuality as a distinct sexual-orientation category, comparable to both homo- and heterosexuality.

Alfred Kinsey (1948, 1953) conceptualized bisexuality not in evolutionary terms, as the Freudians tended to do, but in simple behavioral terms. In his sexual-orientation scale, bisexuality was represented on a continuum between exclusive heterosexuality (the 0 end of Kinsey's scale) and exclusive homosexuality (at 6), with a Kinsey 3 equally attracted to or having had sexual experience with males and females.

Since most humans experience their erotic desires and relationships in a social context, many (perhaps most) bisexuals have more sexual experience with one or the other gender, depending upon whether their social affiliations tend to be mostly heterosexual or homosexual. Indeed, researchers have noted that many people who have displayed "bisexual" behavior over the lifespan—that is, people who have had sexual experience with both males and females—tend to identify sexually according to the gender of their current partner (Blumstein and Schwartz 1983). This is reported as especially true of women. When the current partner is female, women are more likely to identify themselves as lesbian, and when the current partner is male, as heterosexual. Factors such as political or social affiliation can also lead an individual to—or away from—a bisexual identity.

One common stereotype about bisexuals suggests a person is not "really" bisexual unless he or she is a Kinsey 3. This is related to the presumption that the individual is "really" homosexual but hiding behind a heterosexual relationship. The notion that all, or most, people are "really" homosexual or heterosexual has been termed "monosexuality." Monosexuals are individuals who desire members of only one gender, whereas bisexuals desire both. The term was apparently first used to describe hetero- and homosexuals by Stekel (1922). Today this term has gained new currency in the American bisexual community as bisexuals seek to understand and combat the sources of stereotyping and social opprobrium they term "biphobia" (Hutchins and Kaahumanu 1991). Expressions of biphobia encompass caustic dismissals, such as Bergler's (1956) "Nobody can dance at two different weddings at the same time"; difficult relations between bisexual women and some lesbians (Weise 1992); and media-fed concerns that bisexual men are "spreading AIDS" into the heterosexual population. (The latter concern ignores the possibility that bisexual men can be as responsible about safe-sex practices as anyone else, that heterosexuals may also contract HIV from other heterosexuals, and that bisexual men may choose to live monogamous lives with female—or male—partners.)

Until recently, American bisexuals had few sources of support for their sexuality unless they derived it from the gay community—which has been far from uniformly supportive. In fact, it should be noted that many gays deny the reality and/or possibility of bisexuality. In the 1970s, a few support groups for bisexuals were formed; the best known of these was San Francisco's Bisexual Center. By the late 1980s, groups and organizations had emerged that aimed specifically to develop a supportive bisexual community; at the time of this writing, these are extensively networked and are producing their own publications and conferences.

Due to insufficient support, the influence of negative and alienating stereotypes, and the apparent fact that many bisexuals have lived as lesbians, gay men, or heterosexuals, it has been difficult to estimate what percentage of the population is, or has been, bisexual. It is probable that many more people have bisexual histories than would answer affirmatively to a survey researcher asking "Are you bisexual?" Too, many researchers have conflated or collapsed homosexuality and bisexuality (for a recent example, see Laumann et al. 1994), a further indication that many still consider one a variant of the other.

To stress the multidimensional nature of sexuality, Fred Klein (1985) developed his Sexual Orientation Grid, which expands Kinsey's concept of the continuum. He considers not only experience and desire, but also dreams, fantasies, social networks, relationships, ideal sexual orientation, and other variables. Additionally, Klein breaks the scale into temporal units (adolescence; early adulthood; present) so it can better reflect changes in behavior and sexual identity over the lifespan. Coleman (1987) has also developed a scale that takes factors like these into account and that serves as a clinical interview tool. Researchers using these scales, as well as Kinsey's, find that, although some display continuity of sexual identity over the lifespan, other individuals change identity over time. Many rate themselves near the middle of the Kinsey scale when asked their ideal, but report their relationships fall closer to one or the other end.

That behavior and identity are not fixed (and are sometimes not even consonant) is of special interest and relevance to researchers of bisexuality. The differences between homosexual and heterosexual may be less important and intriguing than those between monosexual and bisexual. Why, for example, is a prospective partner's gender of primary importance to some (monosexuals) and not to others (many bisexuals)? Other researchers note that bisexuality assumes different forms in different cultures, subcultures, and individuals. Klein (1978) suggests four primary types: (1) sequential (in which an individual will alternately partner or engage in sex with only men, then only women); (2) concurrent (in which an individual partners and/or engages in sex with both genders during the same period of time); (3) historical (bisexual behavior in an individual's past, especially adolescence); and (4) transitional (through which a heterosexual moves toward homosexuality or a homosexual moves toward heterosexuality).

Other American researchers have concentrated not on the taxonomy of bisexuality, but on the development and adjustment of bisexuals in day-to-day life. Some of this research has been incidental to studies done on gay and lesbian or heterosexual populations; other researchers have looked at self-identified bisexual populations. Just as estimates on the percentage of bisexuals in the population are inconclusive, so is information about what percentage of people who have a history of sexual experience with both genders defines themselves as bisexual. What differentiates those who do from those who do not is still a matter of speculation, although research into the formation of bisexual identity suggests that, at least for them, identity formation is more open-ended than linear.

A common monosexual accusation is that bisexuals are "confused." Although this may be descriptive of some bisexuals before they find the label with which to self-identify, and some may also experience ongoing distress or uncertainty due to the dearth of societal validation (Weinberg and Williams 1994), some research has indicated that self-identified bisexuals are high in self-esteem, self-confidence, and independence of social norms (Rubenstein 1982; Twining 1983).

Much more attention has been given to bisexuals, especially males, who are heterosexually married than to those whose primary relationships are homosexual. These marriages are most successful when the partners communicate openly, the spouse is aware and accepting of the bisexual partner's sexuality, and both partners are committed to the relationship. Especially as the bisexual community brings self-identified bisexual people together, more bisexuals are choosing to partner with other bisexuals. These relationships may be monogamous, open, polyamorous, or—much more rarely—triadic.

Bisexuals bringing issues related to their sexual identities into therapy may seek help in interpreting their attractions to both genders; other issues are isolation and alienation, fears about coming out or about nonvoluntary disclosure of their sexuality, and relationship concerns.

What bisexual community spokespeople call "bisexual invisibility" hinders many individuals from easily resolving their concerns about adopting a non-normative sexual identity. Many do not know about the existence of a community of peers. While some individuals move towards a bisexual identity after considering themselves heterosexual, others have previously been gay- or lesbian-identified. As such, diversity in the bisexual community is broad, and will undoubtedly become broader as more people gain access to its institutions.

7. Cross-Gendered Persons

ARIADNE KANE

A. Conceptualizations

[On March 12, 1993, the "Op-Ed" page of *The New York Times* carried a full-page reflection on "How Many Sexes Are There?" The March/April issue of *The Sciences*, published by the New York Academy of Sciences, featured an article on "The Five Sexes: Why Male and Female Are Not Enough." These articles, by biologist Anne Fausto-Sterling, are evidence of a trend in changing definitions of gender roles over the past decade that is echoed in the appearance in 1995 of *Hermaphrodites with Attitudes*, a newsletter published by cross-gendered persons who endorse Fausto-Sterling's call for the medical profession to recognize gender diversity and cease using surgery and gender reassignment to force true hermaphrodites ("herms"), female pseudohermaphrodites ("ferms"), and male pseudohermaphrodites ("merms") into the dichotomous mold of male or female. (Editor)]

An Indigenous View

American society, with its cultural diversity, has long assumed that one's gender perception, role, and presentation are all a function of biological anatomy, as visually ascertained at birth. This biocentric viewpoint served as the basis for looking at sexual and gender variations for both sexologists and therapists. Until the mid-1970s, many sexual and gender options were seen and diagnosed as deviations of the male/female gender dichotomy and/or as types of sexual dysfunction. Gender options, as style modes of clothing and accouterment, gender shifts, and transsexualism were viewed as dis-eases [sic] of the psyche. Those who chose such options were considered "gender-conflicted" and were treated on the basis of known medical or psychological modalities (Pauly 1994).

Factors contributing to the current trend of changing gender roles include the rise and powerful articulation of feminism among both women and men; the knowledge explosion in molecular biology, specifically genetics and endocrinology, artistic diversity in both the visual arts and music with their individual styles and presentations (with cinema, television, and music increasingly dealing with gender and cross-gender issues), the emergence of an articulate, vocative, and visible gay-lesbian-cross-gender "community," and the influence of computer technology and its application in almost all sectors of American life. The impact of these factors on the daily lives of Americans—how they think, how they feel both about themselves as well as society, and how they act and present themselves to each other—has been awesome.

In this social context, there is a powerful drive to question the biocentric notion about gender being a derivative of the biomorphic nature of *Homo sapiens*, i.e., two sexes implies only two gender forms. This challenge to gender rigidity, in roles and presentations, is seen in many areas of American social and economic life. Women as bus drivers and heavy-equipment operators and men as nurses and secretaries represent only one aspect of the varied paradigm shift occurring in America in the nature of gender identity and its concomitant behaviors. Instead of a two-sexes/two-genders model, one needs a model of two or more sexes and many genders. This gives rise to a sociocentric view of gender, in which one can think of gender in terms of three basic parameters: perception (Jungian constructs of anima/animus), social role (cuing, interactions, and gender-role inventories), and presentation (modes of presenting one's self, for whom, when, motivations, etc.). A person is then seen as a composite of these three parameters, with the gender composite time-dependent and always subject to some change in one or more component over the lifespan.

The shift from focusing on individual gender conflict to looking at facets of gender diversity is evident in the "gender rainbow" paradigm suggested by gender counselors Leah Schaefer and Constance Wheeler, June Reinisch's concept of "gender flavors," and James Weinrich's model of "gender landscapes" (Francoeur 1991, 100-101). In these paradigms, the notion of conflict is broadened to include gender explorations and gender clarifications and how an individual can access these avenues in their search for personal growth in a tolerant and more nurturant society. Armed with this sociocentric model of gender, one can study CD/CG (cross-dressing/cross-gender) behaviors and conflicts with a more-sensitive approach to the issues and problems of gender expression in an ethnoculturally diverse American society.

Traditionally, the terms "transvestite" (TV) and "transsexual" (TS) have been used to label individuals, mostly males, who wear apparel usually associated with the other sex, or who want to cross a gender boundary and seek anatomical congruity with the other sex. These terms are too inclusive and stigmatize the person, who may be on a gender exploration, or who sees personal gender expression as only one piece in their total personality matrix. To deal with this limitation, the following new glossary has been proposed, with the terms serving as "mileposts" on the road to gender "happiness:"

- A "cross-dresser" (CD) is a person, male or female, who wears an item or items of apparel usually worn by the other gender; it is a descriptor of behavior and includes previously used terms like TV (transvestite), FI (female impersonator), and DQ (drag queen).
- "Cross-gender" (CG) refers to a person, male or female, who desires to cross and explore a gender role different from typical gender roles associated with their biologic sex. It can also be used as a behavior descriptor.
- A "transsexual" (TS) is a person, male or female, who has chosen a preferred gender role and wants anatomical congruity with that gender-role preference. This is achieved with an appropriate sex-hormonetherapy program and sex-reassignment surgery (SRS).
- "New Women/Men" refer to persons, male or female, who have transited to a preferred gender role, i.e., transgenderist, and have had sex-reassignment surgery.
- The "CD/CG/TS paraculture" refers to the community of people, males and females, whose general behavior patterns include a major component of gender-diverse activity.

The term "transgender" indicates that a person is crossing gender boundaries usually associated with traditional gender traits of one or the other sex. Transgender, transgendered, and transgenderist are also used to indicate transcending—rising above—traditional gender forms and expressions, a usage that has gained popularity both within the paraculture, as well as in the health-care and academic professions.

A Clinical View

The term "transsexualism" was coined by D. O. Cauldwell, an American sexologist, and popularized by Harry Benjamin in the 1950s and 1960s. Research on this phenomenon was facilitated in 1980 when the concepts of transsexualism and gender disorders were recognized in the American Psychiatric Association's *Diagnostic and Statistical Manual III*. In 1988, transsexualism was defined by the *DSM-III-R* as having the following diagnostic criteria:

1. persistent discomfort and sense of inappropriateness about one's assigned sex;
2. persistent preoccupation for at least two years with getting rid of one's primary and secondary sex characteristics and acquiring the sex characteristics of the other sex; and
3. having reached puberty (otherwise, the diagnosis would be childhood gender identity disorder).

DSM-IV has replaced the term "transsexual" with the generic term "gender disorder."

Transsexualism is estimated to affect at least 1 in 50,000 individuals over the age of 15 years, with a 1:1 male-to-female ratio. The greater visibility of male-to-female transsexuals may reflect a more-negative bias toward male homosexuality or a lack of available female-to-male treatment in a society. Whatever the real incidence, this disorder carries more social significance and impact than the actual prevalence might suggest because of the questions raised for anyone who watches and listens to transsexuals (and transvestites) in their frequent appearances on television talk shows (Pauly 1994, 591).

An individual's perception of his or her own body, and the way she or he feels about these perceptions, are important in the clinical diagnosis of gender disorders. In 1975, Lindgren and Pauly introduced a Body Image Scale, a thirty-item list of body parts, for which the individual is asked to rate her or his feelings on a five-point scale ranging from (1) very satisfied to (5) very dissatisfied. This scale is useful in following the progress and evaluating the success of sex-reassignment treatment.

Evaluating the outcome of sex-reassignment surgery is complicated and difficult. The most recent evaluation leaves little question that the vast majority of post-operative transsexuals claim satisfaction and would pursue the same course if they had to do it again. Post-operative satisfaction ranged from 71.4 percent to 87.8 percent for post-operative male-to-female transsexuals, with only 8.1 percent to 10.3 percent expressing dissatisfaction. Among female-to-male transsexuals surveyed, 80.7 percent to 89.5 percent were satisfied with their outcome, compared with only 6.0 percent to 9.7 percent who are not satisfied. The difference between male-to-female and female-to-male satisfaction was not statistically significant (Pauly 1994, 597).

The publicity that followed the American, Christine Jorgenson's sex-change surgery in Denmark in 1953, led to widespread public and professional discussion, and ultimately a distinction between transsexualism and transvestism. Harry Benjamin developed a three-point scale of transvestism, with transsexuals viewed as an extreme form of transvestism; he later came to regard the two as different entities.

The variety of cross-dressers includes fetishistic males and females who cross-dress for erotic arousal and those who enjoy cross-dressing to express their female persona; it includes individuals who cross-dress and live full-time in the other gender role, and those who cross-dress only occasionally and partially, with the whole range between these two ends of the spectrum.

In the 1960s, Virginia (Charles) Prince, a Los Angeles transvestite, began publishing *Transvestia*, a magazine for heterosexual cross-dressers. Encouraged by the response, Prince organized a "sorority without sisters," the Society for the Second Self or Tri-Ess (SSS), with chapters in several major cities. As a result of her worldwide travels, lectures, and television appearances, research on transvestism increased significantly because of the availability of research subjects.

As the cross-gender movement grew and became more visible, dissident and new voices appeared. At present, there are a variety of support groups for cross-dressers; some accept only heterosexual or homosexual and bisexual members, while others are not concerned with orientation. Some CD groups include transsexuals, others do not. In addition, there is a small industry, including "tall or big girl" fashion shops and mail-order catalogs, that cater to the clothing and other needs of cross-gendered persons.

B. Current Status of American CD/CG Paraculture

It is apparent that many more American males and females are openly cross-dressing than at any other time in this century. The motivations for this activity are quite varied, ranging from female- or male-impersonation (FI, MI) as "Miss Coquette" or "Mr. Baggypants" at a Halloween party, to lip-synching performances at FI and MI reviews (i.e., "La Cage aux Folles" or Mr. Elvis Presley look-alike shows), to femme expressions in daily activities such as work or socializing. While it appears less obvious, there are many more females who cross-dress with the intent of expressing some part of their masculine persona (animus).

In the last decade, there has been a dramatic increase in the number of social contact groups, both for males who cross-dress and want social contact with others of similar persuasion in a secure setting, and for females who want to explore more fully the dimensions of their masculinity. Both female and male adolescents are cross-dressing to reflect feelings of their favorite musical stars, e.g., k.d. lang, RuPaul, Boy George, Melissa Etheridge, Michael Jackson, or the Erasure or Indigo Girls rock groups. (It should be noted that several of these performers are also known to be gay or lesbian, perhaps creating some public confusion about the association between cross-dressing and sexual orientation.) There are also young people who show some affinity for atypical gender-role expression. These may be early phases of mixing aspects of traditional gender norms with explorations of the limits of gender duality, that may benefit from appropriate professional help.

One segment of this paraculture is definitely exploring gender options with the aim of resolving gender conflict. Such conflicts may not be limited to the intrapsychic, but extend into resolving tensions between the rights of individual expression and the norms of conventional gender roles and presentations. When the desire to shift gender is experienced, there is a need for professional help in understanding the motivation for the gender shift and to develop a program that will clarify some of the important questions that individual may have to address in pursuing such a choice. Such a program of gender exploration or gender shift may involve the use of hormones and also the decision to have sex-reassignment surgery. Some of these people label themselves transgenderists, in the sense noted above, and can fully develop and express an alternate gender role and lifestyle. Some may be satisfied with this shift and not want to pursue sex-reassignment surgery. For others, after living full-time for one-and-a-half to two years in the preferred gender role, the decision is to complete the shift with surgery; in which case, the label "transsexual" is appropriate.

Currently, more and more people are challenging the binary gender forms and want to explore other gender options. If surgery is not the ultimate objective, these individuals may choose to blend traits and become more androgynous or gynandrous, expressing a feminine-masculine or masculine-feminine gender. This segment of the paraculture is also receiving some attention.

As for legal issues involving CD/CG behaviors, most states do not have statutes that specifically prohibit the practice of CD/CG presentation in public. However, there may be some local ordinances that restrict this behavior in their jurisdiction. If tested in the judicial system, such laws would probably be ruled unconstitutional. Obtaining a legal change of name is not a problem in most areas of the country, and should be accompanied by some form of public notice for creditors, usually in the classified section of a local newspaper. Change of birth certificate may pose some problems; again each state has its own guidelines.

With regard to sex-reassignment surgery, a medical group created a pamphlet of guidelines for the preoperative transsexual about 1980. *Standards of Care* details guidelines for the client, health-care counselor/therapist, and the surgeon for handling the process of gender shift prior to surgery. This document is available from any of the organizations listed at the end of this section. Few, if any medical-insurance plans pay for this surgery, which for a male-to-female runs about $8,000 to $10,000. In recent years, several reputable gender clinics have discontinued providing this surgery.

For health-care professionals, sex educators, counselors, therapists, physicians, nurses, and sexologists, there are two major programs available to update one's knowledge about gender or to facilitate change in attitudes about gender issues. Segments in the standard Sexual Attitudes Reassessment (SAR) Workshop focus on CD/CG behaviors and lifestyles. In the Gender Attitude Reassessment Program (GARP), the focus is on all aspects of gender and its diversity; ten to fifteen units deal with specific topics in the phenomenon of gender. Both of these programs are given at national professional meetings and in continuing education programs at major universities and mental health centers in the U.S.A.

Within the paraculture structures, there are several programs for CD/TG/TS/AN Americans. Two of the oldest and "personal-growth-oriented" are Fantasia Fair and Be All. Fantasia Fair, founded twenty years ago, provides a living/learning experience for adult male cross-dressers who want to explore the many dimensions of their femme persona in a tolerant open community. Fantasia events, often held at Provincetown on Cape Cod, Massachusetts, emphasize personal growth in all aspects of their programming. Be All, an offshoot of Fantasia Fair, focuses on the practical and social aspects of femme persona development. It is usually held in a motel/inn near a major city and is sponsored by a regional group of social contact organizations.

Organizations providing information on gender issues include:

American Education and General Information Service, P. O. Box 33724, Decatur, Georgia 33033.

Harry Benjamin International Gender Dysphoria Association, P. O. Box 1718, Sonoma, California 95476.

I.C.T.L.E.P., Inc., 5707 Firenza St., Houston, Texas 77035-5515.

Outreach Institute of Gender Studies (OIGS), 126 Western Ave., Suite 246, Augusta, Maine 04330.

The Society for the Second Self (Tri-Ess) (for heterosexual cross-dressers only), P. O. Box 194, Tulare, California 93275. (Publishes a quarterly magazine, *Femme Mirror*, and other support material.)

8. Significant Unconventional Sexual Behaviors

In this section, we consider a group of "other" sexual behaviors. These include sexual coercion (rape, sexual harassment, and child sexual abuse), prostitution, pornography, paraphilias, and fetishes. As a general rule, Americans tend to view heterosexual relations between consenting adults in an ongoing relationship, such as marriage, as the norm. It is true that such sexual relations are the modal pattern in the U.S.A. (Laumann, et al., 1994), as is true of every culture. However, the earlier reviews of extramarital sex, alternative lifestyles, homosexuality, and bisexuality all serve to illustrate that sizable percentages of Americans engage in sexual behavior which departs from this assumed norm. American sexologists have struggled for some time to develop acceptable terminology to describe other sexual practices. The concept of sexual orientation has allowed us to view homosexuality and bisexuality as variations in orientation. Similarly, the concept of gender transposition has provided a terminology for examining cross-gender behaviors.

Typically, non-marital sexual practices have been labeled as sexual deviance or sexual variance. There are, however, at least two problems with such terms. First, no matter what the proper sociological conceptualization, these terms inevitably convey a sense of pathology, dysfunction, or abnormality to behaviors which are situationally defined. For example, consider the act of exhibitionism, exposing one's genitals to another. When practiced in the streets, the act is defined as a crime and is quite rare. When practiced in certain business establishments, the practitioner is paid for the act and clients pay to see it; and when practiced in the privacy of one's home with an intimate partner, it is seen as normal and healthy sexual interaction. Second, some of these behaviors are, in fact, quite common. Muehlenhard reviews evidence that shows many women are victims of sexual coercion. Several recent surveys provide evidence that nearly one quarter of Americans view pornographic video tapes each year (Davis 1990; Laumann, et al. 1994). It appears that relatively small percentages of Americans participate in any one of the various fetish groups reviewed below. However, taken together and added to the forms of non-marital sexual expression we have already reviewed, it seems clear that rather large percentages of Americans do participate in some "other" form of sexual practice [D. L. Weis, Coeditor].

A. Coercive Sex

Sexual Assault and Rape   CHARLENE MUEHLENHARD AND BARRIE J. HIGHBY

Basic Concepts. The conceptualization of rape and the treatment of rapists and rape victims in the United States have changed substantially since the 1970s, largely due to the work of feminists. The situation is complex, however; there are many perspectives on these issues. Even the terminology related to rape is at issue. Some persons have suggested that the term "rape" be replaced by "sexual assault" in order to emphasize the violent nature of the act and to place greater emphasis on the behavior of the perpetrator; recent reforms in the criminal codes of some states no longer speak of rape, but of varying degrees of sexual assault (Estrich 1987; Koss 1993a). Others, however, prefer to retain the term rape "to signify the outrage of this crime" (Koss 1993a, 199). Some regard rape as different and more serious than assault and contend that "to label rape as a form of assault . . . may obscure its unique indignity" (Estrich 1987, 81). There is no clear consensus in the law, the popular media, research literature, or feminist writings. We will use the term rape.

Similarly, some persons have suggested that the term "rape victim" be replaced by "rape survivor." Each term has advantages. The term "victim" highlights the harm that rape causes. The term "survivor" has more optimistic connotations and, thus, may empower someone who has been raped; it also highlights similarities between people who have survived rape and people who have survived other life-threatening events. The term "survivor," however, may perpetuate the stereotype that only rapes that are life-threatening—that is, that involve a great deal of extrinsic violence—are worthy of being regarded as "real rape." Thus, we will use the term rape victim.

Definitions. Rape can generally be defined as one person's forcing another to engage in sex against that person's will. This general definition, however, leaves many questions unanswered (Muehlenhard et al. 1992b). What behaviors count as sex? Whom do these definitions cover? What counts as force? In the United States, thinking about each of these questions has changed since the 1970s, and controversy remains.

Defining rape is complicated by the fact that there are many types of definitions. In the legal domain, the federal government and all fifty states each have their own definition. Legal definitions are written by legislatures, which are composed primarily of men; thus, these definitions are likely to be written from men's perspectives (Estrich 1987). The definitions held by the general public are influenced by the law, the media, folk wisdom, jokes, and so forth. Some researchers base their definitions on legal definitions, which makes them subject to the same biases as legal definitions; others make conscious decisions to deviate from legal definitions, which they find biased or inadequate. Finally, there are political definitions, written by activists wanting to make various political points. For example, MacKinnon (1987, 82) wrote,

> Politically, I call it rape whenever a woman has sex and feels violated. You might think that's too broad. I'm not talking about sending all of you men to jail for that. I'm talking about attempting to change the nature of the relations between women and men by having women ask ourselves, "Did I feel violated?"

Persons who regard legal definitions as the most valid criticize such political definitions as being too broad (e.g., Farrell 1993). Based on the assumption that language is power, however, political activists have resisted the status quo by challenging widely held definitions and encouraging people to think about the assumptions behind these definitions.

Prior to the 1970s, rape definitions of sex often included only penile-vaginal sexual intercourse. This definition has been criticized as too phallocentric, promoting the ideas that an act must involve a man's penis and must have the potential for reproduction to count as "real sex" (Muehlenhard, et al. 1992b; Rotkin 1972/1986). Currently, most definitions of rape use a broader conceptualization of sex, including many kinds of sexual penetration (e.g., penile-vaginal intercourse, fellatio, cunnilingus, anal intercourse, or penetration of the genitals or rectum by an object). Some definitions are even broader, including behaviors such as touching someone's genitals, breasts, or buttocks (Estrich 1987; Koss 1993a).

Another contentious question involves whom these definitions cover. If rape is defined as forced penile-vaginal intercourse, then by definition an act of rape must involve a woman and a man; this definition would exclude coercive sex between two individuals of the same sex. In requiring the perpetrator to penetrate the victim sexually, such definitions would exclude situations in which a woman forced a man to engage in penile-vaginal intercourse, because such situations would involve the victim penetrating the perpetrator (Koss 1993a). Some definitions of rape include only the experiences of adolescents and adults (e.g., Koss et al. 1987), whereas others also include the experiences of children (e.g., Russell 1984).

Prior to the 1970s, rape laws in the U.S. included a "marital exclusion," exempting husbands from being charged with raping their wives. As of the mid-1990s, this marital exclusion has been removed from the laws of all fifty states, as well as from federal law (X 1994). In some states, however, laws still define rape between spouses more narrowly than rape between non-spouses, giving married women less legal protection than unmarried women. Furthermore, some state laws still treat rape less seriously if it occurs between two people who have previously engaged in consensual sex (X 1994).

Yet another contentious question involves what counts as force. Most definitions include physical force and threats of physical force. Many also include sex with someone who is unable to consent due to being intoxicated, asleep, or otherwise unable to consent. There is disagreement, however, regarding how intoxicated one needs to be, whether the alcohol or drugs need to be administered to the victim by the perpetrator, what happens if both persons are intoxicated, and so forth. This is particularly relevant in cases of date or acquaintance rape (Muehlenhard et al. 1992b).

Even regarding threats of physical force, there is disagreement about how direct such threats need to be. For example, in some court cases, appellate judges have made it clear that a woman's acquiescing to sex with a man because she is afraid that he will harm her (e.g., because he has harmed her in the past, or because they are in an isolated location and he is behaving in a way she regards as threatening) is not sufficient to define the incident as rape. Instead, these judges interpreted the law to mean that a woman should not cry and give in; she should fight like a "real man" (Estrich 1987).

Conceptualizations of Rape and Rapists. Prior to the changes initiated by feminists in the 1970s, rape was commonly conceptualized as a sexual act in which a man responded to a woman's sexual provocations. Rapists were often assumed to be either black men who raped white women or else men who were lower class or crazy and who were provoked by women who dressed or behaved too provocatively (Davis 1981; Donat and D'Emilio 1992; Gise and Paddison 1988; LaFree 1982; Mio and Foster 1991). Amir (1971, 273), for example, discussed "victim precipitated rape," which he conceptualized as rape incited by female victims who spoke, dressed, or behaved too provocatively (e.g., who went to a man's residence or who attended "a picnic where alcohol is present." MacDonald (1971, 311) wrote that

> the woman who accepts a ride home from a stranger, picks up a hitchhiker, sunbathes alone or works in the garden in a two-piece bathing suit which exposes rather than conceals her anatomy invites

rape. The woman who by immodest dress, suggestive remarks or behavior flaunts her sexuality should not be surprised if she is attacked sexually. These ladies are referred to as "rape bait" by police officers.

Female victims were often thought to have desired or enjoyed the experience (Gise and Paddison 1988; Griffin 1971; Mio and Foster 1991; Muehlenhard et al. 1992a). For example, Wille (1961, 19) wrote about the typical rape victim's "unconscious desires to be the victim of a sexual assault." Husbands, in effect, "owned" their wives and were entitled to their sexuality; thus, the concept of marital rape was nonexistent (Clark and Lewis 1977; Donat and D'Emilio 1992). Sexual acts that occurred between acquaintances or on dates were often assumed to be sexual encounters that the woman had let get out of hand (Amir 1971).

In the 1970s, feminist writers began to conceptualize rape as violence (e.g., Brownmiller 1975; Griffin 1971). In a classic article, Griffin (1971, 312) wrote that

> rape is an act of aggression in which the victim is denied her self-determination. It is an act of violence which, if not actually followed by beatings or murder, nevertheless always carries with it the threat of death. And finally, rape is a form of mass terrorism, for the victims of rape are chosen indiscriminately.

Griffin also emphasized that the fear of rape limits women's freedom, and as such, rape functions as do other forms of violence. Conceptualizing rape as violence has numerous advantages: acknowledging the serious consequences of rape; highlighting the similarities between the effects of rape and the effects of other kinds of violence; taking the emphasis of rape prevention off restricting women's sexual behavior; and acknowledging that rape affects all women, even those who have not actually been raped, by instilling fear and, thus, restricting women's freedom.

Currently, in the United States, it is common to hear people say, "Rape isn't sex; it's violence." Nevertheless, many writers, both feminist political activists and researchers, have found value in conceptualizing rape as having elements of sex as well as violence (Muehlenhard et al. in press). Feminists have discussed similarities between rape and other sexual situations, which may also be coercive:

> So long as we say that [rape involves] *abuses of violence, not sex,* we fail to criticize what has been made of sex, what has been done to us through sex, because we leave the line between rape and intercourse . . . right where it is. (MacKinnon 1987, 87, emphasis in original)

Understanding rapists has been enhanced by investigating both the sexual and the violent aspects of their behavior and attitudes. Rapists are more likely than nonrapists to become sexually aroused by depictions of sexual violence, as well as to feel hostile toward women, to accept rape myths and violence against women, and to view heterosexual relationships as adversarial. They drink more heavily and are more likely to have drinking problems, which may serve as a release or an excuse for sexually violent behavior. They are also more likely to have witnessed parental abuse or to have been physically or sexually abused in their childhoods. They begin having sexual experiences, either consensual or nonconsensual, earlier than nonrapists (Berkowitz 1992; Burt 1991; Koss and Dinero 1988; Finkelhor and Yllo 1985; Malamuth 1986; Russell 1982/1990).

Drawing on over thirty years of rehabilitation work with convicted sex offenders at the New Jersey State facility, William Prendergast (1991) has described a developmental-descriptive profile of typical compulsive-repetitive sex offenders. This profile involves two childhood experiences or characteristics: an unresolved inadequate personality and an unresolved preadolescent or early adolescent sexual trauma. Rapists try to cope with these unresolved personality traits by denial and overcompensating. In seeking to control their victims, they use terror, physical force, and any behavior that will degrade the victim. Pedophiles, on the other hand, accept their unresolved traits and seek to control their victims by seduction.

Current research has also dispelled other myths about rape. Rapists represent all ethnic groups and social classes (Russell 1984, 1990), and the overwhelming majority of rapes occur between acquaintances (Kilpatrick et al. 1987; Koss et al. 1988; Russell 1984) and between members of the same race or ethnicity (Amir 1971; O'Brien 1987). Research shows that men can be raped and women can be rapists (Brand and Kidd 1986; Muehlenhard and Cook 1988; Sarrel and Masters 1982; Waterman et al. 1989). Still, because rape and the fear of rape affects women more than men, and because of the differences in how women's and men's sexuality is conceptualized in the United States, some claim it would be a mistake to treat rape as a gender-neutral phenomenon (MacKinnon 1990; Rush 1990). Finally, "thanks to the feminist movement, no one any longer defends the dangerous claim that rape is a sexually arousing or sought-after experience on the part of the victim" (Palmer 1988, 514).

Prevalence. How prevalent is rape? Estimates of prevalence depend not only on how rape is defined, but also on the methodology used. Telephone surveys consistently result in lower prevalence estimates than do questionnaires or face-to-face interviews. Conducting interviews in the presence of family members yields low prevalence estimates, which is understandable given that many rape victims do not tell their families about having been raped, and some rape victims have been raped by family members. Asking respondents if they have been "raped" yields low prevalence estimates because many rape victims do not label their experience as "rape." Asking respondents a single question about their experiences generally yields low estimates, perhaps because asking only one such question fails to elicit memories of rapes that may have occurred in numerous contexts (e.g., with strangers, casual acquaintances, dates, or family members, obtained by force or threats of force or when the victim was unable to consent, and so forth; Koss 1993a).

Two sources of information on rape published by the government are generally inadequate: The *Uniform Crime Reports*, published by the Federal Bureau of Investigation (FBI 1993), include only rapes that were reported to the police—a small minority of all rapes (Russell 1984). The *National Crime Victimization Surveys*, conducted by the government's Bureau of Justice Statistics (BJS), also have serious methodological flaws (BJS 1993; Koss 1992; Russell 1984).

The best approach to studying the prevalence of rape involves confidentially asking respondents a series of questions about various experiences that meet the definition of rape. Studies using this procedure have found that approximately 20 percent of adult women in the United States have been raped (see Koss 1993b, for a review). As mentioned previously, most of these rapes occur between acquaintances of the same race. Percentages of men who report being raped or otherwise sexually victimized are generally lower than the percentages of women who report such experiences (Koss 1993a), although because most prevalence studies have focused on female respondents, information on men's being raped is scant.

Consequences for Rape Victims. American research on the consequences of rape has improved dramatically in the past several decades. Prior to the 1970s, studies of rape victims consisted of occasional case studies of victims who sought psychotherapy, a biased sample because most rape victims do not seek therapy and those who do are likely to be atypical (e.g., to be in greater distress, to be of higher socioeconomic status, etc.). The next generation of studies involved assessing rape victims who reported the rapes to police or emergency-room personnel; this practice allowed longitudinal assessment of the effects of rape, but the samples were still biased because most rapes are never reported. Currently, the consequences of rape are often studied by surveying random samples of people; this practice allows comparisons of rape victims with nonvictims, regardless of whether the rape victims had reported the rapes to authorities or had labeled their experiences as rape. Some researchers even conduct prospective studies, in which members of a high-risk group (e.g., first-year college students) are assessed annually; if someone in the sample is raped during the time span of the study, their pre- and postrape adjustment can be compared (Muehlenhard et al. 1992a).

Research shows that most rape victims experience psychological, physical, and sexual problems after being raped. It is important to remember, however, that not all rape victims experience all of these consequences;

some experience many consequences, whereas others experience relatively few consequences.

The psychological consequences of rape can include: depression; fear; anxiety; anger; problems with self-esteem and social adjustment; feeling betrayed, humiliated, or guilty; and experiencing problems with trust (Lystad 1982; Muehlenhard et al. 1991; Resick 1993). Recently, some of these psychological consequences have been conceptualized as post-traumatic stress disorder (PTSD) (American Psychiatric Association 1994). This symptom constellation includes reexperiencing the rape (such as in dreams or flashbacks), feeling numb and avoiding reminders of the rape, and experiencing hyperarousal (such as insomnia, difficulty concentrating, outbursts of anger, or an exaggerated startle response; see Herman 1992; Resnick et al. 1993).

Sexual problems resulting from rape can include avoidance of sex, decreased sexual satisfaction, sexual dysfunctions, and flashbacks to the rape during sex (Kilpatrick et al. 1987; Lystad 1982; Warshaw 1988). Some rape victims engage in sex more than before, perhaps because the rape made them feel devalued, as if "they now have nothing left that's worth protecting" (Warshaw 1988, 74).

The physical consequences of rape can include physical injuries (including injuries from weapons or fists, as well as vaginal or anal injuries), sexually transmitted diseases, pregnancy, reproductive problems causing infertility, and various psychosomatic problems. Physical consequences can also include alcohol and drug abuse and dependency (Koss 1993b; Resick 1993; Warshaw 1988).

Divulging the rape to someone else may result in various problems: feeling embarrassed or uncomfortable; reliving aspects of the experience; being disbelieved or blamed; and being questioned about one's behavior and dress, which might lead victims to feel as if they are "on trial," needing to prove their innocence to others. When rape victims report the rape to the police, their report may be disbelieved or trivialized, although police attitudes and sensitivity have improved during the last several decades. Should the case go to trial, recent "rape shield laws" generally prohibit defense attorneys from inquiring about the victim's sexual past; nevertheless, defense attorneys typically try to discredit victims (Allison and Wrightsman 1993; Estrich 1987; Gelles 1977; Griffin 1971; Roth and Lebowitz 1988).

Contrary to stereotypes, acquaintance or date rape is as traumatic as stranger rape. Victims of acquaintance rape are as likely as victims of stranger rape to experience depression, anxiety, problems with relationships, problems with sex, and thoughts of suicide (Koss et al. 1988). Women who are raped by acquaintances they had trusted may doubt their ability to evaluate the character of others and may be reluctant to trust others. Women raped by acquaintances are less likely than women raped by strangers to be believed and supported by others. If the victim and rapist have mutual friends, the friends may be reluctant to believe that a friend of theirs could be a rapist; they may thus be reluctant to take the victim's side against the perpetrator, and the victim may feel unsupported. If the rapist goes to the same school, workplace, or social functions as the victim, the victim may feel uncomfortable and withdraw from these activities (Kilpatrick et al. 1987; Koss et al. 1988; Russell 1982/90; Stacy et al. 1992; Warshaw 1988). There has been considerable controversy about the prevalence of date or acquaintance rape, especially on college campuses (Roiphe 1993).

People raped by their spouses or cohabiting partners may experience consequences that other rape victims do not experience. Whereas stranger rape is typically a one-time occurrence, the rape of wives and other partners is likely to occur repeatedly and may last for years. The more frequently women are raped by their husbands or partners, the more likely they are to suffer from grave long-term consequences. Many victims of marital or partner rape are also physically abused. Victims raped by a spouse or partner must decide either to live with the perpetrator and risk subsequent rapes or to divorce or separate, which requires many lifestyle adjustments, and which does not guarantee that they will not be raped by their ex-spouse or ex-partner (Koss et al. 1988; Lystad 1982; Russell 1982/90). The consequences may also extend to children living in the household (Mio and Foster 1991). Children may be aware of the problem and may even witness the rapes. They may fear the parent or stepparent who is the perpetrator and may develop negative views of sex and relationships.

Boys and men who have been raped experience many of the same consequences that girls and women do, although being a male victim may result in additional consequences that female victims do not encounter. Being forced into submission is incongruous with the male sex-role stereotype that espouses control and dominance. Males raped by females often confront beliefs that they must have desired and enjoyed the act and that male victims are less traumatized than are female victims. Males raped by other males, regardless of their sexual orientation, often confront homophobic attitudes. Males also confront the belief that, if they had an erection, they must have wanted sex (Groth and Burgess 1980; Russell 1984; Smith et al. 1988; Sarrel and Masters 1982; Warshaw 1988).

Lesbian and gay rape victims may encounter difficulty in attempting to obtain services from crisis-intervention and social-service centers, as these agencies are not prepared to serve lesbian and gay clients (Waterman et al. 1989). Obtaining services may require that gay or lesbian rape victims "come out," revealing their sexual orientation and risking possible discrimination, possibly even losing their jobs, housing, or children should others find out (legal protection of lesbians and gays in the United States varies from city to city and state to state). If rape occurs in a lesbian or gay relationship in which the perpetrator is the biological parent of the children, if the victimized partner leaves the relationship, she or he will probably have to leave the children with the perpetrator. Furthermore, the gay and lesbian community is often tight-knit, so lesbian or gay rape victims may be reluctant to tell mutual friends or to participate in the community's social functions (Grover 1990; Muehlenhard et al. 1991).

Punishment of Rapists. The modal punishment for rapists is no penalty, given that most rapes are not reported to the police (Koss et al. 1988; Russell 1984). Even those that are reported rarely result in arrest and conviction (Allison and Wrightsman 1993). Among those who are convicted of rape, punishment varies from merely being placed on parole to life in prison.

Until the 1970s, the penalty for rape included the death penalty; 89 percent of the men executed for rape in the United States from 1930 to 1967 were African-American (Estrich 1987, 107). In 1977, the U.S. Supreme Court found the death penalty for rape to be unconstitutional (*Coker v. Georgia*, 433 U.S. 584, 1977; see Estrich 1987). Studies of actual sentences given to convicted rapists reveal that the harshest penalties for rape are still imposed on African-American men accused of raping white women (Estrich 1987; LaFree 1980). There is also a bias against convicting affluent, successful men and men who rape women they know or who rape women who do not conform to cultural expectations of how a "good woman" should behave (Estrich 1987; LaFree et al. 1985).

Prevention. Prior to the 1970s, rape prevention was generally regarded as women's responsibility. Because rape was regarded as an act of sex incited by provocative women, rape prevention consisted largely of expecting women to restrict their behavior (expecting women not to talk or dress provocatively, not to go out at night, etc.).

Currently, a variety of prevention strategies are common in the U.S. (Muehlenhard et al. 1992a). There are still those who urge women to restrict their behavior, and research shows that women do indeed restrict their behavior due to the fear of rape: Women report avoiding going outside alone at night, not talking to strangers, wearing bulky clothing, having unlisted phone numbers, and so on (Gordon and Riger 1989). These efforts limit women's freedom and diminish women's quality of life. Furthermore, this approach focuses on stranger rape, a minority of all rapes, and does not address the causes of rape.

There are other prevention strategies that are not predicated on women's restricting their behavior. For instance, many universities have installed extra lighting and emergency telephones (often marked by blue lights) to help women feel safer. These strategies are aimed primarily at preventing stranger rape, however, and will not help women who are raped indoors by husbands, partners, dates, or other acquaintances. To address these problems, many universities have initiated lectures and workshops presented to college dormitory residents, fraternities, sororities, and athletic groups; some high schools and even junior high schools have also initiated such programs, although they sometimes meet resistance from parents and school boards (Donat and D'Emilio 1992). There is evidence that such programs can lead to attitude change (Jones and Muehlenhard 1990), although the effectiveness of these strategies in actually preventing rape is unknown.

Some women take self-defense classes. For example, Model Mugging or En Garde programs teach women self-defense strategies that utilize women's physical strengths, such as lower-body strength (Allison and Wrightsman 1993). Research shows that active-resistance strategies (e.g., physically fighting, screaming, and running away) are generally more effective than the passive-resistance strategies (e.g., coaxing, begging, crying, reasoning, or doing nothing), and active strategies do not increase the risk of physical harm (Bart and O'Brien 1984; Ullman and Knight 1992; Zoucha-Jensen and Coyne 1993). Unfortunately, no strategy is effective all of the time or for all people, and even experiencing an attempted rape can be traumatic. Furthermore, many feminist theorists have argued that, because most rapists are men, it is unfair to place the burden of rape prevention on women (Berkowitz 1992; Koss 1993b).

The most important strategies for preventing rape involve working for broader social change: changing men's and women's attitudes about rape, sex, and gender roles; working toward gender equality; discouraging violence as a problem-solving technique; and emphasizing that coercive sex in any context, whether with a stranger or acquaintance, is never acceptable.

Child Sexual Abuse and Incest   DIANE BAKER AND SHARON E. KING

Knowledge of child sexual abuse (CSA) has undergone cycles of awareness and suppression, as both professionals and the general public have struggled to come to terms with its existence since CSA first gained widespread attention in the 1890s, when Freud proposed that it was at the root of hysterical neurosis. Although modern clinical work tends to confirm the link between CSA and various neuroses, Freud quietly abandoned his early belief in response to the strong opposition from Victorian attitudes of that era. Linking neuroses with repressed childhood sexual conflict, Freud's Oedipal and Electra complexes, was revolutionary, but at least much more acceptable than admitting the reality and prevalence of child sexual abuse.

During the past twenty years, CSA has received renewed attention from American clinicians, researchers, and the general public. Recently, CSA has been the focus of a substantial amount of American research that has, in turn, led to broader recognition of the initial and long-term problems associated with CSA.

Definitions. The definition presented by the National Center on Child Abuse and Neglect is "Contact and interactions between a child and an adult when the child is being used for the sexual stimulation of the perpetrator or another person." This definition is problematic, however, in that it leaves key terms open to question. For example, in considering who is a child, researchers have employed cutoff ages anywhere between 12 and 17 years for victims of CSA. In deciding who is an adult, some researchers have required perpetrators to be at least 16 years of age; others have required age differences between victim and perpetrator of five years or ten years; still others have not required any age difference at all if force or coercion was used. In determining what is sexual stimulation, some authors include noncontact experiences, such as exhibitionism or propositioning, whereas others require manual contact, and still others, genital contact. In a 1987 study designed to determine the effect of varying the operational definition of CSA on its prevalence, the percentage of college men identified as victims ranged from 24 percent to 4 percent based on how restrictive the criteria used were. The parameters defining CSA, therefore, will have strong implications for how widespread a problem society considers it.

A second major issue is determining, in the absence of physical injury, what has been damaged. This issue is complicated by a consistently identified minority of victims who report such experiences as having been positive. Some authors have pointed to this subset and wondered whether the abuse was against the individual or societal values, and further, whether in defining CSA, consideration should be given to the victim's view of the experience as negative or positive. Yet, a victim's view of a CSA experience as positive does not preclude the possibility that it was a harmful or damaging one.

A cogent argument against using the victim's assessment of the experience as positive or negative in defining abuse is that the inequalities of knowledge, sophistication, and power inherent in any child-adult relationship prevent the child from giving informed consent to engage in sexual behavior. From this perspective, it is the emotional and intellectual immaturity of the child that causes the developmentally inappropriate exposure to adult sexuality to be harmful and abusive.

These issues of definition influence the composition of the groups studied by researchers and, thereby, the results obtained. As yet, there has been no completely satisfactory way to define CSA to ensure that the research results are relevant and helpful to the greatest number of people. Currently, the most widely used set of criteria for defining CSA are contact experiences between a child aged 12 or younger with an individual five or more years older, or between a child aged 13 to 16 with an individual ten or more years older. These criteria emphasize the differences in developmental maturity between the victim and perpetrator, while minimizing the inclusion of age-appropriate sexual exploration between peers as sexual abuse.

Prevalence of CSA. Accurate estimates of the prevalence of CSA in either the general population or clinical populations have been difficult to obtain, due in part to the differences in operational definitions discussed above, in part to the sensitive nature of the topic, and in part to differing methods of assessment (e.g., questionnaire, face-to-face interview, or telephone interview). Estimates of the percentage of adult women who have experienced CSA vary from 6 percent to 62 percent and of adult men from 3 percent to 31 percent. In general, percentages are higher among clinical samples than among community-based samples. Additionally, more people disclose abuse histories when information is gathered via an interview rather than by questionnaire, when specific questions about childhood sexual experiences are asked, and when such terms as "sexual abuse" and "molestation" are avoided (see also Prendergast 1993).

More confidence can be placed in the accuracy of prevalence rates when the samples used are large, random, and community-based. In a 1990 random sample of over 2,000 adults across the United States, 27 percent of women and 16 percent of men reported having experienced such abuse as children. In other large-scale studies, about 25 percent of women and 17 percent of college men have been identified as having histories of CSA. The majority of CSA cases are perpetrated by a nonrelative, generally an acquaintance or family friend; about 30 percent of girls are abused by a relative (with about 4 percent involving father-daughter incest), whereas about 10 percent of boys are abused by a relative. Finally, the prevalence of CSA does not seem to vary with social class or ethnicity (Hunter 1990).

Theories Explaining CSA. Upon hearing of CSA, people generally react strongly, wondering how such abuse could occur. Originally, professionals held a simplistic view of CSA, considering it to be the result of the isolated actions of a depraved and flawed perpetrator. In the past several decades, however, two more-complicated theories of CSA have dominated the field.

Family systems theory posits that families function as integrated systems and that irregularities in the system are displayed through symptomatic behavior in one or more family members. From this perspective, the occurrence of incest reflects a distortion in the family system, specifically in the marital subsystem, that is being expressed through a parent's (usually the father's) sexual behavior with a child. This model proposes, then, that CSA occurs as a misguided attempt to cope with problems in the family. Treatment, therefore, involves recognition of the underlying problems and the institution of changes by all family members rather than through removal of the perpetrator.

Although less simplistic than earlier proposals, this model has been criticized for seeming to blame the victims for the abuse and by removing responsibility from the perpetrator. Additionally, the model is relevant only to incest, which is a relatively small fraction of the CSA cases.

In order to address these concerns, Finkelhor proposed a four-factor model of CSA incorporating some aspects of the family systems' perspective, but shifting responsibility for the abuse back to the perpetrator. He conceptualized CSA as resulting from an interaction between environmental circumstances and the personality of the perpetrator, rather than simply as inherent in the perpetrator or in the family system.

In this model, four preconditions must be met for CSA to occur. First, the offender must have some motivation to abuse sexually; thus, CSA satisfies some emotional or sexual need in the perpetrator that is not readily satisfied in other ways. Second, the offender must overcome his or her inhibitions against CSA. Inhibitions may be overcome in a variety of ways, such as substance use, rationalization, the influence of stressors, or personality factors (e.g., impulsivity). Third, environmental impediments to the abuse must be removed; the offender must have private access to a child. Therefore, she or he may target children who are without consistent adult supervision or obtain employment that provides contact with children. Fourth, the offender capitalizes on the lowered resistance of the child; children who are insecure, needy, uneducated about sexuality, and/or have a trusting relationship with the offender have lowered resistance. These children are less likely to be assertive in refusing abusive overtures or to disclose immediately that the abuse took place. All of these factors, working in concert, allow CSA to occur.

Some people remain uncomfortable with the third and fourth preconditions of this model, because they appear to place some responsibility for the CSA outside the perpetrator and onto the child and his or her non-offending parent(s). Finkelhor stresses, however, that without the first and second preconditions, qualities, and behaviors of the offender alone, CSA would never occur. These preconditions place responsibility for the act squarely with the perpetrator.

Who Is at Risk for CSA? The environmental circumstances in which boys are sexually abused versus those in which girls are sexually abused differ in some important ways. Some of these differences were highlighted by Tzeng and Schwarzin (1987), who compared the demographic characteristics of boys and girls in over 15,000 substantiated cases of sexual abuse in Illinois. They found that girls who had been sexually abused tended to live in homes that did not differ from those of the general population in the numbers and kinds of parents/caretakers present, whereas boys who had been sexually abused were significantly more likely to come from single-parent homes and/or from families with either new or many children/dependents. On the other hand, the girls' families tended to display significantly more dysfunction, and caretakers were more physically and/or mentally impaired than caretakers in the boys' families. These results are similar to those of Finkelhor, who found the risk of CSA among girls increased approximately twofold when a mother was absent from the home. These findings point to an increased risk of sexual abuse when parents are absent, impaired, or overworked (see also Prendergast 1993).

Some differences in the perpetrators of abuse of boys versus girls have also been identified. Tzeng and Schwarzin (1987) and others reported that sexual abuse of boys is more likely to be perpetrated by a stranger, whereas abuse of girls is more likely to be perpetrated by a relative. Further, when boys are abused by a relative, these relatives are more likely to be within five years of age of the boys, whereas relatives who abuse girls are more likely to be ten or more years older than the girls. Although the vast majority of perpetrators of both boys and girls are men, boys are more likely to be abused by women than are girls (17 percent versus 2 percent). Thus, for boys, CSA experiences tend to occur outside the home and to be perpetrated by a nonfamily member or, if inside the home and perpetrated by a relative, the relative is less likely to be a parent-figure or to have adult status. Girls are more likely to be abused within the home by a relative ten or more years older. Risk to girls is increased by sevenfold for girls with a stepfather. A general consensus among researchers is that more boys are somewhat more likely to experience severe abuse (actual intercourse) than are girls.

These differences suggest boys and girls may be experiencing CSA situations that require differing coping skills. Girls may, more typically, need to adjust to the notion that an adult in a position of trust has been abusive, and boys may, more typically, need to adjust to the notion that the world outside the home is not safe and may need to react to a more-severe physical experience. It should be stressed that all of these differences are generalizations, and there is substantial overlap in the nature of the CSA experiences of boys and girls.

Initial Effects of CSA. Although researchers have identified a wide array of problems occurring among children who have been sexually abused, most have failed to find any substantial differences in symptomatology between male and female victims. When studying these initial effects, researchers have recently begun to divide subjects into three groups based on their stage of development: preschool (ages 3 to 6), school age (ages 7 to 12), and adolescent (ages 13 to 17). By using these groupings, the presence and frequency of various behaviors and symptoms can be compared to those considered developmentally appropriate for the stage.

Among both preschool boys and girls, the most frequent behavioral symptom associated with CSA experiences is an increase in sexualized behaviors (Beitchman et al. 1991). This increase has been noted in a number of studies using a variety of methodologies, including chart review, parent rating, observed play with anatomically correct dolls, and human-figure drawing. However, the prevalence of this behavior varies widely depending on the context, from 10 percent of the sample in the case of human-figure drawing to 90 percent of the sample in play with anatomically correct dolls; still, this finding is among the most robust in the literature. [*Note:* These studies do not make conparisons to groups of "normal" children and their rate of sexual behavior. (D. L. Weis, Coeditor)]

Emotionally, preschool children are likely to respond to sexual abuse with anxiety, signs of post-traumatic stress (e.g., nightmares, vigilance, or bed wetting), and depression (Kendall-Tackett et al. 1993). These children are also likely to exhibit greater immaturity than nonabused controls, showing increases in both dependency and impulsivity relative to physically abused and nonabused age peers.

Among school-age children, researchers have focused on behavioral problems that interfere with academic and social success. Sexually abused children have been assessed by their teachers as significantly less able than their nonabused peers to learn in the school environment. This difficulty may be a function of the wide range of behavioral and emotional problems they display. For example, approximately half of the school-age girls with histories of CSA show high levels of immaturity and aggression (Kendall-Tacketts et al. 1993). Similarly, both parents and teachers rated sexually abused children as more emotionally disturbed and neurotic than their classmates, displaying both depression and a wide range of fears (Beitchman et al. 1991; Browne and Finkelhor 1986; Kendall-Tackett et al. 1993). Additionally, like preschool children, the sexually abused school-age boys and girls display clear-cut increases in sexualized behaviors, including such problems as excessive and inappropriate masturbation and sexual aggression (Browne and Finkelhor 1986; Kendall-Tackett et al. 1993). All of these symptoms would be expected to lead to problems in school for children, regardless of their intelligence.

A somewhat different presentation has been observed among adolescents with a history of sexual abuse. Although acting-out behaviors, such as running away, substance use, and sexual promiscuity were more common in these adolescents than their nonabused peers, they were less common than among clinical groups of adolescents (Beitchman et al. 1991). The predominant finding among sexually abused adolescents is an increase in depressive symptomatology, such as low self-esteem and suicidal ideation. This depression may be expressed through self-injurious behaviors, as exhibited by more than two thirds of sexually abused adolescents (Kendall-Tackett et al. 1993), or through suicide attempts made by a third of these adolescents in a clinical sample.

Although there is an extensive list of symptoms and problems associated with the initial effects of sexual abuse, it should be noted that not all children display such effects. Indeed, 20 percent to 40 percent of sexually abused children have been found to be asymptomatic at the time of initial assessment (Kendall-Tackett et al. 1993). Unfortunately, some of these children have become symptomatic by the time of later assessments. There is fairly consistent evidence that from a third to a half of sexually abused children show improvement in symptom presentation twelve to eighteen months after the abuse, although another quarter to a third show deterioration in function.

Long-Term Effects of CSA. Although the long-term effects of CSA experiences have been studied in both men and women, the majority of the work has been done with women. Reviews of this research have been conducted by Browne and Finkelhor (1986) and Beitchman et al. (1992). The results vary somewhat, depending on whether the samples were community-based or clinically based; still, there is substantial overlap across the two populations.

In both clinical and community-based surveys of women with histories of CSA, the most common long-term effect is depression. Depression is particularly striking among the community-based samples of victims, in which significantly more women with a history of CSA report both more-severe and more-frequent episodes of depression compared to those without such experiences. Almost one in five college women reporting a history of CSA had been hospitalized for depression compared to one in twenty-five women who had not been abused. In a community-based study of the Los Angeles area, researchers found that a history of CSA was associated with a fourfold increase in the lifetime prevalence rate for major depression among women. Other prominent depression-related symptoms include problems with self-esteem, which appear to intensify as time elapses from the abuse, and an increased risk for self-injurious or destructive behaviors (Browne and Finkelhor 1986).

Increases in problems with anxiety occur among some women with sexual abuse histories. Problems with anxiety are more prominent among clinical samples than community samples (Beitchman et al. 1992; Brown and Finkelhor 1986). Anxiety seems to be particularly prevalent among women sexually abused by a family member and in cases in which force was used during the abuse.

Relationship difficulties are more common among women with histories of CSA compared to nonabused women. Abused women are more likely to fear intimacy and to have sexual dysfunctions, particularly when the abuse was more severe and/or was perpetrated by a father or stepfather (Beitchman et al. 1992). A history of CSA in women is also associated with an increased risk of further revictimization in the forms of rape and domestic violence.

Much less research has been conducted on the long-term effects of sexual abuse in men; much of the information available has been based on clinical case studies or extrapolated from studies with some adult male victims, but in which the majority of the subjects were women. Therefore, conclusions are much more tentative. Several community-based surveys found that men who reported CSA experiences exhibited a higher rate of psychopathology (e.g., depression, anxiety, or symptoms of post-traumatic stress) than those who did not report such experiences. Men who have been sexually abused have reported significant problems with poor self-esteem and self-concept. Men may respond to such feelings by self-medicating with alcohol and drugs, as indicated by the large degree of substance abuse and dependence among male victims; sexually abused women, on the other hand, report greater levels of depression and anxiety.

Clinicians suggest that intense anger, sexual dysfunction, problems with intimacy, gender-identity confusion, and substance abuse are prominent symptoms for males with a history of CSA seeking therapy. Additionally, disclosure of sexual abuse is particularly difficult for men. Issues related to disclosure include fears of not being believed (particularly if the perpetrator was female), fears others will consider them homosexual, concerns that they are homosexual because they have been abused by a man, and issues related to masculine identity.

Correlates of More-Severe Effects. Although the preceding paragraphs present a grim picture of the aftereffects of CSA, not all individuals suffer such severe effects. In fact, in a given sample of abuse survivors, a quarter to a third of the individuals can be expected to appear symptom-free on the chosen assessment instruments (Kendall-Tackett et al. 1993). About one third of these asymptomatic individuals may become symptomatic at later assessments. Still, these differences in outcome have led researchers to examine variables associated with more-severe effects.

One variable consistently associated with more-severe effects is the use of force (Beitchman et al. 1992; Browne and Finkelhor 1986; Kendall-Tackett et al. 1993). This finding has been most robust in studies of the initial effects of CSA among children (Kendall-Tackett et al. 1993). A number of researchers also have identified an association between the use of force and victims' reports of the degree of trauma experienced among adult survivors as well (Beitchman et. al. 1992; Browne and Finkelhor 1986). There is also some evidence that family-background variables, such as high levels of conflict and low levels of support, are related to more-severe effects. The situation is further complicated in that, for some individuals, the use of force has been associated with a decrease in self-blame, thereby reducing the severity of effects.

The relationship of the perpetrator to the victim has also been examined. Among children, the initial effects of abuse are more severe when the perpetrator has a closer relationship to the child (Kendall-Tackett et al. 1993). The situation is less clear for the long-term effects among adults. In general, whether the perpetrator was a family member has little impact on later outcome among adults (Beitchman et al. 1992; Browne and Finkelhor 1986) with one important caveat: Trauma and psychopathology effects are more severe if the abuse was perpetrated by a father or stepfather (Beitchman et al. 1992; Browne and Finkelhor 1986). This difference may represent a greater degree of family dysfunction and a more significant breach of trust when a father perpetrated the abuse (Beitchman et al., 1992). The lack of a general effect of intrafamilial versus extrafamilial abuse among adults may be a reflection that it was the quality of the relationship with the abuser (i.e., how much he was trusted) that influenced outcome rather than whether he was a relative. Finkelhor has extended this notion by proposing that the important variable is the degree to which the child was seduced and persuaded by the perpetrator, whether or not the child had a prior relationship with the perpetrator.

A third major variable examined to determine its relationship to long-term effects has been the duration of the abuse. This variable has been difficult to assess for a number of reasons. First, the criterion for CSA of long duration varies among researchers, from abuse that occurred for more than six months to abuse that occurred for more than five years. Second, as noted by Beitchman et al. (1992), researchers have tended to use very different measures, some assessing a subjective sense of harm, and others assessing a more objective degree of psychopathology. There is some evidence, however, that CSA of longer duration leads to an increase in psychopathology in community-based samples. The two major reviewers of long-term effects of CSA (Beitchman et al. 1992; Browne and Finkelhor 1986) have both concluded that more research must be conducted before firm conclusions can be drawn, whereas reviewers of initial effects have suggested that longer duration is associated with a worse outcome (Kendall-Tackett et al. 1993).

The severity of the CSA experience has also been examined in relation to psychopathology and harm in adulthood; here again, the results are mixed. There is general agreement that increased trauma and maladjust-ment are associated with contact abuse versus noncontact abuse, both initially and in the long term. Further, abuse involving genital contact, whether manual, oral, or invasive, is associated with more-serious outcomes than kissing or clothed contact. Researchers differ, however, in whether invasive contact as compared to manual contact is associated with increased trauma in the long term. Initially, invasive contact is associated with a worse outcome (Kendall-Tackett et al. 1993). Further research is necessary to determine the long-term effects of invasive contact.

One nonabuse-related variable, family support, has also been consistently identified as contributing significantly to both the initial and long-term effects of CSA. Kendall-Tackett et al. (1993) reviewed three studies examin-ing the relationship of maternal support to symptom outcome in children who had been sexually abused. All three studies concluded that children whose mothers were low in support exhibited worse outcomes following the abuse. This conclusion was supported by the findings of other researchers who examined long-term coping among college women with histories of CSA.

Theories about the Nature of the Effects. Researchers have cataloged a multitude of symptoms associated with CSA that therapists have, in turn, attempted to address in treatment. Therapeutic treatment of any type is greatly facilitated by a theory or framework to organize and to approach symptoms. Many clinicians note that it is an impaired trust in self and others that underlies many of the symptoms associated with CSA.

This difficulty with trust has led some researchers and therapists to conceptualize the symptoms associated with CSA as a function of post-traumatic stress disorder (PTSD). This disorder encompasses some of the more-troubling symptoms experienced by sexual abuse survivors, such as depression, nightmares, and affective numbing. All of the PTSD conceptualizations of sexual abuse incorporate the idea that exposure to the abuse is experienced by the victim as overwhelming, due to intense fear and/or to extreme violations of beliefs about the way the world operates. When confronted with the abuse then, the child is unable to cope, given his or her current level of internal resources, and so must distort cognitions and/or affect in an effort to adjust to the experience. These distortions are, then, the basis for the symptoms that appear following the abuse.

However, there are some limitations to the application of PTSD to sexual abuse symptomatology. Among the most compelling of these limitations is the fact that the symptoms of PTSD do not encompass all of the problems associated with CSA. Also, many survivors do not meet the criteria for PTSD. In one group of survivors, only 10 percent could be diagnosed with PTSD at the time of the survey, and only 36 percent could have ever been diagnosed with the disorder. Clearly, more work is needed in the conceptualization of the symptoms associated with a history of CSA.

Toward this end, Finkelhor has proposed a theory of CSA symptomatology, the Traumagenic Dynamics Model of Child Sexual Abuse (TD), which attempts to address the empirical findings more fully. The TD model emphasizes that the trauma associated with CSA may be due to the stress of the ongoing nature of the abuse situation, rather than an isolated event that is overwhelming and far removed from usual human experience (as described by the PTSD criteria in the *Diagnostic and Statistical Manual III Revised* (*DSM III-R*). This differentiation does not suggest that one type of trauma is more harmful than another; it simply highlights a qualitative difference in events that may lead to different coping responses and/or symptomatology.

The TD model includes four dynamics that occur to varying degrees in any CSA situation and that are postulated to contribute to the symptoms identified in the research literature. These dynamics include: (a) Traumatic Sexualization, which occurs when the child is taught distortions about his or her sexuality, and may lead to the increase in sexual dysfunctions observed among adult survivors; (b) Betrayal, which occurs in two ways, either when the child finds that an adult she or he trusted has hurt him or her or when the child discloses the abuse to an adult who refuses to believe or help the child. Finkelhor characterized the increased depression and revictimization seen among survivors as a result of the lost trust and unmet dependency needs. It can also lead to increased anger and hostility as a mechanism of keeping others at a distance; (c) Powerlessness, which occurs in a variety of ways in the CSA situation; for example, when the child finds himself or herself incapable of physically warding off the perpetrator. Powerlessness is further manifest when the child is unable to extricate himself or herself from the abuse situation or unable to do so in a satisfactory way (e.g., without being removed from the home). This powerlessness dynamic leads to anxiety and fear in adult survivors as well as a decreased coping ability; (d) Stigmatization, which occurs either directly through the labeling of the child by others as bad or dirty following disclosure of the abuse or indirectly through the sneaking behavior of the perpetrator and the admonitions that the abuse be kept secret. Stigmatization may be associated with the low self-esteem and the self-destructive behaviors, such as substance abuse and suicide attempts, observed among survivors.

However the effects are conceptualized, recent evidence has demonstrated that CSA is prevalent and commonly results in harmful effects. Finkelhor and others have attempted to make sense of a confusing array of symptoms presented by many, but not all, victims of CSA. More-sophisticated research designs (e.g., involving structural equation modeling) are required before the relationship between various experiences of CSA and outcomes become more clear.

Clergy Sexual Abuse

SHARON E. KING

In the past ten years, sexual abuse of minors by clergy has become a major public scandal and crisis for all the churches, although the public attention is often focused on the Catholic clergy because of their requirement of celibacy. Until recently, charges of sexual abuse by clergy were treated as an internal problem within Church jurisdiction and not reported to police. The main issue for Church officials was to control damage to their institution's image. That silence exploded with national media coverage of the case of James Porter, a Massachusetts priest, who victimized, often sadistically, over 200 minors in several states between 1960 and 1972, and a similar case in Louisiana. Media coverage triggered a flood of new charges of abuse. Ten of 97 priests in a southwestern diocese, nine of 110 in a midwestern diocese, seven of 91 in a southern diocese, and fifteen of 220 and forty of 279 in the eastern United States were charged in civil and criminal suits. In December 1993, twelve of 44 priests in a California minor seminary were charged with having been sexually active with 11- to 17-year-old boys between 1964 and 1987. Between 1984 and 1994, an estimated 5,000 survivors reported their abuse to Church authorities. By early 1995, over 600 cases were pending (Sipe 1995, 26-28). Meanwhile, the Catholic dioceses of Sante Fe and Chicago admitted being in danger of bankruptcy; between 1984 and 1994, Catholic officials admitted to paying out over a half billion dollars in damages to survivors (Rossetti 1991).

Sipe (1995, 26-27) estimates that, at any one time, 6 percent of Catholic clergy are sexually involved with minors; the situation does not appear to be as serious in Protestant and Jewish circles. One third of the cases of abuse by priests can be classified as true pedophiles, with a three-to-one preference for boys. Two thirds of the abusive priests are involved with adolescents with a more even gender distribution. Four times as many priests are involved with adult women as with minors.

"The crisis of image has been compounded by church authorities who were slow, defensive, and even duplicitous in their public response as abuse by clergy became public and other indications of trouble mounted" (Sipe 1995, 8). Even as late as 1992, fully two thirds of the American Catholic bishops were confused or unconvinced that there is a problem of sexual abuse by the clergy, although even the Pope has acknowledged the crisis.

Civil authorities have responded by extending the statutes of limitations on reporting such abuse. New laws in all states require any professional to report suspected sexual abuse of a minor; in many states, any person is required to report suspected abuse. However, such laws are often vague in defining "reasonable suspicion."

The year 1990 was a watershed as confused Church authorities began losing their damage-control efforts to the rising tide of victims' voices expressed in civil and criminal lawsuits against priests, dioceses, and religious orders. Support groups for survivors spread across the nation: Victims of Clergy Abuse LINKUP, Survivors Connections, American Coalition for Abused Awareness, and Survivors Network of Those Abused by Priests (SNAP).

In 1992, the Catholic Archdiocese of Chicago adopted a model plan for processing allegations of clergy abuse; unfortunately, it remains incompletely and unevenly implemented. In 1993, St. John's (Benedictine) Abbey and University in Collegeville, Minnesota, established an ecumenical Interfaith Institute to study this problem.

How survivors are treated by a religious community varies greatly, and survivors should be reminded that, when they set out to seek legal action against anyone, the course may be extremely difficult. Far too often, survivors feel that they are revictimized by a system that protects the abuser, rather than one that is sensitive to the trauma of the victim.

Satanic Ritual Abuse   SHARON E. KING

"Satanic" ritual abuse is another area of recent concern. As the 1989 report by the ritual abuse task force by the Los Angeles County Commission for Women shows, it is a controversial area that requires careful and serious attention. Books and groups dealing with cult and ritual abuse continue to expose this alarming and controversial topic. Unfortunately, it often takes on the atmosphere of a circus and witch hunt. There is no scientific evidence that this type of CSA is widespread or common.

Recovered Memories and False Memory Syndrome   DIANE BAKER AND
                                                                SHARON E. KING

Of great concern recently are a number of cases involving children in day-care centers reporting that they were sexually abused by their caretakers.

Although some investigations have led to convictions, other cases have been found to lack any substance at all. In one case, a middle-aged male retracted his charge that a prominent Catholic cardinal archbishop had sexually abused him when he was in the seminary, claiming that his lawyer had probably prompted or influenced his "recovered memory" of being abused.

Concern over false reporting is not limited to young children. Teachers all over the country report that they no longer touch their students as they once did. Hugging a child, allowing a young child to sit on one's lap, or being alone in a room with a child are just some of the things that teachers must now monitor. Cases in which children have projected sexual abuse that was happening at home onto a teacher, and the false reporting of sexual abuse by a teacher in order to get back at the teacher are now issues that mental-health workers and the legal system must unravel in some of the more unusual cases placed before the courts.

Better questioning of young victims by mental-health and legal workers is one area that continues to improve. As with any inquiry, it has become evident that the invitation to tell what happened cannot, in any way, be colored by suggestive questioning on the part of the interviewer.

Increasing numbers of adult women and men have begun to disclose incidents of sexual abuse that happened to them when they were children. Their sexual abuse occurred during a time when it was not safe for children to disclose such information and when the support systems of the state and therapeutic communities were not in place.

In some incidents where adults disclose what happened to them as children, they have always known what happened to them, but they have never before spoken out or sought help. In some instances, however, adults report "remembering" or retrieving lost memories of childhood sexual abuse. Remembering and dealing with unresolved issues of childhood sexual abuse can often explain to a victim how and why his or her life has been affected by the abuse. Weight problems, depression, sleep disturbances, intimacy and sexual disorders, unexplained fears, compulsive behaviors, self-esteem issues, and psychosomatic disorders are just a few of the symptoms that can be resolved when an adult finally confronts the repressed and unresolved trauma of childhood sexual abuse.

In a response to their own daughter's accusation of being sexually abused by her father, the Freyds' of Philadelphia started an organization that examines the False Memory Syndrome. Dr. Pamela Freyd and her husband have been most public in their denial of their daughter's accusations, basing their response on a belief that her "memories" were suggested by her therapist. After a period of silence on her part, Dr. Jennifer Freyd publicly countered her parents' denial of what happened to her, citing her mother's public debate as yet another example of her intrusiveness. Whatever the struggle between the members of the Freyd family, this small organization has brought forth a concern about the authenticity and reliability of retrieved memories.

Sexual Harassment   ROBERT T. FRANCOEUR

Public awareness of sexual harassment is also a recent phenomenon in American culture, even though sexual discrimination was prohibited by federal law over thirty years ago by Title VII of the 1964 Civil Rights Act. In 1979, Stanford University Law School professor Catharine MacKinnon broadly defined sexual harassment as "the unwanted imposition of sexual requirements in the context of a relationship of unequal power." More-recent definitions include unwanted sexual advances, touches, and actions between peers and coworkers. Sexual harassment can also occur when a subordinate offers sexual favors in return for a promotion, better evaluation, or grade.

A 1976 *Redbook* magazine survey reported that 88 percent of the more than 9,000 women responding reported having experienced overt sexual harassment and regarded it as a serious work-related problem. A 1988 *Men's Health* survey reported 57 percent of the magazine's male readers stated they had been sexually propositioned at work, and 58 percent admitted they had at least occasional sexual fantasies about coworkers.

In a broad survey of over 20,000 federal government workers, 42 percent of the women and 15 percent of the men reported having been sexually harassed at work in the preceding two years. Most of the harassers, 78 percent, were male. Both women and men victims reported that the harassment had negative effects on their emotional and physical condition, their ability to work with others on the job, and their feelings about work. Women were considerably more likely than men to have been harassed by a supervisor, 37 percent versus 14 percent (Levinson et al. 1988).

A random-sample survey of undergraduate women at the Berkeley campus of the University of California found that 30 percent had received unwanted sexual attention from at least one male instructor during their undergraduate years. Examples of harassment included: verbal advances and explicit sexual propositions; invitations to date or to one's apartment; touches, kisses, and fondling; leering or standing too close; writing emotional letters; being too helpful; and offering grades in exchange for sexual favors (see Table 5).

Table 5

Varieties of Sexual Harassment in the Workplace

Type of Harassment	% of Males Reporting	% of Females Reporting
Uninvited sexual attention	20	50
Touching	16	45
Suggestive invitations, talk, joking	15	42
Harassed by same sex	12	7

Based on De Witt 1991; U.S. Merit Systems Board, 1981, 1988, and other sources.

It took over 15 years for the government to identify the sexual-harassment implications of the 1964 Civil Rights Act, and even longer for business corporations to understand the law. In a 1981 *Redbook–Harvard Business Review* survey, 63 percent of the top-level managers and 52 percent of middle managers believed that "the amount of sexual harassment at work is greatly exaggerated." Although the amount of sexual harassment in the workplace has probably decreased because of the growing awareness of its risks, *Working Woman* reported that at least some business managers believe that "More than 95 percent of our complaints have merit" (Gutek 1985).

Although most research on sexual harassment has focused on its occurrence in the workplace and academia, sexual harassment has also been studied in the relationship between psychologists or psychotherapists and their clients, and between physicians and other health-care workers and their patients.

In 1991, televised hearings of Supreme Court nominee Clarence Thomas and Anita Hill captured the nation's attention and sparked considerable debate and a growing awareness of sexual harassment. About the same time, the United States Navy became the focus of congressional investigations and media headlines when close to a hundred male pilots and officers at an annual Tailhook convention were charged with blatant examples of sexual harassment. Sexual harassment was also the subject of *Disclosure*, a popular and powerful 1994 film dealing with a female executive sexually harassing a male employee. As a result, practically every American corporation, professional organization, and educational institution has been forced to develop and adopt a statement defining the nature of sexual harassment and its policies for responding to it.

The "interim guidelines" issued by the Equal Employment Opportunity Commission in 1980, established that "unwelcome sexual advances, requests for sexual favors, and other verbal or physical conduct of a sexual nature constitute sexual harassment" when

1. submission to such conduct is made either explicitly or implicitly a term or condition of an individual's employment,
2. submission to or rejection of such conduct by an individual is used as the basis for employment decisions affecting such individual, or when
3. such conduct has the purpose or effect of substantially interfering with an individual's work performance or creating an intimidating, hostile, or offensive working environment.

In 1985, sociologist Barbara Gutek explained the occurrence of sexual harassment in the workplace in terms of a gender-role spillover model. She defined a work role as "a set of shared expectations about behavior in a job," and a gender role as "a set of shared expectations about the behavior of women and men." Gender-role spillover occurs when gender roles are carried into the workplace, often in inappropriate ways; for example, when the woman in a work group is expected to make coffee or take notes at the meeting. Despite many attitudinal changes in American society, women are still often seen as subservient and sex objects. When these aspects of gender roles spill over into the workplace, sexual harassment can easily occur, despite its negative effects on the employees and organization (Gutek 1985, 17).

B. Prostitution-Sex Workers

ROBERT T. FRANCOEUR AND
PATRICIA BARTHALOW KOCH

Historical Perspective

In the American colonies and early days of the United States, prostitution did not thrive in the sparse rural population. Despite a shortage of women, there were still women on the financial fringe in the small cities—recent immigrants and unattached, single women with few skills—for whom prostitution provided a way of survival and, at times, a way to find a husband or other male supporter. Female servants, apprentices, and slaves were not allowed to marry—a custom that encouraged prostitution. In contrast, indentured male servants are apprentices and could earn money to support themselves and their families, although they received no salary. Until the end of the American Civil War, African and Caribbean women brought to the United States in the slave trade were frequently and regularly exploited sexually by their owners (Barry 1984).

In the nineteenth century, the Industrial Revolution in New England and Middle Atlantic cities precipitated a massive influx of women from rural areas and from abroad looking for work and other opportunities. For example, women preferred the freedom that textile-mill work gave them to the tightly regulated life of a domestic servant, even though the wages were lower. There was little, if any, social life available after work hours for these single persons living apart from their families. Since they often shared a boarding house room with six to eight women, sometimes sleeping three to a bed, they frequently found their only relief at the local tavern. With men moving to the western frontier and a surplus of women, some women turned to prostitution for escape or affection. Too often they found that only sex work offered them a living wage (D'Emilio and Freedman 1988).

Throughout the mid-1800s, waves of immigration created a surplus of males who left their wives and families in Europe. In each new wave of immigration, some of the unattached immigrant women turned to prostitution in an effort to survive; some were already involved in "the trade." Males far outnumbered women in the western frontier towns and mining camps. Thousands of women were imported from Mexico, Chile, Peru, the South Pacific, and China to work in the flourishing brothels. After the Civil War, American cities followed the European practice of segregating prostitutes to certain areas of the city, which came to be known as "red-light" districts, and requiring them to register or be licensed. Regular physical examinations were required of all sex workers.

Between 1880 and 1920, prostitution was commonplace and legal. Since few prostitutes bothered to register, licensing was not effective in controlling disease. Police supervision only spawned crime and corruption via bribes for protection or "looking the other way." In 1910, Congress passed the Mann Act, which forbade the transportation of women across state lines for "immoral" purposes. In the decade before World War I, the Social Hygiene Movement, Women's Christian Temperance Union, Young Men's Christian Association, and other "purity" organizations worked for the criminalization of prostitution. By the end of World War I, these efforts were successful in ending politicians' tolerance of prostitution. "Legal brothels were destroyed and prostitutes were dispersed from stable homes in red-light districts to the city at large where they were less likely to be self-employed or work for other women and more likely to be controlled by exploitive men including pimps, gangsters, slum landlords, unscrupulous club owners, and corrupt politicians" (McCormick 1994, 91).

Currently, prostitution is illegal in all states except Nevada, where a 1971 court decision allowed counties with a sparse population the discretion of legalizing and licensing prostitution. State legal codes forbid making money from the provision of sexual services, including prostitution, keeping a brothel, and pandering, procuring, transporting, or detaining women for "immoral" purposes. Patronizing a prostitute is illegal in some states; a convicted offender may face a fine of $500 or more and a year or more in jail. In some states, pimps may be sentenced to ten to twenty years in jail and fined $2,000 or more.

The Spectrum of Sex Workers and Their Clients

Sex workers vary greatly in status, income, and working conditions, as well as in the services they offer—oral sex being the most common sexual practice offered. The vast majority of sex workers are females with male customers. Most prostitutes view their work as temporary, often on a part-time basis to supplement their traditionally female, poorly paid employment, and to support themselves and their families (McCormick 1994). The average prostitute's career lasts five years since youthful attractiveness is valued by customers. The sexual orientation of female sex workers reflects that of the larger population, and includes heterosexual, lesbian, and bisexual women. While sex workers are predominantly female, the "managers," at all levels, are predominantly male. Pimps—those who live off the earnings of a sex worker—often exploit the workers' romantic feelings, emotional needs, or fear of violence, and often come from disenfranchised groups themselves.

On one hand, many believe that females turn to prostitution because of dysfunctional families and individual psychopathology. The belief that female prostitutes are more likely than other women to be depressed, alienated, emotionally volatile, or engage in criminal activities and excessive use of alcohol and street drugs are often based on small, specialized samples (McCormick 1994). Research is also inconclusive as to the proportion of sex workers who abuse alcohol and other drugs. At least one study has indicated that call girls were as well adjusted as a control group of nonsexworker peers who were matched for age and educational level (McCormick 1994). Yet, for many juveniles, sexual and physical abuse seems to be related, at least indirectly, to their becoming involved with prostitution.

On the other hand, economic survival, not psychopathology, may be the most important contributing factor to engaging in prostitution. Poor and disadvantaged women may engage in sex work because it is the best paying or only job available. More-advantaged women may also engage in sex work because of the often unparalleled economic rewards, coupled with the flexibility in working hours, and the sense of control over clients. Although noncommercial sex is described as more satisfying by most sex workers, many report achieving satisfaction and orgasm though their work (Savitz and Rosen 1988).

On the lowest rung of female and male sex workers are those who solicit on the street; above them are those working in bars and hotel lobbies. Their limited overhead is matched by their low fees. Streetworkers, usually from the lower-socioeconomic class or run-away teenagers, face high risks of violence, robbery, and exploitation, as well as drug addiction, STDs, and HIV infections. Approximately 35 percent of streetwalkers have been physically abused and 30 to 70 percent raped while on the job (Delacoste and Alexander 1987). In addition, because of their visibility, streetworkers are the most vulnerable to harassment and arrest by law enforcement agents. While 10 to 20 percent of sex workers are streetwalkers, they constitute 90 percent of sex-worker arrests. Prostitution is the only crime in America in which the majority of offenders are female. In dealing with prostitutes, the courts often become a "revolving door system," with the sex worker posting bail and back on the street shortly after being arrested. Paradoxically, she is often fined, making it financially important for her to turn again to sex work to survive.

Government estimates suggest that half of the five million teenagers who run away from their homes each year spend at least some time as sex workers. Poor self-images, rejection by peers, few friends, unsupervised homes, and emotional, if not sexual, abuse in the home make them susceptible to the lure of big-city glamor where their survival needs force them to find work on the streets.

Houses of prostitution are less common today than they were in the past. The famous houses of the Storyville area of New Orleans or San Francisco's Barbary Coast were often very luxurious, and women both lived and worked in the same brothel for many years. Because of legal problems, most brothels today are run-down and in disrepair. If tolerated by the local police, they may be better maintained. In many places, regular, "go-go," and "topless" bars and massage parlors double as "fast-service" brothels. Brothels sometimes advertise their services in "underground" newspapers or in the "free press."

Escorts and call girls are at the upper level of sex workers. Young, slender, attractive, middle- and upper-class white women command the highest fees and the best working conditions among sex workers. Call girls typically see a small number of regular, scheduled clients. For them, sex work provides a much higher income than they would earn in almost any other profession, plus better control over their working hours.

The typical customer of a female sex worker, a "john," appears indistinguishable from the average American male. They are often involved in sexual relationships with another woman and report that they purchase sex by choice—perhaps for the adventurous, dangerous, or forbidden aspects of sex with a prostitute. Some frequent prostitutes because their usual sexual partners are unwilling to participate in certain sexual behaviors (like oral or anal sex). Other men frequent prostitutes because they have difficulty in establishing an ongoing sexual relationship because of lack of opportunity or physical or emotional barriers.

Most heterosexual male prostitutes are not street hustlers, but have steady customers or relationships that are ongoing and similar to those of a high-priced call girl. Their clients are often wealthy older women. Much more common are males who sell their sexual services to other males. In fact, most male prostitutes identify themselves as homosexual or bisexual. In large cities, gay male prostitutes cruise gay bars, gay bath houses, public toilets, bus and train stations, and other areas known to local clients.

Sex work also includes a variety of erotic entertainment jobs, including erotic dancing, live pornography or "peep shows," and acting in pornographic films and videos. Female burlesque shows have long been part of the American scene. However, the professional burlesque queens of the past have been replaced by amateur, poorly paid "table dancers." Feminists Barbara Ehrenreich, Gloria Hass, and Elizabeth Jacobs (1987) maintain that male go-go dancers play a role in advancing the rights of women and in breaking down patriarchal biases, because their female viewers treat them as sex objects and reduce their phallic power to impotence within bikini shorts.

The incidence of HIV infection and AIDS varies among sex workers and is increased by IV drug use, untreated STDs, and unsafe-sex practices. In general, it is high among female and gay male sex workers on the street, and lowest among high-priced call girls and heterosexual male prostitutes.

Economic Factors

In the early 1990s, there were an estimated 450,000 female prostitutes working in the United States, a profession lacking job security and fringe benefits, such as health insurance and social security. Most working outside the high-class escort services do not pay taxes. Nor are taxes paid on any of the monies that are exchanged in the underground economy associated with prostitution, such as: the monies that pass between prostitutes and their pimps; the hotel, motel, massage parlor, or bar owners and clerks; or the recruiters like cab drivers and doormen who make prostitution possible.

A 1985 survey of the cost of enforcing antiprostitution laws in the sixteen largest cities of the U.S. estimated police enforcement costs at $53,155,688, court costs at $35,627,496, and correction costs at $31,770,211, for a total 1985 cost of $119,553,395. In 1985, Dallas, Texas, police made only 2,665 arrests for the 15,000 violent crimes reported. They made 7,280 prostitution arrests at a cost of over $10 million and almost 800,000 hours of police work. In 1986, Boston, Cleveland, and Houston police arrested twice as many people for prostitution as they did for all homicides, rapes, robberies, and assaults combined. Meanwhile, 90 percent of perpetrators of violent crimes evaded arrest. Between 1976 and 1985, violent crimes in the sixteen largest cities rose by 32 percent while arrests for violent crimes rose only 3.7 percent, and arrests for robbery and homicide actually dropped by 15 percent. Equally important, the sixteen largest cities continue to spend more on enforcing prostitution laws than they do on either education or public welfare (Pearl 1987).

Working in pairs, police spend an average of twenty-one hours to obtain a solicitation, make an arrest, transport the prostitute to the detention center, process her papers, write up a report, and testify in court. Undercover police cruising the street looking to get a solicitation need frequent changes of disguises and rented cars. Making an arrest of a call girl is even more difficult, requiring greater expense for false identification and credit cards, hotel room, luggage, and other paraphernalia to convince the call girl this is a legitimate customer and not a policeman. The hotel room is usually wiretapped and the solicitation videotaped.

Arrests of prostitutes working in massage parlors present their own difficulties. It usually takes half an hour for an undercover policeman to undress, shower, and get into the massage, before an illegal service is offered. For a while, Houston police ran their own parlor. When that was declared entrapment by the courts, teams of 10 undercover officers began working existing modeling studios as customers. "Ten officers at a time, at $60 each, with no guarantee that we'd get solicited. . . . We could spend $3000 or $4000 and not make a case" (Pearl 1987).

Current and Future Status

Historically, sex workers have been blamed for the spread of sexually transmissible diseases (STDs). However, recent research has indicated that sex workers are much more likely to practice safer sex than the "average teenager" (McCormick 1994). While prostitutes are being blamed for transmitting HIV to their clients, data from the Centers for Disease Control indicate that only a small proportion of persons with AIDS contracted HIV from a prostitute. However, rates of HIV infection are quite high—up to 80 percent—among sex workers who also use intravenous drugs. Unfortunately, sex workers are usually at higher risk of contracting an STD, including HIV, from their lovers with whom they do not use a condom than from their clients with whom they use a condom.

Today in the United States, religious and political conservatives and radical feminists continue to oppose prostitution through such groups as WHISPER (Women Hurt in Systems of Prostitution Engaged in Revolt), an organization devoted to rescuing women and children from sex work. On the other hand, sex workers have begun to organize and advocate better working conditions and treatment through such groups as COYOTE (Call Off Your Old Tired Ethics), Scapegoat, and U.S. PROStitutes. These groups lobby for the decriminalization and legalization of prostitution, inform the public about the realities of prostitution, and offer various services to sex workers. In addition, liberal feminists inside and outside of the sex industry have founded the International Committee for Prostitutes' Rights (ICPR) in order to preserve their rights to life, liberty, and security.

In spite of continued economic inequities in the United States, some observers believe prostitution will decline because of the availability of effective contraceptives, a continued liberalization of sexual attitudes and divorce, a decline in the double standard in employment and sexual expression between the genders, and the risk of AIDS. In the Kinsey study of male sexuality in the late 1940s, 69 percent of white males reported having had at least one experience with a prostitute. The recent national study of 18- to 59-year-olds, *Sex in America*, found that only 16 percent of the men ever paid for sex (Gagnon, Laumann, and Kolata 1994). Yet, it seems that prostitution will continue to exist in some form or another. Although some people support the decriminalization of sexual activity between consenting adults, whether or not money is exchanged, this is not likely to happen in the United States.

C. Pornography and Erotica   ROBERT T. FRANCOEUR

The Legal Context

A landmark legal definition of obscenity was established by the Supreme Court in the 1957 *Roth v. the United States* decision. For a book, movie, magazine, or picture to be legally obscene,

- the dominant theme of the work, as a whole, must appeal to a prurient interest in sex;
- the work must be patently offensive by contemporary community standards; and

- the work must be devoid of serious literary, artistic, political, or scientific value.

This ruling permitted the publication in the U.S.A., for the first time, of such works as D. H. Lawrence's *Lady Chatterly's Lover,* James Joyce's *Ulysses,* and works by Henry Miller. However, this definition left the meaning of the term "community standards" unclear.

In the 1973 *Miller v. the United States* decision, the Supreme Court attempted to tighten the restrictions on obscene material by requiring that defenders of an alleged obscene work prove that it has "serious literary, artistic, or scientific merit." Despite this clarification, the courts still faced the near-impossible task of determining what has "literary, artistic, or scientific merit," who represents the "average community member," and what the "community" is. In 1987, the Supreme Court attempted to refine the *Roth* and *Miller* decisions by saying "a reasonable person," not "an ordinary member of the community," could decide whether some allegedly obscene material has any serious literary, artistic, political, or scientific value. Justice Potter Stewart further confused the situation when he remarked that "You know it when you see it."

In 1969, the Supreme Court ruled that private possession of obscene material was not a crime and is not subject to legal regulation. However, federal laws continue to prohibit obscene material from being broadcast on radio and television, mailed, imported, or carried across state lines. In recent years, pornographic material of any kind involving underaged children has been the target of repeated federal "sting" operations, raising issues of police entrapment.

Research Models

For at least two decades, there has been often-heated debate among the public, among feminists groups, and among scientists regarding the social and psychological impact of pornography, particularly materials that link sex with the objectification of women and with violence. A psychological research theory, the catharsis model, assumes that pornography and other sexually explicit materials provide a "safety valve" in a sexually repressive society. This model views pornography and other sexually explicit materials as "not so good, perhaps disgusting, but still useful" in diverting tensions that otherwise might trigger aggressive antisocial behavior. A different hypothesis suggests an imitation model in which sexually explicit books, pictures, and movies provide powerful role models that can, by conditioning and scripting, promote antisocial, sexually aggressive behavior. A third model of pornography addresses the personal and societal uses of pornography in different cultures, as a product designed as an alternative source of sexual arousal gratification and a way of enhancing masturbation. There are also models of pornography based on communication,

Marxist, psychoanalytic, feminist, and religious theories (Francoeur 1991, 637).

Commission Studies

A 1970 White House Commission funded research by experts in the field and concluded that neither hard-core nor soft-core pornography leads to antisocial behavior and recommended that all obscenity laws except those protecting minors be abolished. The majority of the commission concluded that pornography provides a useful safety valve in an otherwise sexually repressive culture. President Richard Nixon refused to officially accept the commission's report.

A 1986 investigation by then-Attorney General Edwin Meese did not sponsor any new research and took a different approach in reaching its conclusion. This commission reexamined the alleged connection between pornography and child abuse, incest, and rape by inviting anyone interested in speaking to the issue. The commission was widely criticized for having a preset agenda, for appointing biased commission members, and for relying on "the totality of evidence," which gave equal weight to the testimony of fundamentalist ministers, police officers, antipornography activists, and putative victims of pornography. This allowed the commission to conclude there is a "proven" causal connection between violent pornography and sexual assaults. This commission concluded that there is a causal connection between viewing sexually explicit materials, especially violent pornography, and the commission of rape and other sexual assaults. The commission recommended stricter penalties to regulate the pornography traffic, enactment of laws to keep hard-core pornography off home cable television and home telephone service, more vigorous prosecution of obscenity cases, and encouraged private citizens to use protests and boycotts to discourage the marketing of pornography. Among the many criticisms of the Meese Commission, Robert Staples, a black sociologist, pointed out that in the black community, pornography is a trivial issue. It is "a peculiar kind of white man's problem," because blacks see the depiction of heterosexual intercourse and nudity, not as a sexist debasement of women, but as a celebration of the equal rights of women and men to enjoy sexual stimuli and pleasure (Nobile and Nadler 1986).

Concurrent with the *Meese Commission Report*, the 1986 *Report of the U.S. Surgeon General* concluded that we still know little about the patterns of use or the power of attitudes in precipitating sexually aggressive behavior. Much research is still needed in order to demonstrate that the present knowledge of laboratory studies has significant real-world implications for predicting behavior. This report did not call for censorship, boycotts, and other tactics advocated by the Meese Commission. Rather, it recommended development of "street-based, innovative approaches" to educate the public about the different types of sexually explicit material and their possible effects.

Local Efforts at Regulation

In 1985, Andrea Dworkin, Catherine MacKinnon, and Women Against Pornography joined forces with local citizens' groups in Minneapolis, Minnesota, and Long Island, New York, to promote a new kind of pornography legislation. Using a civil rights argument, the proposed legislation stated that

> Pornography is sex discrimination. [Where it exists, it poses] a substantial threat to the health, safety, peace, welfare, and equality of citizens in the community . . . . Pornography is a systematic practice of exploitation and subordination based on sex that differentially harms women. The harm of pornography includes dehumanization, sexual exploitation, forced sex, forced prostitution, physical injury, and social and sexual terrorism and inferiority presented as entertainment.

The proposed legislation would have made producing, selling, or exhibiting pornography an act of sex discrimination. Women forced to participate in pornographic films, exposed by force of circumstances to view pornography in any place of employment, education, home, or public place, or assaulted by a male inspired by pornography could sue in civil court for damages based on sex discrimination. The American Civil Liberties Union (ACLU), Feminist Anti-Censorship Taskforce (FACT), and others challenged this kind of legislation. After considerable nationwide debate about civil rights, sex discrimination, and the constitutional right to free speech, these legislative efforts were abandoned.

Contemporary Aspects

The availability of sexually explicit, X-rated videocassette rentals and sales has become a major factor in American home entertainment. In the past decade, feminist soft-core pornography or erotica has made its mark in the popular media by portraying women as persons who enjoy sexual pleasure as much as men. This material appears in the pages of such mainstream women's magazines as *Cosmopolitan.* It is promoted by sex boutiques, with names like Eve's Garden, Adam and Eve, and Good Vibrations, catering to women. Another growing phenomenon is a variation on the Tupperware and Mary Kay Cosmetics home parties that bring women the opportunity to examine and, of course, purchase sex toys, love lotions, and lingerie in the privacy of their homes, surrounded by other women with whom they are friends. Exotic lingerie is also available in specialty stores in major shopping malls and by mail order from Victoria's Secret and Frederick's of Hollywood. Since 1992, Feminists for Free Expression, opposed to censorship and supported by such notables as Betty Friedan, Erica Jong, and Nancy Friday, has countered the efforts of some feminists to suppress pornography with an alternative view for the feminist community.

Erotic romance novels have become an acceptable form of soft-core pornography for women. Far outselling gothic novels, science fiction, self-help, and other books aimed at women, erotic romances often center around a traditional rape myth, a story in which the woman is at first unwilling, but finally yields in a sensual rapture to a man. In nonsexual characteristics, women who read erotic romantic novels are very much like women who do not. However, they appear to enjoy sex more and have a richer sexual fantasy life (Coles and Shamp 1984; Lawrence and Herold 1988).

Researchers and theorists, both feminist and nonfeminist, have almost completely ignored the existence of gay pornography. Lesbian pornography tends towards two extremes, about evenly divided in popularity, with little middle ground. Small independent presses publish soft-core pornography or erotica. Erotica on audiocassettes are very popular among lesbians. On the other side is a hard-core lesbian literature with a strong SM character that makes some feminists uncomfortable. *On Our Backs*, a tabloid magazine, is the largest publication of this type. *Eidos*, another tabloid, carries numerous ads for lesbians who desire bondage and dominance or sadomasochistic relations.

Considerably more pornography designed for homosexual men is available. Most of this genre is hard-core pornography with an emphasis on leather, SM, and younger males. At the same time, gay videos have pioneered in eroticizing the condom, nonoxynol-9, and safer-sex practices.

Dial-a-porn, or telephone sex, is a multimillion-dollar-a-year business producing massive profits for telephone companies and the companies providing phone-in services. In one year, dial-in services, including dial-a-porn, earned Pacific Bell $24.5 million and the phone-in companies $47.2 million. Because of constitutional concerns, the Public Utilities Commission and Federal Communications Commission (FCC) do not allow telephone companies to censor telephone messages or to discriminate among dial-for-a-message 1-900 services on the basis of content. Telephone companies cannot legally deny telephone lines to adults willing to pay the bill, although at least one court has ruled that it is not unlawful discrimination for a telephone company to refuse to provide services for dial-a-porn services. The FCC does require dial-a-porn services to screen out calls by minors by supplying their customers with special access numbers or having them pay by credit card. Concerned parents may pay a one-time fee to block all phones in a residence from access to dial-a-porn.

D. Paraphilias and Unusual Sexual Practices   BRENDA LOVE

In 1990, a Los Angeles man named Jeff Vilencia formed a group called Squish Productions. Through magazine articles, television appearances, and radio interviews, Vilencia had attracted more than 300 members to his group by 1995, all of whom shared the fetish of becoming aroused by the sight of others stepping on small living things such as snails and insects.

Although the fetish shared by Vilencia and his fellow members in Squish Productions may seem—and may in fact be—novel, paraphilias are nothing new. Paraphilias and fetishes have most likely been in existence in the U.S. for as long as there have been inhabitants on the Western continents. Although while a few immigrants may have brought sexual preferences, such as autoerotic asphyxiation, sadomasochism (SM), foot fetishes, and bestiality with them, other paraphilias have unquestionably developed here. In the world of paraphilias and fetishes, there is always something new. And thanks to increased awareness of and access to information about unorthodox sexual practices and their practitioners, interest in paraphilias appears to be growing in the United States.

Definitions

"Fetish," as defined for the American health professional by the *Diagnostic and Statistical Manual of Mental Disorders III* (*DSM III*), "is the use of nonliving objects (fetishes) as a repeatedly preferred or exclusive method of achieving sexual excitement." Such objects "tend to be articles of clothing, such as female undergarments, shoes, and boots, or, more rarely, parts of the human body, such as hair or nails" (American Psychological Association 1980).

The manual also states that the fetish object "is often associated with someone with whom the individual was intimately involved during childhood, most often a caretaker. . . . Usually the disorder begins by adolescence, although the fetish may have been endowed with special significance earlier, in childhood. Once established, the disorder tends to be chronic" (APA 1980).

"Paraphilias," on the other hand, are defined by *DSM III* as recurrent, fixed, compulsive, sexually motivated thoughts or actions by a personally or socially maladjusted individual that interfere with the individual's capacity for reciprocal affection. It is important to note that a paraphilia is not merely an activity that may appear strange or disgusting to an observer; rather, the activity or compulsion must meet all of the above criteria to be considered a problem requiring therapy.

It is also important to note in the area of paraphilias that many patients mention their unusual sexual interest simply to receive validation. The therapist can do much for the mental health of a patient by mentioning a support group or club for people with the interest, or by giving the patient the clinical name for the practice, stressing that the term paraphilia only applies when the above *DSM III* criteria apply. This can be followed by therapy to improve the person's self-esteem, communication, and social skills. The confession of activities involving minors or nonconsensual activities, however, of course requires immediate intervention by health professionals.

Background on Fetishes and Paraphilias in the U.S.A.

Fetishes change according to current fashions and customs. A hundred years ago, fetishists were aroused by such things as handkerchiefs, gloves, black rubber aprons, garters, corsets, enemas, seeing females wring the necks of chickens, or whipping horses. Today many of these stimuli have been replaced by pantyhose, high heels, tennis shoes, cigarettes, escalators, latex, or phone sex.

In addition, today's technology adds to the variety of ways a fetishist can pursue his or her predilection. In the past, one had either to create one's own drawings, or hope to catch a glimpse of an arousing person, object, or situation. Today, the fetishist has access to television, photographs, Internet newsgroups, clubs, videos, and magazines. Membership in fetish groups has increased during the last decade. And as computer technology has descreased the cost of publishing, groups or individuals have been increasingly able to print their own sex magazines, books, and newsletters, thereby avoiding the censorship imposed by mainstream publications.

At the same time, even the more straitlaced mainstream media have helped to increase the information available about fetishes and paraphilias. Unfortunately, many national television talk shows have "cashed in" on fetishes and victims of sexual trauma by sensationalizing their lives, rather than trying to educate the public. Hollywood also sensationalizes the issue, portraying erotic asphyxia, lust murder, sadomasochism, and nipple piercing. An example of the media's exploitation and sensationalization of unusual sex practices was the hundreds of hours of air time devoted to keeping the public informed of the status of John Wayne Bobbit, the circumstances leading to his castration at the hands of his wife, the subsequent surgical reattachment of his penis, and his appearance in an X-rated video.

Perhaps the most important development in the growth of interest in paraphilias and fetishes has been the Internet, the worldwide computer network through which up to 500,000 "lurkers" a month enter the "alt.sex" newsgroups. Users of these newsgroups, which offer uncensored forums devoted to a wide variety of sexual interests, can exchange or download photos and information, including what would normally be considered illegal in the United States, with other Internet users.

While the Internet has played an increasing role in the lives of fetishists in recent years, it would not be correct to attribute the growing popularity of fetishism and other unorthodox forms of sexuality to the Internet alone, as those in Washington who seek to censor the Internet seem to believe. The role of the Internet is more modest according to Robin Roberts, an Internet guru in California and founder of Backdrop, one of America's oldest fantasy and bondage clubs. Established in 1965, Backdrop promoted itself with discreet ads in the *Berkeley Barb* with post office boxes or mail-drop services as the method of contact. Today, Backdrop has about 5,700 members, but Roberts does not attribute the club's growth to exposure on the Internet.

Roberts explains that Internet lurkers rarely participate in dialog and tend not to join sex clubs. They are typically readers of *Forum* magazine or

"Letters to the Editor" columns. For those users who do participate in sex on-line, computers provide anonymity, and a way to explore taboos in a safe, non-threatening environment. Roberts does note, however, that for those who are active participants in computer sex, rather than just lurkers, the Internet provides twenty-four-hour access to other users, an equal chance to express one's opinions, and an unlimited number of fantasies. At the same time, Roberts does not feel computer sex will replace fetish clubs, due to the simple fact that electronic mail does not provide touch, intonation of the voice, nuances of speech, or visual impressions.

The Growing Popularity of Fetishes and Paraphilias

Not everyone who accesses information about paraphilias and fetishes through these new technological avenues is a fetishist. Many are among the growing number of experimenters who, even though they do not have a fetish, will join groups or purchase sex toys and SM paraphernalia. Such experimentation seems to be on the increase; a 1994 survey conducted in two San Francisco sex boutiques indicated that approximately 55 percent of their customers had at least experimented with SM (Love 1994).

Ann Grogan, owner of San Francisco's Romantasy boutique, has seen an increase in such experimentation among the customers who frequent her sex-accessory establishment, one of two operating in San Francisco in 1995 geared toward women customers.

"Gender play is becoming more and more popular among customers of all ages, primarily ages 30-50 years," Grogan says. "Couples now buy matching corsets and wrist restraints." During the last five years, females in increasing numbers have shown an interest in transgender play, assuming the dominant role in the sexual relationship. Many men are also expressing an interest in anal sexuality, measured in part by the purchase of dildoes and harnesses to be used on men by the women. And a growing number of recently divorced female customers in their 50s have shown a curiosity about safe sex and pleasuring themselves.

Grogan can also testify to the increasing influence of the Internet:

> The latest trend seems to be the appearance of couples who have met on the Internet. They appear together at Romantasy after only one or two meetings, because in previous communications they have gotten far beyond the awkward preliminary dialog about each other's sexual preferences and have jumped into a willingness to act out each other's fantasies. Meeting on the Internet seems to be a "fast track to intimacy." (Grogan 1995)

Ted McIlvenna, president of the Institute for the Advanced Study of Human Sexuality, expects that interest and participation in paraphilias and fetishes will continue to grow. "In the next five years," McIlvenna believes, we will see a group of people seeking information and support groups for their sex interests which, in the past, people have considered excessive or compulsive. This is not an evil path; instead it is remedial sex education. Because of the massive number of people involved—in the U.S. the estimate is forty million people—I have labeled this the "sexual accessories movement." Mental health professionals, including sexual health professionals, must monitor and study but leave this movement alone; their sexuality belongs to them. We can expect people to buy more, join more, and experiment more, and we can only hope that out of this will emerge societal control methods that will enable people to have better and more fulfilling sex lives. (McIlvenna 1995)

Given the recent and anticipated growth of many of the fetish clubs described below, it is important to ask about what causes paraphilias. Although there has been much scientific interest in this question, science has not yet discovered the etiology of fetishes or "paraphilic lovemaps," according to John Money (1988), the leading expert on paraphilias. It does appear, however, that, as is the case with substance abuse and addiction, a small percentage of the population seems more predisposed toward the development of paraphilias, often due to childhood trauma. Money says,

The retrospective biographies of adolescent and adult paraphiles point to the years of childhood sexual rehearsal play as the vulnerable developmental period. . . . The harsh truth is that as a society we do not want our children to be lustfully normal. If they are timorous enough to be discovered engaging their lust in normal sexual rehearsal play or in masturbation, they become, in countless numbers, the victims of humiliation and abusive violence. (Money 1988)

Money has explained how these early traumas can lead to paraphilias:

They [adults who subject sexually curious children to abuse] do not know that what they destroy, or vandalize, is the incorporation of lust into the normal development of the lovemap. The expression of lust is diverted or detoured from its normal route. Thus, to illustrate: those adults who humiliate and punish a small boy for strutting around with an erected penis, boasting to the girls who watch him, do not know that they are thereby exposing the boy to risk of developing a lovemap of paraphilic exhibitionism. (Money 1988)

Fetish and Paraphilia Clubs

The United States is probably home to more fetish clubs than any other country. As Brenda Love (1992) wrote in *The Encyclopedia of Unusual Sex Practices*, which catalogs over 700 sexual practices,

international advertising is fairly inexpensive and computerized printing of newsletters has made it simpler to form clubs. People with fetishes
as obscure as large penises, big balls, hairy bodies, mud wrestlers,
shaving, cigars, used condoms, genital modification, and throwing pies
have been able to find others with similar interests willing to form clubs.

Sadomasochist (SM) clubs are probably the most prevalent type of fetish
clubs in the U.S.A. today, although very few of the members could be
defined as having a true SM fetish or paraphilia.

SM has become an umbrella term for many sexual activities, and because
of its accouterments and role playing, people wanting to experiment with
or improve their sexuality join these groups. "It was only in the late fifteenth
century that the first unambiguous case report of SM was reported, and
then as a medical curiosity rather than a problem" (Ellis 1936). William
Simon has eloquently described the allure of SM:

> The sadomasochistic script plays upon the potential absolutism of
> hierarchy, not merely to experience hierarchy with the relief accompa-
> nying the elimination of its ambiguities but to experience the danger-
> ous emotions that invariably accompany acknowledgment of its exer-
> cise, the rage and fear of rage in both the other and ourselves. (Simon
> 1994)

Charles Moser (1988) estimates that approximately 10 percent of the
adult population are SM practitioners. This estimate is based on Kinsey's
report that approximately 50 percent reported some erotic response to
being bitten (Kinsey 1953). However, there is no direct empirical evidence
verifying this estimate. Moser divides SM behaviors

> into two types, physical and psychological. . . . Physical behaviors may
> be further subdivided into the following categories: bondage, physical
> discipline, intense stimulation, sensory deprivation, and body altera-
> tion. . . . Psychological pain is induced by feelings of humiliation,
> degradation, uncertainty, apprehension, powerlessness, anxiety, and
> fear. . . . Both physical and psychological behaviors are devised to
> emphasize the transfer of power from the submissive to the dominant
> partner. SM practitioners often report it is this consensual exchange of
> power that is erotic to them and the pain is just a method of achieving
> this power exchange. (Moser 1988)

Moser lists the common types of clinical problems presented by SM
practitioners to their therapists as: "1) Am I normal? 2) Can you make these
desires go away? 3) SM is destroying our relationship; 4) I cannot lead this
double life anymore; 5) I cannot find a partner; and 6) Is it violence or SM?"
(Moser 1988). All but the last question are also the concern of most fetishists.

Foot-fetish club members have a more focused interest than do SM practitioners. Weinberg et al. (1994) conducted a survey of 262 members of a gay foot-fetishist group called the Foot Fraternity that had approximately 1,000 members in 1990, but had grown to over 4,000 by 1995. These sexologists also compared the ratio of self-masturbation during sexual encounters to that of oral-genital activity and to anal intercourse. Fetishists tended to masturbate to orgasm while engaging in foot play rather than experiencing orgasm as a result of some type of penetrative sex with a partner. Furthermore, the researchers discovered that 76 percent responded that they masturbated themselves to orgasm frequently, whereas 48.1 percent performed oral-genital activity, and only 9.55 percent performed anal intercourse.

Weinberg et al. (1994) reported that their research highlighted the psychological importance a support group or club has for fetishists.

> Despite the lack of a widespread fetish subculture, the Foot Fraternity itself can be considered an embryonic subculture. Almost 70 percent of the respondents said membership in the Foot Fraternity allowed them to pursue their fetish interests more easily. Some 66 percent said membership increased their interest in feet and footwear, and over 40 percent said that they learned new ways of expressing their sexuality. Thus, the organization helped to sustain, as well as expand, its members' unconventional sexual interest. Almost 70 percent said the Foot Fraternity got them to correspond with others with similar interests, 50 percent that it got them to meet others with similar interests, and 40 percent that this led them to engage in foot play with another member. Finally, over 40 percent said that membership in the Foot Fraternity helped remove confusion about their interest in feet and footwear and almost 60 percent that it increased their self-acceptance. (Weinberg et al. 1994)

These statistics regarding benefits of membership can most likely be applied to other sexual interest groups as well.

Doug Gaines, founder of this Cleveland-based club, estimates that 15 percent of the U.S. population has a foot or related fetish, an opinion based on the fact that he has received 80,000 requests for club information. He promotes the group in magazines, radio interviews, and a foot-fetish Internet newsgroup.

Interestingly, Gaines seconded the findings of researchers on the genesis of fetishes by identifying childhood experiences, such as being tickled, riding on the foot of a parent ("playing horsey"), or seeing a parent's foot immediately prior to being picked up and nurtured, as predominant memories of most of his members. The Foot Fraternity offers a newsletter, glossy magazine, and videos of men modeling their feet. The selection of photos is determined by a detailed membership questionnaire which asks what type of shoe, sock, or foot the new member finds erotic.

The activities in which foot enthusiasts participate include masturbation while looking at photos of feet, slipping off a partner's shoes in order to smell the stockings and foot, or placing oneself underneath the foot in a submissive posture. The foot is massaged and licked completely (toes, between toes, bottom, etc.). SM dominance and submission scenes, for example, where a partner takes on the role of a policeman and the fetishist must kiss his boot to get out of being given a traffic ticket, are popular.

Another common scene consists of acting out the roles of principal and student. Foot fetishists rarely use pain in their dominance/submission; rather, these scenes simply serve as an excuse for foot worship. A few foot fetishists attend auctions where they are able to purchase shoes once belonging to their favorite sports figures or movie stars hoping that the "scent" of the person remains in the shoe.

Squish Productions, mentioned earlier, can also be viewed as a foot-fetish club. Unlike the Foot Fraternity, Squish has yet to be the subject of any in-depth survey by sexologists. Even so, the genesis of the Squish fetish appears to be similar to that found in other fetishes, as evidenced by Squish founder Jeff Vilencia's recollections of his childhood. Identifying what he considers to be his childhood trigger point in the development of his fetish, Vilencia recalled that, as the younger of two children, he was the "victim" of an older sister who enjoyed kicking and stepping on him. Upon reaching puberty, he discovered feeling aroused when seeing females step on bugs. The bug apparently only serves as a projection of himself, because his fantasy involves taking the bug's place under the woman's foot.

Cross-dressing and other forms of transgender activity are found in many countries. The new *DSM IV* no longer lists this activity as a paraphilia, but rather as "gender dysphoria." Clubs such as ETVC in San Francisco have an extensive library for members, social outings, support-group hot line, newsletter, make-up classes, and lingerie modeling. Membership in ETVC increased from 329 in 1988 to a total of 433 in 1995.

Another group, Texas Tea Party, sponsors an annual party that, after eight years of existence, drew about 400 people in 1995. Estimates on the percentage of the population who have ever cross-dressed range from 1.5 to 10 percent. Groups attract new members with newspaper and magazine advertisements, appearances on television and radio, magazine articles on the subject, and by staffing a booth at the annual San Francisco Lesbian and Gay Freedom Day Parade and Celebration.

A recent survey of 942 transgenderists by Linda and Cynthia Phillips indicates that most members experienced cross-dressing in puberty, although one member did not begin cross-dressing until the age of 72. The average transgenderist did not seek out a transgender club until his early 40s. Sexual arousal while cross-dressing is also more common during adolescence, and appears to diminish as the boy grows older. Therefore, an adult male transgenderist dresses to feel "feminine," whereas an underwear fetishist uses the lingerie for sexual arousal. (Females who cross-dress do not tend to experience arousal while cross-dressing) (Phillips 1994).

No one knows how many cross-dressers or clubs exist in the U.S., but it is known that many people purchase special-interest cross-dressing magazines. One of these, *Tapestry*, had a 1995 quarterly distribution of 10,000 issues compared to 2,000 five years earlier. And a fairly new magazine, *Transformation*, had an international distribution of 50,000 in 1995.

Infantilism is fairly unique to the U.S. and growing in popularity. Its practitioners take on the persona of infants or young children. They may wear diapers under their business suits, drink from a baby bottle, use an assortment of toys and baby furniture, and, if they have a partner, they may participate by reading bedtime stories, diapering, spanking, or using other forms of affection or punishment.

One practitioner, who asked to be identified only as Tommy, is the founder of Diaper Pail Friends. Inside his home in a prestigious San Francisco suburb, a visitor will find an adult-sized high chair, bibs, and numerous baby bottles in the kitchen. Downstairs, Tommy's bedroom features a large crib with a view of the Bay area, a collection of adult-sized baby clothes, and a trail of toys leading to a train set that fills the center of an adjacent room.

Diaper Pail Friends is about 15 years old, and grew from about 1,000 members in 1990 to more than 3,000 in 1995. Most of the members discovered the group through articles in magazines or books, television talk shows, or an Internet newsgroup. The club publishes a newsletter, short stories, videos, and distributes adult-sized baby paraphernalia.

A group of sexologists conducted an extensive survey of the Diaper Pail Friends, but had not yet published their findings as of 1995. Tommy, however, concluded from an informal survey of the group's members that

> Even a casual review of infantilists in the DPF Rosters show that there are tremendous differences between one infantilist and another. In fact, there would seem to be as many personal, individual variations as there are people. Nevertheless, certain patterns do seem to become evident, patterns that seem to encompass a very large percentage of the environmental and inborn factors that are involved with the creation of Infantilism in human personality. These patterns are [in order of prevalence] (1) deficient early nurturing, (2) rejection of Softness, (3) childhood sexual abuse [primarily in female members], and (4) bed wetting. Every infantilist probably has one or more of these patterns in their history, and each infantilist combines them in varying degrees. The variations are limitless. (Tommy 1992)

A Chicago-based national acrotomophile club (people aroused by seeing amputees) has a membership of about 300. They sponsor an annual conference during the first week of June and have spawned local chapters that also hold meetings. Quarterly pamphlets are sent to members and a couple of Internet newsgroups exist. New membership is not aggressively recruited, but the number of self-identified acrotomophiles has increased since 1989 publication of Grant Riddle's book, *Amputees and Devotees*, which examines the psychological basis of this phenomenon.

According to Riddle, many "devotees" are aware of this preference as a child, but there seems to be a wide variety of reasons for its development. One of these is being overly criticized by parents and wishing to be like a handicapped neighbor, assuming this would relieve some of the pressure. Another cause is being taught that sex is dirty, and from there, having to rationalize that if one cares for someone handicapped, one can justifiably ask for sex in return. Activities of acrotomophiles include having a healthy partner pretend to limp or use crutches; most acrotomophiles, however, content themselves with viewing photos (mostly of clothed females) or possibly catching a glimpse of an amputee on the street (Riddle 1989).

Autoerotic asphyxia (self-strangulation) seems originally to have been carried to Europe by French Foreign Legionnaires returning from war in Indochina (Michaldimitrakis 1986). Erotic asphyxia involves using a pillow, gag, gas mask, latex or leather hood, plastic bag, or other object to block oxygen intake. It may also involve strangulation by a partner's hands, or with a scarf or Velcro blood-pressure cuff. Corseting of the waist is another less obvious method of impeding oxygen intake.

This practice takes the lives of an estimated 250 to 1,000 Americans each year. It is believed that many more people experiment with asphyxia safely alone and/or with a partner, but because this act carries great legal liability if things go wrong, it is impossible to estimate the number of people who engage in it. During the early 1990s, a Seattle man made an effort, through workshops and lectures, to teach safety techniques to practitioners. Although he found many interested parties, he had to limit his public appearances and advice due to legal concerns.

Although there is little information available about the asphyxiphile's childhood, John Money has described one case in his book, *Breathless Orgasm*. This subject recalled first becoming interested in asphyxia when his childhood sweetheart drowned. He began by thinking of her drowning experience and soon discovered he was becoming aroused by visualizing her nude body under water and thinking about her suffocating (Money et al. 1991).

Another asphixiphile, who related his experience to the audience at a San Francisco lecture on the subject, described being raised as a Jehovah's Witness and taught that masturbation was a sin. This did not deter him from engaging in masturbation, but rather made it much more exciting, because he felt he could be "struck by lightning." After giving up his religious practice in his late teens, he immediately discovered that masturbation lost its intensity. He then found that by putting himself in a life-or-death situation, i.e., asphyxia, he could recover this lost intensity.

Most data on asphyxiphiles have been collected from the death scene of the victims. Ray Blanchard and Stephen J. Hucker have collected a vast data bank of coroner's reports and other materials on the subject. In their study of 117 incidents, they discovered that older men

> were more likely to have been simultaneously engaged in bondage or transvestitism, suggesting elaboration of the masturbatory ritual over time. The greatest degree of transvestitism was associated with intermediate rather than high levels of bondage, suggesting that response competition from bondage may limit asphyxiators' involvement in a third paraphilia like transvestitism. (Blanchard et al. 1991).

Sexual asphyxia is rarely depicted in print media, but has been shown in a few films, such as the 1993 movie, *The Rising Sun,* and also in the 1976 French-Japanese movie, *In the Realm of the Senses.*

Chubby Chasers, a San Francisco club of men attracted to the obese, almost doubled in membership between 1990 and 1995 and grew to include 50 different international groups. This club was involved on the Internet early and recruited many of its members there. This club also staffs a booth at the annual San Francisco Lesbian and Gay Freedom Day Parade. Membership in the organization includes a newsletter and invitation to many social activities. Many, but not all, "chasers" had a parent or close relative who was very obese, and recall having a preference for "chubbies" when they were as young as 4 or 5. For those with this interest, there are full-color commercial magazines depicting obese nude females, sometimes with a slender male partner, available in adult book stores.

There are a number of food fetishists or "piesexuals," a word coined by a well-known pie enthusiast, Mike Brown, who began his affair with pies at age 13. Mr. Brown produces pie videos and also hosts annual "bring your own pie" throwing parties, where couples undress and hit each other with pies. There is an Internet newsgroup and also several clubs catering to this interest. *Splosh* magazine, although not sexual, features attractive females smeared with an assortment of food and mud, another messy fetish.

Other more obscure fetish/paraphilia organizations include WES (We Enjoy Shaving) of Reno, Nevada; the Wisconsin STEAM journal for agoraphiles, who enjoy engaging in sex in public; and Hot Ash, a New York club for people aroused by partners who smoke. Hot Ash publishes a newsletter and sells videos for those with this interest.

New York is also the home of a vampire sex club whose members make small cuts on others and rub or lick the blood off. Blood sports are also common among some SM practitioners in forms of caning, cutting, or piercing. San Francisco had coprophilia (feces) and urophilia (urine) clubs before the AIDS epidemic. Some of the newest groups include Fire Play, whose members drip hot wax on their partners, rub lit cigarettes on their bodies, and/or use chemical irritants. Some with this interest rub a small part of the body with diluted alcohol and ignite it.

In another new paraphilic activity, some men catch bees and use them to sting the penis. The venom not only doubles the size of the penis for a few days, but also seems to bring about a change in the neural system that enhances the arousal stage.

The foregoing are but a few of the many unorthodox sexual practices now being pursued in the United States. Many more exist, and new ones are being invented all the time. And thanks to technology, including the Internet, advances in the quality and availability of home-based desktop publishing, and the rise of sensationalist television talk shows, interest and participation in these activities is on the increase.

In the coming years, the continuing growth of fetish/paraphilia sex groups will require therapists to learn to make clear determinations among people who experiment with various activities, those who self-report to have a fetish but five years later become bored with it, and the few clinically defined paraphiles who truly need some type of intervention or treatment.

9. Contraception, Abortion, and Population Planning
PATRICIA BARTHALOW KOCH

[In the final sections of this review of sexuality in American culture, we consider several areas which are concerned with health and/or technology. The areas of contraception, abortion, and sexually transmitted disease each have rather obvious health implications, but each is also influenced by growing medical technology and illustrates a relationship between sexual conduct and technological advances. We would note that the question of effective social policy in each of these areas remains a matter of considerable social conflict within the U.S.A. The identification and treatment of sexual "dysfunctions" reflect these same concerns. In fact, the growing recognition that various sexual conditions can be diagnosed and treated, and the growing public acceptance of the legitimacy of such treatment, may be one of the more profound, if subtle, changes in American sexuality in the last century. In no small way, this process has served to fuel the growth of an array of sexual professions with a corresponding need to provide graduate education for such professionals and the emergence of professional organizations. We provide a brief review of each of these professional developments. Finally, we close with a brief review of how one recent technological development, the Internet, may be changing the way that at least some Americans receive sexual information and communicate with each other about sexuality. Some mention of this was already made earlier in the section on fetishes and paraphilias (see Section 8D). As always seems to be the case with sexual issues within the U.S.A., this technology has already generated a fair amount of political activity and social conflict over its use. (D. L. Weis, Coeditor)]

A. Contraception   PATRICIA BARTHALOW KOCH

A Brief History

"The struggle for reproductive self-determination is one of the oldest projects of humanity; one of our earliest collective attempts to alter the biological limits of our existence" (Gordon 1976, 403). Throughout U.S. history, as elsewhere, many have been desperate to learn safe and effective ways to prevent conception and induce abortion, while others have believed artificial contraception is unacceptable because it interferes with the course of nature.

Brodie (1994) conducted a historical analysis of efforts for reproductive control in colonial and nineteenth-century America. New England fertility rates in colonial times were higher than those in most of Europe. Colonists had little real ability, and perhaps little will, to intervene in their reproduction. It has been estimated that one third of the brides of this time were pregnant. Although the Puritans viewed marriage with children as the highest form of life, the prevalence of premarital pregnancy was not viewed as a threat to this value, because virtually all such pregnancies led to marriage (Reiss 1980).

On the other hand, Native Americans seemed to possess knowledge and cultural practices—breast-feeding, periodic abstinence, abortion, and infanticide—specific to their particular tribes, enabling them to maintain small families. Fertility among the African and Caribbean women brought as slaves varied widely, depending on the region of the United States—in some places, fecundity reaching human capacity and in other places, fertility rates decreasing. According to Brodie (1994, 53): "Fecundity assured slave women that they were valuable to the master and offered some hope against being sold. Yet preventing the birth of new slaves for the master could be a form of resistance to slavery."

The three most common forms of birth control during this time were coitus interruptus (withdrawal), breast-feeding, and abortion. The effectiveness of breast-feeding in preventing another pregnancy depended on how long the woman breast-fed, on when her menstruation resumed after childbirth, and on how long and how often the infant suckled. However, by the nineteenth century, the option of bottle feeding infants was becoming more available and popular.

Abortion methods included violent exercises, uterine insertions, and the use of drugs. These methods may have been no more dangerous than the pregnancy and childbirth complications of the time, but it has been suggested that these methods were also a common cause of death for women. American folk medicine was evolving from the knowledge and indigenous practices of the Native Americans, European settlers, and African/Caribbean slaves. Many abortificients were made from plants, such as pennyroyal, tansy, aloe, cohash, and squaw root. Such "remedies" were often passed down through family Bibles and cookbooks. Over 1,500 medical almanacs, many containing herbal remedies to "bring on a woman's courses," were circulated before the American Revolution. Yet there was little public discussion of birth control and no laws or statutes governing information or practice.

Brodie documents that reproductive control during most of the nineteenth century in America was neither rare nor taboo. Information was available about withdrawal, douching (the "water cure"), rhythm (although the information was not very accurate), condoms, spermicides, abortion-inducing drugs, and early varieties of the diaphragm. When other contraceptive options were available, couples seemed to prefer them over withdrawal; sexual abstinence was not one of the chief means of controlling birth rates. Abortion was not illegal until "quickening" (movement of the fetus).

Beginning in the 1830s, reproductive control became a commercial enterprise in the expanding American market economy. Douches and syringes, vaginal sponges, condoms, diaphragms (or "womb veils"), cervical caps, and pessaries (intravaginal and intrauterine devices) began to be widely advertised through a burgeoning literature on the subjects of sexuality and reproductive control, euphemistically called "feminine hygiene." Education through this means was made possible by the technological improvements in printing and the increased basic literacy of the American public.

The self-help literature instructed readers on how to make contraceptive and abortion agents at home from products readily available in the household or garden. Douching was the most frequent method for reproductive control used by middle- and upper-class women. The invention of the vulcanization process for rubber by Goodyear in the 1840s enabled condoms to be made more cheaply. In addition, the appearance of the mail-order catalog allowed the public to "shop" for contraceptive devices confidentially.

The birthrate of white native-born married women was reduced almost by half between 1800 and 1900, coinciding with the major social upheaval of industrialization and urbanization. Many American couples wanted fewer children and greater spacing between them. This became possible with the evolving availability of information about and access to more-effective contraceptive techniques.

By the mid-1800s, the abortion rate among the white middle class increased sharply with greater access to diverse sources of information about abortion, abortion drugs and instruments, and persons offering abortion services. There was little outcry about abortion being "immoral" until the American Medical Association launched a campaign to curb it at mid century. Historians have debated whether the new opposition to abortion by male physicians was due more to the threat of competition from female midwives or to a concern about the dangers of unsafe abortion.

As reproductive control became commercialized after 1850, and as some women became increasingly able to assert a degree of independent control over their fertility through contraception and abortion, the deep ambivalences with which many Americans regarded such changes came increasingly into play. In the second half of the nineteenth century, diverse groups emerged to try to restore

> American "social purity," and one of the issues they focused on was restricting sexual freedom and control of reproduction. . . . All branches of government were their allies; their goals were won through enactments of federal and state legislation and sustained by judicial decisions that criminalized contraception and abortion, both of which had in earlier decades been legal. (Brodie 1994, 253)

Laws began to alter two hundred years of American custom and public policy towards contraception and abortion. Federal and state laws made it a felony to mail products or information about contraception and abortion. Such materials were then labeled "obscene." In 1873, Congress passed "The Act for the Suppression of Trade in, and Circulation of Obscene Literature and Articles of Immoral Use," which tightened the loopholes on interstate trade and importation of birth-control materials from abroad. This law was better known as the Comstock Law, named after Anthony Comstock, a leading "social purity" proponent and crusader against "obscenity." Comstock was even appointed a special agent of the U.S. Post Office and allowed to inspect and seize such "illegal" material until his death in 1915.

> The combined force of the social purity legions and of overwhelming public acquiescence overrode a generation of commercialization and growing public discourse and drove reproductive control, if not totally back underground, at least into a netherworld of back-fence gossip and back-alley abortion. (Brodie 1994, 288)

The Comstock Law would stand until a federal appeals court would overturn its anticontraceptive provisions in 1936 (*United States v. One Package*) on the grounds that the weight of authority of the medical world concerning the safety and reliability of contraception was not available when the law was originally passed. (The anti-obscenity provisions of the Comstock Law remained intact for several more decades.)

What is referred to as "the birth-control movement" was begun in the United States shortly before World War I, primarily by socialists and sexual liberals as both a political and moral issue. Margaret Sanger's leadership, in the early 1900s, was responsible for gaining support from mainstream America and centralizing the cause through her American Birth Control League. Sanger attributed her indomitable dedication to making birth-control information and methods available to American women, particularly of the working class, to her nursing experiences with poor women during which they would beg her to tell them the "secrets" of the rich for limiting children.

In 1915, she began publishing *Woman Rebel*, a monthly magazine advocating birth control. She was indicted for violating the Comstock Law, but the case was dropped and she continued dispensing birth-control information through lectures and publications. In 1916, she was arrested again for opening the first birth-control clinic in the United States in a poor slum in Brooklyn, New York. She served thirty days in jail; however, the testimonials of her poor birth-control clients at the trial helped to fuel the birth-control movement.

Gordon (1976) documents the birth-control movement throughout the twentieth century in the United States. In the early 1920s, most doctors were opposed to contraception. However, through the efforts of Margaret Sanger and Dr. Robert Latou Dickenson, contraception was scientifically studied and became accepted as a health issue, not simply a moral one. Clergy, particularly of the Protestant and Jewish faiths, also began to view contraceptive choice as an individual moral decision when it affected the health of a family. To this day, however, the Catholic Church has remained staunch in its opposition to "artificial birth control." Yet, this opposition has not deterred Catholic women in the United States from using birth-control methods as frequently as women of other or no faiths.

The Great Depression of the 1930s forced many more Americans into accepting and practicing birth-control measures. Social workers, based on their interactions with many poor and struggling families, became proponents in support of better education about, and access to, birth control for all women, not just the middle class and wealthy. The manufacturing of condoms became a large industry. In the 1930s, with the formation of the American Birth Control League, over three hundred clinics throughout the United States were providing contraceptive information and services; this increased to more than eight hundred clinics by 1942.

Yet, despite the fact that a 1937 poll indicated that 79 percent of American women supported the use of birth control, those who did not have access to private doctors were limited in their access to birth-control information and devices. However, judges, doctors, government officials, entrepreneurs, and others were beginning to respond to grassroots pressure. For example, in 1927, the American Medical Association officially recognized birth control as part of medical practice. In 1942, Planned Parenthood Federation of America (PPFA) was founded with a commitment to helping women better plan family size and child spacing. PPFA was greatly responsible for making birth control more accessible to women of various backgrounds, particularly those of lower-socioeconomic levels, throughout the United States.

Development of the Oral Contraceptive Pill and IUD

During the 1950s, research was progressing in the United States that would transform contraceptive technology and practice worldwide. Asbell (1995) details the biography of the "drug that changed the world." The quest for a female contraceptive that could be "swallowed like an aspirin" began when Margaret Sanger and Katherine McCormick, a wealthy American woman dedicated to the birth-control movement, enlisted Gregory Pincus, an accomplished reproductive scientist, to develop a contraceptive pill. Applying the basic research findings of others, particularly Russel Marker, who produced a chemical imitation of progesterone from the roots of Mexican yam trees, Pincus developed just such a pill combining synthetic estrogen and progesterone.

With the help of John Rock, a noted Harvard gynecologist and researcher, the oral contraceptive was initially given to fifty Massachusetts volunteers, and then field tested with approximately 200 women in Puerto Rico in 1956, where it was believed opposition to such a drug would be less than in the United States. However, the pill was heartily condemned by the Catholic Church, leaving Puerto Rican women to face the dilemma of choosing to be in the trials (and committing a mortal sin) or bearing more children which they could not adequately support. In addition, the standards for informed consent for research subjects were not as strict as they are today, so that participants in these trials were not thoroughly informed as to the experimental procedures being used and the potential risks involved (which were generally unknown).

In 1957, the pill was first approved by the Food and Drug Administration (FDA) for treatment of menstrual disorders. At this time, it was observed that many women who had never before experienced menstrual disorders suddenly developed this problem and sought treatment with the pill. By 1960, the pill was formally approved by the FDA as a contraceptive following double-blind clinical trials with 897 Puerto Rican women. Such a procedure would well be considered ethically questionable today.

The pill was extremely attractive to many potential users because of its convenience and efficacy. Women now had the option of engaging in intercourse with minimal threat of pregnancy. This method separated the act of coitus from the action taken to restrict fertility (ingestion of the pill). In addition, the woman was in sole charge of this method of birth control and did not need any cooperation from her male partner. Many believed this innovation in birth control was responsible for a "sexual revolution" in which women were to become more "sexually active," displaying patterns of sexual attitudes and behaviors more like men, although there is little scientific evidence to support this claim. As Ira Reiss explained the evolutionary changes taking place in American sexual expression:

> Sexual standards and behavior seem more closely related to social structure and cultural and religious values than to the availability of contraceptive techniques . . . [increased premarital sexuality] was promoted by a courtship system that had been evolving for a hundred years in the United States permitting young people to choose their own marriage partners, and which therefore encouraged choice of when as well as with whom to share sex. (Asbell 1995, 201)

By 1967, the Population Council estimated that 6.5 million women were using the birth-control pill in the U.S., while 6.3 million women were using it in other parts of the world. Some were concerned as to whether millions of women were serving as guinea pigs in a massive experiment, since careful large-scale studies of its safety had not been conducted before it was marketed (Seaman 1969). Disturbing side effects, including deep-vein thrombosis, heart disease and attacks, elevated blood pressure, strokes, gallbladder disease, liver tumors, and depression, were being reported. In the first few years of use in the U.S., more than one hundred court claims were filed against its manufacturer. Some countries, including Norway and the Soviet Union, banned the pill. Some American women mobilized to create a women's health movement, spearheaded by the National Women's Health Network, to help the public become better informed about the benefits and risks of pill use, as well as other medical procedures and drugs. Yet, accurate information about the benefits and risks of pill use was often unavailable, difficult to access, and distorted and sensationalized. In the 1970s, pill sales dropped 20 percent.

Twenty-five years later, oral contraception has become one of the most extensively studied medications ever prescribed. Today, pills with less than 50 micrograms of estrogen are associated with a significantly lower risk of serious negative effects and are as effective in preventing pregnancy as the higher-dose pills of the past (Hatcher et al. 1994).

The intrauterine device (IUD) also became popular in the United States as the "perfect" alternative to the pill because of its effectiveness and convenience. However, the Dalkon Shield, which was marketed from 1971 to 1975, was implicated in a number of cases of pelvic inflammatory disease and spontaneous septic abortions resulting in the deaths of at least twenty women. In 1974, the Shield was taken off the U.S. market, although it was still distributed abroad. Currently, there are only two IUDs for sale in the United States, the TCu-380A (ParaGard) and the Progesterone T device (Progestasert).

Government Policy and Legal Issues

While research was expanding birth-control options, the 1950s and 1960s saw the development and implementation of federal policies supporting population control programs designed to deal with overpopulation throughout the world. Birth control was offered as a "tool" for economic development to Third World countries. The 1960 budget of $2 million for family-planning programs grew to $250 million in 1972 (Asbell 1995). However, American goals were often in conflict with the cultural beliefs of the people in various countries. Reproductive options cannot be separated from the economic options and social mores of a culture.

Governmental policies on birth control were also changing at home. In 1964, President Lyndon B. Johnson, over strong political opposition, provided federal funds to support birth-control clinics for the American poor. These efforts were continued by President Richard M. Nixon, who in 1970 declared "a new national goal: adequate family-planning services within the next five years for all those who want them but cannot afford them" (Asbell 1995).

Important legal changes were also occurring in the U.S. during this time. In 1965, the Supreme Court decided, in *Griswold v. Connecticut,* that laws prohibiting the sale of contraceptives to married couples violated a constitutional "right of privacy." Writing the majority opinion, Justice William O. Douglas declared:

> we deal with a right of privacy older than the Bill of Rights—older than our political parties, older than our school system. Marriage is a coming together for better or worse, hopefully enduring and intimate to the degree of being sacred. (Asbell 1995, 241)

The court asked, "Would we allow the police to search the sacred precincts of marital bedrooms for telltale signs of the use of contraceptives?" The judges responded, "The very idea is repulsive to the notions of privacy surrounding the marital relationship."

In 1972, the Supreme Court extended this "right to privacy" for contraceptive use to unmarried people (*Eisenstadt v. Baird*) on the basis that a legal prohibition would violate the equal protection clause of the 14th Amendment. A 1977 Supreme Court decision (*Carey v. Population Services*) struck down laws prohibiting the sale of contraception to minors, the selling of contraception by others besides pharmacists, and advertisements for or displays of contraceptives.

Recent Developments in Birth Control

More-recent developments in contraceptive technology receive tougher scrutiny than in the past before winning FDA approval. For example, Norplant was developed by the international nonprofit Population Council, which began clinical trials including half a million women in 46 countries, not including the U.S.

However, Norplant was not approved for use in the United States by the Food and Drug Administration (FDA) until 1990. This approval was opposed by the National Women's Health Network because the long-term safety of Norplant had not been established. Wyeth-Ayerst, the U.S. distributor, is required by law to report any unusual events associated with Norplant use to the FDA, while an internationally coordinated surveillance of Norplant use and its effects is being conducted by the World Health Organization and others in eight developing countries. Currently, a class-action suit is being formulated by a group of Norplant users in the U.S., primarily because of the difficulties they experienced in having the Norplant rods removed. Such complications are a serious impediment keeping American pharmaceutical companies from researching and developing new contraceptives.

Depro-Provera (Depo-medroxyprogesterone acetate or DMPA) is the most commonly employed injectable progestin used in over ninety countries worldwide. However, it was not approved for use in the U.S. by the FDA until 1992. Women's health activists, organized by the National Women's Health Network, had opposed its approval in the absence of more long-term studies of its safety.

In 1993, the FDA approved the first female condom, called Reality, for over-the-counter sale in the United States. The female condom, or vaginal pouch, is a polyurethane lubricated sheath that lines the vagina and partially covers the perineum. Although the method failure rate of the female condom (5 percent) is similar to that of the male condom (3 percent), it has a higher failure rate with typical use (21 percent) than does the male condom (12 percent) (Hatcher et al. 1994). This may reflect the "newness" of this female method and inexperience with its use. Yet, in a study of 360 women using female condoms, only 2 discontinued its use.

Although a combination of RU-486 (mifespristone) and prostaglandin has been tested in over a dozen countries, particularly in France, it has generated controversy in the U.S. and was only approved for use here in 1996. Because RU-486, when combined with a prostaglandin, is an effective early abortifacient, its use has been opposed by anti-abortion proponents, even for research purposes or its potential use in the treatment of breast cancer, Cushing's syndrome, endometriosis, and brain tumors. Because it was so politically controversial, RU-486 had not been expected to be approved for any use in the United States, which turned out not to be the case.

What is the future for the development of new birth-control methods in the United States? Contraceptive-vaccine researchers acknowledge that a new form of birth control for men is badly needed. Yet, it is believed that immunizing men against their own sperm would risk destroying the testes. However, researchers in the U.S. are talking with the FDA to test a vaccine with women that induces the woman's immune system to attack sperm. Previously, such vaccines have been tested on mice, rabbits, and baboons with an effectiveness rate of 75 to 80 percent.

In the past, Federal agencies have shied away from supporting such work because "right-to-lifer" advocates view such a vaccine as abortive and, therefore, unacceptable. In addition to the possibility of medical liability, American pharmaceutical companies are unlikely to market such a vaccine because of the protests and boycotts that "right-to-life" groups threaten to organize. Because of the threat of boycotts from adversarial groups and lawsuits from persons claiming to be harmed by new contraceptive technologies, only one American company remains active in contraceptive research and development. In the late 1960s, nine American drug companies were competing to find new and better birth-control methods.

Current Contraceptive Behavior

Between 1988 and 1990, the proportion of women in the United States, from the age of 15 to 44, who had never had vaginal-penile intercourse declined from 12 percent to 9 percent. (Data used in this section are based on the 1982 and 1988 *National Survey of Family Growth (NSFG)* and the 1990 *NSFG Telephone Reinterview*) (Peterson 1995). The proportion of 15- to 44-year-olds who were at risk for unintended pregnancy but were not contracepting increased from 7 percent to 12 percent. This increase was most pronounced among 15- to 44-year-olds (8 percent to 22 percent), never-married women (11 percent to 20 percent), and non-Hispanic white women (5 percent to 11 percent).

In 1990, 34.5 million women, or 59 percent of those aged 15 to 44, in the United States were using some type of contraception—with almost three quarters (70.7 percent) of married women using contraception; see Table 6. There is little difference in contraceptive use based on religious background between Catholic, Protestant, and Jewish women. The leading methods used by contraceptors were female sterilization (29.5 percent), the contraceptive pill (28.5 percent), and the male condom (17.7 percent). (Information on the use of three newer methods—Norplant, the female condom, and Depo-Provera—was not available at the time of the surveys). Overall, the use of female and male sterilization, the condom, and periodic abstinence had increased from 1988, whereas the use of the pill, IUD, and diaphragm had decreased.

Female sterilization is most widely used among older and less-educated women who have completed their childbearing, with over one half (52.0 percent) of female contraceptors age 40 to 44 having been sterilized. Anglo-American women are much more likely to have male partners with a vasectomy (15.5 percent) than are African-American women (1.3 percent). The aging of the baby-boom generation in the United States portends a continued rise in female sterilization rates throughout the next decade and a rise in vasectomies among the better educated.

The increased use of the condom was most pronounced among young (aged 15 to 44), African-American, never-married, childless, or less-educated women, and those living below the poverty level. For example, condom use among never-married women tripled between 1982 and 1990 (4 percent to 13 percent). The percentage of adolescents using condoms rose from 33 percent to 44 percent between 1988 and 1990. Almost all contracepting teenagers used either the pill (52 percent) or condom (44 percent) in 1990. However, it must be kept in mind that only 56 percent of condom users report using them consistently every time they have intercourse.

The use of contraception at first intercourse by adolescents has increased significantly since the early 1980s. For example, during 1980-1982, 53 percent of unmarried women aged 15 to 19 used contraception during their first intercourse experience. By 1988-1990, this percentage rose to 71

Table 6

Number of Women 15-44 Years of Age, Percent Using Any Method of Contraception, and Percent Distribution of Contraceptors by Method, According to Age, Race and Origin, and Marital Status, 1988 and 1990

Age, Race, and Marital Status	Number of Women Using a Method (in Thousands)	Percent Using Any Method	Female Sterilization	Male Sterilization	*Read across >>>>>* Pill
1990²					
All women	34,516	59.3	29.5	12.6	28.5
Age					
15-19	2,623	31 5	0.0	0.0	52.0
15-17	1,165	24.3	0.0	0.0	41.1
18-19	1,458	41.2	0.0	0.0	60.7
20-24	5,065	55.3	8.0	1.8	55.4
25-29	6,385	60.0	17.4	5.0	47.3
30-34	7,344	66.2	32.7	13.0	23.9
35-39	7,138	70.6	44.2	19.8	10.6
40-44	5,962	66.9	52.0	26.5	2.2
Race and Origin					
Hispanic	2,856	52.2	33.1	6.4	31.4
White non-Hispanic	25,928	60.5	27.3	15.5	28.5
Black non-Hispanic	4,412	58.7	41.0	1.3	28.5
Marital Status					
Currently married	21,608	70.7	33.5	33.5	19.2
Divorced, separated, widowed	4,026	57.3	52.1	2.8	22.4
Never married	8,882	43.0	9.6	1.1	50.5
1988					
All women	34,912	60.3	27.5	11.7	30.7
Age					
15-19	2,950	32.1	1.5	0.2	58.8
15-17	1,076	19.9	0.0	0.0	53.3
18-19	1,874	49.6	2.4	0.4	61.9
20-24	5,550	59.0	4.6	1.8	68.2
25-29	6,967	64.5	17.0	6.0	44.5
30-34	7,437	68.0	32.5	14.0	21.5
35-39	6,726	70.2	44.9	19.7	5.2
40-44	5,282	66.0	51.1	22.2	3.2

<<<<< *Read across*

Age, Race, and Marital Status	IUD	Diaphragm	Condom	Periodic Abstinence[1]	Other
1990[2]					
All women	1.4	2.8	17.7	2.7	4.8
Age					
15-19	0.0	0.0	44.0	1.0	3.0
15-17	0.0	0.0	51.9	2.2	4.7
18-19	0.0	0.0	37.6	0.0	1.7
20-24	0.8	0.6	25.3	2.8	5.3
25-29	0.4	2.3	19.0	2.7	5.9
30-34	0.9	4.7	15.9	3.5	5.4
35-39	3.3	3.3	10.3	3.4	5.2
40-44	1.8	3.8	9.2	1.6	2.9
Race and Origin					
Hispanic	1.9	1.5	17.1	3.7	5.1
White non-Hispanic	1.3	3.0	17.0	2.7	4.7
Black non-Hispanic	1.4	1.6	19.4	1.2	5.6
Marital Status					
Currently married	20.6	1.4	14.0	3.5	3.8
Divorced, separated, widowed	2.5	0.9	9.7	0.6	9.0
Never married	0.8	0.6	30.1	1.8	5.5
1988					
All women	2.0	5.7	14.6	2.3	5.4
Age					
15-19	0.0	1.0	32.8	0.8	4.8
15-17	0.0	0.7	40.4	0.9	4.7
18-19	0.0	1.2	28.4	0.8	4.9
20-24	0.3	3.7	14.5	1.7	5.2
25-29	1.3	5.5	15.6	2.4	7.6
30-34	2.9	8.9	12.0	2.7	5.5
35-39	2.7	7.7	11.8	3.0	5.1
40-44	3.7	3.9	10.5	2.2	3.2

continued

Table 6 continued

Age, Race, and Marital Status	Number of Women Using a Method (in Thousands)	Percent Using Any Method	Female Sterilization	Male Sterilization	*Read across* >>>>> Pill
1988					
Race and Origin					
Hispanic	2,799	50.4	31.7	4.3	33.4
White non-Hispanic	25,799	62.9	25.6	14.3	29.5
Black non-Hispanic	4,208	56.8	37.8	0.9	38.1
Marital Status					
Currently married	21,657	74.3	31.4	17.3	20.4
Divorced, separated, widowed	4,429	57.6	50.7	3.6	25.3
Never married	8,826	41.9	6.4	1.8	59.0

[1]Includes natural family planning and other types of periodic abstinence.

[2]Percentages for 1990 were calculated excluding cases for whom contraceptive status was not ascertained. Overall, contraceptive status was not ascertained for 0.3 percent of U.S. women in1990.

Source: Peterson, L. S. (1995, February). "Contraceptive Use in the United States: 1982-1990." From *Vital and Health Statistics. Advanced Data No. 260*, Hyattsville, MD: National Center for Health Statistics.

percent, mainly attributable to rising condom use (from 28 percent to 55 percent). The increase in condom use was particularly striking among Hispanic teens, with a threefold increase from 1980 to 1990 (17 percent to 58 percent).

Table 7 depicts the latest estimates of pregnancy prevention with typical use (indicating user failure) and perfect use (indicating method failure) among the contraceptive methods currently available in the United States (Hatcher et al., 1994). The most effective methods are Norplant, the oral contraceptive pill, male and female sterilization, Depo-Provera, and IUDs.

B. Childbirth and Single Women

Each year, one million American teenage girls become pregnant, a per-thousand rate twice that of Canada, England, and Sweden, and ten times that of the Netherlands. A similar disproportionately high rate is reported for teenage abortions (Jones et al. 1986).

The birthrate for unmarried American women has surged since 1980, with the rate for white women nearly doubling, and the rate for teenagers dropping from 53 percent of the unwed births in 1973, to 41 percent in 1980, and 30 percent in 1992. One out of every four American babies in 1992 was born to an unmarried woman. The unwed birthrate rose sharply for women 20 years and older. The highest rates were among women ages 20 to 24 (68.5 births per 1,000), followed by 18- and 19-year olds (67.3 per

<<<<< *Read across*

Age, Race, and Marital Status	IUD	Diaphragm	Condom	Periodic Abstinence[1]	Other
1988					
Race and Origin					
Hispanic	5.0	2.4	13.6	2.5	7.1
White non-Hispanic	1.5	6.6	15.2	2.3	5.0
Black non-Hispanic	3.2	2.0	10.1	2.1	5.9
Marital Status					
Currently married	2.0	6.2	14.3	2.8	5.6
Divorced, separated, widowed	3.6	5.3	5.9	1.9	3.8
Never married	1.3	4.9	19.6	1.3	5.7

1,000) and 25- to 29-year-olds (56.5 per 1,000). Overall, according to a 1995 report from the National Center for Health Statistics, the unmarried birthrate rose 54 percent between 1980 and 1992, from 29.4 births per 1,000 unmarried women ages 15 to 44 in 1980 to 45.2 births per 1,000 in both 1991 and 1992 (Holmes 1996a).

In 1970, the birthrate for unmarried black women was seven times the rate for white women, and four times the rate for white women in 1980. Since 1980, the white unmarried birthrate has risen by 94 percent while the rate for blacks rose only 7 percent. By 1992, the birthrate for single black women was just 2.5 times the rate for white women. In 1992, the out-of-wedlock birthrates were 95.3 for Hispanic women, 86.5 for black women, and 35.2 for white women (Holmes 1996a).

Commenting on the social implications of these statistics, Charles F. Westoff, a Princeton University demographer, said they "reflect the declining significance of marriage as a social obligation or a social necessity for reproduction." Poorly educated, low-income teenage mothers and their children are overwhelmingly likely to experience long-term negative consequences of early childbearing as single parent (Associated Press News Release, June 7, 1995). A 1996 study, sponsored by the charitable Robin Hood Foundation, estimated the public cost of unwed teenage pregnancy at $7 billion. The study looked at the consequences for teenage mothers, their children, and the fathers of the babies, compared with people from the same social background when pregnancy was delayed until the woman

Table 7

Percentage of Women Experiencing a Birth Control Failure During the First Year of Typical Use and the First Year of Perfect Use and the Percentage Continuing Use at the End of the First Year

Method	% of Women Experiencing an Accidental Pregnancy Within the First Year of Use		% of Women Continuing Use at One Year
	Typical Use	Perfect Use	
Chance	85	85	
Spermicide	21	6	43
Periodic Abstinence	20		67
Calendar		9	
Ovulation Method		3	
Sympto-Thermal		2	
Post-Ovulation		1	
Withdrawal	19	4	
Cap (with spermicide)			
Parous Women	36	24	45
Nulliparous Women	18	9	58
Sponge			
Parous Women	36	20	45
Nulliparous Women	18	9	58
Diaphragm (with spermicide)	18	6	58
Condom			
Female (Reality)	21	5	56
Male	12	3	63
Pill	3		
Progestin Only		0.5	N.A.
Combined		0.1	N.A.
IUD			
Progesterone T	2.0	1.5	81
Copper T 380A	0.8	0.6	78
Depo-Provera	0.3	0.3	70
Norplant (6 Capsules)	0.09	0.09	85
Female Sterilization	0.4	0.4	100
Male Sterilization	0.15	0.10	100

Source: Hatcher, R. et al. (1994). *Contraceptive Technology* (16th rev. ed.) p. 13. New York: Irvington.

was 20 or 21. The breakdown of annual costs included $2.2 billion in welfare and food-stamp benefits, $1.5 billion in medical-care costs, $900 million in increased foster-care expenses, $1 billion for additional prison construction, and $1.3 in lost tax revenue from the reduced productivity of teenage women who bear children (Holmes 1996a).

At the present rate, something like 50 percent or more of America's children will spend at least part of their childhood in a single-parent family. About half of this number will be the result of divorce or separation; the rest will be born to a mother who has never been married (Luker 1996).

In any given year, roughly 12 percent of American infants are born to teenage mothers. However, the vast majority of these teenage mothers are 18 or 19 years old, and thus only technically teenagers. American teenagers have been producing children at about the same rate for most of this century. Fewer than a third of all single mothers are teenagers, even when we include the 18- to 19-year-olds. And this proportion is declining. What is different in recent decades is that increasing numbers of teenage mothers are unmarried when they give birth. In 1970, only 30 percent of teenage mothers had never been married; by 1995, 70 percent of teenage mothers had never been married (Luker 1996).

While there is no good reason to suppose that the teenage birthrate is going up in any significant way—it was, in fact, higher in the 1950s—one must admit that the rate of single parenting is going up. In 1947, virtually all single mothers were widows, or living apart from their mate after separation or divorce. In 1947, fewer than one in a hundred had never been married. Today, overall, never-married single mothers account for one in three, and the percentage is rising. The number of single teenage mothers is going up at a rapid rate, but so is the number of single mothers at every age.

These data suggest that we are participants in, or at least witness to, an important shift in the nature of American family life that is echoing throughout the industrialized world. According to Luker (1996), the last years of this century may turn out to be the beginning of a time when the very notions of childrearing on the one hand and family life on the other are increasingly disconnected. While the rate of out-of-wedlock births is clearly on the way up, the rate of marriage may be declining, and the age of first marriage is clearly being delayed. In 1995, 60 percent of American families were headed by a single parent, half of them never-married. Luker (1996) suggests two possible outcomes. The present situation may prove to be only a temporary deviation from a stable pattern of long-standing. Or it may mark the first hesitant appearance of an important new pattern.

If the latter interpretation turns out to have substance, one can ask why this is happening. Luker cites several influential shifts in social attitudes and behavior. First, "illegitimacy" has lost its moral sting. Second, many women are realizing that they do not need to put up with the abuse, domination, and other burdens they associate with married life. This has special resonance for women in poverty, who ask why they should live with a male who is unreliable and has no skills or job. Third, although welfare benefits are declining throughout the industrialized world, teenage pregnancies are on the rise regardless of the level of welfare benefits. Finally, the vast majority of teenage pregnancies are unintended and not linked with the availability of welfare aid.

So long as teenagers are sexually active, the most effective way to reduce the incidence of childbearing is to assure that they have access to contraception before the fact, and abortion, if needed, after the fact. The many Americans who oppose sexuality and contraceptive education in the schools, distribution of contraceptives in schools, and abortion can only hope that someone discovers a way to reduce teenage sexual activity itself. That seems unlikely, given the decreasing age of puberty among American youth, the declining age of first sexual intercourse, and the clear trend to delay marriage well into the 20s or even 30s. Admonitions to "Just say 'No'" are scarcely going to suffice as a workable national policy. In analyzing the politics of teenage pregnancy and single mothers in the United States, Kristin Luker (1996) concluded that:

> Americans have every right to be concerned about early childbearing and to place the issue high on the national agenda. But they should think of it as a *measure*, not a cause, of poverty and other social ills. A teenager who has a baby usually adds but a slight burden to her life, which is already profoundly disadvantaged. . . . Early childbearing may make a bad situation worse, but the real causes of poverty lie elsewhere.

C. Abortion

In America today, it seems that two camps are at war over the abortion issue. "Pro-choice" supporters advocate the right of the individual woman to decide whether or not to continue a pregnancy. They contend that the rights of a woman must take precedence over the "assumed" rights of a fertilized human egg or fetus. They believe that a woman can never be free unless she has reproductive control over her own body. Pro-choice advocates in the United States include various Protestant and Jewish organizations, Catholics for Free Choice, Planned Parenthood, the National Organization for Women (NOW), National Abortion Rights Action League (NARAL), and the American Civil Liberties Union (ACLU), among others.

Anti-abortion groups have politically identified themselves as "pro-life" supporters of "the right to life" for the unborn. This coalition involves such constituents as Eastern Orthodox, charismatic and conservative Roman Catholics, fundamentalist Protestants, and Orthodox Jews, in influential groups like Operation Rescue, Focus on the Family, and the Christian Coalition. These groups use various methods in order to prevent women from being able to have abortions, including, in some cases, personal intimidation of abortion providers and clients and political action.

The basic motivation of the protection of human life of those in the anti-abortion movement has, however, been questioned. For example, an analysis of the voting records of U.S. senators who are anti-abortion advocates indicates that they had the lowest scores on votes for family-support issues, bills for school-lunch programs, and for aid to the elderly (Prescott and Wallace 1978).

A Brief Legal History

As documented by Brodie (1994), early American common law accepted abortion up until "quickening" (movement of the fetus). Not until the early 1800s did individual states begin to outlaw abortion at any stage of pregnancy. By 1880, most abortions were illegal in the United States, except those "necessary to save the life of the woman." However, since the right and practice of early abortion had already taken root in American society, abortionists openly continued to practice with public support and little legal enforcement. In the 1890s, doctors estimated that there were approximately two million abortions performed each year in the U.S. (Brodie 1994).

Before 1970, legal abortion was not available in the United States (Gordon 1976). In the 1950s, about one million illegal abortions were performed a year, with more than one thousand women dying each year as a result. Three quarters of the women who died from abortions in 1969 were women of color. Middle- and upper-class women, often with difficulty and great expense, could get "therapeutic abortions" from private physicians. By 1966, four fifths of all abortions were estimated to be for married women, and the ratio of legal to illegal abortions was 1 to 110.

In 1970, New York State passed legislation that allowed abortion on demand through the twenty-fourth week if it was done in a medical facility by a physician. However, on January 22, 1973, the U.S. Supreme Court decided a landmark case on abortion—*Roe v. Wade*. The Court stated the "right of privacy . . . founded in the Fourteenth Amendment's concept of personal liberty . . . is broad enough to encompass a woman's decision whether or not to terminate her pregnancy" (Tribe 1992). The major points of this decision were:

1. An abortion decision and procedure must be left up to the pregnant woman and her physician during the first trimester of pregnancy.
2. In the second trimester, the state may choose to regulate the abortion procedure in order to promote its interest in the health of the pregnant woman.
3. Once viability occurs, the state may promote its interest in the potentiality of human life by regulating and even prohibiting abortion except when judged medically necessary for the preservation of the health or life of the pregnant woman.

Although induced abortion is the most commonly performed surgical procedure in the United States, various restrictions continue to be placed upon the accessibility of abortion for certain groups of women. For example, in 1976, the Hyde Amendment, implemented through the United States Congress, prohibited federal Medicaid funds from being used to pay for abortions for women with low incomes. This is believed to contribute to the fact that low-income women of color are more likely to have second-trimester abortions, rather than first-trimester ones, since it takes time for them to save enough money for the procedure.

In addition, the Supreme Court has upheld various state laws that have been instituted to restrict abortions. In 1989, a Missouri law prohibiting the use of "public facilities" and "public employees" from being used to perform or assist abortions not necessary to save the life of the pregnant woman was upheld (*Webster v. Reproductive Health Services*). The court also upheld one of the strictest parental notification laws in the country in 1990 (*Hodgson v. Minnesota*). This law required notification of both of a minor's parents before she could have an abortion, even if she had never lived with them. Along with this restriction came a "waiting period" provision. A court decision in *Rust v. Sullivan* (1991) upheld a "gag rule" that prohibited counselors and physicians in federally funded family-planning clinics from providing information and making referrals about abortion. In 1992, the court upheld many restrictions set forth in a Pennsylvania law (*Planned Parenthood v. Casey*). These restrictions included requiring physicians to provide women seeking abortions with pro-childbirth information, followed by a twenty-four-hour "waiting period," and parental notification for minors (Tribe 1992).

Nineteen years after the *Roe* decision, the *Casey* decision demonstrated that the Supreme Court was divided more sharply than ever over abortion. While a minority of justices wanted to overturn the *Roe* decision outright, the majority did not allow a complete ban of abortion. However, by enacting the "undue burden" standard, they did lower the standard by which abortion laws are to be judged unconstitutional. This standard places the burden of proof on those challenging an abortion restriction to establish that it is a "substantial obstacle" to their constitutional rights.

The various state laws now restricting abortion are particularly burdensome for younger and poorer women, and open the way for the creation of increasing obstacles to women's access to abortion. Currently, only thirteen states provide funding for poor women for abortions, and thirty-five states enforce parent-notification/consent laws for minors seeking abortions. At the same time, the Supreme Court has upheld the right to abortion in many cases.

The recent murders of physicians and staff at abortion clinics, arson and bombing of abortion clinics, and the blocking of abortion clinics by anti-abortion protesters have contributed to women's difficulty in receiving this still-legal medical procedure. Over 80 percent of all abortion providers have been picketed, and many have experienced other forms of harassment, including bomb threats, blockades, invasions of facilities, property destruction, assault of staff and patients, and death threats.

In 1988, Operation Rescue, the term adopted by anti-abortion groups, brought thousands of protesters to Atlanta to blockade the abortion clinics. Using an 1871 statute enacted to protect African-Americans from the Ku Klux Klan, the federal courts invoked injunctions against the protesters. However, in 1993, this decision was overturned, leading to Operation Rescue blockades of abortion clinics in ten more U.S. cities. The federal government moved to apply the Racketeer Influenced and Corrupt Organization (RICO) Act against such blockades on the grounds that it was a form of extortion and part of a nationwide conspiracy. This application of the RICO Act was upheld unanimously by the Supreme Court in 1994. Despite this protection, there has nevertheless been a serious decline in the number of facilities and physicians willing to perform abortions.

Current Abortion Practice

Legally induced abortion has become the most commonly performed surgical procedure in the United States. In 1988, 6 million pregnancies and 1.5 million legal abortions were reported. One in five women (21 percent) of women of reproductive age have had an abortion (Hatcher et al. 1994). If current abortion rates continue, nearly half of all American women will have at least one abortion during their lifetime.

Women having abortions in the United States come from every background and walk of life (Koch 1995). Abortion rates are highest among 18- to 19-year-old women, with almost 60 percent being less than 25 years old. One in eight (12 percent) are minors, aged 17 or younger. Of these minors, over 98 percent are unmarried and in school or college, with fewer than one tenth having had any previous children.

The vast majority (80 percent) of adult women having abortions are separated, divorced, or never married, with 20 percent currently married. One third of American women seeking abortions are poor. Almost half are currently mothers, with most of them already having two or more children. Half of the women seeking abortions were using a form of birth control during the month in which they conceived. About one third of abortion clients are employed, one third attend public school or college, and the other third are unemployed. The majority of women (69 percent) getting abortions are Anglo-American. Latinas are 60 percent more likely than Anglos to terminate an unintended pregnancy, but are less likely to do so than are African-American women.

Women with a more-liberal religious or humanist commitment are four times more likely to get an abortion than those adhering to conservative religious beliefs, according to Alan Guttmacher Institute surveys in 1991 and 1996. Catholic women are just as likely as other women to get abortions.

Catholic women, who constitute 31% of the female population, had 31 percent of the abortions in 1996. In 1991, one sixth of abortion clients in the U.S. were born-again or evangelical Christians (Alan Guttmacher Institute 1991). In a similar 1996 survey, evangelical or born-again Christians, who account for almost half the American population, had 18% of the abortions.

Women give multiple reasons for their decision to have an abortion, the most important reasons being financial inability to support the child and inability to handle all the responsibilities of parenting. Three quarters of abortion clients believe that having a baby would interfere with work, school, or their other family responsibilities. Over half are concerned about being single parents and believe that the relationship with the father will be ending soon. Adolescent women, in particular, usually believe that they are not mature enough to have a child. One fifth of the women seeking an abortion are concerned that either the fetus or they, themselves, have a serious health problem which necessitates an abortion. One in a hundred abortion clients are rape or incest survivors. Most abortion clients (70 percent) want to have children in the future.

Half of the abortions in the U.S. are performed before the eighth week of gestation and five out of six are performed before the thirteenth week (Hatcher et al. 1994). The safest and easiest time for the procedure is within the first three months. Most (97 percent) women receiving abortions during this time have no complications or postabortion complaints. Vacuum curettage is the most widely used abortion procedure in the United States, accounting for 97 percent of abortions in 1989. Intra-amniotic infusion is the rarest form of abortion performed, accounting for only 1 percent of abortions in 1989.

The weight of research evidence indicates that legal abortion, particularly in the first trimester, does not create short or long-term physical or psychological risks for women, including impairment of future fertility (Russo and Zierk 1992). In 1985, the maternal death rate for legal abortions was 0.5 per 100,000 for suction methods, 4.0 for induced labor, and one in 10,000 for childbirth (Hatcher et al. 1994).

Attitudes Toward Abortion

The National Opinion Research Center has been documenting attitudes toward abortion since 1972 (Smith 1996). Throughout this time period, public support for abortion under various circumstances has increased (see Table 8). The vast majority of Americans approve of abortion if a pregnancy seriously endangers the health of the mother, if the fetus has a serious defect, or if the pregnancy resulted from a rape or incest. Approximately half of the American public approves of abortion if the woman does not want to marry the father or if the parents cannot afford a child or do not want any more children. Close to half of Americans approve of abortion if

Table 8

Percentage of U.S.A. Adults Approving of Legal Abortion for Various Reasons

Reason	1972	1985	1996
Pregnancy poses serious health endangerment for woman	87.4	89.9	91.5
Strong chance of serious defect of fetus	78.6	78.9	81.1
Pregnancy resulted from rape	79.1	81.5	83.7
Parent(s) low income—cannot afford a child	48.9	43.2	45.7
Unmarried woman who does not want to marry father	43.8	41.2	44.3
Married woman who does not want more children	40.2	40.7	46.2
Woman wants an abortion for any reason	N.A.*	37.0	44.6

*Not asked

Source: Smith, T. W. (1996, December). Unpublished data from 1972-1996. *General Social Surveys.* Chicago: National Opinion Research Center.

the woman wants it for any reason. Level of education has the strongest effect on people's attitudes, with college-educated people being significantly more approving than those who are less educated. Catholics, fundamentalist Protestants, and Mormons who have a strong religious commitment are the most likely to disapprove of abortion. Anglo-Americans are somewhat more approving than African-Americans; men and adults under 30 are slightly more approving than women and adults over 65. In general, approval of legal abortion and the right of women to control their reproductive ability is associated with a broad commitment to basic civil liberties.

America is at a crossroads in terms of protecting the access of all women to abortion (Tribe 1992, 6). (See comments on efforts of the Christian Coalition to enact laws that restrict and limit access to abortion and abortion information in Section 2A). The era of absolute judicial protection of legal abortion rights that began with the Supreme Court's 1973 decision in *Roe v. Wade* ended with that Court's 1989 decision upholding certain state regulations of abortion in the case of *Webster v. Reproductive Health Services.* Thus, a woman's right to decide whether to terminate a pregnancy was placed in the arena of rough-and-tumble politics, subject to regulation, and possibly even prohibition, by federal and state elected representatives. The range of abortion rights that many Americans have taken for granted are now in jeopardy. Even as the public agenda is stretched to address such new questions as the right to die, the use of aborted fetal tissue in treating disease, and the ethics and legal consequences of reproductive technologies, no issue threatens to divide Americans politically in quite as powerful a way as the abortion issue still does.

10. Sexually Transmitted Diseases
ROBERT T. FRANCOEUR

It is impossible to obtain reliable statistics about the incidence of STDs, because American physicians are only required by law to report cases of HIV and syphilis to the Centers for Disease Control and Prevention (CDC). Public clinics keep fairly reliable statistics, but many private physicians record syphilis and other STDs as urinary infections and do not report them to the CDC. A second, equally important factor leading to the lack of data is the number of persons infected with various STDs who are without symptoms and do not know they are infectious. This "silent epidemic" includes most males infected with candidiasis, 10 percent of males and 60 to 80 percent of females infected with chlamydia, 5 to 20 percent of males and up to 80 percent of females with gonorrhea, and many males and females with hemophilus, NGU, and trichomonas infections.

In 1995, the nation's three most commonly reported infections were sexually transmitted, according to statistics from the federal Centers for Disease Control and Prevention released in October 1996. Chlamydia, tracked for the first time in 1995, topped the list with 477,638 cases. Gonorrhea, the most commonly reported infectious disease in 1994 with 418,068 cases dropped to second in 1995 with 392,848 cases. AIDS dropped from second place in 1994 (78,279 cases) to third place in 1995 (71,547 cases). In 1995, five sexually transmitted diseases, chlamydia, gonorrhea, AIDS, syphylis, and hepatitis B, accounted for 87 percent of the total number of infectious cases caused by the top ten maladies. Chalmydia was more commonly reported among women, striking 383,956 in 1995; gonorrhea and AIDS were more common with men, with 203,563 and 58,007 cases, respectively.

The latest data suggest that the national incidence of gonorrhea and syphilis has continued to decline (U.S. Department of Health and Human Services 1994). Reported cases of gonorrhea peaked at a million cases in 1978 and declined to about 700,000 cases in 1990. With a realistic estimate suggesting two million new cases annually, gonorrhea is one of the most commonly encountered STDs, especially among the young. About 50,000 new cases of syphilis are reported annually; an estimated 125,000 new cases occur annually. Syphilis is primarily an adult disease, mostly concentrated in larger cities, and one of the least common STDs. The incidence of syphilis rose sharply between the late 1980s and the early 1990s, and then continued its more long-term decline. Congenital syphilis rates have decreased in parallel to declining rates of syphilis among women. Infants most at risk were born to unmarried, African-American women who receive little or no prenatal care. Syphilis and gonorrhea have consistently been more common in the southern states. Reasons for this are not well understood, but may include differences in racial and ethnic distribution of the population, poverty, and the availability and quality of health-care services.

Chlamydia is the most prevalent bacterial STD in the United States, with four million adults and possibly 10 percent of all college students infected. It is more common in higher socioeconomic groups and among university students. Prevention and control programs were begun in 1994, and are a high priority because of the potential impact on pelvic inflammatory disease (PID) and its sequelae, infertility and ectopic pregnancy. Twenty to 40 percent of women infected with chlamydia develop PID. Many states have implemented reporting procedures and begun collecting case data for chlamydia.

Three million new cases of trichomonas are reported annually, but probably another six million harbor the protozoan without symptoms. Fifteen million Americans have had at least one bout of genital herpes. About a million new cases of genital warts are reported annually.

STD rates continue to be much higher for African-Americans and other minorities than for white Americans, sixtyfold higher for blacks and fivefold higher for Latinos. About 81 percent of the total reported cases of gonorrhea occur among African-Americans, with the risk for 15- to 19-year-old blacks more than twentyfold higher than for white adolescents. Similarly, the general gonorrhea rate is fortyfold higher for blacks and threefold higher for Latinos than it is for white Americans. There are no known biologic reasons to explain these differences. Rather, race and ethnicity in the United States are risk markers that correlate with poverty, access to quality health care, health-care-seeking behavior, illicit drug use, and living in communities with a high prevalence of STDs.

11. HIV/AIDS

A. A National Perspective   ANDREW D. FORSYTH

In a single decade, human immunodeficiency virus (HIV), the agent that causes acquired immunodeficiency syndrome (AIDS), has become one of the greatest threats to public health in the United States. By 1992, AIDS surpassed heart disease, cancer, suicide, and homicide to become the leading cause of death among men between ages 25 and 54 (CDC 1993a). Similarly, AIDS became the fourth leading cause of death among women between ages 25 to 44 in 1992 and the eighth leading cause of death among all United States citizens. Over one million people are estimated to be infected with HIV in the United States—approximately 1 in 250—and over 441,528 cases of AIDS have been diagnosed, 62 percent of which have already resulted in death (CDC, 1994a).

Trends suggest that AIDS will continue to have significant impact in the United States in coming years. Throughout the 1980s and early 1990s, there was a steady increase in the number of documented AIDS cases. However, between 1993 and 1994, the number of AIDS cases reported to public health departments nationwide dramatically increased due to the implementation of an expanded surveillance definition of AIDS, which included cases of severe immunosuppression manifesting in earlier stages of HIV infection. Although the number of AIDS cases declined in 1994 relative to the previous year, it still represents a considerable increase over cases reported in 1992 (CDC 1995a).

Consistent with previous years, the most severely affected segment of the U.S. population in 1994 was men who have sex with men. Although men constitute 82 percent of all AIDS cases reported among adults and adolescents (13 years or older), men who have sex with men represent the single largest at-risk group, constituting 44 percent of all nonpediatric AIDS cases (CDC 1994a). Young men who have sex with men (between ages 20 and 24) constitute a particularly salient at-risk group for HIV infection, representing 60 percent of AIDS cases among all men of that same age. In contrast, 53 percent of all men with AIDS occur in men who have sex with men.

Even so, the number of AIDS cases reported among men who have sex with men decreased by 1.1 percent for the second consecutive year in 1992, suggesting that infection rates among this segment of the population may be leveling off (CDC 1993a). The same cannot be said for heterosexual men who inject drugs and men who inject drugs and have sex with men; they represent the second and third largest at-risk groups among men, explaining 24 percent and 6 percent of AIDS cases, respectively (CDC 1994b). Newly reported AIDS cases for these groups continue to increase sharply. Although only 4 percent of all men diagnosed with AIDS by 1994 were infected via sexual contact with an infected woman, they had the largest proportionate increase in AIDS cases among all men in recent years (CDC 1994a).

The proportion of AIDS cases reported among women has more than doubled since the mid-1980s (CDC 1994b). In 1994, 58,448 cumulative cases of AIDS were documented among women, comprising 13 percent of all adults and adolescents (13 years or older) diagnosed with AIDS in the United States (CDC 1994a). Although they represent a minority of all AIDS cases, the incidence of AIDS among women has increased more rapidly than have rates for men, with over 24 percent of all cases of AIDS among women reported in the last year alone (CDC 1994b). The impact of the CDC's implementation of the expanded case definition for AIDS is particularly salient for incidence rates among women: In 1994, 59 percent of cases of women with AIDS were reported based on the revised surveillance definitions. Correspondingly, the incidence of AIDS opportunistic illness (AIDS-OI) has increased more rapidly among women than it has for men. Overall, the modes of HIV transmission for women also differ considerably from those for men: Women are most likely to be infected via intravenous drug use (41 percent) or sex with infected men (38 percent). Although 19 percent of women with AIDS reported no risk of exposure to HIV, follow-up data from local public health departments suggested an inverse trend. Most of those with previously unidentified risk exposure were infected via heterosexual contact (66 percent) or intravenous drug use (27 percent (CDC 1994b).

Because women of childbearing age (i.e., 15 to 44 years old) represent 84 percent of AIDS cases among women, perinatal transmission of HIV presents itself as a serious problem (CDC 1994b). In comparison with the statistics for HIV transmission for all women cited above, the most frequently reported modes of HIV transmission for seropositive new mothers were by heterosexual contact with infected male partners (36 percent) and injection drug use (30 percent) (CDC 1994a). However, it is often impossible to separate these two avenues of infection, because women may be having sex with of an infected male while also using IV drugs, both before and during pregnancy. According to recent trends, approximately 7,000 HIV-infected women gave birth to infants in the United States in 1993; about 30 percent of these infants may have contracted HIV perinatally (Gwinn et al. 1991). In 1994, 1,017 cases of AIDS were documented among children less than 13 years of age, an increase of 8 percent from 1993. In 92 percent of these cases, children contracted HIV perinatally (CDC 1994a). Demographically, there were no apparent differences in perinatal transmission rates between boys and girls; however, most newly reported cases of pediatric AIDS occurred among African-American (62 percent) and Hispanic (23 percent) children (CDC 1995a). By December 1994, a cumulative total of 6,209 AIDS cases were documented among children 13 years or younger (CDC 1994a).

In any discussion of incidence, etiology, and the avenues of infection for HIV/AIDS, the official CDC statistics are quite misleading, especially when comparing figures for different years. The clinical definition of the AIDS syndrome has been expanded several times, making the incidence seem comparatively lower in earlier years. In addition, the CDC has not been consistent in studying modes of infection, especially for women. The intake interview questions asked of men and women seeking HIV testing have changed significantly over the years; they also differ significantly for men and women, with several possible avenues of infection left out in the questions for women. In the 1980s, being born in a developing country could be listed as an avenue for men and women testing HIV-positive; women, but not men, were asked if they had had sex with a person from a developing nation. Also, the criteria for assignment to the "unidentified risk" category has changed back and forth, which in turn raises or lowers the number of infected individuals in other categories.

Clearly, adolescents and young adults are at-risk for HIV infection as well, although modes of transmission for them vary considerably. In 1994, there was a cumulative total of 1,965 cases of AIDS among adolescents between ages 13 and 19 years (CDC 1994a). For this age group, males represented 66 percent of AIDS cases and most frequently contracted HIV through receipt of infected blood products (44 percent), through sex with men (32 percent), or through injection drug use (7 percent). In contrast, females between the ages of 13 and 19 most frequently contracted HIV through sexual contact with infected men (52 percent) or injection drug use (18 percent); 22 percent of these young women failed to identify an exposure category. For young adults between the ages of 20 and 24, men represented 77 percent of AIDS cases, most of whom contracted HIV through sex with men (63 percent), injection drug use (13 percent), or sex with men and injection drug use (11 percent). Young women in this group were most likely to be infected with HIV through sexual contact with infected men (50 percent) or injection drug use (33 percent). Another 14 percent of women in this age group failed to identify an exposure category, although it is possible that the most frequent mode of transmission for them and their younger peers parallels that of older women who initially failed to report an exposure category, most of whom were infected via sexual contact with infected men (CDC 1994a).

The impact of the AIDS epidemic has been especially devastating in communities of color in the United States, largely due to a number of socioeconomic factors that disproportionately affect racial and ethnic minorities (CDC 1993b). Although they represent only 21 percent of the population, racial and ethnic minorities presently constitue 47 percent of cumulative AIDS cases among adult and adolescent men, 76 percent of cases among adult and adolescent women, and 81 percent of all pediatric AIDS cases (CDC 1994a). In 1994, African-Americans and Hispanics alone represented 58 percent of the 80,691 reported AIDS cases for that year, and they had the highest rates of infection per 100,000 people (100.8 and 51.0, respectively). In contrast, Asian/Pacific Islanders and American Indians/Alaska Natives comprised 577 (0.007 percent) and 227 (0.003 percent) of AIDS cases, respectively, reported in 1994 and had the lowest rates of infection per 100,000 people (6.4 and 12.0 percent, respectively). Whites comprirsed 33,193 (41 percent) of AIDS cases reported in 1994 and had the third highest infection rate per 100,000 people (17.2 percent).

The disproportionate effects of AIDS on racial minorities in the U.S. are most salient among women and children. In 1994, infection rates among African-American and Hispanic adult and adolescent women (i.e., 13 years and older) were 16.5 and 6.8 times higher than were rates for white women of the same ages, respectively (CDC 1994a). Likewise, infection rates among African-American and Hispanic children (i.e., less than 13 years old) were 21 and 7.5 times higher than were rates for white children, respectively. Although racial and ethnic status do not themselves confer risk for HIV/AIDS, a number of sociocultural factors inherent to many communities of color increase the risk of HIV infection, including chronic underemployment, poverty, lack of access to health-education services, and inadequate health care (CDC 1993b).

Clearly, AIDS has quickly emerged as a leading threat to public health facing United States citizens. Although there appear to be trends indicating that the impact of AIDS is leveling off in some risk groups (e.g., men who have sex with men), it is increasing steadily in others (e.g., African-American and Hispanic women and children). Furthermore, it is possible that additional segments of the population are currently "at risk" for HIV infection, including the severely mentally ill, older adults, and women who have sex with women. AIDS cases among them may constitute a third wave in the AIDS epidemic.

Because there is no cure for AIDS, behavioral change that reduces risk of exposure to HIV (e.g., unprotected sex and sharing of needles while injecting drugs) is paramount. Interventions focusing on AIDS education, self-protective behavioral change, and utilization of existing medical and testing services together represent the most promising course of action in the prevention of HIV infection and AIDS in the United States.

The clinical definition of AIDS has been revised twice by the Centers for Disease Control, first in 1987 and then in 1993, when new female symptoms for invasive cervical (stage 4) and other disease were added, along with a revision in the T4 (helper) cell count. These redefinitions need to be considered when interpreting statistics on the rates of AIDS infection.

Confidential testing for HIV status is available nationwide, with a free or sliding-scale fee and counselors available to assist in informing partners of HIV-positive persons. Several states have won the right to test all prospective employees for HIV and share this information with related agencies. The American Civil Liberties Union has won a court decision denying mandatory testing. Legal and ethical challenges posed by HIV/AIDS are far-reaching, and it may be another decade before consistent, reasonable, and effective guidelines emerge.

Although African-Americans constitute 12 percent of the population, they represent 27 percent of the reported AIDS cases (CDC 1992), these infections being due more to heterosexual intercourse and IV drug use than to gay and bisexual men. Hispanics are also overrepresented, with 16 percent of reported cases. Consequently, there is an urgent need for development of the education and prevention programs in the African-American and Latino communities.

College students pose a particular problem. Changes in college-student behaviors between 1982 and 1988 were not encouraging. In a comparison of student behavior among 363 unmarried students in 1982 (when the term AIDS was coined and few articles were published on the subject) and 273 students in 1988, the number of students having intercourse, the number of partners, and the lifetime incidence of intercourse all increased. In 1988, 72 percent of men and 83 percent of women had received oral sex, and 69 percent of males and 76 percent of females had given oral sex; 14 and 17 percent respectively had engaged in anal sex. Twenty percent of males and 12 percent of females in 1988 had four or more partners. Students with multiple or casual partners were less likely to use condoms; there also was no increase in condom use from first to most recent intercourse (Bishop and Lipsitz 1991).

Despite the need and proven effectiveness of sterile needle-exchange programs for IV drug users and the free distribution of condoms in high schools, both programs have met considerable opposition from conservative groups and the religious right. At the same time, the need for safer-sex education for all segments of the population has allowed educators to make considerable progress in general sexuality education that might not have been possible if AIDS did not pose such a major public health problem.

B. Five Specific Emerging Issues   LINDA L. HENDRIXSON

AIDS as a Family Dilemma

As the AIDS pandemic continues through its second decade in the United States, unforeseen issues have emerged as important considerations in attempts to meet the needs of people living with AIDS (PLWAs).

What began as a disease syndrome affecting individuals has become a problem which confronts whole families in America. Researchers, health providers, and policymakers have had to re-work their approaches to take into account the impact that AIDS has on family members, both immediate and extended. Our definition of "family" has undergone much change throughout this pandemic. As we consider the people who care for PLWAs, and those who care about them, family has come to be defined much more broadly than before. The family of origin has been replaced or extended to include non-blood-related friends, lovers, AIDS buddies, and others who provide emotional and instrumental support.

For many PLWAs, estrangement from birth families is a way-of-life. AIDS exacerbates those earlier problems. Others become estranged after their diagnosis is discovered. Families who have not disclosed the illness of their family member live with fear of ostracism and discrimination. If an AIDS diagnosis is kept secret within the family, social isolation becomes a continuing problem. Family pressures escalate if children are involved, especially if those children are infected. The financial strain of caring for adults and/or children with AIDS can be considerable. Finding competent doctors is an additional serious challenge throughout the country. Medical costs, health insurance, adequate health care, and social support, caregiving, child custody, disclosure, stigma, discrimination, loss, and grieving are among the troubling issues facing families and others living with AIDS (Macklin 1989).

Emerging Populations and Changing Locales

AIDS is no longer found in what were originally perceived to be the only affected American AIDS populations—white, middle-class gay men and minority intravenous drug users in the inner cities (Voeller 1991; Wiener 1991). AIDS is now found in:

- people who live in rural locations;
- middle- and upper-class women, many of whom do not misuse drugs or alcohol;
- women who have only vaginal sex with men;
- women who have rectal sex with men, but do not report this behavior;
- women who have received contaminated donor semen;
- women who have had oral sex with other women;
- middle- and upper-class men;
- men who have only vaginal sex with women, and do not have sex with other men;
- black, Hispanic, and Asian gay and bisexual men;
- teenagers who have been sexually abused as children;
- people who use drugs, such as heroin, but do not use needles;
- athletes who use contaminated needles while injecting illegal steroids;
- women with blood-clotting disorders;
- people who have received contaminated organ transplants and other body tissues;
- senior citizens; and
- babies who nurse from infected mothers

There is no longer a statistically precise AIDS profile or pattern. To a great extent, epidemiological categories have become meaningless.

The spread of AIDS to rural and small-town locations is worth noting. Most people still equate AIDS with major urban areas, and, true, the numbers of cases are highest there. However, the pandemic has diffused from urban epicenters, past suburbia, and into small, rural enclaves in the U.S. (Cleveland and Davenport 1989) The spread of AIDS in Africa along truck routes, as men seek sex away from home, is not unlike the spread of AIDS along major highways in the U.S., as people travel in and out of metropolitan AIDS epicenters. The government is paying little attention to rural AIDS in America; it is the least understood and least researched part of our national epidemic, with numbers of infected rising dramatically.

Limited research shows that some PLWAs who left their rural birthplaces for life in the city, are now returning to their rural families to be cared for. But many PLWAs who grew up in cities are leaving their urban birthplaces and moving to the country where they believe it is healthier for them, mentally and physically. This is especially true for recovering addicts whose city friends have died of AIDS, and who hope to escape a similar fate.

Besides the "in-migration" of people with AIDS to rural locations, there are many indigenous people in small towns who are infected as well. The numbers of cases of HIV/AIDS is increasing rapidly in rural America, where social services are inadequate, medical care is generally poor, and community denial is a reality. Federal and state monies continue to be channeled to inner-city agencies, leaving rural and small-town providers with scant resources to ease increasing caseloads (Hendrixson 1996).

Complexion of the Pandemic

The face of AIDS is changing in other ways, as well. There is now a considerable number of infected people who have outlived medical predictions about their morbidity and mortality. These are divided into two groups: asymptomatic non-progressors, and long-term survivors. Both groups test HIV-antibody-positive, indicating past infection with human immunodeficiency virus.

Despite being HIV-antibody-positive, the first group shows no other laboratory or clinical symptoms of HIV disease. The second group has experienced immune suppression and some opportunistic infections, and is diagnosed as having AIDS, but continues to live beyond its expected lifespan (Laurence 1994). In addition, there are others who are inexplicably uncharacteristic:

- people who have been diagnosed with AIDS, but who do not test HIV-antibody-positive, meaning that there is no indication of previous exposure to the virus, despite their illnesses
- people who have "retro-converted" from testing HIV-antibody-positive to now testing HIV-antibody-negative
- people who are repeatedly exposed to HIV through sex or contaminated blood and who do not become infected

Scientists have no explanation for these anomalies. Little research has been done on people who do not fit the accustomed pattern physicians look for. Yet, the very fact that they challenge medical expectations is a clue that they hold answers that may help thousands of others in this country.

In many ways, some new drug treatments have helped infected people forestall serious illnesses, turning AIDS into more of a chronic than an acute-illness syndrome. Yet many PLWAs have renounced AZT and other toxic anti-retroviral drugs, because of their serious side effects. Increasing numbers of patients are embracing alternative therapies—physical, mental, and spiritual—rather than taking potent AIDS drugs. Others are combining the best of conventional and unconventional medicine in their own self-styled treatment plans. The new protease inhibitors offer much promise, but it is too early to know what side effects they may produce. The bottom line is that AIDS no longer automatically equates with death ("The End of AIDS" 1996).

HIV-Positive Children Coming of Age

As life is extended, more and more children born with the virus are moving through late childhood and early adolescence in relatively good physical health. New challenges await them and their families. Some children may know they are infected with HIV; others may not. They continue to grow socially, with sexual feelings beginning to emerge. How do we help them fit in with their uninfected peers? How do we teach them about their sexuality? How do we prepare them for dating situations? What do we say when they speak of marriage hopes? How do we teach them about safer sex? What new approaches in HIV/AIDS education should health teachers consider as these children enter their classes? Parents, teachers, and youth leaders are wrestling with new questions that were unanticipated ten years ago when we believed that HIV-antibody-positive children would not live much beyond toddlerhood.

New Paradigms, New Theories

At least one revolutionary theory about AIDS is gaining prominence, as a cure for the syndrome continues to elude us. Dr. Peter Duesberg, a cancer geneticist, virologist, and molecular biologist at the University of California–Berkeley, and a member of the elite National Academy of Sciences, along with other well-established scientists, has challenged the standard medical and scientific HIV hypothesis. He maintains that AIDS researchers have never definitively proven that HIV alone causes AIDS. He theorizes that HIV cannot be the sole cause of such a complex cascade of physiological events as the complete suppression of the entire human immune system, eventually leading to fatal opportunistic infections and conditions such as cancer and dementia.

Duesberg, one of the first scientists to discover retroviruses, the family of viruses to which HIV belongs, contends that HIV is a benign "carrier" retrovirus which a healthy immune system inactivates as it would any intruder. HIV antibodies result from this normal defense response. Being HIV-antibody-positive only means that a person's immune system is working properly. It does not mean that the person will develop AIDS.

Duesberg and others believe that the serious immune suppression which manifests as severely lowered T-cell counts and opportunistic infections that may become fatal, can result from one or more of the following factors, all of which are immune-suppressive:

- continuous, long-term misuse of legal and illegal recreational drugs, including sexual aphrodisiacs such as nitrite inhalants, used by men to facilitate rectal sex with other men;
- over-use of prescription drugs, including antibiotics, anti-virals, and anti-parasitics, often taken for repeated sexually transmitted infections;
- toxic effects of AZT and other anti-retroviral drugs, which are intended to interfere with cell DNA replication ("DNA chain terminators"), and, therefore, kill *all* body cells without discrimination;
- malnutrition, which often accompanies long-term illicit drug and alcohol use; or
- untreated sexual diseases and other recurring illnesses, which also suppress immunity.

One or a combination of these factors eventually brings on the potentially fatal condition which the CDC arbitrarily calls "AIDS."

Duesberg points to the number of people with AIDS who do not test HIV-antibody-positive, as well as those who are HIV-antibody-positive but are not symptomatic. He questions why scientists are not interested in studying these people who defy the accepted AIDS dogma. Duesberg's efforts to have his research papers published by the mainstream American scientific press, to present his views at scientific AIDS conferences, and to be awarded funding to do additional AIDS research have met with virtual failure in this country.

Duesberg (1996) has been shut out by the powerful medical/scientific establishment which pretends to be open to new ideas and theories, but which, he maintains, is chained to the HIV-equals-AIDS hypothesis. He presented his challenge in a 1996 book entitled *Inventing the AIDS Virus*.

Conclusion

In the fifteenth year of the AIDS pandemic, we have no cure and no vaccine for this disease. Thousands have died in our country, most of them young people. Thousands more have died in other countries. New advances in drug treatments and alternative/holistic modalities have helped some American PLWAs, but many families continue to silently mourn the death of their loved ones. The stigma of AIDS is ever-present; the fear continues. Yet, compassion and love have emerged, as well, as caring people reach out to help those who are suffering. AIDS appears to have "dug in" for the long term while science looks for answers. In the meanwhile, we need to ask two questions. First, as scientists search for the truth of AIDS, are they asking the right questions? Second, as the disease shifts from its former pattern of early, premature death to a more manageable long-term chronic illness, are we meeting the needs of all the people infected and affected by this disease—PLWAs, their families, and their loved ones?

C. The Impact of AIDS on Our Perception of Sexuality   RAYMOND J. NOONAN

Little has been written on the impact that AIDS has had and continues to have on our collective sensibilities about sexuality and our innate needs to express aspects of our sexual selves. Research has been sparse, if non-existent, on the various meanings ascribed—both by professionals in the sexual sciences and members of the general public—to either sexuality itself or to the disease complex of AIDS.

Professionals in any field often serve to support and maintain the various cultural norms of any given society. As such, with the exception of the safety-valve role of those who might be referred to as the "loyal opposition," rarely are there expressions of sentiments or ideas that seriously challenge widely held beliefs and assumptions. Within the various disciplines encompassing the sexual sciences, the struggling theory, for example, that HIV may not be the direct cause of AIDS (see previous section), is one of the few examples of such reassessments. Among the popular press, nevertheless, various accounts have sporadically appeared with critical appraisals of either our general or specific approaches to current AIDS perspectives, including Farber (1993; 1993a; 1993b), Fumento (1990), Patton (1990), and others.

Current Trends

It cannot be denied that AIDS is a serious, debilitating, and potentially deadly disease. Yet, the American response to it has often been one in which the reality of the disease, as well as myths promoted as facts, have been appropriated to further some related or unrelated political aim. Metaphorical allusions are often used to discuss the issue, not to impart factual information about or to motivate persons to AIDS prevention, but to further a political agenda or even to attack some political group(s) perceived as adversaries. Such political goals and targets have included:

- claims that AIDS is God's punishment for sexual impropriety made by some homophobic religious leaders and others;
- instituting and promoting sex education by supporters;
- the promotion of male contraceptive responsibility by some health and sexuality professionals;
- AIDS used as a scare tactic to discourage sexual activity, particularly among the young, by some parents and others;
- providing the "scientific" reason for postponing sexual activity, being more selective about who one's sexual partners are, and reducing the number of sexual partners, by some educational, political, and health authorities;
- the promotion of monogamy and abstinence;
- the promotion of community and solidarity among compatriots, from gays to fundamentalist Christians, who perceive they are under attack;
- the use of AIDS to promote anti-male, anti-white, and/or anti-Western attitudes; and
- the advocacy of some noncoital sex practices to communicate covert negative (heterophobic) views of heterosexuality and penile-vaginal intercourse (see Noonan 1996, pp. 182-185).

For most sexologists and sexuality educators, the co-opting of the issues of protection and responsibility, especially for young people, reflects the intrinsically good part of human nature that seeks to find the "silver lining" in the dark cloud of HIV/AIDS. Although these political goals and targets probably do not apply to all people who are concerned about HIV/AIDS, these philosophies have had a more profound effect on overall public and professional approaches to sexuality and related issues than the number of their supporters would suggest. Some examples follow.

Although it is well known that anal intercourse offers the most effective way for HIV to be transmitted sexually, and that vaginal-penile intercourse is far less risky, rarely have investigators asked those whose infections are suspected to have been heterosexually transmitted, particularly women, whether and how often they engaged in anal intercourse. Instead, heterosexually transmitted HIV infections are assumed to be vaginally transmitted, although this is generally unlikely on the individual scale, and not likely to result in an HIV epidemic in the heterosexual population (Brody 1995; National Research Council 1993).

Concentrating only on the condom for both contraception and STD/AIDS prevention ignores the effectiveness of spermicidal agents with nonoxynol-9 in the prevention of pregnancy and infection as a reasonable alternative for couples who object to condom use (North 1990) (see Table 7 in Section 9A). It also ignores the negative impact condoms have on sexual intimacy for some couples (Juran 1995).

In addition, our terminology with respect to AIDS has had a profound impact on our perception of sexuality. For example, the well-known slogan, "When you sleep with someone, you are having sex with everyone she or he has slept with for the last x-number of years," is believed to be literally true by many people. The effectiveness of this slogan is seriously undermined when questions are raised about the kind of statistical and/or epidemiological evidence available to support this statement. To many, such slogans imply a view of sexuality that denigrates *all* sexual experiences, no matter how valid or valuable they are or have been. The "epidemic" of AIDS is another phrase that many, if not most, people believe to be literally true. They fail to realize that the word is being used in its metaphorical sense, with its emotional connotations being more important than its literal truth. The same can be said for the statement, "Everyone is equally at risk for AIDS." Granted this statement is true, but only in the trivial sense that we are all, as mortal human beings, prone to sickness and death. The fact that ethnic and racial minorities in the U.S. are disproportionately represented in the AIDS and HIV-positive statistics (CDC 1996) should dispel that myth completely. Brandt (1988) has insightfully analyzed the notion of AIDS-as-metaphor:

> At a moment when the dangers of promiscuous sex are being emphasized, it suggests that every *single* sexual encounter is a promiscuous encounter. . . . As anonymous sex is being questioned, this metaphor suggests that no matter how well known a partner may be, the relationship is *anonymous*. Finally, the metaphor implies to heterosexuals that if they are having sex with their partner's (heterosexual) partners, they are in fact engaging in homosexual acts. In this view, every sexual act becomes a homosexual encounter. (p. 77, emphasis in original)

In fact, our very use of the terms "safe" or "safer sex" implies that all sex is dangerous, when in fact it usually is not (Noonan 1996a).

It is typical within the American culture to ignore the chronic problems that result from the general American uncomfortableness with sexuality and sexual pleasure. In terms of responding to the health issues surrounding AIDS, Americans have two choices:

1. We can continue to respond as we have to other sexual issues, by spotlighting them and ignoring the broader issues of sane healthy sexuality, which includes the celebration of sexual intimacy and pleasure. This narrow panic response is typical of American culture and its dealing with such issues as teenage pregnancy, child sexual abuse, satanic ritual practices, sexual "promiscuity," the "threats" to heterosexual marriage and the family posed by recognition of same-sex marriages, and the "epidemics" of herpes and heterosexual AIDS; or

2. We can respond to the AIDS crisis within the context of positive broad-based accommodation to radical changes in American sexual behavior and relationships. This broad-based, sex-positive approach could well include: the availability of comprehensive, more affordable, and more reliable sexual-health and STD evaluations for men, comparable to the regularly scheduled gynecological exams generally encouraged for women; the development of effective alternatives to the condom, including the availability of effective male contraceptives that are separated from the sexual act of intercourse, easy to use, and reliable; making birth control as automatic for men as the pill has been for women (ideally, they would also work to prevent STDs); the expansion of research to make all contraceptives safe for both women and men; the elimination of fear as a method to induce the suppression of sexual behavior; and sex-positive encouragement for making affirmative intentional decisions to have sex, in addition to the "traditional" support for deciding not to do so (Noonan 1996a).

At this time, it remains unclear whether the American response to AIDS will follow its customary pattern of initial panic in the mass media, followed by a benign neglect and silence prompted by our traditional discomfort with sex-positive values, or whether this country will, at long last, confront the issue of AIDS, and deal with it in the broader context of a safe, sane, and healthy celebration of sexuality.

12. Sexual Dysfunctions, Counseling, and Therapies

A. Brief History of American Sexual Therapy

WILLIAM HARTMAN AND
MARILYN FITHIAN

The scientific study of sexual dysfunctions and the development of therapeutic modalities in the United States started with Robert Latou Dickinson (1861-1950). Born and educated in Germany and Switzerland, he earned his medical degree in New York and began collecting sex histories from his patients in 1890. In the course of his practice, he gathered 5,200 case histories of female patients, married and single, lesbian and heterosexual, and published extensively on sexual problems of women (Brecher 1979; Dickinson and Beam 1931, 1934; Dickinson and Person 1925).

The turn-of-the-century popularity of Sigmund Freud's psychoanalysis strongly influenced early American sexual therapy. Although its popularity has faded significantly, the psychoanalytic model is still practiced or integrated with other modalities by some therapists working with sexual problems. The 1948 and 1953 Alfred Kinsey studies brought an increased awareness of human sexuality as a subject of scientific investigation that could include the treatment of sexual disorders as part of psychiatry and medicine. The pioneering work of Joseph Wolpe and Arnold Lazarus (1966) in adapting behavioral therapy, shifted sexual therapy away from the analytical and medical model, as therapists began to view dysfunctional sexual behavior as the result of learned responses that can be modified.

William Masters and Virginia Johnson began their epoch-making study of the anatomy and physiology of human sexual response in 1964. Their initial research with 312 males and 382 females, published as *Human Sexual Response* (1966), remains the keystone of modern sex therapy, not just in the United States, but anywhere sex therapy is studied or practiced. *Human Sexual Inadequacy* followed in 1970. Masters and Johnson used a male-female dual-therapy team, and a brief, intensive, reeducation process that involved behavior-oriented exercises like sensate focus. It appeared to be highly successful because they worked with a select population of healthy people in basically solid relationships. After their success with relatively simple cases, they and other therapists began to encounter more difficult cases, which could not be solved with the original behavioral approach.

In the early 1970s, Joseph LoPiccolo advocated the use of additional approaches designed to reduce anxiety within the behavioral therapy model suggested by Masters and Johnson (LoPiccolo and LoPiccolo 1978; LoPiccolo and Lobitz 1973; Lobitz and LoPiccolo 1972). LoPiccolo's (1978) analysis of the theoretical basis for sexual therapy identified seven major underlying elements in every sex therapy model: (1) mutual responsibility, (2) information, education, and permission giving, (3) attitude change, (4) anxiety reduction, (5) communication and feedback, (6) intervention in destructive sex roles, lifestyles, and family interaction, and (7) prescribing changes in sex therapy.

John Gagnon and William Simon (1973) stressed the importance of addressing social scripting in sex therapy. Harold Lief, a physician and family therapist, pointed out the importance of nonsexual interpersonal issues and communications problems as factors in sexual difficulties. Lief (1963, 1965) also advocated incorporating the principles of marital therapy into sex therapy. As therapists began to integrate other modes of psycho-therapy, such as cognitive, gestalt, and imagery therapies, it soon became apparent that there was no single "official" form of sex therapy. In addition, some sex therapists became sensitive to the impact and influence of ethnic values on some sexual problems (McGoldrick et al. 1982).

Helen Singer Kaplan, a psychiatrist at Cornell University College of Medicine, made an important and profound contribution to sex therapy when she blended traditional concepts from psychotherapy and psycho-analysis with cognitive psychology and behavioral therapy. Kaplan's *New Sex Therapy* (1974) explored the role of such important therapeutic issues as resistance, repression, and unconscious motivations in sex therapy. This new approach focused not only on altering behavior with techniques like the sensate-focus exercises, but also with exploring and modifying covert or unconscious thought patterns and motivations that may underlie a sexual difficulty (Kaplan 1974, 1979, 1983).

Specific areas of sexual therapy have been developed, including Lonnie Barbach's (1980) and Betty Dodson's (1987) independent work with non-orgasmic women, Bernard Apfelbaum and Dean Dauw's use of surrogates in their work with single persons, William Hartman and Marilyn Fithian's (1972) integration of films, body imagery, and body work with dysfunctional couples, and Bernie Zilbergeld's (1978, 1992) focus on male sexual health and problems.

There have been no major innovative treatments developed in sex therapy programs in recent years, although new refinements continue to occur. Some would comment that one does not have to reinvent the wheel when the results are good, but the early success rates have declined as the presenting problems have become more complicated and difficult to treat. Nevertheless, self-reported success rates from reputable sex therapy clinics run between 80 percent and 92 percent. However, critical reviews of sex therapy treatment models emphasize the paucity of scientific data in de-termining the effectiveness of such programs.

Today, few professionals who counsel clients with sexual difficulties see themselves as pure sex therapists. More and more, the term "sex therapy" refers to a focus of intervention, rather than to a distinctive and exclusive technique. Individual psychologists, psychotherapists, marriage counsel-ors, and family therapists may be more or less skilled in providing counsel-ing and applying therapeutic modalities appropriate to specific sexual problems, but each tends to apply those interventions and techniques with which they are more comfortable.

Informal support groups also provide opportunities for dealing with sexual problems and difficulties. Many hospitals and service organizations provide workshops and support groups for patients recovering from heart attacks, for persons with diabetes, emphysema, multiple sclerosis, cystic fibrosis, arthritis, and other chronic diseases. These support groups usually include both patients and their partners.

B. Current Status   JULIAN SLOWINSKI AND WILLIAM R. STAYTON

Recently, American sex therapy has incorporated important advances in medicine and pharmacology. More-precise knowledge and techniques now allow a therapist to develop a hormone profile for a patient, monitor nocturnal penile tumescence, and check penile and vaginal blood flow. With patients now reporting the negative side effects of medications on their sexual responses, doctors have developed strategies for altering the course of medication. New surgical methods improve penile blood supply. Moreover, prosthetics and other aids, like injections and electrical devises to stimulate erection, have been developed.

Breakthroughs are also occurring in female sex research with direct implications for sex therapy. Examples include the efforts of sex-affirming women to redefine sexual satisfaction in women's terms and expand our appreciation of the spectrum of erotic/sexual responses beyond the phallic/coital (Ogden 1995), Joanne Loulan's (1984) exploration of lesbian sexual archetypes, sexual responses of women with a spinal cord injury, the effects on women's libido of homeopathics to increase the bioavailability of testosterone, and work combining testosterone with estrogen replacement to increase both sexual desire and pleasure in perimenopausal women.

One sidelight in this exciting female sex research is that the old methods of sensate focus and pleasuring exercises are still working successfully. For example, the self-help materials are still very useful in working with preorgasmic women. The traditional sensate-focus exercises are still effective in working with desire issues, painful intercourse, and vaginal spasms.

More good news are the trends in treating male sexual dysfunction today. For the motivated and cooperative male, there is treatment for virtually every dysfunction. In addition to the ever-helpful sensate-focus exercises, we have medications for increasing desire and arousal, such as yohimbe, a bark extract of the African tree yohimbe, and a combination of green oat and palmetto-grass extract. These are available through a physician's prescription, at health food stores, or through mail-order catalogs. As of mid-1995, there is enthusiastic anecdotal feedback from individual therapists who are using yohimbe and oat extract with their clients, but what is anxiously awaited—and needed—in this area are the results of controlled clinical studies to document the actual therapeutic effects, if any.

The vacuum pump for erections has been much improved with automatic monitoring of blood flow. With some clients, penile injections produce remarkable results. Monoxydyl and nitroglycerin are being used as topical preparations, as are prostaglandin E1 suppositories inserted into the urethral meatus. Taken alone, these medications are not effective. Without therapy, the person will often stop using the medication or method. However, when sex therapy is added, the success rate increases dramatically, because both the relationship and the dysfunction are being treated.

Problems

Several problems currently impede the delivery of sex therapy to clients. Primary among these is the state of flux in the insurance industry (third-party payers) with the shift toward managed care, health maintenance organizations, and provider networks. The availability of third-party payment makes it much more feasible for patients to avail themselves of sex therapy. The insurance industry has changed the entire health-care-provider field by creating the impression that therapists, like others in the medical field, are not to be trusted to know how long therapy should last, or what methods should be used to treat psychodynamic problems. This has created the image that all psychological problems can be treated by brief therapy within a predetermined number of sessions. The insurance industry has also made confidentiality problematic, because clients must sign away the right to confidentiality in order to receive mental-health coverage. Increasingly, insurance plans refuse to pay for sex therapy. This has prompted many therapists to give a diagnosis that is acceptable to the plan, and then include sex therapy as an Axis II diagnosis.

Secondly, the rise of the religious right appears to have had a negative impact on sex therapy in America. Although there has been no general decline in premarital sex in America, the "abstinence only until marriage" ethic can be a considerable barrier to normal adolescent sexual rehearsal explorations for some people, and may well result in trauma and dysfunction when newlywed couples confront their sexuality and sexual functioning on the wedding night. Thirty years ago, Masters and Johnson found that religious orthodoxy was a primary cause of sexual dysfunction. Two responses are likely, the individuals and/or couple may become so stressed that it is difficult for them to function naturally within the permitted circumstances, or they may rebel even before marriage and get involved in promiscuous and/or risky practices.

A third concern is a growing challenge as to whether sex therapy is even a separate discipline. There are those who believe that sex therapy needs to be subsumed under psychology, marriage and family therapy, social work, or psychiatry. The fact is that few of these disciplines have educational or training programs that teach about the healthy aspects of sex and sexuality or the creative treatment of sexual problems.

Finally, the amount of money and effort given to research on female sexuality significantly lags behind research on male sexuality (di Mauro 1995).

Because humans are born sexual but not lovers, sex therapy is increasingly seen as including good sex education, good medicine, and good psychotherapy/counseling. In the last ten years, sex therapy has added important concerns related to gender-identity dysphoria, sexual (gender) orientations, and lifestyle issues.

C. Recent Developments JULIAN SLOWINSKI AND WILLIAM R. STAYTON

Psychotropic Drugs

Antidepressants, antianxiety, and antipanic medications are being used with psychotherapy in treating desire-phase problems and in treating paraphilic compulsive-obsessive behaviors (Coleman 1991). Recent anecdotal reports and some early controlled studies are finding a category of antidepressant medications useful in treating sexual disorders. SSRIs, such as Zoleft, Paxix, and Prozac, are useful in increasing the latency time for ejaculation, and thus are helping some men who present with problems of ejaculatory control (early ejaculation). Another medication, Anafranil, and antidepressants used in treating obsessive-compulsive disorders, have been demonstrated in at least one study to help in the treatment of premature ejaculation. Of course, these results occur when therapy is provided, for if medication is discontinued, there can be a resumption of symptoms. That suggests the presence of untreated anxiety, relationship problems, or a constitutional tendency towards difficulty with ejaculation control.

An unfortunate side effect of SSRIs is the frequent complaint by patients of some loss of sexual desire. This has been reported by patients on these medications for depression. In some patients, however, the lifting of their depression symptoms alone is enough to increase their libido, despite the use of medication. Wellbrutrin, a relatively recent antidepressant, is claimed to have few negative effects on sexual desire. A newly marketed antidepressant, Serzone, is also being hailed for having no negative effects on libido.

Vulvodynia, a Newly Identified Syndrome

One of the new challenges facing American sex therapists and gynecologists today is the occurrence in many women of a painful burning sensation in the vulvar and vaginal area. This condition, recently named vulvodynia, or burning vulva syndrome, is a form of vestibulitis that can have a number of causes, from microorganisms that cause dermatosis to inflammation of the vestibular glands. The presenting complaint of these women is burning and painful intercourse. Some women develop secondary vaginismus. Discomfort varies from constant pain to localized spots highly sensitive to touch. In many cases, the psychological and relationship consequences are grave. Many women become depressed as a result and frustrated by attempts at treatment.

Current treatment includes topical preparations, laser surgery to ablate affected areas, dietary restrictions, and referral to a physical therapist to realign pelvic structure and reduce pressure on the spinal nerves serving the genital area. Some affected women have sought relief with acupuncture. Therapy may be enhanced by focusing on the effects of the condition on the sexual functioning of the patient, her relationship with her partner, and self-image. Pain-reduction techniques, including self-hypnosis, have proven valuable in some cases. Low doses of an antidepressant, including some SSRIs, may reduce the pain.

There is much work to be done in the treatment of vulvodynia, including making the public aware of this condition and educating physicians in the role that sex therapists can play in supporting these women and their partners.

The Medicalization of Sex Therapy

There is an increasing medicalization in sex therapy today. Although this may at first seem to benefit many patients—and it does—there is a concern among sex therapists that many conditions will be summarily treated through medications by primary physicians, with a corresponding failure to address the dynamic and interpersonal aspects of the patient. In short, there is a danger of incomplete evaluation of the patient's status if only the medical aspects are considered and the therapist is left out of the process. In the ideal situation, the sex therapist and physician would collaborate on the treatment plan, using medication as indicated.

D. Education and Certification of Sex Therapists JULIAN SLOWINSKI AND WILLIAM R. STAYTON

Since American sex educators, counselors, and therapists are not licensed by any government agency, reputable professionals in the field operate under one of several traditional professional licenses, as part of their practice as a physician, psychologist, psychoanalyst, social worker, marriage and family counselor, or pastoral counselor.

The American Association of Sex Educators, Counselors, and Therapists (AASECT) does offer its own certification for sex educators, counselors, and therapists following successful completion of specified training programs that include supervised practice. Continuing education credits are required for renewal of this certification.

E. Sex Surrogates: The Continuing Controversy RAYMOND J. NOONAN

Three decades after Masters and Johnson pioneered modern sex therapy, the use of sexual partner surrogates continues despite a long history of controversy, largely because it has been found by some professionals to be an effective therapeutic modality in certain circumstances for persons without partners and for specially challenged persons with physical limitations. Still, as Dauw (1988) has noted, little in-depth research has been conducted about surrogates, their effectiveness, or their appropriateness in working with specific sexual dysfunctions. Misconceptions about surrogates are widespread (Apfelbaum 1984), in part, because of a common confusion between the roles of sex surrogates and prostitutes, based on the potential for intimate sexual interaction and the surrogate being paid for her or his work. Roberts (1981) has suggested that "the most common misconception" is of the surrogate as "an elitist type of prostitute." In addition, some authors have commented on the effects of media accounts of sex surrogates, which have tended to focus on the bizarre, the sensational, and even the untrue (Braun 1975; Lily 1977).

The distinction commonly noted between surrogates and prostitutes usually relies on the intent of the sexual interaction: the prostitute's intent being immediate gratification localized on genital pleasure, whereas the surrogate's intent is long-term therapeutic reeducation and reorientation of inadequate capabilities of functioning or relating sexually (Brown 1981; Jacobs et al.,1975; Roberts 1981). In 1970, Masters and Johnson noted that ". . . so much more is needed and demanded from a substitute partner than effectiveness of purely physical sexual performance that to use prostitutes would have been at best clinically unsuccessful and at worst psychologically disastrous."

IPSA, the International Professional Surrogates Association (n.d.), wrote,

> A surrogate partner is a member of a three-way therapeutic team consisting of therapist, client and surrogate partner. The surrogate participates, as a partner to the client, in experiential exercises designed to build the client's skills in the areas of physical and emotional intimacy. This partner work includes exercises in communication, relaxation, sensual and sexual touching and social skills training.

Others, including Allen (1978), Apfelbaum (1977, 1984), Brown (1981), Dauw (1988), Masters and Johnson (1970), Roberts (1981), Symonds (1973), Williams (1978), and Wolfe (1978) have described, either briefly or in part, typical surrogate sessions or alternative models. According to Jacobs, et al. (1975): "The usual therapeutic approach is slow and thorough. Exercises are graduated and concentrate on body awareness, relaxation and sensual/sexual experiences that are primarily non-genital." Where appropriate, the surrogate also teaches "vital social skills and traditional courtship patterns which finally include sexual interaction." However, none of these writers gave a perspective of the relative amount of time or importance that each aspect of the surrogate therapy session or program places on the entire process. Such a perspective would give a clearer understanding of the true functions of a sex surrogate that would allow the integration of the use of surrogate therapy into a useful theoretical perspective relative to clinical sexology, as well as to normative sexual functioning.

The use of sex surrogates was introduced by Masters and Johnson (1970) as a way to treat single men who did not have partners available to participate in their couple-oriented sex-therapy program. As the practice evolved, surrogates sometimes specialized in working with specific populations, such as single heterosexual or homosexual men, with couples as a coach, or with people with physical disabilities.

Today, the use of surrogates remains controversial with complex legal, moral, ethical, professional, and clinical implications. Although Masters and Johnson abandoned the practice (Redlich, 1977), the use of professional sex surrogates has been ethically permissible as part of the sex therapist's armamentarium, according to the American Association of Sex Educators, Counselors, and Therapists (AASECT 1978, 1987). Still, the most recent version of AASECT's (1993) *Code of Ethics* has ceased to mention the use of surrogates explicitly. Instead, the 1993 code merely states that a member of AASECT should not make a "referral to an unqualified or incompetent person" (p. 14), which would presumably refer to surrogates, among others.

In their 1987 *Code of Ethics*, however, and in at least one earlier version, AASECT addressed the issue of surrogates directly, and promulgated the parameters for their ethical use, including the understanding that the surrogate is not a sex therapist or psychotherapist, and that the therapist must protect the dignity and welfare of both the client and the surrogate. In addition, it outlined how issues of confidentiality and consent should be addressed. In many ways, this document is similar in putting the client's welfare first to the *Code of Ethics* espoused by the International Professional Surrogates Association (IPSA, 1989). Among IPSA's strict requirements for members are the necessity that surrogates practice only within the context of the therapeutic triangle consisting of the client, surrogate, and supervising therapist, that the relationship with the client always be within the context of the therapy, that the surrogate recognize and act in accordance with the boundaries and limitations of her competence, and that the surrogate be responsible for all precautions against pregnancy and disease. Confidentiality and continuing-education requirements are also among the seventeen items listed in the code, although the surrogate's primary role as a co-therapist or substitute partner in any given therapeutic situation is left open to agreement between the therapist and surrogate.

In 1997, there are estimated to be fewer than 200 surrogates worldwide, according to Vena Blanchard, president of IPSA (personal communication, March 15, 1997), with maybe 100 practicing in the U.S.A. This number is down by about two thirds from the 300 estimated to be practicing in the U.S.A. in 1983-1984 (Noonan 1995/1984), a time when the number of surrogates peaked. However, the downward trend of the subsequent decade, caused primarily by fears surrounding AIDS, has been showing signs of reversing since the mid-1990s, according to Blanchard, who pointed to the number of new surrogates being trained and requesting training by IPSA. Still, according to Blanchard, only a few urban areas, primarily on the two coasts, have surrogates working, with most of the country not being served.

Noonan (1995/1984) surveyed fifty-four sex surrogates who were part of a surrogates' networking mailing list representing about 65 to 70 percent of all known legitimate trained surrogates in 1983-1984. The fifty-four surrogate respondents represented about 36 percent of the 150 estimated known surrogates, who were estimated to be approximately one half of all surrogates practicing in the U.S. at the time. In addition to demographic data, the instrument asked respondents to estimate the percentage of time they spent in each of seven activities with clients. The data gathered seemed to support strongly the hypothesis that sex surrogates provide more than sexual service for their clients, spending about 87 percent of their professional time doing non-sexual activities. In addition to functioning as a sexual intimate, Noonan found that the surrogate functions as educator, counselor, and co-therapist, providing sex education, sex counseling, social-skills education, coping-skills counseling, emotional support, sensuality and relaxation education and coaching, and self-awareness education. The results indicated that a majority of time is spent outside of the sexual realm, suggesting further that surrogate therapy employs a more holistic methodological approach than previous writings, both professional and lay, would seem to indicate. Clearly, the sex surrogate functions far beyond the realm of the prostitute.

Specifically, Noonan's (1995/1984) results showed that the surrogate spends much of her or his time talking with the client, with approximately 34 percent of the time spent giving sexual information, as well as reassurance and support. Almost one half of the surrogate's time (48.5 percent) is spent in experiential exercises involving the body non-sexually, with the majority of that time devoted to teaching the client basically how to feel—how to be aware of what is coming in through the senses. Combining the two averages, we find that the surrogate typically spends 82.5 percent of the therapeutic time enhancing the cognitive, emotional, and sensual worlds of the client. Only after this foundation is developed does the surrogate spend almost 13 percent of the time focusing on erotic activities, including sexual intercourse, cunnilingus, and fellatio, and teaching sexual techniques. The remaining 4.5 percent focuses on social skills in public settings, clearly the least important aspect of what the surrogate deals with.

Finally, a profile emerged of the "average" sex surrogate in 1983-1984: she is a white female, in her late 30s/early 40s, and not very religious. She is one way or another single with 1.4 children, college-educated, lives in California, has been practicing as a surrogate for four years three months, and sees twenty-seven clients per year. Finally, she is a heterosexual who does not need to concern herself or her partner with chemical or mechanical methods of contraception, because she has been sterilized (Noonan 1995/1984). It is interesting to note that among the fifty-four respondents, six of the surrogates had earned doctorates, with the average being a bachelor's degree plus some advanced study, indicating the atypically high level of educational achievement in this group.

Present and Future Issues

Surrogate therapy has no doubt changed somewhat over the past decade and a half for various reasons. These changes need to be elucidated, documented, and incorporated into our collective knowledge about normative sexuality and how to address the various problems we have created or maintained around its expression.

Since 1983, the impact of AIDS has become a deep concern of both surrogates and therapists. Exactly how it has affected the work of surrogates remains to be studied. Certainly in the years immediately following Noonan's (1995/1984) study of the functions of sex surrogates, many surrogates, who in retrospect were not particularly at risk for HIV infection, stopped practicing or modified their practice as surrogates out of fear. Many therapists also stopped referring clients to surrogates out of fear of legal liability. As the reality of HIV infection has become better known, surrogates, who are mostly female working with heterosexual males, are continuing to help clients function better sexually while promoting responsible sexual behavior at all levels. Little or no research exists that has investigated how gay male surrogates, who worked mostly with gay male clients in the 1980s, have changed their practice.

Since the 1980s, women have become more aware of how surrogates might help them effectively deal with various sexual dysfunctions. Some female clients will ask their therapists, or seek out therapists who are open to the possibility, to find a male surrogate with whom they might work. Largely because of the sexual double standard that continues to operate in many, if not most, therapists, however, most clients of surrogates continue to be male. The degree to which women have begun to work with surrogates to solve their sexual problems, or who consider it a viable option, are questions that require additional research. In addition, the differences that may exist in the design of the therapy program itself and how a female client might work with a surrogate, as compared to how males work with surrogates, is also a topic open to research. It appears that heterosexual male surrogates remain today the rarest of sex surrogates, as in the early 1980s.

Despite these research needs, the population of surrogates is likely to remain resistant to study, both because of the legal ambiguities often involved with their practice and the fact that the use of surrogates retains a relatively high visibility in public consciousness, although surrogates themselves are usually quite invisible. Because they are a small group, they will be difficult to study with any reasonable assurances of confidentiality.

The most troubling aspect of research on sex surrogates may be the indication, yet to be verified by any research, that there are probably many more surrogates working with clients and therapists in the United States, who are independently trained by varying standards by the therapists with whom they may be working, and who are both isolated from other surrogates and from researchers. This leaves them unaware of the most recent knowledge and advances in the field, because rarely are therapists trained in working with surrogates. It also deprives us of the knowledge gained from experience that these "hidden" surrogates may have learned.

13. Research and Advanced Education

A. A Research Assessment   ROBERT T. FRANCOEUR

The United States has a long tradition and unequaled wealth of sexological research. The survey work of Alfred Kinsey and his colleagues in the 1940s and 1950s and the clinical/therapeutic research of William Masters and Virginia Johnson are but tips of the iceberg, referred to and cited in almost any discussion of sexological research anywhere in the world (Brecher 1979; Bullough 1994; Pomeroy 1972).

Sexological research in the United States today is vital to the management of many social and public health problems. Each year, one million teenage girls become pregnant, a per-thousand-rate twice that of Canada, England, and Sweden, and ten times that of the Netherlands; the disproportion is similar for teenage abortions (Jones et al. 1986). The nation spends $25 billion on families begun by teenagers for social, health, and welfare services. One million Americans are HIV-positive and almost one quarter of a million have died of AIDS. Yet only one in ten American children receives sexuality education that includes information about HIV/AIDS transmission and prevention. One in five adolescent girls in grades eight through eleven is subject to sexual harassment, while three quarters of girls under age 14 who have had sexual relations have been raped. These and other public health problems are well documented and increasingly understood in the context of poverty, family trauma, ethnic discrimination, lack of educational opportunities, and inadequate health services. However, there is little recognition of the need for sexological research to deal effectively with these problems. Congress has several times refused or withdrawn funding for well-designed and important surveys because of pressure from conservative minorities (di Mauro 1995).

In 1995, the Sexuality Research Assessment Project of the Social Science Research Council (605 Third Avenue, 17th Floor. New York, New York 10158) published a comprehensive review of *Sexuality Research in the United States: An Assessment of the Social and Behavioral Sciences* (di Mauro 1995). This report identified and described major gaps and needs in American sexological research. There is a serious lack of a framework for the analysis of sexual behaviors in the context of society and culture. This framework is needed to examine how sexual socialization occurs in families, schools, the media, and peer groups, and to address the complex perspectives of different situations, populations, and cultural communities. Areas of need identified by the project include: gender, HIV/AIDS, adolescent sexuality, sexual orientation, sexual coercion, and research methodology. Three major barriers hindering sexuality research are (1) the lack of comprehensive research training in sexuality, (2) inadequate mechanisms and efforts to disseminate research findings to policymakers, advocates, practitioners, and program representatives in diverse communities who need this information, and (3) the lack of federal, private-sector, and academic funding for research.

B. Advanced Sexological Institutes, Organizations, and Publications

MARTHA CORNOG

Advanced Sexuality Education and Institutes

The premier American sexological research institute is the Kinsey Institute for Research in Sex, Gender and Reproduction, based at Indiana University, Bloomington, Indiana. Two other major institutes are: the Institute for the Advanced Study of Human Sexuality (Address: 1525 Franklin Street, San Francisco, CA 94109); and the Mary Calderone Library at the Sexuality Information and Education Council of the United States). A more complete selection of libraries specializing in various sexuality topics may be found by consulting the index to the *Directory of Special Libraries and Information Centers* (Gale Research).

About two dozen universities grant degrees with majors or concentrations in sexology and/or sex education, counseling, or therapy. These include Indiana University, the University of Minnesota, New York University, and the University of Pennsylvania. A full list is available from the national office of the Society for the Scientific Study of Sexuality (see address below).

In the late 1960s, several medical schools introduced programs in human sexuality into their curricula for training physicians. These programs reached their zenith in the early 1980s. By the late 1980s, many of them were under fire from newly appointed conservative administrators, and threatened with cutbacks and elimination. Indications suggest a significant decline in sexuality training for physicians and other health-care professionals, but the picture is not clear because no one has studied the situation nationwide (see Section E below). Likewise, students seeking an advanced degree or major concentration in sexology find the current situation of prospects for the future of individual graduate study cloudy.

Sexological Organizations

There are four major American sexological organizations:

The Society for the Scientific Study of Sexuality (SSSS). Founded in 1957; currently over 1,000 members. Address: P. O. Box 208, Mt. Vernon, Iowa 52314.

The American Association of Sex Educators, Counselors, and Therapists (ASSECT). Founded in 1967; currently over 3,000 members. Address: 435 North Michigan Avenue, Suite 1717, Chicago, Illinois 60611.

The Sexuality Information and Education Council of the United States (SIECUS). Founded in 1964; currently about 3,600 members. Address: 130 West 42nd Street, Suite 350, New York, NY 10036.

The Society for Sex Therapy and Research (SSTAR). Founded in 1974; currently about 300 members. Address: c/o Candyce Risen, The Center for Sexual Health, 2320 Chagrin Boulevard, 3 Commerce Park, Beachwood, Ohio 44122.

Several dozen other groups are oriented to various types of professionals concerned with sexuality. Typical among these are: Association for the Behavioral Treatment of Sexual Abusers, Association of Nurses in AIDS Care, National Council on Family Relations, Society for the Psychological Study of Lesbian and Gay Issues, and Society for the Study of Social Problems. (For addresses of many of these groups, see the listing in the Directory of Sexological Organizations at the end of this volume.)

There are at least one hundred advocacy and common-interest organizations that deal in one way or another with advocacy for gay and lesbian viewpoints, or provide a vehicle for the gay and lesbian practitioners of a profession or hobby to socialize or work together. The largest and most comprehensive are the National Gay Rights Advocates, the Lambda Defense and Education Fund, and the National Gay and Lesbian Task Force, each with 15,000 or more member-contributors and budgets in the millions of dollars. Typical of smaller special-interest groups are: Federal Lesbians and Gays (federal government workers), International Gay Travel Association, Good Gay Poets, Lesbian and Gay Bands of America, Girth and Mirth (overweight gay men), and Gay and Lesbian History on Stamps Club.

Similar organizations exist for many sexual viewpoints and behaviors other than homosexuality—and for sexual matters perceived as problems. An all-too-brief sampling from the *Encyclopedia of Associations* (*EoA*) (Gale Research Publications) includes: Americans for Decency, American Coalition for Traditional Values, American Sunbathing Association (nudism), Adult Video Association (pro-pornography/erotica), Christian Voice, Eagle Forum, Focus on the Family, North American Swing Club Association and Lifestyles (both recreational nonmonogamy), National Clearinghouse on Marital and Date Rape, National Task Force on Prostitution (pro-prostitution, formerly COYOTE), PONY (Prostitutes of New York), Society's League Against Molestation (child sexual abuse), Society for the Second Self (TRI-Ess) (transvestites), Sexaholics Anonymous, Impotents Anonymous, People with AIDS Coalition, Women Exploited by Abortion, Renaissance (Philadelphia-based with a dozen local chapters for transvestites and transsexuals), and Women Against Pornography. Check *EoA* for a full listing. Other special-interest groups are not listed in the *EoA* but can be located by scanning sex-related publications. Such groups include: Club Latexa (rubber fetishists), DPF (Diaper Pail Friends; infantilism and nepiophilia), Janus (bisexuals), SAMOIS (lesbian sadomasochism), and Eulenspiegel (sadomasochism).

Sexological Journals and Sexually-Oriented Magazines

Professional journals that publish sexuality-related research include: *Archives of Sexual Behavior, Annual Review of Sex Research, Journal of Gay and Lesbian Psychotherapy, Journal of Gender Studies, Journal of Homosexuality, Journal of Marriage and the Family, Journal of Psychology and Human Sexuality, Journal of Sex and Marital Therapy, Journal of Sex Education and Therapy, Journal of Sex Research, Marriage and Family Review, Journal of Social Work and Human Sexuality, Journal of the History of Sexuality, Maledicta* (language), *Medical Aspects of Human Sexuality,* and the *SIECUS Report.*

Major popular magazines that publish sexually oriented nonfiction and sometimes fiction include: *Eidos, Frighten the Horses, Libido, Penthouse, Playboy, Screw, Tantra,* and *Yellow Silk* (entirely literary). Resource directories include: *Gayellow Pages, Gaia's Guide,* and *Gay and Lesbian Library Service.* The major gay/lesbian nationwide periodicals are: *Advocate* (out of Los Angeles) and *Blade* (out of Washington, D.C.). Dozens of other publications exist, such as *Deneuve* and *On Our Backs* (for lesbians). Addresses for these and similar journals and magazines can be found in the *Gale Directory of Publications and Broadcast Media, Ulrich's International Periodical Directory, The Standard Periodical Directory,* or other directories.

C. Sexuality Education of Physicians and Clergy

Medical School Sexuality Education   RICHARD J. CROSS

Medical schools have always taught certain aspects of sexuality, e.g., the anatomy of the male and female sex organs, the menstrual cycle, basic obstetrics, and some psychology and psychiatry. That picture began to change about thirty years ago when Harold I. Lief (1963, 1965), a psychiatrist at Tulane University Medical School in Louisiana, wrote articles pointing out that most Americans regarded physicians as authorities on human sexuality, that the field of sexology was changing fast, and that only three medical schools in the country were even trying to teach modern sexology. The situation gradually improved, and when Harold Lief and Richard J. Cross, a physician who had introduced sexology education at the Robert Wood Johnson Medical School at Rutgers University in New Jersey, sent a questionnaire to all medical schools in the U.S. and Canada in 1980, they found only three schools that said they did not teach sexuality. However, they did not publish their results because of the poor response rate and apparent unreliability of self-serving responses from medical school administrators. It was clear, however, that the improvement was limited; part of the change reported was due to different interpretations of the question-naire and differing definitions of "sexuality." No one knows just what is being taught in the different medical schools today.

Part of the problem is that medical schools have traditionally defined education as the acquisition of factual information and certain skills by students. In the field of sexuality education, affective learning is also important. The greatest shortcoming of most practicing physicians is their discomfort. Since early childhood, they have been taught that sex is a private subject and that it is impolite and/or improper to talk about it. Physicians, who have not learned to confront and overcome their discomfort in talking about sex, transmit to their patients nonverbal, and sometimes verbal, messages that they do not want to hear about sexual problems. Their patients, who are often equally uncomfortable, cooperate by not raising any sexual issues. The result, too often, is "a conspiracy of silence," in which sexual issues that sometimes have a great impact on health never get discussed.

A number of medical schools have instituted courses or short programs in sexuality that emphasize attitudes, values, and feelings, rather than the memorization of factual information. These courses make extensive use of sexually explicit, educational films and videos and panels of people who are willing and able to talk about their personal sexual experiences. Fol-lowing each large-group session, the students break into smaller groups who meet with facilitators to process what they have heard and seen with an emphasis on their personal feelings and reactions. Such programs seem to give medical students a better understanding of their own sexuality, a greater tolerance for unusual sexual attitudes they may encounter in their patients, and greater comfort in dealing with and discussing sexual issues.

Unfortunately, these programs rarely elicit enthusiastic support from the medical school faculties, who, after all, have been selected for their exper-tise in analyzing scientific data. Time is jealously guarded in the medical school curriculum. Money has always been a concern in higher education, but money gets tighter year by year, and small groups are expensive to organize and run. Many sexuality programs in medical schools are elective, which is sad, because the students who need these courses most are often the least likely to register for them.

Despite thirty years of improved sexuality education, most American doctors still do an inadequate job of helping patients with sexual problems. Comprehensive courses seem to help, but in the current conservative political and economic climate, it seems unlikely that they will be greatly expanded in the near future. In fact, there are indications that some programs are in danger of being cut back. There is, on the other hand, a small but growing move in the Association of American Medical Colleges to go beyond stuffing facts into students by dealing with attitudes and feelings in the medical school curricula. If this takes hold, sexuality courses may lead the way. Time alone will tell.

Sexuality Education for Clergy in   PATRICIA GOODSON AND
Theological Schools and Seminaries   SARAH C. CONKLIN

History. Protestantism has historically enjoyed the status of dominant religion in this country, but democracy, with its emphasis on religious freedom
and pluralism, has nourished the establishment of countless religious
groups. Because these groups are numerous, and the education of their
leadership varies considerably, a discussion of clergy training in sexuality
requires qualification.

The main focus here will be on the seminaries and students included in
the studies conducted by Conklin (1995) and Goodson (1996). Denomi-
nationally, the emphasis in these studies was mainly on Protestant and
Roman Catholic clergy, although Jewish seminary faculty members were
interviewed for the study by Conklin. By including both conservative and
liberal schools and denominations, the largest religious groups are represented, but the samples are neither random nor the results generalizable.

Seminaries and theological schools are defined, here, as institutions of
higher education accredited by the Association of Theological Schools
(ATS). They offer post-baccalaureate degrees leading to ordination and
licensure of pastors, priests, ministers, rabbis, chaplains, and pastoral counselors (categories broadly referred to as clergy).

Traditionally, clergy students have been characterized as young, white,
and male, but this profile is slowly changing. First, it is becoming an older
population composed of more part-time and second-career students. Second, diversity in both ethnicity and gender is increasing. In a comparison
of motivations, women were more inclined to report entering seminary to
discover "ways to best serve Christ in the church and the world" or "personal
spiritual growth and faith development" rather than "preparing to be a
parish minister," which was the overwhelmingly reported motivation for men
entering seminary (Aleshire in Hunter 1990, p. 1265). In terms of sexuality
education, seminary students are now perceived as being "more diverse in
attitudes, more willing to share personal experiences, and more open about
sexual orientation" than in previous generations (Conklin 1995, p. 231).

Conflict over whether seminary education accents professional training
or personal formation may be a factor accounting for the apparent lack of
emphasis on sexuality content (Kelsey 1993). As the percentage of female
students has increased, greater awareness and sensitivity about the negative
sexual experiences of women has been accompanied by curricular changes.
As clinical settings for counseling practice have been included in most
seminary curricula, less emphasis has been placed on foundational education (languages, such as Latin, Greek, and Hebrew, are less often required),
but issues of training remain problematic, especially concerning sexuality
education.

The scientific literature contains abundant evidence of the positive role
that clergy may have in health promotion generally and in sexual health

promotion, specifically. One study affirmed, for instance, that nearly half of all referrals made by clergy to mental-health professionals "involved marriage and family problems" (Weaver 1995, p. 133).

Recently, however, this supportive role has come into question as trust in clergy generally has been undermined by the misconduct of a few. Fortune (1991) contends that omission of sexuality components in professional training misses an intervention opportunity for clergy students to explore ethical boundary issues concerning what appropriate sexual conduct consists of prior to entering the profession. Such evidence clearly points to the appropriateness of marriage, family, and sexuality content in clergy training, but such content seems lacking or is limited by various internal and external restrictions.

Prevalence. When seminary course offerings were surveyed in the early 1980s, only a small number of courses included the term sex or sexuality in their title or description (McCann-Winter 1983). It might be assumed that sexual content is included in courses not so named, but this low prevalence still indicates that sexuality content is not prevalent in most clergy training programs.

A review of literature on training in pastoral counseling cites one study in which 50 to 80 percent of the sampled clergy thought their training in pastoral counseling was inadequate and did not equip them to deal with marital counseling issues (Weaver, 1995). A study by Allen and Cole (1975) comparing samples of Protestant seminary students in 1962 and 1971 found that the students in the more recent sample did not perceive themselves as better trained in family-planning issues than those students in 1962. A recent study by Goodson (1996) documented that 82 percent of the Protestant seminary students surveyed declared having had zero hours of training in family planning in their seminaries, and 66 percent expressed desire for more training on this topic.

When seminary faculty members who include some aspect of sexuality in their courses were interviewed (Conklin, 1995), they indicated that they did not identify themselves as sexuality educators, and they expressed anxiety about how their teaching of sexuality content would be viewed by others. Yet, they expressed optimism and hope, because sexuality content and courses are sought and positively evaluated by students, even though not required. There is eagerness and enthusiasm by students, congregants, and clergy to have sexuality issues addressed openly and to move in the direction of health, justice, and wholeness.

Content. Profound changes have occurred in the past four decades regarding sexuality education in seminaries. Resources which were once viewed as advantageous are now seen as outdated. More use is being made of commercial films, literature, and case studies. Printed materials with sexuality content have vastly increased in both quantity and quality. The Sexual

Attitude Reassessment (SAR) model, providing intense and condensed exposure to a range of explicit materials, panels, and speakers interspersed with small-group processing, is still viewed with both affirmation as effective and with suspicion as risky (Rosser et al. 1995).

Increased awareness of the pervasiveness of negative outcomes related to sexuality has provided the impetus for continuing-education requirements, mandatory screening of various sorts, development of training programs, trainers, centers, and professional counselors, therapists, and consultants focusing on prevention of various kinds of violations. An understanding of sexuality based upon the content of sexual relationships, rather than the form of sexual acts, is described as a paradigmatic change now underway.

In the Conklin study (1995), sexual orientation and related terms were included, either as central concerns or peripherally, in all but one of the thirty-nine interviews with seminary faculty. Prevention of harm seemed a more common goal than promotion of sexual health, and resources, language, and experiences for classroom use which focus on positive aspects of sexuality seem to be lacking. Examples of content frequently mentioned in the interviews included sexual violence, such as rape, abuse, and incest, sexual harassment and misconduct, sexually transmitted diseases, and sexual compulsivity. Content having religious connections included ordination, celibacy, incarnation, sexual theology, and sacrament.

Support and Resistance. While the need for professional sexuality education within seminaries has been documented in a few studies, and Conklin's qualitative assessment has indicated strong faculty support for teaching sexuality content, some resistance is still expected. Limitations may arise from diverse sources, such as denominational executives and curriculum committees, seminary reward and assignment systems for faculty, financial restrictions, and students' reluctance to deal with sexual issues or be in value conflict with their institution or instructor's teaching.

Goodson's survey (1996) of the attitudes of Protestant seminary students toward family planning identified 4.5 percent of conservative students, as compared to 0.9 percent of non-conservative students ($p < .05$), espousing unfavorable views of family planning, and potentially opposing its teaching in seminary. With this same sample, when analyzing a statistical model to predict intention to promote family planning in their future careers, the variable "attitudes toward sexuality" emerged as a strong mediator of the relationship between the variables "religious beliefs" and "attitudes toward family planning." While "religious beliefs" exhibited a correlation of 0.81 with the "attitudes toward sexuality" variable, conservative students had, on average, more negative views of sexuality when compared to their non-conservative counterparts. The difference was statistically large: 1.04 standard deviation units, and significant at the 0.001 level of probability.

Resources and Intervention Needs. Given these findings, it is clear that religious beliefs need to be considered when selecting resources and planning interventions. At present, it seems broad-based support for sexuality education comes from insurers encouraging risk-reduction measures to prevent actionable behaviors which could lead to claims or litigation. Some administrative encouragement of faculty efforts has been reported, especially in response to student pressure or suggestions from peers or superiors. However, this support seems to be far outweighed by administrative indifference or caution, although perceived hostility has decreased.

A high standard has been set by faculty members who have taught and written about sexuality. Impetus to do more, not less, seems dominant, especially among faculty. However, no one has clearly articulated as a unified plan of action what there should be more of in this area. There is, however, some openness toward planning and development rather than a rigid adherence to an already conceived plan or model. A current resource encouraging the development of plans or models is the Center for Sexuality and Religion in Wayne, Pennsylvania.

As we see it, a two-pronged approach to sexuality education is needed, in which promotion of assets and prevention of deficits are both necessary (Conklin 1995). Clearly, the main assets of Protestant and Catholic churches include their nurturing, caring, and supportive environments, as well as maintenance of centers for dissemination of knowledge and training of their leaders. Nevertheless, such training has been characterized as deficient, and the need to plan, implement, and evaluate appropriate sexuality programs is notorious. The outcomes of a successful two-pronged intervention, which balances emphasis on both sexual health and sexual harm, may be worth pursuing, if we consider the important role clergy and churches have had and may continue to have in promoting the health and well-being of people in this country.

A Door to the Future: Sexuality on the Information Superhighway

Sexuality and the Internet   SANDRA BARGAINNIER

People interested in sexual topics have always been quick to explore a new mode of communication—from graffiti on a prehistoric cave wall, movable type, photography, and radio, to video cameras, VCRs, and videocassette rentals and sales—as a way around the censorship society uses to regulate and limit the dissemination of sexual information. The most recent new mode of communication, the computer-based "information superhighway," the Internet or simply "the Net," is no exception. From its birth, the Net has raised images of erotica, pornography, and cybersex available in the privacy of one's home. The Net does provide sexuality information for the general "on-line" public, but it can also provide a wealth of reliable information for sex researchers, sex educators, and sex therapists. However, the use of the Net to access sexuality information has also brought the inevitable sequel of society's effort to regulate this new avenue of sex information.

The Internet is not a physical or tangible entity, but rather a giant network which interconnects innumerable smaller groups of linked computer networks. In early 1995, the global network of the Internet had 2 million Internet hosts; in late 1995-1996, 5 million hosts; and in early 1996, 9.5 million hosts. This is expected to double to 20 million hosts sometime in 1997. However, the number of Internet hosts is misleading, because many hosts limit access of their users with firewalls and other electronic barriers.

Gateways to a variety of electronic messaging services allow Internet users to communicate with over 15 million educational, commercial, government, military, and other types of users throughout the worldwide matrix of computer networks that exchange mail or news. These rapidly developing, and constantly changing, network information and retrieval tools are transforming the way people learn, interact, and relate. These networks provide users with easy access to documents, sounds, images, and other file-system data; library catalog and user-directory data; weather, geography, and physical-science data; and other types of information (Schwartz and Quarterman 1993). Professional journals, papers, conferences, courses, and dialogues are increasingly delivered electronically.

Although the federal government initiated the Internet during the "Cold War" as a way to send top-secret information quickly and securely, no government or group controls or is in charge of the Internet today. The Internet depends on the continuing cooperation of all the interconnected networks (Butler 1994). Because there is no proprietary control, anyone can send e-mail (electronic mail), start a newsgroup, develop a listserv, download files, and/or have their own World Wide Web (WWW) home page or Web site. This freedom has opened the cyberspace doors to the sexuality arena.

For sexuality professionals, the opportunities in cyberspace are limitless. E-mail is just one of many functions. This one-on-one mode of electronic communication allows colleagues to communicate and collaborate in their research worldwide, pursue new leads quickly, test new ideas and hypotheses immediately, and build networks of like-minded colleagues. Whole documents can be attached to e-mail, sent electronically around the globe, and downloaded by the recipients almost instantly. Both time and money can be saved by editing on-line and bypassing postal delays and costs.

Many American university professors communicate with their students by e-mail. Lessons, syllabi, and homework are passed back and forth with e-mail. E-mail can also provide the shy or quiet students in a class another venue for participation.

Listserv mailing lists are similar to e-mail, but instead of communicating with only one other person, communication takes place between many. Many Americans of all ages subscribe to a mailing list and use it as a good place to debate issues, share professional ideas, and try out new concepts with others. Subscribers automatically receive correspondence from others who belong to the list. It is like reading everyone's e-mail about a particular topic. Hundreds of listservs exist, including those that address rape, gay and bisexual issues, feminist theory, women's health, AIDS, addictions, survivors of incest, and advocacy, to name a few.

In addition to sending e-mail to individuals or to a mailing list, Americans are increasingly meeting people and sharing interests through newsgroups. Like listservs, newsgroups are open discussions and exchanges on particular topics. Users, however, need not subscribe to the discussion mailing list in advance, but can instead access the database at any time (Butler 1994). One must access a special program called a news reader to retrieve messages/discussions from a newsgroup. A local site may have many newsgroups or a few.

Newsgroups are as diverse as the individuals posting on them. Usenet newsgroups are arranged in a hierarchical order, with their names describing their area of interest. The major hierarchies are talk, alt, biz, soc, news, rec, sci, comp, and misc. Some examples of newsgroups in the field of sexuality are: sci.med.aids, talk.abortion, soc.women, soc.men, soc.bi, alt.sex, alt.transgendered, alt.sexual.abuse.recovery, and alt.politics.homosexuality. This hierarchy and system of naming help the user decide which groups may be of interest.

Many groups provide informative discussions and support. Other groups are often magnets for "flamers" (those who insult) or people posing as someone else (i.e., a young adult male posing on-line as a lesbian). One benefit of the newsgroup is that anyone can read the articles/discussions but not participate. These voyeurs are called "lurkers." This may be a safe starting point for a few months until one has an understanding of the group, their history, and past discussions. "Newbies" (newcomers to groups) are often flamed if they ask neophyte questions in some newsgroups. Reading a newsgroup's "FAQ" (frequently asked questions) page prior to inquiring on-line is one way newbies can avoid being flamed for naive or inappropriate inquiries.

In addition to transmitting messages that can be read or accessed later, Internet users can also engage in an immediate dialogue (called "chat") in "real time" with other users. Real-time communication allows one-to-one communication, and "Internet Relay Chat" (IRC) allows two or more people to type messages to each other that almost immediately appear on the other's computer screen. IRC is analogous to a telephone party line. In addition, most commercial on-line services have their own chat systems allowing members to converse. An example of a chat system is the Human Sexuality Forum on CompuServe, a proprietary on-line network that also offers members access to the Internet.

In addition to e-mail, newsgroups, listservs, and chats, one can access information by transferring files from one computer to another with FTP (file transfer protocol). One important aspect of FTP is that it allows files to be transferred between computers of completely dissimilar types. It also provides public file sharing (*The Internet Unleashed*, 1994). These files may contain text, pictures, sound, or computer programs.

Another method of connecting with remote locations is through Telnet. Telnet allows the user to "log in" on a remote machine in real time. For example, a student can use Telnet to connect to a remote library to access the library's online card catalog.

American sexuality professionals now communicate, collaborate, and discuss issues with colleagues around the globe. They can also access information from around the world. Two of the more common methods for accessing information are Gopher and the World Wide Web (WWW). A user can collect data, read conference proceedings, tap into libraries, and even search for jobs on-line.

Gopher guides an individual's search through the resources available on a remote computer. It is menu driven and easy to use. Most American colleges and universities have a local Gopher menu. Gopher can also be accessed through most commercial on-line services. Gopher allows users to access information from various locations. The National Institute for Health, the Centers for Disease Control and Prevention, and the National Library of Medicine are just a few examples of sites that are accessible via Gopher.

Most information sites that can be reached through Gopher can also be accessed via the World Wide Web (WWW). The "Web" uses a "hypertext" formatting language called hypertext markup language (HTML). Programs called Web browsers that "browse" the Web can display HTML documents containing text, images, sound, animation, and moving video. Any HTML document can include links to other types of information or resources. These hypertext links allow information to be accessed and organized in very flexible ways, and allow people to locate and efficiently view related information, even if the information is stored on numerous computers all around the world.

Many organizations now have "home pages" on the Web. The home page typically serves as a table of contents for the site, and provides links to other similar sites. Some Web sites that may be of interest to the sexuality professional are: the Society for the Scientific Study of Sexuality (SSSS) [http://www.ssc.wisc.edu/ssss/]; the Kinsey Institute [http://www.indiana.edu/~kinsey/]; the Sexuality Information and Education Council of the United States (SIECUS) [http://www.siecus.org/]; the Queer Resources Directory [http://www.qrd.org/qrd/]; and Tstar [http://travesti.geophys.mcgill.ca/~tstar/]. TStar provides resources and information for the transgendered community. The TStar home page is also a gateway to other resources on the Web, such as the Lesbian, Gay, Transgendered Alliance, and the Gay, Bi-Sexual, Lesbian, and Transgender

Information from the United Kingdom. [*The SexQuest Web Index for Sexual Health* provides links to most sexuality research, education, and therapy sites on the Web: http://www.SexQuest.com/SexQuest.html. (Editor)]

Sex researchers, educators, and therapists can use e-mail, listservs, newsgroups, and the WWW for updated information and resources. Sexuality professionals can also use the Internet as a new frontier for sex research. Approximately 200 active Usenet newsgroups deal with sex and variations of some sexual theme (Tamosaitis 1995). Very few have researched who these newsgroup users are, what sexuality knowledge they possess, what sexual attitudes they hold, or in which types of behavior they engage.

In the fall of 1994, a modified version of the Kinsey Institute Sex Knowledge Test was distributed to 4,000 users on-line (Tamosaitis 1995). The results showed that over 83 percent were male, white, highly educated, single, middle- to upper-class, and not afraid of technology. The majority were in their 20s and 30s and predominantly bicoastal, with 63 percent living either on the West or East coasts. The survey demonstrated that both the sexually oriented and general on-line user group respondents are more knowledgeable about women's sexuality issues than they are about comparable men's issues when compared to the general off-line population polled (Tamosaitis 1995). This study, the first of its kind, could provide the impetus for further on-line research. Of the twenty most popular Usenet newsgroup forums, half are on sex-related topics (Lewis 1995).

Several universities are also concerned about sexually explicit material and are limiting or prohibiting access to certain newsgroups. In November 1994, Carnegie Mellon University moved to eliminate all sexually oriented Usenet newsgroups from its computers. Stanford, Penn State, Iowa State and other universities have also attempted to limit access (Tamosaitis 1995).

Legal Challenges to Free Speech on the Internet   BARBARA GARRIS

Politically, any mention of sexuality in international cyberspace, from the most benign to the most perverse, is currently under scrutiny in the Supreme Court. In June 1995, Senator James Exon offered the Communications Decency Act of 1995 as an amendment to the Telecommunications Act of 1996, which was then included in the Telecom Act as Title 5, Section 507. The Communications Decency Act (CDA) expands regulations on obscene and indecent material to minors which would be transmitted to them through the telephone lines by way of the worldwide Internet, or any other on-line service (Itialiano 1996; Lewis 1995; Lohn 1996).

The bill included, in a very subtle unthreatening way, elements of the old Comstock Act of 1873 which, in the past, made it a crime to send material on birth control and abortion through the postal service (Schwartz 1996a). This archaic act, inserted by Representative Henry J. Hyde, a longtime abortion foe, remains on the legislative books today as 18 U.S.C. Sec. 1462. Elements of the Comstock Act prohibiting dissemination of contraceptive information and the sale of contraceptives to married and single women had been declared unconstitutional in various decisions, the last two in 1966 and 1972. However, the prohibition against providing information about abortion remains on the books to the present. In the new Communications Decency Act, the maximum fine for providing information about abortion has been raised from $5,000 to $250,000 for anyone convicted of knowingly transmitting any "obscene, lewd, lascivious, filthy, or indecent" communications on the nation's telecommunications networks including the Internet. Meanwhile, other legislators sponsored legislation, the Comstock Clean-up Act of 1996, to repeal completely the remnants of the Comstock Act.

The Telecommunications Act of 1996 was signed by President Clinton on February 8, 1996. Although the President signed the bill into law, he immediatedly issued a disclaimer, saying that

> I do object to the provision in the Act concerning the transmission of abortion related speech and information.... The Department of Justice has advised me of its long-standing policy that this and related abortion provisions in current law are unconstitutional and will not be enforced because they violate the First Amendment [protecting freedom of speech].

The CDA was included in the Telecommunications Act supposedly to squelch on-line pornography and make the World Wide Web and the Internet, as well as other on-line services, "safe" for children. But the wording crafted by Internet-illiterate congressmen was so vague and overly broad that even the most innocent use of health-related information could result in a $250,000 fine and two years in prison. Free-speech activists, spearedheaded by the American Civil Liberties Union, Electronic Freedom Foundation, American Library Association, and many others, were appalled and filed suit to keep at bay any prosecution and punishment for this alleged on-line crime until the case can be heard by the United States Supreme Court.

Suit was immediately filed by the American Library Association and the Citizen's Internet Empowerment Coalition in the United States District Court for the Eastern District of Pennsylvania seeking a preliminary injunction against the CDA on the constitutional grounds of the right to free speech. "Plaintiffs include various organizations and individuals who, inter alia, are associated with the computer and/or communications industries, or who publish or post materials on the Internet, or belong to various citizen groups." The case was heard before Judge Sloviter, Chief Judge, United States Court of Appeals for the Third Circuit, and Judges Buckwalter and Dalzell, Judges for the Eastern District of Pennsylvania.

An injunction was granted on June 11, 1996, after all three judges had schooled themselves with hands-on experience with the Internet. The basis for the injunction was three-fold:

1. That whatever previous decisions had been handed down limiting indecent expression on other media (such as cable television and radio) could not be applied to cyberspace,
2. Control over pornography aimed at children rested with the parents and schools, not with the government nor with on-line services transmitting the offensive material, and
3. There was no technological way available to the Internet of checking the age of Internet users, except the use of credit card numbers, to access hard-core pornography.

All three judges saw the CDA as patently unconstitutional and asked the Supreme Court for a final ruling (EPIC 1996; McCullaugh 1996; *The New York Times* 1996; Quinttner 1996; Schwartz 1996b).

On July 1, 1996, the U.S. Department of Justice officially filed an appeal. In its September 30, 1996, edition, *HotWired* magazine reported that the U.S. Department of Justice was stalling for time, and the U.S. Supreme Court granted them an extra month to submit filings. The case was supposed to have been heard in the Supreme Court in October 1996, but no new hearing date had been published as of November 1996. As of March 1997, the CDA was going to the Supreme Court, with a decision expected in June.

Judge Dalzell's opinion sums up the on-going debate over sex on the Internet:

> True it is that many find some of the speech on the Internet to be offensive, and amid the din of cyberspace many hear discordant voices that they regard as indecent. The absence of govermental regulation of Internet content has unquestionably produced a kind of chaos, but as one of plaintiffs' experts put it with such resonance at the hearing: "What achieved success was the very chaos that the Internet is. The strength of the Internet is that chaos."
>
> Just as the strength of the Internet is chaos, so the strength of our liberty depends upon the chaos and cacophony of the unfettered speech the First Amendment protects.
>
> For these reasons, I without hesitation hold that the CDA is unconstitutional on its face.

Since the filing of this case, three other state cases have been brought to court. A New York City case, filed April 30, 1996, by Joe Shea, reporter for the *American Reporter*, sought to overturn the CDA, claiming that the law limits freedom of speech for the press. On July 29, 1996, the court ruled in favor of Shea. This case is expected to be folded into the primary case brought to the Supreme Court by the American Civil Liberties Union (ACLU) et al. suit mentioned above. At the same time, journalism professor Bill Loving of the University of Oklahoma filed suit against the university charging that it blocked access on April 1, 1996 to a newsgroup, "alt.sex," after the university received complaints from a fundamentalist religious organization. Loving claimed that restricting students' access to the Internet is a violation of their First Amendment rights. (As of late 1996, he was awaiting the University's response.) Finally, effective July 1, 1996, the Georgia State General Assembly passed a law providing criminal sanctions against anyone falsely identifying themselves on the Internet. A suit (*ACLU of Georgia et al. vs. Miller et al.*), seeking a preliminary injunction against the Georgia statue, was filed September 24, 1996, by the ACLU, Electronic Frontiers Georgia, Georgia State Representative Mitchell Kaye, and others. As of late 1996, the hearing had not been held.

Summing Up   SANDRA BARGAINNIER

What is considered sexually explicit? Are safe-sex guidelines considered sexually explicit? Obviously, this type of law could disband the educational and informative sex-related Internet resources and the sex-related newsgroups.

Another concern associated with the Internet is the loss of community in the real world and the formation of on-line communities. Opponents believe that people are not honest about who they are in cyberspace, which is a fantasy land. Proponents say that virtual communities provide a place for support, information, and understanding. Many feel that gender, race, age, orientation, and physical appearance are not apparent in cyberspace unless a person wants to make such characteristics public. People with physical disabilities or less-than-glamorous appearances find that virtual communities treat them as they always wanted to be treated—as thinkers and transmitters of ideas and feelings, not just an able body or a face (Rheingold 1995). Many young people can be part of a community for the first time in their life by interacting with an on-line community. An on-line community might, for example, provide a teenage lesbian who feels alienated at school and home with a sense of self-worth and understanding.

Not since the invention of television has a technology changed how a nation and a world spend their time, gather information, and communicate, as has the Internet. Sexuality professionals and the public have the capacity to access tremendous amounts of sexual information, some of it valid and educational, some of it entertaining, and some that others might label "obscene." But who is to judge? Sexuality professionals need to get involved before others judge what is deemed acceptable sexuality information. The Internet will also serve as a new frontier for sex research, sex education, sex information, collaboration, and communication (Tamosaitis 1995).

15. Current Developments

PATRICIA BARTHALOW KOCH

A note to our readers:

Although we retained our original format of 14 sections from *The International Encyclopedia* for practical reasons, we have carefully replaced some slightly dated material with more current information. We have also added this new section to cover some important recent developments. Our "Concluding Remarks" for this volume reemphasize the three major themes of change, diversity, and conflict, which are evident throughout this work.

For your convenience, page references are often provided below to related material in the previous sections, along with a supplementary bibliography for the updated material in this volume on page 332.

A. The Interaction of Gender and Race

Sexuality and African-American Women

Gender and race have traditionally been defined and operationalized as fixed biological categories into which people could neatly be sorted. However, many scholars now consider gender and race as social constructions, based on social and political influences, rather than on biological characteristics (Irvine 1995; Simon 1996). Additionally, many research studies have confounded socioeconomic status with race. Shortcomings often encountered in sexuality research include the lack of historical context, cultural insensitivity, and generalizations or assumptions about gender (Burgess 1994). Various aspects of African-American women's sexuality are quintessential examples of the salience and interaction of gender and race upon sexuality in the United States. African-American women's sexual attitudes, values, behaviors, and relationships have been shaped by their gender and racial heritage, including the historical experience of slavery and continued marginalization in American society (Staples and Johnson 1993).

To the extent that African-American males have been "emasculated" by gender-role stereotyping, as described by Samuels (pp. 42-49), African-American females have often been "defeminized" by this same process. By virtue of the historical legacy of slavery and continuing discrimination against African-American men in the labor force and other aspects of "mainstream" American society, e.g., housing and education, African-American women have always needed to be in the labor force to support their families (Anderson 1996). This economic necessity has contributed to the myth of the "black matriarchy," which has then been blamed for the deterioration of the black family. African-American women have been described as domineering authoritarians who drive away their husbands and destroy their sons' ability to perform effectively as productive adults.

These "castrating matriarchs" and "lazy black men" have been chided as the "cause" of poverty among African-American families, avoiding any search for causes in a political and economic system that provided African-Americans with few opportunities to successfully support intact families (Anderson 1996; Staples and Johnson 1993).

In essence, there tends to be more egalitarian gender-roles and fluidity among African-Americans than among Anglo-Americans (Broman 1991; Farley and Allen 1987). White stereotypic norms seem to be violated when black women have greater participation in family decision-making than has been present within a dominant Anglo society where male control is more the "rule." Therefore, according to Burgess (1994), African-American women are seen as domineering. African-American women have most often been portrayed in some combination of four primary images: (1) as highly maternal, family-oriented, and self-sacrificing "Mammies" or "Aunt Jemimas"; (2) as threatening and argumentative "Sapphires"; (3) as seductive, sexually irresponsible, promiscuous "Jezebels"; and (4) as ignorant, lazy, greedy, breeding "Welfare Mothers" (Collins 1990; Weitz 1993; West 1995).

In reality, African-American women must play dual roles. They are pressured to be more androgynous or masculine in order to make it in the work world, since they are often more successful at gaining employment than are African-American men. Yet, they also often try to maintain traditional female gender roles, especially that of mothering, to sustain relationships within their domestic networks (Binion 1990). As a hedge against failure, poor black men may limit their affective and economic commitments to family, approaching marriage and fatherhood ambivalently (Anderson 1996). Black women often want to be supportive of their men, yet sometimes find the men's behavior to be distancing, oppressive, or abusive (Lorde 1984). Lorde has noted that female-headed households in the black community do not always occur by default. She and others contend that black women are less likely to accept oppressive conditions in their marriages than white women, and, therefore, are much more likely to leave abusive unions with males. African-American women often develop matrifocal kin networks in which female family members, e.g., grandmothers and aunts, share the family and child-care responsibilities. Compared to their Anglo-American counterparts, African-American women are less likely to marry, more likely to be divorced or separated, and less likely to remarry (Anderson 1990).

Regarding specific sexual behaviors, black men and women appear to engage in cunnilingus and fellatio less often than their white peers (Belcastro 1985; Hunt 1974; Laumann et al. 1994). A lack of foreplay is a grievance often expressed by married black women (Staples 1981), although black women report a higher frequency of intercourse per week than white women (Fisher 1980). Concerning such differences, Staples (1972:9) suggests that:

Unlike many white women who see sexual relations as primarily an activity designed to give men pleasure, black women expect their sexual partners to try and sexually satisfy them, and criticize him if he doesn't. Sex is not necessarily something that is done to them.... Also in contrast to many white women, the black woman tends to be open within the peer group about her sexual experiences.... [This] allows black women to develop standards of sexual conduct to which males must address themselves.

Rape and sexual assault have a unique history for African-American women because of the sexual exploitation of slaves for over 250 years before the American Civil War (Getman 1984). Throughout America's history, sexual assault on African-American women has been perceived and treated with less concern than for Anglo-American women (Wyatt 1992). For example, by 1660 in the American South, there were laws supporting sex between black women and white men in order to insure that interracial children would be slaves owned by the white slave masters. However, sex between a black man and white woman was severely punished with the alleged black "assailant" being castrated or sentenced to death, usually by lynching. Yet, there were no penalties for the rape of black women by white men. The stereotype that black women are "oversexed" by nature and, thus, cannot be rape victims still exists in America today (Getman 1984). When both a rape victim and defendant are black, there is less likelihood of conviction compared to both victim and defendant being white (LaFree, Ruskin, and Visher 1985). Because of this and discriminatory police practices toward other crimes in the black community, black victims may feel less support and are, therefore, less likely to report being raped (Wyatt, Newcomb, and Notgrass 1990). Hooks (1990) has emphasized that sexism and racism are "interlocking systems of domination that maintain each other."

B. Sexuality Education

Abstinence-Only Sexuality Education

Under the 1996 Welfare Reform Law, funds were made available to the states to establish programs that have as their "exclusive purpose" the "promotion of abstinence-only education." Funding of $50 million a year is guaranteed for these programs for the next five years. To qualify for a federal grant, a state abstinence-only program must teach:

1. The social, psychological, and health gains to be realized by abstaining from sexual activity;
2. Abstinence from sexual activity outside marriage as the expected standard for all school-age children;

3. Abstinence from sexual activity is the only certain way to avoid out-of-wedlock pregnancy, STDs, and other associated health problems;
4. A mutually faithful monogamous relationship in the context of marriage is the expected standard of human sexuality;
5. Sexual activity outside of the context of marriage is likely to have harmful psychological and physical effects;
6. Bearing children out-of-wedlock is likely to have harmful consequences for the child, the child's parents, and society;
7. How to reject sexual advances, and how alcohol and drug use increase vulnerability to sexual advances; and
8. The importance of attaining self-sufficiency before engaging in sexual activity.

All fifty states have submitted abstinence-only education proposals; many of them are school-based. Yet, national and worldwide research have found abstinence-only programs to be considerably less effective, if effective at all, when compared with comprehensive sexuality education programs, in preventing unintended pregnancy and STDs among youth (Brick and Roffman 1993, Nelson 1996). Yet, no federal funding is forthcoming to support comprehensive sexuality education.

It is safe to predict that the trend of increasing sexual experience among adolescents will continue, and that young people will not respond favorably to these abstinence-only programs. Perhaps when the general public realizes the ineffectiveness of these programs, greater support for and expansion of more comprehensive sexuality education will result. (See also pages 70-88.)

C. Intersexuality and the Politics of Difference   ROBERT T. FRANCOEUR

In the past ten years, female impersonators, transvestites, and other gender-bending images have become popular subjects of television talk shows and prime-time television "magazines" like Prime Time Live and 60 Minutes. Major films have made cross-dressing and transvestite issues a common theme—to mention a few: *La Cage Aux Folles* and its remake *The Bird Cage; Yentl* (with Barbra Streisand); *Victor/Victoria* (with Julie Andrews); *Tootsie* (with Dustin Hoffman); *Mrs. Doubtfire* (with Robin Williams); *M Butterfly; Adventures of Priscilla, Queen of the Desert; Glen or Glenda; Farewell My Concubine; Just Like a Woman; Different for Girls; The Sheltering Sky* (with Debra Winger); *Bull Durham* (featuring a rookie pitcher who wears a garter belt under his uniform); *Love Compassion and Valor;* and *To Wong Foo, Thanks for Everything, Julie Newmar* (featuring Wesley Snipes, John Leguizamos, and Patrick Swayze). RuPaul, a stunning six-foot-seven African-American drag queen has gained national recognition as a model for GLAM Lipstick and as a popular television talk show host and radio disk jockey. Rudolph Giuliani, the mayor of New York, appeared comically at several public events in drag. Dennis Rodman, Chicago Bulls professional basketball player, has also appeared in drag several times, including once dressed as a bride. Female impersonation, cross-dressing, and transvestism seem to be "in vogue camp." (See also pages 165-171.)

In 1992, the polymorphous San Francisco culture saw the birth of Transgender Nation, an energetic transgender political movement, developed out of Queer Nation, a post-gay/lesbian group, which sought to transcend gender-identity politics. Transgender Nation made news when some members were arrested for protesting the psychiatric labeling of transsexuality as a mental illness at the American Psychiatric meeting. About the same time, openly transsexual scholars, including Susan Stryker and Sandy Stone, became visible in academic positions at leading universities.

Whether this broad spectrum of transgendered persons becomes significant in the long term of American sexual culture is not at present clear, but its synchronicity with the recent emergence of a very small but potentially important activist group of transgendered persons is worth investigation. In 1993, Chase founded the Intersex Society of North America. ISNA's immediate goal was to "create a community of intersex people who could provide each other with peer support to deal with their shame, stigma, grief, and rage, as well as with practical issues such as how to obtain old medical records or how to locate a sympathetic psychotherapist or endocrinologist." According to Cheryl Chase,

> ISNA's longer-term and more fundamental goal, however, is to change the way intersex infants are treated. We advocate that surgery not be performed on ambiguous genitals unless there is a medical reason (such as blocked or painful urination) and that parents be given the conceptual tools and emotional support to accept their children's physical differences. While it is fascinating to think about the potential development of new genders or subject positions grounded in forms of embodiment that fall outside the familiar male/female dichotomy, we recognize that the two-sex/gender model is currently hegemonic and, therefore, advocate that children be raised either as boys or girls according to which designation seems likely to offer the child the greatest future sense of comfort. Advocating gender assignment without resorting to normalizing surgery is a radical position given that it requires the willful disruption of the assumed concordance between body shape and gender category. However, this is the only position that prevents irreversible physical damage to the intersex person's body, that preserves the intersex person's agency regarding their own flesh, and that recognizes genital sensation and erotic functioning to be at least as important as reproductive capacity. If an intersex child or adult decides to change gender or to undergo surgical or hormonal alteration of his/her body, that decision should also be fully respected and

facilitated. The key point is that intersex subjects should not be violated for the comfort and convenience of others (Chase 1998).

ISNA has publicized its message and activist agenda with an astute and effective use of the media, including: Public Broadcast Radio and Television; publications like *The New York Times, New York Post, Mademoiselle* (February 1998), *Rolling Stone* (December 11, 1997); a special issue of *Chrysalis* (published by AEGIS, the American Educational Gender Information Service); a newsletter titled *Hermaphrodites with Attitude*, dialogues and protest demonstrations at medical meetings; and articles in professional journals, such as *Urology Times* and *Archives of Pediatric and Adolescent Medicine.*

Of particular interest is the use ISNA has made of the Internet to connect and cooperate with other groups, including: the Turner Syndrome Society, Androgen Insensitivity (AIS) Support Group, Klinefelter's Syndrome (K.S.) & Associates, the Ambiguous Genital Support Network, Hermaphrodite Education and Listening Post (HELP), the Gay and Lesbian Medical Association, the Workgroup on Violence in Pediatrics and Gynecology, the Genital Mutilation Survivors' Support Network (organized by German intersexuals), and Hijra Nippon (organized by activist intersexuals in Japan).

It is estimated that one in a hundred infants are born with some anomaly in sex differentiation, and about one in two thousand newborns are different enough to make their gender assignment as "boy" or "girl" problematic. Thus, the members of ISNA would appear to have minuscule potential for achieving their goal of persuading society to accept a "politics of difference" with recognition and valuing of other-gendered persons. A minority as small as ISNA would seem to have little chance of successfully challenging the prevailing medical paradigm of immediate surgical intervention to remedy sexual ambiguity (Coleman 1991). However, as medical ethicist Karen Lebacqz (1997) has observed,

> The politics of difference has emerged out of the self-identification of groups that may be minorities in society but that are large enough to become a political force. . . . [T]he advent of new technologies such as the Internet may facilitate the process, as individuals who are widely scattered geographically can find each other and form connections and agendas.

Only the future will tell whether American society is at a watershed where reconstructions of societal and individual responses to gender are possible. Whether the mass media and Internet are powerful enough to enable American culture to replace its all-prevailing gender dichotomy with a "politics of difference," similar in some respects to the valuing of "third-gendered persons" in other cultures, remains to be seen.

D. Sexual Health

Puberty and Menarche ROBERT T. FRANCOEUR

A puzzling phenomenon has been noted in new data regarding the onset of female puberty in the United States (see Table 9). According to a 1997 study of 17,000 girls ages 3 through 12 seen in 65 pediatric practices around the country, American girls are reaching puberty earlier than previously believed. Nearly half of African-American and 15 percent of white girls are beginning to develop sexually by age 8 (Herman-Giddens 1997). The average age of menstruation for white girls has been unchanged for 45 years. For black girls—about 9.6 percent of the 17,000 girls in the study—the average age of menarche is about four months younger than it was 30 years ago, when poor nutrition and poverty, which can delay puberty, afflicted more blacks.

Table 9

The Onset of Puberty in American Girls

	Breast and Pubic Hair Development			
	By Age 8	By Age 7	By Age 3	Average Age of Menarche
African-American girls	48.3%	27.2%	3%	12.16 years
White girls	14.7%	6.7%	1%	12.88 years

Preliminary comparisons of these data with puberty onset and menarche data from a variety of other countries indicate that the age of menarche is roughly similar around the world, while the onset of puberty is about two years earlier in the United States than it is in other countries.

The study raises questions about whether environmental estrogens, chemicals that mimic the female hormone estrogen, are inducing earlier puberty among some girls. Environmental estrogens occur from the break-down of chemicals in products ranging from pesticides to plastic wrap. Natural estrogen is used in some hair products, including pomades marketed to blacks. Research is needed to ascertain whether and to what extent natural and environmental estrogen may be affecting sexual development.

As the study's lead author, Marcia Herman-Giddens of the University of North Carolina at Chapel Hill, noted, the new data also suggest that sex education should begin sooner than is current practice. "I don't think parents, teachers, or society in general have been really thinking of children that young having to deal with puberty." (See also pages 91-105.)

Infertility and Assisted Pregnancy ROBERT T. FRANCOEUR

America's romance with assisted reproductive technology began a hundred years ago when J. Marion Sims made 55 attempts at "ethereal copulation," as artificial insemination with donor semen (AID) was then known. His success rate at Jefferson Medical School in Philadelphia was only 4 percent because insemination was performed just before or after menstruation, which was wrongly believed at the time to be a woman's most fertile period. In 1960, Bunge and Sherman experimented with artificial insemination using frozen donor semen at the State University of Iowa, whereas Behrman and associates at the University of Michigan reported 29 successful pregnancies using frozen semen. By 1974, America had 28 private and public sperm banks with approximately 20,000 pregnancies a year from artificial insemination, double the mid-1960s' rate (Francoeur 1977).

In 1981, reproductive specialists at Eastern Virginia Medical Center produced American's first in-vitro fertilized (IVF) baby, three years after the world's first IVF baby in Cambridge, England. Some American feminists organized a Feminist International Network on the Reproductive Technologies to protest "female slavery and exploitation by male infertility specialists and patriarchal husbands" (Ardetti, Klein, and Minder 1984).

Other forms of assisted reproductive technology have followed, including embryo transplants, surrogate motherhood, embryo lavage for harvesting ova from donors, epididymal aspiration of sperm, and microinsemination of ova with single sperm. Social complications quickly followed. The court fight of Mary Beth Whitehead, a New Jersey surrogate mother, to retain custody of "Baby M," whom she had contracted to carry for an infertile couple, made national news. In the aftermath, several states outlawed surrogate-mother contracts and prohibited payment. In 1990, when a divorcing couple fought over custody of seven frozen embryos remaining from fertility treatments, the court declared the frozen embryos "human life from the moment of conception," and awarded custody to the mother (Holmes, Hoskins, and Gross 1981; Corea 1985). The 1990s have witnessed a flood of new technologies, including insertion of sperm and zygotes into the fallopian tube (GIFT and ZIFT), postmenopausal pregnancies, and frozen eggs.

Three major psychological, social, and ethical controversies have emerged from these technologies. The first involves "designer and discount designer embryos." Several American infertility clinics now offer infertile couples the option of paying $20,000 or more to select donor sperm and egg from a select list of designer donors. After IVF, several designer zygotes are implanted in the adoptive woman's uterus. If any embryos are left in cryogenic storage after a successful pregnancy, they may be sold at a discount to other infertile couples.

The high risk of multiple births is a second issue. England, Australia, and most European countries have laws prohibiting transfer of more than two or three embryos in each pregnancy attempt. These clinics have a success rate about 20 percent lower than American clinics, which are not subject to any limit on the number of embryos they transfer. American clinics typically transfer four or five embryos per attempt, but some clinics transfer as many as ten. The result is a high risk of multiple pregnancies that are themselves dangerous to both mother and offspring. In a survey of 281 American infertility clinics in 1995, 37 percent of all births were multiple births, contrasted with 2 percent in the general population. Woman under age 35 experienced a 17 percent pregnancy rate and a 3 percent multiple-pregnancy risk when two embryos were transferred. Transfer of four embryos gave a 34 percent pregnancy rate, but a multiple-pregnancy risk of 15 percent. Transferring more than four embryos does not improve the fertility rate, but it does increase the multiple births. In 1997, infertility treatment resulted in the survival of the McCaughey septuplets, the world's second set of surviving septuplets, the first being in Saudi Arabia.

Some clinics transfer multiple embryos in the hope of raising their fertility rate, in order to attract more clients. A clinic that reduces the risk of multiple pregnancy faces a lower fertility rate and may not survive in the competition for clients. The present practice is not pleasant for infertile couples who have to decide whether to let a multiple pregnancy go to full term and risk losing all or some of the offspring, or to resort to "selective reduction," which aborts several of the multiple embryos early in pregnancy. Selective reduction improves the survival of the one or two remaining embryos, but it may also trigger a miscarriage of all the embryos.

Finally, there is the issue of payment for donor eggs. When egg donation was first introduced, donors were paid a few hundred dollars. More recently, the standard fee has been $2,500. In early 1998, a major New Jersey hospital offered donors $5,000, because their clients were being forced to wait up to a year for an egg. The shortage of donor eggs has brought private egg brokers into the market, with some brokers offering $35,000 for a suitable donor.

Abortion—The Twenty-Fifth Anniversary of the Roe v. Wade Decision

A 1998 report on the status of abortion rights in the United States documents that there are more obstacles today for women seeking their constitutional right to abortion than ever before since the Supreme Court's *Roe v. Wade* decision in 1973 (NARAL 1998). The report documents the increasing risk of unintended pregnancy with concomitant increasing difficulties in obtaining abortions resulting in increased risks to women's health and well-being. The factors contributing to this include increased anti-abortion legislation enacted at the state and federal levels, an acute shortage of medical providers being trained in abortion procedures in medical schools, a parallel shortage of medical providers willing to contend with constant harassment from anti-choice activists, lack of sexuality education, and denial of insurance coverage for contraception. As Chief Justice William Renquist stated in the Supreme Court's *Planned Parenthood v. Casey* decision, "Roe continues to exist but only in the way a storefront on a western movie exists: a mere facade to give the illusion of reality" (*Planned Parenthood of Southeastern PA v. Casey* 1992).

In 1998, states were enforcing an unprecedented number of abortion restrictions, including: mandatory waiting periods, Medicaid funding bans, parental notification and consent laws, bans on the use of public facilities for abortion, prohibitions on the participation of public employees in providing abortion services, bans on actual abortion procedures (e.g., "partial-birth" abortions), and prohibitions on the use of public funds to counsel women about or provide referrals for abortion services. In 1998, for example, seventeen states were enforcing three or more abortion restrictions, a 467 percent increase from 1992. Over half the states enacted some restriction on access to abortion in 1997. An anti-abortion bill introduced into a state legislature in 1997 was more than twice as likely to be enacted than in 1996. Efforts to ban "partial-birth" or "late-term" abortions dominated legislative debate at both the federal and state levels in 1997. This resulted in sixteen states banning this rare procedure and the U.S. Congress passing a bill to ban it. The bill was not signed by President Clinton, because it contained no provision to protect the mother's health or life. (See also pages 233-234.)

There is also diminishing access to abortion providers due to increased harassment and violence by anti-abortion groups and a shortage of physicians trained and willing to provide abortion services. Between 1982 and 1992, the number of abortion providers nationwide decreased by 18 percent. Many residency programs have eliminated abortion instruction from the curriculum altogether or have relegated it to an elective course. Currently, there are no abortion providers in 84 percent of the counties in the United States. The American Medical Association has concluded that the shortage of abortion providers has "the potential to threaten the safety of induced abortion" (AMA 1992).

Private insurance companies, often with the blessing of state legislatures, are cutting back on coverage for contraceptive services. Almost half—49 percent—of the typical large insurance plans exclude coverage for prescription contraception, although for women this often constitutes their major medication expenses. Illinois, North Dakota, and Texas have even enacted state legislation allowing health-care institutions or insurers to refuse to provide or counsel patients for health-care services that violate their "organizational conscience," including family planning, infertility services, vasectomy, female sterilization, and abortion procedures.

These increasing obstacles to obtaining legal abortions demonstrate the successes of the anti-abortion groups, particularly in electing supporters into state and federal legislatures. It seems likely that the trend to erode access to abortion services will continue, at least in the short term.

E. Condom Distribution in the Schools ROBERT T. FRANCOEUR

Seventy-two percent of American high school seniors, on average, have engaged in sexual intercourse, although the percent is higher for teenagers in large cities and their suburbs. At the same time, American teenagers have the highest rate of teenage pregnancy and abortion in North America and Europe. They are also rapidly becoming the highest risk group for HIV/AIDS infection in the United States. American parents, educators, and health care professionals are consequently struggling to decide on ways to deal with this reality. Typical of the conflicted, schizophrenic American approach to sexual issues, religious conservatives call for teaching abstinence-only education and saying nothing about contraceptives and other ways of reducing the risk of contracting sexually transmissible diseases and HIV infections. At the same time, others advocate educating and counseling: "You don't have to be sexually active, but if you are, this is what you can do to protect yourself." However, the problem is so serious in New York, Baltimore, Chicago, Los Angeles, San Francisco, Philadelphia, Miami, and other large cities that school boards in these cities now allow school nurses and school-based health clinics to distribute free condoms to students, usually without requiring parental notification or permission (Guttmacher 1997; Richardson 1997).

Typical of the opposition is Dr. Alma Rose George, president of the National Medical Association, who opposes schools giving condoms to teens without their parents knowing about it: "When you give condoms out to teens, you are promoting sexual activity. It's saying that it's all right. We shouldn't make it so easy for them." Faye Wattleton, former president of the Planned Parenthood Federation of America, approves of schools distributing condoms, and maintains that "mandatory parental consent would be counterproductive and meaningless." Some critics claim that condom distribution programs are inherently racist and a form of genocide because the decisions are mostly made by a white majority for predominantly black schools. (See also pages 216-230.)

Recently, a study comparing the sexual activity and condom use of 7,000 students in New York City high schools, and 4,000 similar high school students in Chicago, supported the effectiveness of school condom distribution (Guttmacher 1997). The New York schools combined HIV/AIDS education with free condoms, while the Chicago schools had similar HIV/AIDS education but no condom distribution. In both cities, 60 percent of the students were sexually active regardless of whether or not their schools distributed condoms. However, students in schools that distributed condoms were significantly more likely to have used a condom in their last intercourse than teens in schools that did not distribute condoms. Regardless of the data available on the ineffectiveness of abstinence-only education and the effectiveness of condom distribution, this debate will continue.

F. Sexually Transmissible Diseases

In 1997, a Committee on Prevention and Control of Sexually Transmitted Diseases issued an important analysis of the epidemiology of STDs (except for HIV) and effectiveness of public health strategies to prevent and control them in the United States (Eng and Butler 1997).

The Committee, sponsored by the Institute of Medicine, an adviser to the federal government, concluded that STDs are hidden epidemics of enormous health and economic consequence in the United States. The incidence rates of curable STDs in the United States are the highest in the developed world, with rates that are 50 to 100 times higher than other industrialized nations. For example, the reported incidence of gonorrhea in 1995 was 150 cases per 100,000 persons in the United States versus three cases per 100,000 in Sweden. STDs continue to have a disproportionate impact on women, infants, young people, and racial/ethnic minorities. The estimated overall costs from STDs in the United States was nearly $17 billion in 1994.

Updates concerning the epidemiology and consequences of STDs in the United States are provided by the Centers for Disease Control and Prevention (CDC, 1998). Chlamydia (an estimated 4,000,000 new cases each year) and gonorrhea (800,000 new cases each year) are a major cause of pelvic inflammatory disease (PID). Among American women with PID, 20 percent will become infertile, and 9 percent will have an ectopic pregnancy, which is the leading cause of first-trimester pregnancy-related deaths in American women. The ectopic pregnancy rate could be reduced by as much as 50 percent with early detection and treatment of STDs. In addition, fetal or neonatal death occurs in up to 40 percent of pregnant women who have untreated syphilis. There are an estimated 101,000 new cases of syphilis each year, with 3,400 infants born with congenital syphilis.

Genital herpes may now be the most common STD in the United States, with perhaps more than 45 million Americans, including 18 percent of whites and 46 percent of blacks, carrying the herpes virus. Despite an emphasis on safe sex to prevent HIV/AIDS, the Centers for Disease Control reported that genital herpes had increased fivefold since the late 1970s among white teenagers and doubled among whites in their 20s. In all, about one in five Americans is infected with genital herpes. There are an estimated 200,000 to 500,000 new symptomatic cases each year. In addition, it is likely that more than 24 million Americans are infected with Human Papillomavirus (HPV), with an estimated 500,000 to a million new infections each year. Sexually transmitted HPV is the most important risk factor for cervical cancer, which was responsible for about 5,000 deaths in 1995.

To deal with this silent epidemic in the United States, the Institute of Medicine Committee made a strong advocacy statement in support of establishing an effective national system for STD prevention. To accomplish this, four major strategies were recommended for implementation by public- and private-sector policymakers at the local, state, and national levels:

1. Overcome barriers to adoption of healthy sexual behaviors, particularly through a nationally organized mass-media campaign;

2. Develop strong leadership, strengthen investment, and improve information systems for STD prevention;
3. Design and implement essential STD-related services in innovative ways for adolescents and underserved populations; and
4. Ensure access to and quality of essential clinical services for STDs.

The report concluded that the veil of enforced secrecy about sexual health must be lifted, public awareness raised, and bold national leadership must come from the highest levels in order to overcome the public health shame of STD epidemics. However, it is unlikely that these recommendations will be put into action, and Americans will needlessly continue to suffer the physical, emotional, social, and financial consequences of these preventable diseases. (See also pages 238-239.)

G. HIV Disease

A major development in the course of the AIDS epidemic in the United States was heralded in 1996. For the first time, there was a marked decrease in deaths among people with AIDS (PWAs)—12 percent less during the first two quarters of 1996 as compared to 1995 (CDC 1996). This decline in deaths is likely due to two factors:

1. The slowing of the epidemic overall, due in part to the effectiveness of prevention efforts, with an increase in people diagnosed with AIDS of only 2 percent in 1995; and
2. Improved treatments, including the use of protease inhibitors, which lengthen the lifespan of PWAs.

Yet, it must be noted that AIDS deaths are not declining among all groups. For example, deaths declined among men by 15 percent but increased among women by 3 percent. Deaths declined among men who have sex with men by 18 percent, among injecting-drug users by 6 percent, but increased among people contracting AIDS through heterosexual contact by 3 percent. The death rate is also not decreasing equally among various racial/ethnic groups. Declines were greater among whites (21 percent) than among Hispanics (10 percent) or blacks (2 percent).

The cumulative number of AIDS cases reported to the CDC through June 30, 1997, was 612,078. Adult and adolescent cases totaled 604,176, with 511,934 (85 percent) cases in males and 92,242 (15 percent) cases in females. An additional 7,902 cases were reported in children under age 13. Racial/ethnic minorities continued to be disproportionately affected by AIDS, as illustrated by the breakdown of AIDS cases by race/ethnicity: white, not Hispanic—279,072 (46 percent); black, not Hispanic—216,980 (36 percent); Hispanic—109,252 (18 percent); Asian/Pacific Islander—4,370 (7 percent); American Indian/Alaskan Native—1,677 (3 percent).

With the increasing number of people living with HIV and AIDS, additional resources will be needed for services, treatment, and care. A major breakthrough in the treatment of HIV disease has been the use of "drug cocktail" therapy, which combines the use of multiple drugs, usually a protease inhibitor with one or two reverse transcriptase inhibitors. Research has shown that this combination-drug therapy can dramatically prolong survival and slow disease progression in people with advanced AIDS, as well as holding the virus for many months below minimum detectable blood levels (Smart 1996). In fact, AIDS deaths in the United States declined 44 percent between 1996 and 1997. As of mid-1998, the long-term effectiveness of these treatments is unknown, with concern over the development of resistance leading to more virulent strains of HIV. Also, the expense of these drugs (approximately $20,000 or more per year) prohibits large segments of HIV-infected people, often from minority groups, from receiving treatment. Prevention efforts must still be emphasized, since they remain the best and most cost-effective strategies for containing HIV and saving lives. (See also pages 239-251.)

H. Sexual Dysfunctions, Counseling, and Therapies

Incidence Rates

Although it is extremely difficult to ascertain accurately the occurrence of the various sexual disorders and dysfunctions in the United States, research on various clinical and community samples has provided a glimpse as to their prevalence (Spector and Carey 1990). Sexual desire problems are the most common complaint seen in sex therapy in the United States, with affected men outnumbering women. It is also the most common sexual complaint of lesbian couples (Nichols 1989). Community studies indicate that 16 to 34 percent of the population experience inhibited sexual desire. Between 11 and 48 percent of the female population may experience arousal phase disorder, whereas 4 to 9 percent of males report this disorder. Erectile disorder is the most common complaint of men, and inhibited orgasm is the most common complaint of women seeking sex therapy in the United States. It is estimated that 5 to 10 percent of women in the general population experience persistent or recurrent inhibited orgasm. On the other hand, inhibited orgasm is one of the least common dysfunctions among American males (1 to 10 percent). It seems to be a more common difficulty among gay men than among heterosexual men, however. The most common dysfunction of heterosexual men is rapid ejaculation, with 36 to 38 percent reporting persistent or recurrent rapid ejaculation. Dyspareunia is much more common in women than men, with 8 to 23 percent of women experiencing genital pain. Yet, few lesbian women report this difficulty. Over a hundred diseases and disorders of the urogenital system have been linked with painful intercourse. (See also pages 91-105.)

Culturally Appropriate Counseling and Therapy

Minority women and men in the United States experience the entire range of sexual problems and dysfunctions as those experienced by Anglo-Americans (Wyatt et al. 1978). However, most of the research has been conducted with samples of white, middle-class clients. This has left a critical need for research regarding the effectiveness of various sex counseling and therapy techniques among males and females from various racial/ethnic groups (Christensen 1988).

A primary issue is that most minority clients do not have the confidence in or financial resources for professional help and are most likely to turn to extended family or close friends—if anyone—with a sexual concern. Discussion of most sexual matters may be considered too intimate or shameful to discuss with anyone but a long-trusted confidante. People from minority groups may also have experienced prejudicial treatment from professionals in the dominant group, that has led them to have mistrust, hostility, or expectations that their problem will not be understood. Thus, they usually come into contact with professionals only in a crisis when seeking help for legal, financial, reproductive, gynecological, or other medical problems, rather than for relationship or mental health issues.

Professional helpers are overwhelmingly drawn from the white middle-class and generally are male, middle-aged, and well-educated (Atkinson et al. 1983). Their personal attitudes, values, and behaviors usually represent those of the dominant, more privileged culture. Unfortunately, the training of most sex counselors and therapists has not provided opportunities to become aware of and informed about the effects of gender, race/ethnicity, and class on their treatment of minority clients. An Anglo-American ethnocentrism may result in: misunderstanding, misdiagnosing, and/or mistreating a minority client's problem; trying to control aspects of the client's sexuality or fertility rather than helping him or her to make personally satisfying and culturally sensitive choices; or ignoring sources of help and support from within the client's culture (Christensen 1988; McGoldrick, Pearce, and Giordano 1982). The therapist may need to focus, not just on the individual, but also on the institutions and sexist/racist policies that may be affecting the client adversely (systemically induced dysfunction).

Sexuality of Menopausal Women

As America's baby boomers experience mid-life and older age, the sexual concerns of peri- and post-menopausal women have gained greater attention. Older women have been increasingly discussing sexual issues, along with their other health concerns (such as hot flashes, osteoporosis, and heart disease), with their physicians, and are turning to sex counselors and therapists for help. Some of the chief complaints experienced by mid-life heterosexual women are decreased sexual desire, decreased frequency and intensity of orgasm, and decreased frequency of sexual behaviors with a partner, although some women experience heightened sexual response and satisfaction during this time (Mansfield, Voda, and Koch 1995). Interestingly, mid-life lesbian women report less decline in sexual functioning and satisfaction than do their heterosexual peers (Cole 1988).

Hormone replacement therapy (HRT) has been widely touted as a "miracle" drug to help women fight the "estrogen deficiency disease" of menopause and maintain their youth (e.g., smoother skin and elimination of hot flashes) and health (e.g., decreased risk of heart disease, osteoporosis, and perhaps, Alzheimer's disease). However, others have addressed the naturalness of menopause and raised questions as to the actual and relative health risks involved with the use of HRT (such as increased breast cancer) (Love 1997). Regarding sexual functioning, estrogen seems to be important in maintaining vaginal lubrication and perhaps, vaginal vasocongestion, whereas testosterone seems to be important for the pleasurable sensations associated with sexual arousal (Anderson 1991). There are also natural ways to replace estrogen, such as a diet high in soy-based foods, and vaginal dryness may be reduced with a vaginal lubricant, such as K-Y jelly.

It should not be assumed that sexual concerns of mid-life women are always related to hormonal menopausal changes since various research studies have found no connection, or only a weak link, between sexual functioning and menopausal status (Mansfield, Voda, and Koch 1995). Growing older in our culture also creates difficulties for women, such as perceived loss of attractiveness and value, that can affect self-esteem and sexuality. Continued or new difficulties in an ongoing sexual relationship can precipitate sexual concerns. As women reach mid-life, they may become more assertive about having their needs met rather than fulfilling the more traditional gender roles and male phallocentric definitions of sexual satisfaction (Ehrenreich, Hass, and Jacobs 1987, 153; Ogden 1995). Indeed, a partner's ill health or declining sexual responsiveness may also affect the couple's sexual relationship. Thus, in diagnosing and treating a mid-life woman's sexual concerns, physiological, psychological, relational, and sociocultural factors should all be considered (Mansfield and Koch 1997).

Male Erectile Problems   ROBERT T. FRANCOEUR

Throughout recorded history, impotence or erectile dysfunction (ED) has been a major concern of men, and the curing of this sexual dysfunction one of medicine's shadiest niches populated by hundreds of bizarre remedies ranging from ground rhinoceros horns, boar gall, and tiger-penis soup to mail-ordered electrified jockstraps. Pharmaceutical companies concerned about their public images and the stockholders' focus on the bottom line have studiously avoided entering this area, despite the enormous profit that would follow development of a proven safe remedy for erectile dysfunction.

In 1966, inflatable and flexible penile implants were introduced, followed by surgery to boost penile arterial flow in 1973. In 1982, the Food and Drug Administration approved a vacuum pump that pulls blood into the penis by creating a vacuum around a sheathed penis. In the same year, a milestone demonstration by Giles Brindley, a British physician, opened a new door to a major medical breakthrough in the treatment of ED. On stage at a medical conference in Las Vegas, Brindley demonstrated the result of injecting the penis with papaverine, a drug that lowers blood pressure. Several penile injection therapies were soon being tested and welcomed by patients, including: alprostadil; "cocktails" of papaverine, phentolamine, and prostaglandin E1; and phentolamine combined with the protein VIP. Urethral suppositories containing alprostadil were approved by the FDA in 1997. In 1998, pills containing sildenafil, apomorphine, and phentolamine were in various stages of testing and FDA approval (Stipp and Whitaker 1998).

In December 1992, the National Institutes of Health convened a Consensus Development Conference to address the issue of male erectile dysfunction (National Institutes of Health 1992). Specific issues investigated included:

1. The prevalence and clinical, psychological, and social impact of erectile dysfunction;
2. The risk factors for erectile dysfunction and how they might be used in preventing its development;
3. The need for and appropriate diagnostic assessment and evaluation of patients with erectile dysfunction;
4. The efficacies and risks of behavioral, pharmacological, surgical, and other treatments for erectile dysfunction;
5. Strategies for improving public and professional awareness and knowledge of erectile dysfunction; and
6. Future directions for research in prevention, diagnosis, and management of erectile dysfunction.

Among their findings, the panel concluded that:

1. The term "erectile dysfunction" should replace the term "impotence";
2. The likelihood of erectile dysfunction increases with age, but is not an inevitable consequence of aging;
3. Embarrassment of patients and reluctance of both patients and health care providers to discuss sexual matters candidly contribute to underdiagnosis of erectile dysfunction;
4. Many cases of erectile dysfunction can be successfully managed with appropriately selected therapy;

5. The diagnosis and treatment of erectile dysfunction must be specific and responsive to the individual patient's needs, and compliance as well as the desires and expectations of both the patient and partner are important considerations in selecting appropriate therapy;

6. Education of health care providers and the public on aspects of human sexuality, sexual dysfunction, and the availability of successful treatments is essential; and

7. Erectile dysfunction is an important public health problem, deserving increased support for basic science investigation and applied research.

In the early 1980s, an estimated 10 million Americans suffered from erectile dysfunction. In 1987, a federally funded survey, the Massachusetts Male Aging Study led by Boston University urologist Irwin Goldstein, provided evidence for NIH to triple the early estimate of ED to 30 million Americans. When Pfizer Pharmaceutical released the first erection pill in April 1998, the demand by men—and women—for this prescription medication far exceeded the expected market. For many weeks after Viagra's release, television programs, newspapers, and magazines were filled with discussions of the erection pill, of other possible modes of delivery including a transdermal gel, and the use of this medication by both men and women. While early reports and discussions focused on the "miracle of better loving through chemistry," it quickly shifted to broader psychological and relationship repercussions, both beneficial and harmful, for both men and women who have lived with impotence for some time. Health insurance companies quickly moved to limit their coverage of the medication, leaving potential users wondering about the cost of $10 per pill and their ability to pay. At the same time, questions are being asked how the insurance companies can justify paying for the erection pill while they refuse to pay for the cost of the birth control pill and mammograms. Sex therapists, like Leonore Tiefer, have warned that the erection pill is yet another example of the tendency of Americans to medicalize sex and seek "magic bullet" therapy:

> The primary disadvantage of medicalization is that it denies, obscures, and ignores the social causes. . . . [T]he spotlight directed on "the erection" within current medical practice isolates and diminishes the man even as it offers succor for his insecurity and loss of self-esteem. Erections are presented as understandable and manipulable in and of themselves, unhooked from person, script, or relationship (Tiefer 1995, 155, 167).

One beneficial effect has been that discussion of male impotence entered the public domain, where men can openly admit their dysfunction and a desire to try the new medication. This public discussion of male impotence, like the open discussion of oral sex that followed allegations of sexual impropriety against the President, will definitely alter American sexual life.

I. Concluding Remarks

In the beginning of this book, we identified the assessment of how change occurs in a context of conflict between diverse social groups as a major theme in our analysis of sexual behaviors and values in the United States. Subsequent pages are rich in details relating to this theme. The reader is encouraged to savor the entire book and digest all of these details. However, we would like to conclude by recapitulating and integrating some of the major points related to this theme.

Change

Over a quarter of a billion Americans, representing a wide variety of ethnic, racial, and religious traditions, continue to struggle with the interface of science, technology, and society in all domains of life, nowhere less or more intimately than in our sexual behaviors and values. Recent computerized technology has enabled us to produce, access, and consume more information than has ever been possible in the history of the world. As we noted elsewhere, professionals and the public can now turn to the Internet, rather than to more traditional sources, to obtain sexual information, receive counseling, and even interact sexually. This provides many redundant opportunities. For example, persons who have felt alienated and isolated from the sexual "mainstream," such as the physically disabled and trans-gendered, have found information, support, and a new medium for self-expression on the Net. Yet, the use of this technology is not without conflict. The war over censorship versus freedom of speech and self-expression, waged with other print and broadcast media, is continuing with renewed fervor as state-of-the-art technology tests the limits of access to sexual information and sexually explicit dialogues and materials.

As we have seen in every aspect of our sexuality examined in these pages, numerous changes are taking place in Americans' collective and individual sexual lives. As Weis described in the "Demographic Overview," various factors are impacting the experience of sexuality: the changing racial/ethnic fabric; the "graying" of America; and more-varied lifestyle patterns (e.g., increases in wives/mothers working outside of the home, and in the number of cohabiting couples, and a growing disconnection between child rearing and married life).

Yet, the public representation and institutionalized values of American sexuality are often not keeping pace with the realities of people's private lives. For example, it is well documented that television, considered the most influential medium in American life, continues to present stereotypical views of gender roles, which do not reflect the realities of people's personal, family, sexual, and work lives. As Weis noted in Section 8, while heterosexual marriage is the modal pattern for sexual relations in the United States, sizable percentages of Americans depart from this assumed norm to engage in nonmarital sexual expressions, including premarital,

extramarital, same-gender, and unconventional sexual behaviors and relationships. Contrary to the goals of most public policies and programs
dealing with adolescent sexuality, the facts demonstrate that "premarital
virginity" has largely disappeared in the United States.

Because change is actually a constant within people's sexual lives on both
the individual and societal levels, research must focus more on the process
and dynamics of sexuality rather than simply recording "social bookkeeping." More-varied and complex qualitative and quantitative research methodologies and analyses must be applied to the study of human sexuality.

Diversity

The theme of diversity is woven throughout every thread of sexual life
within the United States. Our country is known for being a "salad bowl" of
diversity with a continuous struggle to achieve its promise of human
rights—no matter one's gender, racial/ethnic background, socioeconomic
status, religious persuasion, or physical characteristics.

Much of our public and scholarly discourse about sexuality still relies
heavily on simplistic, often dichotomous, categorizations for complex phe-
nomena, such as gender, race, ethnicity, and sexual orientation. However,
the sexologists who contributed to this book have tried to expose perspectives and research supporting the complexity of personal characteristics as
they interface with sexual expression. Although this was not always possible,
since scholarly research and information about diversity and sexuality tend
to be limited, it is important to note the many aspects of diversity that are
treated in some detail. The complexity of gender is evident in the paradigms
of the "gender rainbow" (Leah Schaefer and Constance Wheeler), "gender
flavors" (June Reinisch), "gender landscapes" (James Weinrich), and the
identification of five sexes (Anne Fausto-Sterling). Samuels, Pérez, and
Pinzón emphasize the varied characteristics and cultures of those labeled
"African-Americans" or "Latinos," and the effects of these upon individuals'
sexuality. Koch dispels the myth of "the feminist" representing a monolithic
ideology. Francoeur and Perper explore the varieties and complexities of
fixed and processual religious groups, a diversity highlighted by Forrest's
discussion of the sexual values found among members of the Church of
Jesus Christ of Latter-Day Saints, or Mormons. The work of Kinsey, Klein,
Weinberg, Williams, Pryor, and Moses and Hawkins, among many others,
illuminates the diversity among homosexually and bisexually oriented
people. In discussing adult heterosexualities, Weis describes the varieties
of sexual expression and relationships among married and nonmarried
individuals. Francoeur and Koch describe the diversity among sex workers,
while Love points out that the United States has more fetish clubs than any
other country in the world, and discusses some common and unique
fetishes. These are but a few examples of how every aspect of sexuality is
reflective of and affected by diversity. It is obvious that a major challenge

to American thinking about sexuality requires that we stop viewing sexuality in simplistic terms of male or female, black or white, gay or straight, marital or nonmarital, or normal or abnormal.

We still have great strides to make in closing the gaps in our knowledge and understanding of how sexuality is affected by and reflective of diversity. The majority of past and current research does not conceptualize or operationalize many personal and social variables as multidimensional (e.g., gender, race, sexual orientation)—when they are addressed at all. Koch's 1997 study of the twelve quantitative research articles published in *The Journal of Sex Research* in 1996 reveals, for example, that the race/ethnicity of the subjects is not reported in two thirds of the studies. For the other third of the studies, no statistical analyses are presented to examine similarities or differences, based on race/ethnicity, in the sexual topics being examined. Similarly, in half of the 12 quantitative studies, the sexual orientation of the subjects was not reported. In the one study that identified the subjects' sexual orientation, no analyses of similarities or differences, based on sexual orientation, was conducted on the independent variables under study. None of the research examined the interaction among variables such as gender, race/ethnicity, and sexual orientation. As we have repeatedly seen throughout this book, these interactions are paramount for an accurate and realistic understanding of human sexuality. The sexual experiences of Anglo-American heterosexual men often differ from those of Anglo-American heterosexual women, which also differ from those of Anglo-American gay men, which also differ from those of African-American gay men, which also differ from those of African-American lesbians, which also differ from those of Latina lesbians, and so on. Our research sensibilities and methodologies must become more sensitive and sophisticated if we are to truly advance sexual science, education, therapy, and policy.

Without adequate research, and sometimes even with it, people rely on stereotypes to form personal opinions and public policy. Too often these stereotypes lead to adverse judgments or prejudices. These prejudices then influence individual and collective actions, resulting in discrimination against under-represented groups. This text was filled with examples of discrimination affecting people's sexual relationships, sexual health, and sexual rights. For example, women of lower socioeconomic status in the U.S.A. have much more restricted access to legalized abortion services than do women of higher economic status. Individuals from marginalized groups are disproportionately affected by sexually transmissible diseases, including HIV disease, due to poverty and poorer education and health care. Gay men and lesbian women are the last large minority group in the U.S.A. that generally has no legal protections against discrimination. They are subjected to discrimination in all areas of their lives: housing, employment, health care, relationship and family formation, and military service, as well as being targets of gay bashing and other hate crimes. Sexual scientists, researchers, educators, and other professionals, as well as citizens at large, must take action to stop ignorance and prejudicial attitudes from continuing to shape public policy, resulting in harm to people's health and well-being.

Conflict

With the advancements in science and technology, the diverse groups in our society have not been able to keep abreast by implementing concomitant social progress. It seems that the more things change, the more they stay the same. As described in the section on "Contraception, Abortion, and Population Planning," abortion, especially until "quickening," was widely practiced throughout the history of the United States until the second half of the nineteenth century. At that time, various factions of "social purity" groups banded together with branches of government to restrict sexual freedoms and control reproduction. Laws, including the "Comstock Law," began to alter two hundred years of American custom and public policy towards contraception and abortion. The anti-contraceptive provisions of the Comstock Law were enforced until 1936 when finally a federal appeals court overturned them based on the medical authorities who supported the safety and reliability of contraception.

Following are examples that illustrate the "point" and "counterpoint" of sexual conflicts in the United States.

Points

- Today we are experiencing a well-organized and often successful resurgence of the social purity movement, which is restricting sexuality education, sexual health, sexual research, and many sexual freedoms. For example, there are currently more barriers to U.S. women's access to abortion than since the Supreme Court's 1973 *Roe v. Wade* decision. The moral issues of groups of religious and political conservatives are more influential in determining legislated public policy than the well-researched and documented public health concerns surrounding non-access to legalized abortion. New "Comstock laws" are being enacted that once again restrict access to birth control information and services, even though the weight of the authority of the medical world supports their safety, reliability, and necessity.
- Federal funding of abstinence-only education is another example of policy and practice being driven by special interest groups' concern with moral issues rather than by knowledge gained through experience and research. Abstinence-only education has been shown, both nationally and worldwide, to be less effective in preventing unintended pregnancy and sexually transmissible disease risk than more comprehensive forms of sexuality education. Yet, some effective sexuality education programs are being replaced throughout the country with

the less-than-effective abstinence-only ones. At the same time that a nationwide study of puberty documents that half of America's black girls and one in five white girls has begun puberty by age 8 (the third grade), school boards, administrators, and parents are abandoning sexuality education or postponing it until junior or senior high schools, even in states with sex education mandates.

• In addition, our knowledge of normative sexual development throughout the lifespan, particularly in childhood and adolescence, is severely hampered by lack of funding and other barriers established by conservative "social purity" groups that wield power through federal, state, and local governments. Funding for sexuality research by well-respected scientists, like Udry and Laumann, has been blocked, despite the fact that such research is critical to expanding our basic knowledge of sexual development, practices, and relationships, as well as reducing sexual health risks, including HIV disease.

Counterpoints

• Despite long-term opposition of some groups to contraception and abortion—the Comstock Laws, arrests of Margaret Sanger for distributing birth control, opposition of the Popes to "artificial" birth control, and the recent successes of the "pro-life" movement to restrict access to abortion—the general trend over the course of the last century has been a greater ability of women and couples to control their fertility and greater use of a variety of family planning practices.

• Despite a century of efforts by various adult groups to limit adolescent premarital sexual behavior, the clear trend of the twentieth century has been increasing percentages of adolescents engaging in premarital sexual practices at progressively earlier ages. By the 1990s, fewer than 10 percent of American youth are virgins on their wedding day. Attitudes have also become progressively more permissive.

• Despite the efforts of some groups to restrict the availability of sexual information and to block sex education in the schools (again, a century-long effort), the general trend has been toward more sex education in the schools and greater availability of information through a number of sources, particularly various media. Nevertheless, conservative members of the Senate and House of Representatives did pass a bill limiting sexual information on the Internet; however, the Supreme Court ruled the law unconstitutional.

• Although many sexual issues remain controversial, discourse about sex has become freer and more open. More people talk about sex in public settings and discuss a wider variety of sexual practices than in the past. For example, public discussions of homosexuality are much more common now; and everyone seems to be talking about oral sex in the wake of the sexual allegations against the president. There is also more sexual content on American television, both on the networks and cable; in movies, including in the theaters and on videocassettes; in all forms of printed material, such as general-circulation and sexually explicit magazines; and in all forms of popular music, from heavy metal and rap to country music.

- Homosexuality has become increasingly visible. The "coming out" of Ellen in a television sitcom series of that name is one example of this greater visibility. In addition to Ellen, there are more gay characters being portrayed on American television and in movies than ever before. There is also a growing availability of gay-related fiction. Disney and other corporations have begun to extend job benefits to gay couples, although conservative groups threatened to boycott Disney because of this. Hawaii is considering some kind of legal recognition of homosexual unions or marriage, although other states have stated that they will refuse to legally recognize such unions. Even the U.S. Supreme Court has ruled that same-gender sexual harassment does exist. However, gays still have not been granted full equality in the U.S. and face continuing challenges to their civil rights.

- Finally, the rising age at marriage and the growing divorce rate throughout this century have increased the relative percentage of unmarried adults, at any one time, who are pursuing various non-marital lifestyles and relationships. There seems to be greater awareness of this trend and acceptance of this trend in adult sexual expression.

Some of the obstacles we face in better understanding American sexual values and behavior originate and work within the scientific community itself. Scientists from various disciplines must learn to work together in a more collaborative fashion to examine the various contributing factors and outcomes of specific sexual development, health, and educational issues. Competition between biological, psychological, and sociocultural research perspectives and practices needs to be minimized and a more holistic biopsychosocial perspective adopted.

Looking forward to the twenty-first century, the historical theme of sexuality being embedded in change, occurring within a context of conflict among diverse social groups in the United States, will certainly continue. The spheres of influence of various social groups will ebb and flow with changing demographics and social consciousness. The dimensions of change will be directly affected by the speed and direction of technological development. As in the past, persons with fixed-world ideological views will continue to try to impede social progress in adapting to change and diversity. Yet, on balance, the trend throughout American history has been towards liberalization in sexual attitudes and behaviors. It is our belief that education, research, and human rights will continue to be critically needed guideposts in the determination of sexual values, practices, policies, and programs in the United States in the future.

References and Suggested Readings*

Adler, J. 1994 (January 10). "Farewell, Year of the Creep." *Newsweek,* 59.

Ahlburg, D. A., and C. J. DeVita. 1992. "New Realities of the American Family." *Population Bulletin,* 47(2).

Alan Guttmacher Institute. 1991. *Abortion in the United States: Facts in Brief.* New York: Alan Guttmacher Institute.

Alberda, R., and C. Tilly. 1992. "All in the Family: Family Types, Access to Income, and Family Income Policies." *Policy Studies Journal,* 20(3):388-404.

Alcalay, R., P. M. Sniderman, J. Mitchell, and R. Griffin. 1990. "Ethnic Differences in Knowledge of AIDS Transmission and Attitudes Among Gays and People with AIDS." *International Quarterly of Community Health Education,* 10(3):213-222.

Alcorn, R. C. 1990. *Is Rescuing Right? Breaking the Law to Save the Unborn.* Downers Grove, IL: InterVarsity Press.

Alexander, J. M. 1992 (April). "Meeting Changing STD Counseling Needs: A Glossary of Contemporary Mexican Sexual Terms." Prepared for the Resource Book of the Third Annual New Orleans HIV/AIDS Conference for Primary Health Care Providers.

Allen, J. E., and L. P. Cole. 1975. "Clergy Skills in Family-Planning Education and Counseling." *Journal of Religion and Health,* 14(3):198-205.

Allen, N. 1978 (June). "Sex Therapy and the Single Woman." *Forum,* pp. 44-48.

Allen, W. R., and B. A. Agbasegbe. 1980. "A Comment on Scott's 'Black Polygamous Family Formation.'" *Alternative Lifestyles,* 3:375-381.

Allgeier, A. R., and E. R. Allgeier. 1988. *Sexual Interactions* (2nd ed.). Lexington, MA: D. C. Heath.

Allison, J. A., and L. S. Wrightsman. 1993. *Rape: The Misunderstood Crime.* Newbury Park, CA: Sage Publications.

Altman, L. K. 1997 (February 28). "U.S. Reporting Sharp Decrease in AIDS Deaths." *The New York Times,* pp. A1 and A24.

Amaro, I. 1991. *Hispanic Sexual Behavior: Implications for Research and HIV Prevention.* Washington, DC: National Coalition of Hispanic Health and Human Services Organizations.

American Association of Sex Educators, Counselors, and Therapists (AASECT). 1978 (March, rev.). *AASECT Code of Ethics.* Washington, DC: Author.

American Association of Sex Educators, Counselors, and Therapists (AASECT). 1987. *AASECT Code of Ethics.* Washington, DC: Author.

American Psychiatric Association. 1980. *Diagnostic and Statistical Manual of Mental Disorders III (DSM III)* (3rd ed. 302.81, pp. 268). Washington, DC: American Psychiatric Association.

American Psychiatric Association. 1994. *Diagnostic and Statistical Manual of Mental Disorders* (4th ed.). Washington, DC: American Psychiatric Association.

Amir, M. 1971. *Patterns in Forcible Rape.* Chicago: University of Chicago Press.

Anderson, P. B., D. de Mauro, and R. J. Noonan, eds. 1996. *Does Anyone Still Remember When Sex Was Fun? Positive Sexuality in the Age of AIDS* (3rd ed.). Dubuque, IA: Kendall/Hunt Publishing Co.

Aneshensel, C. S., R. M. Becerra, E. P. Fiedler, and R. H. Schuler. 1990. "Onset of Fertility Related Events during Adolescence: A Prospective Comparison of Mexican American and Non-Hispanic White Females." *American Journal of Public Health,* 80(8):959-963.

Annon, J. S. 1974. *The Behavioral Treatment of Sexual Problems Volume 1: Brief Therapy.* Honolulu, HI: Kapiolani Health Services.

Acknowledgment: The editors appreciate the assistance of William Taverner, M.Ed., in checking many of these bibliographic references. See also the Supplementary References on page 332.

Ansen, D. 1994 (April 18). "Boy Meets Girl Meets Boy." *Newsweek*, p. 60.

Apfelbaum, B. 1977. "The Myth of the Surrogate." *Journal of Sex Research*, 13(4):238-249.

Apfelbaum, B. 1984. "The Ego-Analytic Approach to Individual Body-Work Sex Therapy: Five Case Examples." *Journal of Sex Research*, 20(1):44-70.

Asbell, B. 1995. *The Pill: A Biography of the Drug that Changed the World.* New York: Random House.

Atwater, L. 1982. *The Extramarital Connection: Sex, Intimacy, and Identity.* New York: Irvington.

Baldwin, W. 1980. "The Fertility of Young Adolescents." *Journal of Adolescent Health Care*, 1:54-59.

Barbach, L. 1980. *Women Discover Orgasm: A Therapist's Guide to a New Treatment Approach.* New York: Free Press.

Barry, K. 1984. *Female Sexual Slavery.* New York: New York University Press.

Bart, P. B., and P. H. O'Brien. 1985. "Stopping Rape: Effective Avoidance Strategies." *Signs*, 10:83-101.

Bartell, G. D. 1971. *Group Sex: A Scientist's Eyewitness Report on the American Way of Swinging.* New York: Wyden.

Bauman, K. E., and R. R. Wilson. 1974. "Sexual Behavior of Unmarried University Students in 1968 and 1972." *Journal of Sex Research*, 10:327-333.

Beach, R. A. 1976. "Sexual Attractivity, Proceptivity and Receptivity in Female Mammals." *Hormones and Behavior*, 7:105-138.

Beitchman, J. H., K. Zucker, J. Hood, G. DaCosta, and D. Akman. 1991. "A Review of the Short-Term Effects of Childhood Sexual Abuse." *Child Abuse and Neglect*, 15:537-556.

Beitchman, J. H., et al. 1992. "A Review of the Long-Term Effects of Child Sexual Abuse." *Child Abuse and Neglect*, 16:101-118.

Belcastro, P. A. 1985. "Sexual Behavior Differences Between Black and White Students." *Journal of Sex Research*, 21:56-67.

Bell, A. P.1968 (October). "Black Sexuality: Fact and Fancy." Paper presented to Focus: Black American Series, Indiana University, Bloomington, IN.

Bell, A. P., and M. Weinberg. 1978. *Homosexualities: A Study of Diversity Among Men and Women.* New York: Simon and Schuster.

Bell, A. P., M. S. Weinberg, and S. K. Hammersmith. 1981. *Sexual Preference: Its Development in Men and Women.* Bloomington, IN: Indiana University Press.

Bell, R. R., and P. I. Bell. 1972 (December). "Sexual Satisfaction Among Married Women." *Medical Aspects of Human Sexuality*, 136-144.

Bell, R., and J. B. Chaskes. 1968. "Premarital Sexual Experience Among Coeds, 1958 and 1968." *Journal of Marriage and the Family*, 30:81-84.

Bell, R. R., S. Turner, and L. Rosen. 1975. "A Multivariate Analysis of Female Extramarital Coitus." *Journal of Marriage and the Family*, 37(2):375-384.

Berger, R. J., P. Seales, and C. E. Cottle. 1991. *Pornography.* New York: Praeger.

Bergler, E. 1956. *Homosexuality: Disease or Way of Life.* New York: Collier.

Berkowitz, A. 1992. "College Men as Perpetrators of Acquaintance Rape and Sexual Assault: A Review of Recent Research." *Journal of American College Health*, 40:175-181.

Bernstein, A. C., and P. A. Cowan. 1975. "Children's Concepts of How People Get Babies." *Child Development*, 46:77-91.

Berscheid, E. 1983. "Emotion." In H. H. Kelley, et al., eds. *Close Relationships* (pp. 110-168). New York: W. H. Freeman and Co.

Biale, D. 1992. *Eros and the Jews: From Biblical Israel to Contemporary American.* New York: Basic Books.

Biddlecom, A. E., and A. M. Hardy. 1991. "AIDS Knowledge and Attitudes of Hispanic Americans: United States, 1990." *Advance Data. Number 207.* Washington, DC: U.S. Department of Health and Human Services.

Billy, J. O. G., K. Tanfer, W. R. Grady, and D. H. Klepinger. 1992. "Sexual Behavior of Men in the United States." *Family Planning Perspectives*, 25(2):52-60.

Bishop, P. D., and A. Lipsitz. 1991. "Sexual Behavior Among College Students in the AIDS Era: A Comparative Study." *Journal of Psychology and Human Sexuality*, 4:467-476.

Blanchard, R. and S. J. Hucker. 1991 (September0. "Age, Transvestism, Bondage, and Concurrent Paraphilic Activities in 117 Fatal Cases of Autoerotic Asphyxia." *British Journal of Psychiatry*, 159:371-377.

Blumstein, P., and P. Schwartz. 1983. *American Couples*. New York: William Morrow.

Bolin, A. 1988. *In Search of Eve: Transsexual Rites of Passage*. South Hadley, MA: Bergin and Garvey Publishers.

Bonilla, L., and J. Porter. 1990. "A Comparison of Latino, Black, and Non-Hispanic White Attitudes Toward Homosexuality. Hispanic." *Journal of Behavioral Sciences*, 12(4):437-452.

Boswell, J. 1980. *Christianity, Social Tolerance, and Homosexuality*. Chicago: University of Chicago Press.

Boswell, J. 1994. *Same-Sex Unions in Premodern Europe*. New York: Villard Books.

Brand, P. A., and A. H. Kidd. 1986. "Frequency of Physical Aggression in Heterosexual and Female Homosexual Dyads." *Psychological Reports*, 59:1307-1313.

Brandt, A. M. 1988. AIDS and Metaphor. *Social Research*, 55(3, Autumn), p. 430. Cited in M. Fumento, 1990, *The Myth of Heterosexual AIDS*. New York: Basic Books.

Braun, S. ed. 1975. *Catalog of Sexual Consciousness* (pp. 135-137). New York: Grove Press.

Brayshaw, A. J. 1962. "Middle-Aged Marriage: Idealism, Realism, and the Search for Meaning." *Marriage and Family Living*, 24:358-364.

Brecher, E. M. 1979. *The Sex Researchers*. San Francisco: Specific Press.

Brecher, E. M., and the Editors of Consumer Reports Books. 1984. *Love, Sex, and Aging: A Consumer Union Report*. Boston: Little, Brown.

Bretschneider, J. G., and N. L. McCoy. 1988. "Sexual Interest and Behavior in Healthy 80- to 101-year-olds." *Archives of Sexual Behavior*, 17(2):109-129.

Brett, G. H. 1993. "Networked Information Retrieval Tools in the Academic Environment: Towards a Cybernetic Library." *Internet Research*, 3(3):26-36.

Brindis, C. 1992. "Adolescent Pregnancy Prevention for Hispanic Youth: The Role of Schools, Families, and Communities." *Journal of School Health*, 62(7):345-351.

Brindis, C. 1997. "Adolescent Pregnancy Prevention for Hispanic Youth. *The Prevention Researcher*, 4(1):8-10.

Brindis, C., A. L. Wolfe, V. McCater, and S. Ball. 1995. "The Association Between Immigrant Status and Risk-Behavior Patterns in Latino Adolescents." *Journal of Adolescent Health*, 17(2):99-105.

Bringle, R. G. 1991. "Psychosocial Aspects of Jealousy: A Transactional Model." In P. Salovey, ed. *The Psychology of Jealousy and Envy* (pp. 103-131). New York: Guilford Press.

Bringle, R. G., and K. L. G. Boebinger. 1990. "Jealousy and the 'Third' Person in the Love Triangle." *Journal of Social and Personal Relationships*, 7:119-133.

Broderick, C. B. 1965. "Social Heterosexual Development Among Urban Negroes and Whites." *Journal of Marriage and the Family*, 27(2):200-203.

Broderick, C. B. 1966a. "Socio-Sexual Development in a Suburban Community." *Journal of Sex Research*, 2:1-24.

Broderick, C. B. 1966b. "Sexual Behavior Among Pre-Adolescents." *Journal of Social Issues*, 22:6-21.

Broderick, C. B., and S. E. Fowler. 1961. "New Patterns of Relationships Between the Sexes Among Preadolescents." *Marriage and Family Living*, 23:27-30.

Brodie, J. F. 1994. *Contraception and Abortion in Nineteenth-Century America*. Ithaca, NY: Cornell University Press.

Brody, S. 1995. "Lack of Evidence for Transmission of Human Immunodeficiency Virus Through Vaginal Intercourse." *Archives of Sexual Behavior*, 24(4):383-393.

Brooks-Gunn, J., and F. F. Furstenberg. 1989. "Adolescent Sexual Behavior. *American Psychologist*, 44:249-259.

Brown, D. A. 1981. "An Interview with a Sex Surrogate." In D. A. Brown & C. Chary, eds. *Sexuality in America* (pp. 301-317). Ann Arbor, MI: Greenfield Books.

Browne, A., and D. Finkelhor. 1986. "Impact of Child Sexual Abuse: A Review of Research." *Psychological Bulletin*, 99:66-77.

Brownmiller, S. 1975. *Against Our Will: Men, Women, and Rape* New York: Bantam.

Bukstel, L. H., G. D. Roeder, P. R. Kilmann, J. Laughlin, and W. M. Sotile. 1978. "Projected Extramarital Sexual Involvement in Unmarried College Students." *Journal of Marriage and the Family*, 40:337-340.

Bullough, V. L. 1994. *Science in the Bedroom: A History of Sex Research.* New York: Basic Books.

Bullough, V. L., and B. Bullough. 1987. *Women and Prostitution: A Social History.* Buffalo, NY: Prometheus Press.

Bullough, V. L., and B. Bullough. 1992. *Annotated Bibliography of Prostitution, 1970-1992.* New York: Garland.

Bullough, V. L., and B. Bullough. 1993. *Cross Dressing, Sex, and Gender.* Philadelphia: University of Pennsylvania Press.

Bullough, V. L., and B. Bullough. 1994a. "Prostitution." In V. L. Bullough and B. Bullough, eds. *Human Sexuality: An Encyclopedia.* New York: Garland Publishing.

Bullough, V. L., and B. Bullough. 1994b. "Cross-dressing." In V. L. Bullough and B. Bullough, eds. *Human Sexuality: An Encyclopedia* (pp. 156-160). New York: Garland Publishing.

Bureau of Justice Statistics. 1993. *Sourcebook of Criminal Justice Statistics—1992.* Washington, DC: U.S. Government Printing Office.

Burgess, E. W., and P. Wallin. 1953. *Engagement and Marriage.* Philadelphia: Lippincott.

Burt, M. R. 1991. "Rape Myths and Acquaintance Rape." In A. Parrot and L. Bechhofer, eds. *Acquaintance Rape: The Hidden Crime.* New York: Wiley.

Buss, D. M. 1994. *The Evolution of Desire: Strategies of Human Mating.* New York: Basic Books.

Butler, M. 1994. *How to Use the Internet.* Emeryville. CA: Ziff & Davis Press.

Buunk, B. 1980. "Sexually Open Marriages: Ground Rules for Countering Potential Threats to Marriage." *Alternative Lifestyles*, 3:312-328.

Buunk, B. 1981. "Jealousy in Sexually Open Marriages." *Alternative Lifestyles*, 4:357-372.

Buunk, B. 1982. "Strategies of Jealousy: Styles of Coping with Extramarital Involvement of the Spouse." *Family Relations*, 31:13-18.

Byrne, D., and W. A. Fisher. eds. 1983. *Adolescents, Sex, and Contraception.* Hillsdale, NJ: Erlbaum.

Call, V., S. Sprecher, and P. Schwartz. 1995. "The Incidence and Frequency of Marital Sex in a National Sample." *Journal of Marriage and the Family*, 57:639-652.

Cannon, K. L., and R. Long. 1971. "Premarital Sexual Behavior in the Sixties." *Journal of Marriage and the Family*, 33:36-49.

Carballo-DiÉguez, A. 1989. "Hispanic Culture, Gay Male Culture, and AIDS: Counseling Implications." *Journal of Counseling and Development*, 68:26-30.

Carrier, J. M. 1976. "Cultural Factors Affecting Urban Mexican Male Homosexual Behavior." *Archives of Sexual Behavior*, 5(2):103-124.

Carrier, J. M., and R. Bolton. 1987. "Anthropological Perspectives on Sexuality and HIV Prevention." *Annual Review of Sex Research*, 2:49-75.

Carrier, J. M., and J. R. Magaña. 1991. Use of Ethnosexual Data on Men of Mexican Origin for HIV/AIDS Prevention Programs. *Journal of Sex Research*, 28(2):189-202.

Castex, G. M. 1994. "Providing Services to Hispanic/Latino Populations: Profiles in Diversity." *Social Work*, 39(3):288-296.

Cazenave, N. A. 1979. "Social Structure and Personal Choice: Effects on Intimacy, Marriage and the Family Alternative Lifestyle Research." *Alternative Lifestyles*, 2:331-358.

Cazenave, N. A. 1981. "Black Men in America: The Quest for Manhood." In H. P. McAdoo, ed. *Black Families* (pp. 176-185). Beverly Hills: Sage.

Centers for Disease Control. 1992. "HIV Infection, Syphilis, Tuberculosis, Screening Among Migrant Farm Workers—Florida 1992." *Morbidity and Mortality Weekly Report*, 41(39):723-725.

Centers for Disease Control. 1993a. "The Scope of the HIV/AIDS Epidemic in the United States." *Fact Sheet. (Publication no. D-534)*. Rockville, MD: CDC National AIDS Clearinghouse.

Centers for Disease Control. 1993b. "HIV/AIDS and Race/Ethnicity." *Fact Sheet. (Publication no. D-293)*. Rockville, MD: CDC National AIDS Clearinghouse.

Centers for Disease Control. 1993c, August. "Study of Non-Identifying Gay Men." *HIV/AIDS Prevention Newsletter*, 4(2):6-7.

Centers for Disease Control. 1994a. *HIV/AIDS Surveillance Report*, 6(2):1-39.

Centers for Disease Control. 1994b. *HIV/AIDS Surveillance Report. Year-End Edition*, 6:11.

Centers for Disease Control. 1994c. "Women and HIV/AIDS." *Fact Sheet. (Publication no. D-290)*. Rockville, MD: CDC National AIDS Clearinghouse.

Centers for Disease Control. 1995a. "Update: Acquired Immunodeficiency Syndrome—United States, 1994." *Morbidity and Mortality Weekly Report*, 44(4):64-67.

Centers for Disease Control. 1995b. "Update: AIDS Among Women." *Morbidity and Mortality Weekly Report*, 44(5):81-84.

Centers for Disease Control and Prevention (CDC). 1996. *HIV/AIDS Surveillance Report, Year-End 1995 Edition*, 7(2):1-18.

Chefetz, J. S., and A. G. Dworkin. 1986. *Female Revolt: Women's Movements in the World and Historical Perspective*. New Jersey: Rowman & Allanheld.

Chideya, F., et al. 1993 (August 30). "Endangered Family." *Newsweek*, 17-27.

Choi, K. H., J. A. Catania, and M. Dolcini. 1994. "Extramarital Sex and HIV Risk Behavior Among U.S. Adults: Results from the National AIDS Behavior Survey." *American Journal of Public Health*, 84(12):2003-2007.

Christensen, F. M. 1990. *Pornography: The Other Side*. New York: Praeger.

Christensen, H. T. 1962a. "Value-Behavior Discrepancies Regarding Premarital Coitus in Three Western Cultures. *American Sociological Review*, 27:66-74.

Christensen, H. T. 1962b. "A Cross-Cultural Comparison of Attitudes Toward Marital Infidelity." *International Journal of Comparative Sociology*, 3:124-137.

Christensen, H. T. 1973. "Attitudes Toward Infidelity: A Nine-Culture Sampling of University Student Opinion." *Journal of Comparative Family Studies*, 4:197-214.

Christensen, H. T., and G. R. Carpenter. 1962. "Timing Patterns in the Development of Sexual Intimacy: An Attitudinal Report on Three Modern Western Societies." *Marriage and Family Living*, 24:30-35.

Christensen, H. T., and C. F. Gregg. 1970 (November). "Changing Sex Norms in America and Scandinavia." *Journal of Marriage and the Family*, 616-627.

Christensen, H., and L. Johnson. 1978. "Premarital Coitus and the Southern Black: A Comparative View." *Journal of Marriage and the Family*, 40:721-732.

Christopher, F. S., and R. M. Cate. 1985. "Premarital Sexual Pathways and Relationship Development." *Journal of Social and Personal Relationships*, 2:271-288.

Christopher, F. S., and R. M. Cate. 1988. "Premarital Sexual Involvement: A Developmental Investigation of Relational Correlates." *Adolescence*, 23:793-803.

Church of Jesus Christ of Latter-Day Saints. 1989. *Pearl of Great Price*. Salt Lake City, UT.

Church of Jesus Christ of Latter-Day Saints. 1990. *For the Strength of Youth*. Salt Lake City, UT.

Church News. 1978, December 16. Volume 6. Salt Lake City: Church of Jesus Christ of the Latter-Day Saints Publication.

Clark, L., and D. J. Lewis. 1977. *Rape: The Price of Coercive Sexuality*. Toronto: Women's Press.

Claude, P. 1993. "Providing Culturally Sensitive Health Care to Hispanic Clients." *Nurse Practitioner*, 18(12):40-51

Clayton, R. R., and J. L. Bokemeier. 1980. "Premarital Sex in the Seventies." *Journal of Marriage and the Family*, 42:759-776.

Cleveland, P. H. and J. Davenport. 1989 (Summer). "AIDS: A Growing Problem for Rural Communities." *Human Services in the Rural Environment*, 13(1):23-29.

Clunis, D. M., and G. D. Green. 1988. *Lesbian Couples*. Seattle, Washington: Seal Press.

Cobliner, W. G. 1974. "Pregnancy in the Single Adolescent Girl: The Role of Cognitive Functions." *Journal of Youth and Adolescence*, 3:17-29.

Cohn, B. 1994 (December 19). "Goodbye to the 'Condom Queen.'" *Newsweek*, 26-27.

Coleman, E. 1987. "Assessment of Sexual Orientation." *Journal of Homosexuality*, 14(1/2):9-24.

Coleman, E. 1991. "Compulsive Sexual Behavior: New Concepts and Treatments." *Journal of Psychology and Human Sexuality*, 4(2):37-52.

Coles, C. D., and M. J. Shamp. 1984. "Some Sexual, Personality, and Demographic Characteristics of Women Readers of Erotic Romances." *Archives of Sexual Behavior*, 13:187-209.

Conklin, S. C. 1995. *Sexuality Education of Clergy in Seminaries and Theological Schools: Perceptions of Faculty Advocates Regarding Curriculum Implications*. Unpublished doctoral dissertation. University of Pennsylvania, Philadelphia.

Constantine, L. L. 1973. *Group Marriage: A Study of Contemporary Multilateral Marriage*. New York: Macmillan.

Coontz, S. 1992. *The Way We Never Were: American Families and the Nostalgia Trap*. New York: Harper Collins Basic Books.

Cornog, M. 1994. "Appendix on Sexological Research." In V. L. Bullough and B. Bullough, eds. *Human Sexuality: An Encyclopedia* (pp. 607-617). New York: Garland Publishing.

Cornog, M., and T. Perper. 1996. *For Sex Education, See Librarian*. New York: Greenwood Press.

Countryman, L. W. 1988. *Dirt, Greed and Sex: Sexual Ethics in the New Testament and Their Implications for Today*. Philadelphia: Fortress Press.

Curran, C. E., and R. A. McCormick, eds. 1993. *Dialogue about Catholic Sexual Teaching*. Mahwah, NJ: Paulist Press.

Current Population Reports. 1985. *Marital Status and Living Arrangements. March, 1984*. United States Department of Commerce, Bureau of the Census.

Darabi, K. F., and V. Ortiz. 1987. "Childbearing Among Young Latino Women in the United States." *American Journal of Public Health*, 77(1):25-28.

Dauw, D. C. 1988. "Evaluating the Effectiveness of the SECS' Surrogate-Assisted Sex Therapy Model." *Journal of Sex Research*, 24:269-275.

Davidson, J. K., and C. Anderson Darling. 1993. "Masturbatory Guilt and Sexual Responsiveness Among Post-College-Age Women: Sexual Satisfaction Revisited." *Journal of Sex and Marital Therapy*, 19(4):289-300.

Davis, A. Y. 1981. *Women, Race and Class.* New York: Vintage Books.

Davis, J. A. 1990. *General Social Surveys, 1972-1990: Cumulative Codebook.* Chicago: National Opinion Research Center, University of Chicago.

Davis, J. A., and T. W. Smith. 1994. *General Social Surveys, 1979-1994: Cumulative Codebook.* Chicago: National Opinion Research Center.

Davis, K. B. 1929. *Factors in the Sex Life of Twenty-Two Hundred Women.* New York: Harper and Row.

Davis, S. M., and M. B. Harris. 1982. "Sexual Knowledge, Sexual Interest, and Sources of Sexual Information of Rural and Urban Adolescents from Three Cultures." *Adolescence,* 17:471-492.

Dawson, D. A. 1990. "AIDS Knowledge and Attitudes for January-March 1990. Provisional Data from the National Health Interview Survey." *Advanced Data from Vital and Health Statistics. Number 193.* Hyattsville, MD: National Center for Health Statistics.

Dawson, D. A., and A. M. Hardy. 1989. *AIDS Knowledge and Attitudes of Hispanic Americans. Provisional Data from the 1988 National Health Interview Survey. Advanced Data from Vital and Health Statistics. Number 166.* Hyattsville, MD: National Center for Health Statistics.

de la Cancela, V. 1989. "Minority AIDS Prevention: Moving Beyond Cultural Perspectives Towards Sociopolitical Empowerment." *AIDS Education and Prevention,* 1(2):141-153.

Delacoste, F., and P. Alexander. 1987. *Sex Work: Writings by Women in the Sex Industry.* Pittsburgh, PA: Cleis Press.

de la Vega, E. 1990. "Considerations for Reaching the Latino Population with Sexuality and HIV/AIDS Information and Education." *SIECUS Report,* 18(3).

DeLamater, J. D., and P. MacCorquodale. 1979. *Premarital Sexuality: Attitudes, Relationships, Behavior.* Madison, WI: University of Wisconsin Press.

D'Emilio, J., and E. B. Freedman. 1988. *Intimate Matters: A History of Sexuality in America.* New York: Harper and Row.

Denfeld, D. 1974. "Dropouts from Swinging." *Family Coordinator,* 23:45-59.

DeRachewitz, B. 1964. *Black Eros: Sexual Customs of Africa from Prehistory to the Present Day.* New York: Lyle Stuart.

DeWaal, F. 1982. *Chimpanzee Politics: Power and Sex Among Apes.* New York: Harper Colophon Books.

DeWitt, K. 1991 (October 13). "As Harassment Plays, Many U.S. Employees Live It." *The New York Times,* p. 24.

Dickinson, R. L., and L. Bean. 1931/1932. *A Thousand Marriages: A Medical Study of Sex Adjustment.* Baltimore: Williams & Wilkins.

Dickinson, R. L., and L. Bean. 1934. *The Single Woman.* Baltimore: Williams and Wilkins.

Dickinson, R. L., and H. H. Pierson. 1925. "The Average Sex Life of American Women." *Journal of the American Medical Association,* 85:1113-1117.

Dietz, P. 1989/1990 (December/January). "Youth-Serving Agencies as Effective Providers of Sexuality Education." *SIECUS Report,* 18:16-20.

di Mauro, D. 1995. *Sexuality Research in the United States: An Assessment of the Social and Behavioral Sciences.* New York: Social Sciences Research Council.

di Mauro, D. 1989/1990 (December/January). "Sexuality Education 1990: A Review of State Sexuality and AIDS Education Curricula." *SIECUS Report,* 18:1-9.

Dixon, D. 1985. "Perceived Sexual Satisfaction and Marital Happiness of Bisexual and Heterosexual Swinging Husbands." Special Issue: Bisexualities: Theory and Research. *Journal of Homosexuality,* 11(1-2):209-222.

Dixon, J. K. 1984. "The Commencement of Bisexual Activity in Swinging Married Women over Age 30." *Journal of Sex Research.* 20:71-90.

Docter, R. F. 1988. *Transvestites and Transsexuals: Toward a Theory of Cross-Gender Behavior.* New York: Plenum Press.

Doddridge, R., W. Schumm, and M. Berger. 1987. "Factors Related to Decline in Preferred Frequency of Sexual Intercourse Among Young Couples." *Psychological Reports*, 60:391-395.

Dodson, B. 1987. *Sex for One: The Joy of Selfloving*. New York: Harmony Books. Published in 1974 and 1983 under the titles of *Selflove and Orgasm* and *Liberating Masturbation*.

Donat, P. L. N., and J. D'Emilio. 1992. "A Feminist Redefinition of Rape and Sexual Assault: Historical Foundations and Change." *Journal of Social Issues*, 48(1):9-22.

Donnerstein, E., D. Linz, and S. Penrod. 1987. *The Question of Pornography: Research Findings and Policy Implications*. New York: The Free Press.

Duberman, M., M. Vicinus, and G. Chauncey, eds. 1989. *Hidden from History: Reclaiming the Gay and Lesbian Past*. New York: New American Library.

Duesberg, P. H. 1996. *Inventing the AIDS Virus*. Washington, DC: Regnery Press.

Dugger, Celia W. 1996a (December 28). "Tug of Taboos: African Genital Rite vs. U.S. Law." *The New York Times*, pp. 1 and 9.

Dugger, Celia W. 1996b (October 12). "New Law Bans Genital Cutting in United States." *The New York Times*, pp. 1 and 28.

Duncan, D. F., and T. Nicholson. 1991. "Pornography as a Source of Sex Information for Students at a Southeastern State University." *Psychological Reports*, 68:802.

Durant, R. 1990. "Sexual Behaviors Among Hispanic Female Adolescents in the U.S." *Pediatrics*, 85(6):1051-1058.

Eckard, E. 1982. *Contraceptive Use Patterns, Prior Source, and Pregnancy History of Female Family Planning Patients: United States, 1980*. Washington, DC: United States Department of Health and Human Services, Public Health Service, Vital Statistics, No. 82.

Edwardes, A., and R. E. L. Masters. 1963. *The Cradle of Erotica: A Study of Afro-Asian Sexual Expression and an Analysis of Erotic Freedom in Social Relationships*. New York: The Julian Press.

Edwards, J. N., and A. Booth. 1976. "Sexual Behavior In and Out of Marriage: An Assessment of Correlates." *Journal of Marriage and the Family*, 38(1):73-81.

Ehrenreich, B., G. Hass, and E. Jacobs. 1987. *Remaking Love: The Feminization of Sex*. New York: Doubleday/Anchor.

Ehrmann, W. W. 1959. *Premarital Dating Behavior*. New York: Holt, Rinehart and Winston.

Ehrmann, W. W. 1964. "Marital and Nonmarital Sexual Behavior." In H. T. Christensen, ed. *Handbook of Marriage and the Family* (pp. 585-622). Chicago: Rand McNally.

Elias, J., and P. Gebhard. 1969. "Sexuality and Sexual Learning in Childhood." *Phi Delta Kappan*, 50:401-405.

Ellis, A. 1969. "Healthy and Disturbed Reasons for Having Extramarital Relations." In G. Neubeck, ed. *Extramarital Relations* (pp. 153-161). Englewood Cliffs, NJ: Prentice-Hall.

Ellis, H. 1936. *Love and Pain, Studies in the Psychology of Sex. Vol. 1* (originally published 1903). New York: Random House.

EPIC (on-line) 1996 (September 30). "CDA Ruled Unconstitutional?".

Eskridge, W. N. 1996. *The Case for Same-Sex Marriage*. New York: Free Press.

Estrich, S. 1987. *Real Rape*. Cambridge, MA: Harvard University Press.

Faderman, L. 1991. *Odd Girls and Twilight Lovers*. New York: Columbia University Press.

Fanon, F. 1967. *Black Skin, White Mask*. New York: Grove Press.

Farber, C. 1993 (March). "Out of Africa." *Spin*, pp. 60-63, 86-87.

Farber, C. 1993a (April). "Out of Africa: Part Two." *Spin*, pp. 74-77, 106-107.

Farber, C. 1993b (April). "Sex in the '90s." *Spin*, p. 15.

Farrell, W. 1990. "The Last Taboo?: The Complexities of Incest and Female Sexuality." In M. Perry, ed. *Handbook of Sexology: Volume 7: Childhood and Adolescent Sexology*. New York: Elsevier.

Farrell, W. 1993. *The Myth of Male Power: Why Men Are the Disposable Sex.* New York: Simon & Schuster.

Federal Bureau of Investigation. 1993. *Uniform Crime Reports for the United States 1992.* Washington, DC: U.S. Government Printing Office.

Fennelly, K. 1988. *El Embarazo Precoz: Childbearing Among Hispanic Teenagers in the United States.* New York: Columbia University, School of Public Health.

Fennelly, K. 1992. "Sexual Activity and Childbearing Among Hispanic Adolescents in the United States." In R. Lerner, et al., eds. *Early Adolescence: Perspectives on Research, Policy and Intervention.* Hillsdale, NJ: Eldbaum Press.

Fennelly, K., V. Kandiah, and V. Ortiz. 1989. "The Cross-Cultural Study of Fertility Among Hispanic Adolescents in the Americas." *Studies in Family Planning,* 20(2):96-101.

Fennelly-Darabi, K., and V. Ortiz. 1987. "Childbearing Among Young Latino Women in the United States." *American Journal of Public Health,* 77(1):25-28.

Fine, M., and A. Asch, eds. 1988. *Women with Disabilities: Essays in Psychology, Culture, and Politics.* Philadelphia: Temple University Press.

Finger, F. W. 1975. "Changes in Sex Practices and Beliefs of Male College Students Over 30 Years." *Journal of Sex Research,* 11:304-317.

Finkelhor, D. 1980. "Sex Among Siblings: A Survey on Prevalence, Variety, and Effects." *Archives of Sexual Behavior,* 9:171-194.

Finkelhor, D., and K. Yllo. 1985. *License to Rape: Sexual Abuse of Wives.* New York: Free Press.

Fischer, G. J. 1987. "Hispanic and Majority Student Attitudes Towards Forcible Date Rape as a Function of Differences in Attitudes Towards Women." *Sex Roles,* 17(2):93-101.

Fisher, H. E. 1992. *Anatomy of Love: The Natural History of Monogamy, Adultery, and Divorce.* New York: Norton.

Fisher, T. D. 1986. "An Exploratory Study of Parent-Child Communication About Sex and the Sexual Attitudes of Early, Middle, and Late Adolescents." *Journal of Genetic Psychology,* 147:543-557.

Floyd, H. H. Jr., and D. R. South. 1972. "Dilemma of Youth: The Choice of Parents or Peers as a Frame of Reference for Behavior." *Journal of Marriage and the Family,* 34:627-634.

Ford, C. S., and F. A. Beach. 1951. *Patterns of Sexual Behavior.* New York: Harper and Brothers.

Ford, K., and A. Norris. 1991. "Methodological Considerations for Survey Research on Sexual Behavior: Urban African American and Hispanic Youth." *Journal of Sex Research,* 28(4):539-555.

Ford, K., and A. E. Norris. 1993. "Urban Hispanic Adolescents and Young Adults: Relationship of Aculturation to Sexual Behavior." *Journal of Sex Research,* 30(4):316-323.

Forrest, J. D., and R. R. Fordyce. 1988. "U.S. Women's Contraceptive Attitudes and Practices: How Have They Changed in the 1980s?" *Family Planning Perspectives,* 20(3):112-118.

Forrest, J. D., and J. Silverman. 1989. "What Public School Teachers Teach about Preventing Pregnancy, AIDS and Sexually Transmitted Diseases." *Family Planning Perspectives,* 21:65-72.

Forrest, J. D., and S. Singh. 1990. "The Sexual and Reproductive Behavior of American Women, 1982-1988." *Family Planning Perspectives,* 22(5):206-214.

Fortune, M. M. 1991. *Is Nothing Sacred? When Sex Invades the Pastoral Relationship.* San Francisco: Harper.

Fox, M. 1983. *Original Blessing.* Sante Fe, New Mexico: Bear and Company.

Fox, M. 1988. *The Coming of the Cosmic Christ: The Healing of Mother Earth and the Birth of a Global Renaissance.* San Francisco: Harper and Row.

Fox, R. 1995. "A History of Bisexuality Research." In Anthony D'Augelli and Charlotte Patterson, eds. *Lesbian, Gay and Bisexual Identities Over the Lifespan.* New York: Oxford University Press.

Francoeur, R. T. 1987. "Human Sexuality." In M. B. Sussman and S. K. Steinmetz, eds. *Handbook of Marriage and the Family.* New York: Plenum Press.

Francoeur, R. T. 1988. "Two Different Worlds, Two Different Moralities." In: Jeannine Gramick and Pat Furey, eds. *The Vatican and Homosexuality.* New York, NY: Crossroads.

Francoeur, R. T. 1990. "Current Religious Doctrines of Sexual and Erotic Development in Childhood." In M. Perry, ed. *Handbook of Sexology: Volume 7: Childhood and Adolescent Sexology.* New York: Elsevier.

Francoeur, R. T. 1991a. *Becoming a Sexual Person* (2nd ed.). New York: Macmillan.

Francoeur, R. T. 1991b. *Taking Sides: Clashing Views on Controversial Issues in Human Sexuality* (3rd ed.). Guilford, CT: Dushkin Publishing Group.

Francoeur, R. T. 1992 (April/May). "Sexuality and Spirituality: The Relevance of Eastern Traditions." *SIECUS Report,* 20(4):1-8.

Francoeur, R. T. 1994. "Religion and Sexuality." In V. L. Bullough and B. Bullough, eds. *Human Sexuality: An Encyclopedia* (pp. 514-520). New York: Garland.

Francoeur, A. K., and R. T. Francoeur. 1974. *Hot and Cool Sex: Cultures in Conflict.* New York: Harcourt, Brace, Jovanovich.

Frank, E., and C. Anderson. 1979 (July/August). "Sex and the Happily Married." *The Sciences,* 10-13.

Frank, E., C. Anderson, and D. Rubinstein. 1978. "Frequency of Sexual Dysfunction in 'Normal' Couples." *New England Journal of Medicine,* 299:111-115.

Frayser, S. 1985. *Varieties of Sexual Experience: An Anthropological Perspective on Human Sexuality.* New Haven, CT: HRAF Press.

Freeman, J. 1995. "From Suffrage to Women's Liberation: Feminism in Twentieth-Century America." In J. Freeman, ed. *Women: A Feminist Perspective.* Mountain View, CA: Mayfield.

Freud, S. 1938. Three Contributions to the Theory of Sex. In A. A. Brill, ed. *The Basic Writings of Sigmund Freud* (originally published in 1905). New York: The Modern Library.

Friend. R. A. 1987. "The Individual and Social Psychology of Aging: Clinical Implications for Lesbians and Gay Men." *Journal of Homosexuality,* 14(1-2):307-331.

Fumento, M. 1990. *The Myth of Heterosexual AIDS.* New York: Basic Books [A New Republic Book].

Gagnon, J. H. 1977. *Human Sexualities.* New York: Scott, Foresman.

Gagnon, J. H. 1985. "Attitudes and Responses of Parents to Preadolescent Masturbation." *Archives of Sexual Behavior,* 14:451-466.

Gagnon, J. H., and W. Simon. 1973. *Sexual Conduct: The Social Sources of Human Sexuality.* Chicago: Aldine.

Gaines, D. 1995 (June 30). *Founder of the Foot Fraternity.* Interview with Brenda Love. San Francisco.

Galenson, E. 1990. "Observation of Early Infantile Sexual and Erotic Development." In M. Perry, ed. *Handbook of Sexology: Volume 7: Childhood and Adolescent Sexology.* New York: Elsevier.

Galenson, E., and H. Roiphe. 1980. "Some Suggested Revisions Concerning Early Female Development." In M. Kirkpatrick, ed. *Women's Sexual Development: Exploration of Inner Space* (pp. 83-105). New York: Plenum.

Garcia, C. 1993. "What Do We Mean by Extended Family? A Closer Look at Hispanic Multigenerational Families." *Journal of Cross Cultural Gerontology*, 8(2):137-146.

Garcia, F. 1980. "The Cult of Virginity." In *Program on Teaching and Learning: Conference on the Educational and Occupational Needs of Hispanic Women* (pp. 65-73). Washington, DC: National Institute of Education.

Gardella, P. 1985. *Innocent Ecstasy: How Christianity Gave America an Ethic of Sexual Pleasure.* New York: Oxford University Press.

Gebhard, P. H. 1968. "Postmarital Coitus Among Widows and Divorcees." In P. Bohannan, ed. *Divorce and After* (pp. 81-96). New York: Doubleday.

Gebhard, P. H. 1993 (September/October). "Kinsey's Famous Figures." *Indiana Alumni Magazine*, p. 64.

Gelles, R. J. 1977. "Power, Sex, and Violence: The Case of Marital Rape." *Family Coordinator*, 26:339-347.

Gibson, J. W., and J. Kempf. 1990. "Attitudinal Predictors of Sexual Activity in Hispanic Adolescent Females." *Journal of Adolescent Research*, 5(4):414-430.

Giles, J., and C. S. Lee. 1994 (August 15). "There's Nothing Like a Dame." *Newsweek*, p. 69.

Gilmartin, B. G. 1978. *The Gilmartin Report.* Secaucus, NJ: Citadel.

Gise, L. H., and P. Paddison. 1988. "Rape, Sexual Abuse, and Its Victims." *Psychiatric Clinics of North America*, 11:629-648.

Givens, D. 1978. "The Nonverbal Basis of Attraction: Flirtation, Courtship, and Seduction." *Psychiatry*, 41:346-359.

Glass, S. P., and T. L. Wright. 1977. "The Relationship of Extramarital Sex, Length of Marriage and Sex Differences on Marital Satisfaction and Romanticism: Athanasiou's Data Reanalyzed." *Journal of Marriage and the Family*, 39:691-703.

Glass, S. P., and T. L. Wright. 1985. "Sex Differences in Type of Extramarital Involvement and Marital Dissatisfaction." *Sex Roles*, 12:1101-1120.

Glazer, N., and D. P. Moynihan. 1964. *Beyond the Melting Pot: The Negroes, Puerto Ricans, Jews, Otawoams, Italians, and Irish of New York City.* Cambridge, MA: MIT Press.

Glenn, N. D. and C. N. Weaver. 1979. "Attitudes Toward Premarital, Extramarital, and Homosexual Relations in the U.S. in the 1970s." *Journal of Sex Research*, 15:108-118.

Glick, P. C. 1984. "Marriage, Divorce, and Living Arrangements: Prospective Changes." *Journal of Family Issues*, 5:7-26.

Glick, P. C., and A. Norton. 1977. *Marrying, Divorcing, and Living Together in the U.S. Today.* Washington, DC: Population Reference Bureau.

Gold, Rabbi Michael. 1992. *Does God Belong in the Bedroom?* Philadelphia: The Jewish Publication Society.

Goldfarb, L., M. Gerrarc, F. X. Gibbons, and T. Plante. 1988. "Attitudes Toward Sex, Arousal, and the Retention of Contraceptive Information." *Journal of Personality and Social Psychology*, 55:634-641.

Goldman, R. J., and J. G. D. Goldman. 1982. *Children's Sexual Thinking.* Boston: Routledge & Kegan Paul.

Goodson, P. 1996. *Protestant Seminary Students' Views of Family Planning and Intention to Promote Family Planning Through Education.* Unpublished doctoral dissertation. The University of Texas at Austin, TX.

Gordon, L. 1976. *Woman's Body, Woman's Right: A Social History of Birth Control in America.* New York: Penguin.

Gordon, M. T., and S. Riger. 1989. *The Female Fear.* New York: Free Press.

Greeley, A. 1995. *Sex: The Catholic Experience.* Allen, TX: Thomas More Press.

Greeley, A. M. 1991. *Faithful Attraction: Discovering Intimacy, Love, and Fidelity in American Marriage.* New York: Doherty.

Greeley, A. M., R. T. Michael, and T. W. Smith. 1990. "Americans and Their Sexual Partners." *Society*, 27(5):36-42.

Green, R. 1987. *The "Sissy Boy Syndrome" and the Development of Homosexuality.* New Haven, CT: Yale University Press.

Greenblat, C. S. 1983. "The Salience of Sexuality in the Early Years of Marriage." *Journal of Marriage and the Family*, 45:289-299.

Grier, W., and W. Cobbs. 1968. *Black Rage.* New York: Basic Books.

Griffin, S. 1971. "Rape: The All-American Crime." *Ramparts*, 10:26-35.

Griffit, W. September 1985. "Some Prosocial Effects of Exposure to Consensual Erotica." Paper presented at annual meeting of the Society for the Scientific Study of Sex, San Diego, CA.

Grogan, Ann. 1995 (July 5). Owner of Romantasy Boutique. Interview with Brenda Love. San Francisco.

Groth, A. N., and A. W. Burgess. 1980. "Male Rape: Offenders and Victims." *American Journal of Psychiatry*, 137:806-810.

Grover, J. 1990. "Is Lesbian Battering the Same as Straight Battering? Children from Violent Lesbian Homes. Battered Lesbians Are Battered Women." In: *Confronting Lesbian Battering: A Manual for the Battered Women's Movement* (pp. 41-46). St. Paul, MN: Minnesota Coalition for Battered Women.

Gutek, B. A. 1985. *Sex and the Workplace.* San Francisco, CA: Jossey-Bass.

Gwinn, M., M. Pappaioanou, J. R. George, et al. 1991. "Prevalence of HIV Infection in Childbearing Women in the United States." *Journal of the American Medical Association*, 265(13):1704-1708.

Haffner, D. W. 1989 (March/April). "SIECUS: 25 Years of Commitment to Sexual Health and Education." *SIECUS Report*, 17:1-6.

Haffner, D. W. 1992 (February/March). "1992 Report Card on the States: Sexual Rights in America." *SIECUS Report*, 20:1-7.

Haffner, D. W. 1994 (August/September). "The Good News about Sexuality Education." *SIECUS Report*, 17-18.

Haffner, D. W., and M. Kelly. 1987 (March/April). "Adolescent Sexuality in the Media." *SIECUS Report*, 9-12.

Hahn, H. and R. Stout. 1994. *The Internet Yellow Page.* Berkeley, CA: Osborne McGraw-Hill.

Hall, T. 1987 (June 1). "Infidelity and Women: Shifting Patterns." *The New York Times.*

Halverson, H. M. 1940. "Genital and Sphincter Behavior of the Male Infant." *Journal of Genetic Psychology*, 56:95-136.

Hamer, D., S. Hu, V. Magnuson, N. Hu, and A. Pattatucci. 1993. "A Linkage Between DNA Markers on the X Chromosome and Male Sexual Orientation." *Science*, 261:321-327.

Hamilton, G. V. 1948. *A Research in Marriage.* New York: Lear Publications.

Hamm, Lisa M. (Associated Press). 1996 (November 4). "Not Just Africa: Female Circumcision Even Happens in U.S." *New Jersey On-Line—Newark Star Ledger's Electronic Edition.*

Hartman, W. E., and M. A. Fithian. 1972. *Treatment of Sexual Dysfunction: A Bio-Psycho-Social Approach.* Long Beach, CA: Center for Marital and Sexual Studies.

Haseltine, F. P., S. S. Cole, and D. B. Gray, eds. 1993. *Reproductive Issues for Persons with Physical Disabilities.* Baltimore: Paul H. Brookes Publishing Co.

Hass, A. 1979. *Teenage Sexuality.* New York: Macmillan.

Hass, K., and A. Hass. 1993. *Understanding Sexuality.* St. Louis: Mosby.

Hatcher, R., J. Trussell, F. Stewart, G. Stewart, D. Kowal, F. Guest, W. Cates, Jr., and M. Pokicar. 1994. *Contraceptive Technology* (16th rev. ed.). New York: Irvington.

Hawkins, G., and F. E. Zimring. *Pornography in a Free Society.* Cambridge: Cambridge University Press.

Heiby, E., and J. D. Becker. 1980. "Effect of Filmed Modeling on the Self-Reported Frequency of Masturbation." *Archives of Sexual Behavior,* 9(2):115-120.

Helminiak, D. A. 1994. *What the Bible Really Says about Homosexuality.* San Francisco: Alamo Press.

Hendrixson, L. L. 1996. *The Psychosocial and Psychosexual Impact of HIV/AIDS on Rural Women: A Qualitative Study.* Unpublished doctoral dissertation, New York University.

Hengeveld, M. W. 1991. "Erectile Disorders: A Psychological Review." In U. Jonas, W. F. Thon, C. G. Stief, eds. *Erectile Dysfunction* (pp. 207-235). Berlin: Springer-Verlag.

Herman, J. L. 1992. *Trauma and Recovery.* New York: Basic Books.

Herold, E. S., and M. S. Goodwin. 1981. "Adamant Virgins, Potential Nonvirgins and Nonvirgins." *Journal of Sex Research,* 17:97-113.

Hershey, M. 1978. "Racial Differences in Sex-Role Identities and Sex Stereotyping: Evidence Against a Common Assumption." *Social Science Quarterly,* 58:584-596.

Heyward, C. 1989. *Touching Our Strength: The Erotic as Power and the Love of God.* San Francisco: HarperSanFrancisco.

Hite, S. 1976. *The Hite Report* New York: Dell.

Hite, S. 1983. *The Hite Report on Male Sexuality.* New York: Knopf.

Hofferth, S. L., J. R. Kahn, and W. Baldwin. 1987. "Premarital Sexual Activity Among U.S. Teenage Women over the Past Three Decades." *Family Planning Perspectives,* 19(2):46-53.

Holmes, S. A. 1996a (June 13). "Public Cost of Teen-Age Pregnancy Is Put at $7 Billion This Year." *The New York Times,* p. A19.

Holmes, S. A. 1996b (October 5). "U.S. Reports Drop in Rate of Births to Unwed Women." *The New York Times,* pp. 1 and 9.

Holzman, H., and S. Pines. 1982. "Buying Sex: The Phenomenology of Being a John." *Deviant Behavior,* 4:89-116.

Hooker, E. E. A. 1957. "The Adjustment of the Male Overt Homosexual." *Journal of Projective Techniques,* 21:17-31.

Hopkins, J. 1977. "Sexual Behavior in Adolescence." *Journal of Social Issues,* 33:67-85.

Houston, L. 1981. "Romanticism and Eroticism Among Black and White College Students." *Adolescence,* 16:263-272.

Hu, D. J., and R. Keller. 1989. "Communicating AIDS Information to Hispanics: The Importance of Language in Media Preference." *American Journal of Preventive Medicine,* 54:196-200.

Hunt, M. 1974. *Sexual Behavior in the 1970s.* Chicago: Playboy Press.

Hunt, T. 1994 (December 10). "Clinton Fires Surgeon General" (AP News Service). *Bowling Green Sentinel Tribune,* p. 3.

Hunter, H. W. 1995. *Being a Righteous Husband and Father.* Salt Lake City, UT: Church of Jesus Christ of Latter-Day Saints.

Hunter, M. 1990. *The Sexually Abused Male.* Lexington, MA: Lexington Books.

Hunter, R. J., ed. 1990. *Dictionary of Pastoral Care and Counseling.* Nashville, TN: Abingdon Press.

Hurlbert, D. F. 1992. "Factors Influencing a Woman's Decision to End an Extramarital Sexual Relationship." *Journal of Sex and Marital Therapy,* 18(2):104-113.

Hutchins, L. and L. Kaahumanu, eds. 1991. *By Any Other Name: Bisexual People Speak Out.* Boston: Alyson.

International Professional Surrogates Association (IPSA). 1989 (June). *Code of Ethics* [Brochure]. Los Angeles: Author.

International Professional Surrogates Association (IPSA). n.d. "General Information about IPSA and Surrogates." *Surrogate Partner Therapy* [Brochure]. Los Angeles: Author.

The Internet Unleashed. 1994. Indianapolis, IN: SAMS Publishing.

Irvine, J. 1990. *Disorders of Desire: Sex and Gender in Modern American Sexology.* Philadelphia: Temple University Press.

Itialiano, Laura. 1996 (March). "Communications Decency Act: Threat to Cyber Space? Or Much Ado About Nothing?" *NJ Online.*

Jacobs, M., L. A. Thompson, and P. Truxaw. 1975. "The Use of Sexual Surrogates in Counseling." *The Counseling Psychologist,* 5(1):73-77.

Jacobus, X. 1937. *Untrodden Fields of Anthropology.* New York: Falstaff Press.

James, W. H. 1981. "The Honeymoon Effect on Marital Coitus." *Journal of Sex Research,* 17:114-123.

James, W. H. 1983. "Decline in Coital Rates with Spouses' Ages and Duration of Marriage." *Journal of Bioscience,* 15:83-87.

Jasso, G. 1985. "Marital Coital Frequency and the Passage of Time: Estimating the Separate Effects of Spouses' Ages and Marital Duration, Birth, and Marriage Cohorts, and Period Influences." *American Sociological Review,* 50:224-241.

Jefferson, T. 1954. *Notes on the State of Virginia.* Chapel Hill, North Carolina: University of North Carolina Press.

Jenks, R. J. 1985. "Swinging: A Test of Two Theories and a Proposed New Model." *Archives of Sexual Behavior,* 14:517-527.

Jesser, C. J. 1978. "Male Responses to Direct Verbal Sexual Initiatives of Females." *Journal of Sex Research,* 14:118-128.

Jessor, S. L., R. Jessor. 1977. *Problem Behavior and Psychosocial Development: A Longitudinal Study of Youth.* New York: Academic Press.

Johnson, L. B. 1978. "Sexual Behavior of Southern Blacks." In R. Staples, ed. *The Black Family: Essays and Studies.* Belmont, CA: Wadsworth Press.

Johnson, L. B. 1986. "Religion and Sexuality: A Comparison of Black and White College Students in Three Regions of the U.S." Unpublished manuscript.

Johnson, R. E. 1970. Some correlates of extramarital coitus. *Journal of Marriage and the Family,* 32:449-456.

Jones, E., J. Forrest, N. Goldman, S. Henshaw, R. Lincoln, J. Rossoff, C. Westoff, and D. Wulf. 1985. "Teenage Pregnancy in Developed Countries: Determinants and Policy Implications. *Family Planning Perspectives,* 17:53-63.

Jones, E. F., et al. 1986. *Teenage Pregnancy in Industrialized Countries.* New Haven, CT: Yale University Press.

Jones, J., and C. L. Muehlenhard. 1990 (November). "Using Education to Prevent Rape on College Campuses." Presented at the annual meeting of the Society for the Scientific Study of Sex, Minneapolis, MN.

Joseph Smith's Testimony. Salt Lake City: Church of Jesus Christ of the Latter-Day Saints Publication.

Juran, S. 1995. The 90's: Gender Differences in AIDS-Related Sexual Concerns and Behaviors, Condom Use and Subjective Condom Experience. *Journal of Psychology & Human Sexuality,* 7(3):39-59.

Kahn, J. R., and J. R. Udry. 1986. "Marital Coital Frequency: Unnoticed Outliers and Unspecified Interactions Lead to Erroneous Conclusions." *American Sociological Review,* 51:734-737.

Kallen, D., and J. Stephenson. 1982. "Talking about Sex Revisited." *Journal of Youth and Adolescence.* 11:11-23.

Kaplan, D. A. 1993 (November 22). "Take Down the Girlie Calendars." *Newsweek,* p. 34.

Kaplan, H. Singer. 1979. *Disorders of Sexual Desire and Other New Concepts and Techniques in Sex Therapy.* New York: Brunner/Mazel.

Kaplan, H. Singer. 1983. *The Evaluation of Sexual Disorders: Psychological and Medical Aspects.* New York: Brunner/Mazel.

Kaplan, H. Singer. 1974. *The New Sex Therapy: Active Treatment of Sexual Dysfunctions.* New York: Brunner/Mazel.

Kelsey, D. H. 1993. *Between Athens and Berlin: The Theological Education Debate.* Grand Rapids, MI: Eerdmans.

Kendall-Tackett, K., L. A. Williams, and D. Finkelhor. 1993. "Impact of Sexual Abuse on Children: A Review and Synthesis of Recent Empirical Studies." *Psychological Bulletin,* 113:164-180.

Kenney, A., S. Guardado, and L. Brown. 1989. "Sex Education and AIDS Education in the Schools: What States and Large School Districts Are Doing. *Family Planning Perspectives,* 21:56-64.

Kilpatrick, D. G., C. L. Best, B. E. Saunders, and L. J. Veronen. 1987. "Rape in Marriage and in Dating Relationships: How Bad Is It for Mental Health?" *Annals of the New York Academy of Sciences,* 528:335-344.

Kinsey, A. C., W. Pomeroy, and C. Martin. 1948. *Sexual Behavior in the Human Male.* Philadelphia: Saunders.

Kinsey, A. C., W. Pomeroy, C. Martin, and P. Gebhard. 1953. *Sexual Behavior in the Human Female.* Philadelphia: Saunders.

Kirby, D. 1985. "Sexuality Education: A More Realistic View of Its Effects." *Journal of School Health,* 55(10):421-424.

Kirby, D., J. Atter, and P. Scales. 1979. *An Analysis of U.S. Sex Education Programs and Evaluation Methods: Executive Summary.* Atlanta, GA: U.S. Department of Health, Education, and Welfare.

Kirkendall, L. A., and I. G. McBride. 1990. "Preadolescent and Adolescent imagery and Sexual Fantasies: Beliefs and Experiences." In M. Perry, ed. *Handbook of Sexology: Volume 7: Childhood and Adolescent Sexology.* New York: Elsevier.

Kilpatrick, A. C. 1986. "Some Correlates of Women's Childhood Sexual Experiences: A Retrospective Survey." *Journal of Sex Research,* 22:221-242.

Kilpatrick, A. C. 1987. "Childhood Sexual Experiences: Problems and Issues in Studying Long-Range Effects." *Journal of Sex Research,* 23:173-196.

Klein, M. 1994. "Response to the FBI—The Rest of the 'Child Porn' Story." *AASECT Newsletter.*

Klein, F. 1978. *The Bisexual Option: A Concept of One Hundred Percent Intimacy.* New York: Arbor House.

Klein, F., B. Sepekoff, and T. J. Wolf. 1985. "Sexual Orientation: A Multi-Variable Dynamic Process." *Journal of Homosexuality,* 11(1/2):35-50.

Koch, P. B. 1988. "The Relationship of First Sexual Intercourse to Later Sexual Functioning Concerns of Adolescents." *Journal of Adolescent Research,* 3:345-352.

Koch, P. B. 1995. *Exploring Our Sexuality: An Interactive Text.* Dubuque, IA: Kendall/Hunt.

Kosnick, A., W. Carroll, A. Cunningham, R. Modras, and J. Schulte. 1977. *Human Sexuality: New Directions in American Catholic Thought.* New York: Paulist Press.

Koss, M. P. 1992. "The Underdetection of Rape: Methodological Choices Influence Incidence Estimates." *Journal of Social Issues,* 48(1):61-75.

Koss, M. P. 1993a. "Detecting the Scope of Rape: A Review of Prevalence Research Methods." *Journal of Interpersonal Violence,* 8:198-222.

Koss, M. P. 1993b. "Rape: Scope, Impact, Interventions, and Public Policy Responses." *American Psychologist,* 48:1062-1069.

Koss, M. P., and T. E. Dinero. 1988. "Predictors of Sexual Aggression Among a National Sample of Male College Students." In R. A. Prentky and V. L. Quinsey, eds. *Human Sexual Aggression: Current Perspectives* (pp. 133-147). New York: New York Academy of Sciences.

Koss, M. P., T. E. Dinero, C. A. Seibel, and S. L. Cox. 1988. "Stranger and Acquaintance Rape: Are There Differences in the Victim's Experience?" *Psychology of Women Quarterly*, 12:1-24.

Koss, M. P., C. A. Gidycz, and N. Wisniewski. 1987. "The Scope of Rape: Incidence and Prevalence of Sexual Aggression and Victimization in a National Sample of Higher Education Students." *Journal of Consulting and Clinical Psychology*, 55:162-170.

Kraditor, A. 1965. *The Ideas of the Women's Suffrage Movement.* New York: Columbia University Press.

Krivacska, J. J. 1990. "Child Sexual Abuse and Its Prevention." In M. Perry, ed. *Handbook of Sexology: Volume 7: Childhood and Adolescent Sexology.* New York: Elsevier.

Kutsche, P. 1983. "Household and Family in Hispanic Northern New Mexico." *Journal of Comparative Family Studies*, 14(2):151-165.

LaFree, G. D. 1982. "Male Power and Female Victimization: Toward a Theory of Interracial Rape." *American Journal of Sociology*, 88:311-328.

LaFree, G. D., B. F. Reskin, and C. A. Visher. 1985. "Jurors' Responses to Victims' Behavior and Legal Issues in Sexual Assault Trials." *Social Problems*, 32:389-407.

Langfeldt, T. 1979. "Processes in Sexual Development." In M. Cook and G. Wilson, eds. *Love and Attraction.* Oxford: Pergamon Press.

Larson, D. L., E. A. Spreitzer, and E. E. Snyder. 1976. "Social Factors in the Frequency of Romantic Involvement Among Adolescents." *Adolescences*, II:7-12.

Laumann, E. O., J. H. Gagnon, R. T. Michael, and S. Michaels. 1994. *The Social Organization of Sexuality: Sexual Practices in the United States.* Chicago: University of Chicago Press.

Laurence, J. 1994 (March/April). "Long-Term Survival Versus Nonprogression." *The AIDS Reader*, 4(2):39-40, 71.

Lawrence, K., and E. S. Herold. 1988. "Women's Attitudes Toward and Experience with Sexually Explicit Materials." *Journal of Sex Research*, 24:161-169.

Lawrence, R. J. 1989. *The Poisoning of Eros: Sexual Values in Conflict.* New York: Augustine Moore Press.

Leaper-Campbell, V. D. 1996. "Predictors of Mexican American Mothers' and Fathers' Attitudes Toward Gender Equality. Hispanic." *Journal of Behavioral Sciences*, 18:343-355.

Lefley, H. P., C. S. Scott, M. Llabre, and D. Hicks. 1993. "Cultural Beliefs about Rape and Victims' Response in Three Ethnic Groups." *American Journal of Orthopsychiatry*, 63(4):623-632.

LeGates, M. 1995. "Feminists Before Feminism: Origins and Varieties of Women's Protests in Europe and North America before the Twentieth Century. In: J. Freeman, ed. *Women: A Feminist Perspective.* Mountain View, CA: Mayfield.

LeHaye, T., and B. LeHaye. 1976. *The Act of Marriage: The Beauty of Sexual Love.* Grand Rapids, MI: Zondervan.

Leiblum, S. R., and L. A. Pervin, eds. 1980. *Principles and Practice of Sex Therapy.* New York: Guilford Press.

Leiblum, S. R., and R. C. Rosen, eds. 1988. *Sexual Desire Disorders.* New York: Guilford Press.

LeVay, S. 1991. "A Difference in Hypothalamic Structure Between Heterosexual and Homosexual Men." *Science*, 253:1034-1037.

Levin, R. J. 1975 (October). "The Redbook Report on Premarital and Extramarital Sex. *Redbook*, 38-44 and 190-192.

Levinson, D. R., M. L. Johnson, and D. M. Devaney. 1988. *Sexual Harassment in the Federal Government: An Update.* Washington, DC: U.S. Merit Systems Protection Board.

Lewis, P. H. 1995 (March 26). "Cybersex Stays Hot, Despite a Plan for Cooling It Off." *The New York Times News Service* (on-line).

Lewis, R. J., and L. H. Janda. 1988. "The Relationship Between Adult Sexual Adjustment and Childhood Experiences Regarding Exposure to Nudity, Sleeping in the Parental Bed, and Parental Attitudes Toward Sexuality." *Archives of Sexual Behavior,* 17:349-362.

Lewis, W. C. 1965. "Coital Movements in the First Year of Life." *International Journal of Psychoanalysis,* 46:372-374.

Libby, R. W. and R. N. Whitehurst, eds. 1977. *Marriage and Alternatives: Exploring Intimate Relationships.* Glenview, IL: Scott-Foresman.

Lief, H. I. 1963. "What Medical Schools Teach About Sex." *Bulletin of the Tulane University Medical Faculty,* 22:161-168.

Lief, H. I. 1965. "Sex Education of Medical Students and Doctors." *Pacific Medical Surgery,* 73:52-58.

Lifshitz, A. 1990. "Critical Cultural Barriers that Bar Meeting the Needs of Latinas." *SIECUS Report,* 18(3):16-17.

Lily, T. 1977 (March). "Sexual Surrogate: Notes of a Therapist." *SIECUS Report,* 12-13.

Lobitz, W. C., and J. LoPiccolo. "New Methods in the Behavioral Treatment of Sexual Dysfunction." *Journal of Behavior Therapy and Experimental Psychiatry,* 3(4):265-271.

Lohr, S. 1996 (June 13). "A Complex Medium That Will Be Hard to Regulate." *The New York Times.*

LoPiccolo, J., and W. C. Lobitz. 1973. "Behavior Therapy of Sexual Dysfunction." in L. A. Hammerlynck, L. C. Handy, and E. J. Mash, eds. *Behavior Change: Methodology, Concepts and Practice.* Champaign, IL: Research Press.

LoPiccolo, J., and L. LoPiccolo, eds. 1978. *Handbook of Sex Therapy.* New York: Plenum Press.

Lorch, D. 1996 (February 1). "Quinceañera" A Girl Grows Up. *The New York Times,* pp. C1 and C4.

Loulan, J. 1984. *Lesbian Sex.* San Francisco: Spinsters/Aunt Lute.

Love, B. 1992. *The Encyclopedia of Unusual Sex Practices.* New York: Barricade Books.

Love, B. 1994. "Interviews and Surveys of 200 Adult Book Store Customers and Analysis of Same, 1994." In: *A Longitudinal Study of Sexuality.* San Francisco: The Institute for the Advanced Study of Sexuality, (in press).

Ludlow, D. H., ed. 1992. *The Encyclopedia of Mormonism.* New York: McMillan Publishing Co.

Luker, K. 1996. *Dubious Conceptions: The Politics of Teenage Pregnancy.* Cambridge, MA: Harvard University Press.

Lyons, R. D. 1983 (October 4). "Sex in America: Conservative Attitudes Prevail." *The New York Times.*

Lystad, M. H. 1982. "Sexual Abuse in the Home: A Review of the Literature." *International Journal of Family Psychiatry,* 3:3-31.

Maccoby, E. E., and J. A. Martin. 1983. "Socialization in the Context of the Family: Parent-Child Interaction." In P. H. Mussen, ed. *Handbook of Child Psychology: Volume 4* (4th ed., pp. 1-101). New York: J. Wiley.

MacDonald, J. M. 1971. *Rape Offenders and Their Victims.* Springfield, IL: Thomas.

MacKinnon, C. 1982. "Marxism, Method, and the State: An Agenda for Theory." *Signs,* 7:515-544.

MacKinnon, C. A. 1987. *Feminism Unmodified: Discourses on Life and Law.* Cambridge, MA: Harvard University Press.

MacKinnon, C. A. 1990. "Liberalism and the Death of Feminism." In D. Leidholdt and J. G. Raymond, eds. *The Sexual Liberals and the Attack on Feminism* (pp. 3-13). New York: Pergamon.

Macklin, E. D. 1980. "Nontraditional Family Forms: A Decade of Research." *Journal of Marriage and the Family,* 42:905-920

Macklin, E. D. ed. 1989. *AIDS and Families: Report of the AIDS Task Force. Groves Conference on Marriage and the Family.* Binghamton, NY: Harrington Park Press.

Magaña, A., and N. M. Clark. 1995. "Examining a Paradox: Does Religiosity Contribute to Positive Birth Outcomes in Mexican American Populations?" *Health Education Quarterly*, 22(1):96-109.

Malamuth, N. M. 1986. "Predictors of Naturalistic Sexual Aggression." *Journal of Personality and Social Psychology*, 50:953-962.

Malin, M. H. 1987 (June 14-20). "A Preliminary Report of a Case of Necrophilia." Paper presented at the Eighth World Congress for Sexology, Heidelberg.

Maltz, D. N., and R. A. Borker. 1983. "A Cultural Approach to Male-Female Miscommunication." In J. J. Gumperz, ed. *Language and Social Identity* (pp. 195-216). New York: Cambridge University Press.

Mansfield, P. K., A. Voda, and P. B. Koch. 1995. "Predictors of Sexual Response Changes in Heterosexual Midlife Women." *Health Values*, 19:10-20.

Marciano, Teresa Donati. 1987. "Families and Religion." In M. B. Sussman and S. K. Steinmetz, eds. *Handbook of Marriage and the Family* (pp. 285-316). New York: Plenum Press.

Marcus, I. M., and J. F. Francis, eds. 1975. *Masturbation from Infancy to Senescence.* New York: International Universities Press.

Marín, B. V., C. A. Gomez, and N. Hearst. 1993. "Multiple Heterosexual Partners and Condom Use Among Hispanics and Non-Hispanic Whites." *Family Planning Perspectives*, 25:170-174.

Marín, B. V., G. Marín, and R. Juárez. 1990. "Differences Between Hispanics and Non-Hispanics in Willingness to Provide AIDS Prevention Advice." *Hispanic Journal of Behavioral Sciences*, 12(2):153-164.

Martinson, F. M. 1973. *Infant and Child Sexuality: A Sociological Perspective.* St. Peter, MN: The Book Mark.

Martinson, F. M. 1976. "Eroticism in Infancy and Childhood." *Journal of Sex Research*, 12:251-262.

Martinson, F. M. 1990. "Current Legal Status of the Erotic and Sexual Rights of Children." In M. Perry, ed. *Handbook of Sexology: Volume 7: Childhood and Adolescent Sexology.* New York: Elsevier.

Martinson, F. M. 1995. *The Sexual Life of Children.* Westport, CT: Greenwood Press.

Marty, M. E., and R. Scott Appleby, eds. 1992. *Fundamentalisms Observed, Volume 1.* Chicago: University of Chicago Press.

Marty, M. E., and R. Scott Appleby, eds. 1993. *Fundamentalism and Society, Volume 2.* Chicago: University of Chicago Press.

Marty, M. E., and R. Scott Appleby, eds. 1993. *Fundamentalism and the State, Volume 3.* Chicago: University of Chicago Press.

Marty, M. E., and R. Scott Appleby, eds. 1994. *Accounting for Fundamentalism, Volume 4.* Chicago: University of Chicago Press.

Masters, W. H., and V. E. Johnson. 1966. *Human Sexual Response.* Boston: MA: Little Brown.

Masters, W. H., and V. E. Johnson. 1970. *Human Sexual Inadequacy.* Boston, MA: Little Brown.

Mays, V. M. and S. D. Cochran. 1988. "Issues in the Perception of AIDS Risk and Risk Reduction by Black and Hispanic/Latino Women." *American Psychologist*, 43(11):949-957.

Mays, V. M. and S. D. Cochran. 1990. "Methodological Issues in the Assessment and Prediction of AIDS Risk-Related Sexual Behaviors Among Black Americans." In B. Voeller, J. M. Reinisch, and G. M. Gottlieb, eds. *AIDS and Sex: An Integrated Biomedical and Biobehavioral Approach.* New York: Oxford University Press.

McCann, J., and M. K. Biaggio. 1989. "Sexual Satisfaction in Marriage as a Function of Life Meaning." *Archives of Sexual Behavior*, 18:59-72.

McCann-Winter, E. J. S. 1983. *Clergy Education about Homosexuality: An Outcomes Analysis of Knowledge, Attitudes, and Counseling Behaviors.* Unpublished doctoral dissertation, University of Pennsylvania, Philadelphia.

McCleary, K. 1992 (May). "The Chastity Revolution." *Reader's Digest*, 69-71.

McCormick, N. B. 1994a. "Feminism and Sexology." In V. L. Bullough and B. Bullough, eds. *Human Sexuality: An Encyclopedia* (pp. 208-212). New York: Garland Publishing, Inc.

McCormick, N. B. 1994b. *Sexual Salvation: Affirming Women's Sexual Rights and Pleasures.* Westport, CT: Praeger.

McCullagh, Declan. 1996 (August 20). "CDA Update." *The Netizen.*

McGoldrick, J. K. Pearce, and J. Giordano, eds. 1982. *Ethnicity and Family Therapy.* New York: Guilford Press.

McIlvenna, T. 1995 (July 3). Telephone interview with Brenda Love, Palo Alto, California.

McNeil, J. 1976. *The Church and the Homosexual.* Kansas City, Missouri: Sheed Andrews and McMeel.

McWhirter, D., and A. Mattison. 1984. *The Male Couple: How Relationships Develop.* Englewood Cliffs, NJ: Prentice-Hall.

Medina, C. 1987. "Latino Culture and Sex Education." *SIECUS Report*, 15(3):1-4.

Medora, N., and M. Burton. 1981. "Extramarital Sexual Attitudes and Norms of an Undergraduate Student Population." *Adolescence*, 16:251-262.

Michael, R. T., J. H. Gagnon, E. O. Laumann, and G. Kolata. 1994. *Sex in America: A Definitive Survey.* Boston: Little, Brown.

Michaldimitrakis, M. 1986. "Accidental Death During Intercourse by Males." *American Journal of Forensic Medicine and Pathology*, 7:74.

Mikawa, J. K., et al. "Cultural Practices of Hispanics: Implications for the Prevention of AIDS." *Hispanic Journal of Behavioral Sciences*, 14(4):421-433.

Miller, B. C., J. K. McCoy, T. D. Olson, and C. M. Wallace. 1986. "Parental Discipline and Control Attempts in Relation to Adolescent Sexual Attitudes and Behavior." *Journal of Marriage and the Family*, 48:503-512.

Miller, B. C., and K. A. Moore. 1990. "Adolescent Sexual Behavior, Pregnancy, and Parenting: Research Through the 1980s." *Journal of Marriage and the Family*, 52:1025-1044.

Miller, P. Y., and W. Simon. 1981. "The Development of Sexuality in Adolescence." In J. Adelson, ed. *Handbook of Adolescent Psychology* (pp. 383-407). New York: J. Wiley.

Mio, J. S., and J. D. Foster. 1991. "The Effects of Rape upon Victims and Families: Implications for a Comprehensive Family Therapy." *American Journal of Family Therapy*, 19:147-159.

Money, J. 1976. "Childhood: The Last Frontier in Sex Research." *The Sciences*, 16:12-27.

Money, J. 1985. *The Destroying Angel.* Buffalo, NY: Prometheus Press.

Money, J. 1986/1994. *Lovemaps: Sexual/Erotic Health and Pathology, Paraphilia, and Gender Transposition in Childhood, Adolescence, and Maturity* Buffalo, NY: Prometheus.

Money, J. 1988. *Gay, Straight, and In-Between: The Sexology of Erotic Orientation.* New York: Oxford University Press.

Money, J. 1995. *Gendermaps: Social Constructionism, Feminism, and Sexosophical History.* New York: Continuum.

Money, J., and A. A. Ehrhardt. 1972. *Man & Woman, Boy & Girl.* Baltimore: Johns Hopkins University Press.

Money, J., and R. W. Keyes. 1993. *The Armed Robbery Orgasm.* Amhearst, NY: Prometheus Books.

Money, J., and M. Lamacz. 1989. *Vandalized Lovemaps: Paraphilic Outcome of Seven Cases in Pediatric Sexology.* Buffalo, NY: Prometheus Press.

Money, J., G. Wainwright, and D. Hingsburger. 1991. *The Breathless Orgasm: A Lovemap Biography of Asphyxiophilia.* Buffalo, NY: Prometheus Books.

Moore, M. M. 1985. "Nonverbal Courtship Patterns in Women: Context and Consequences." *Ethology and Sociobiology,* 6:201-212.

Moore, M. M., and D. L. Butler. 1989. "Predictive Aspects of Nonverbal Courtship Behavior in Women." *Semiotica,* 76:205-215.

Moran, J. R., and M. D. Corley. 1991. "Source of Sexual Information and Sexual Attitudes and Behaviors of Angle and Hispanic Adolescent Males." *Adolescence,* 26(104):857-864.

Morgan, R. 1984. *Sisterhood Is Global.* Garden City, NY: Anchor Press.

Moser, C. 1988. *"Sadomasochism" The Sexually Unusual Guide to Understanding and Helping.* New York: Harrington Park Press.

Moses, A. and R. Hawkins, Jr. 1982/1986. *Counseling Lesbian Women and Gay Men: A Life-Issues Approach.* Englewood Cliffs, NJ: Paramount Publishing.

Mosher. Clelia Duel. 1980. *The Mosher Survey: Sexual Attitudes of Forty-Five Victorian Women.* James Mahood and Kristine Wenburg, eds. New York: Arno Press.

Mosher, D. L. 1994. "Pornography." In V. L. Bullough and B. Bullough, eds. *Human Sexuality: An Encyclopedia.* New York: Garland Publishing.

Muehlenhard, C. L., and S. W. Cook. 1988. "Men's Self-Reports of Unwanted Sexual Activity." *Journal of Sex Research,* 24:58-72.

Muehlenhard, C. L., S. Danoff-Burg, and I. G. Powch. 1996. "Is Rape Sex or Violence? Conceptual Issues and Implications." In D. M. Buss and N. Malamuth, eds. *Sex, Power, Conflict: Evolutionary and Feminist Perspectives.* New York: Oxford University Press.

Muehlenhard, C. L., M. F. Goggins, J. M. Jones, and A. T. Satterfield. 1991. "Sexual Violence and Coercion in Close Relationships." In K. McKinney and S. Sprecher, eds. *Sexuality in Close Relationships.* Hillsdale, NJ: Lawrence Erlbaum Associates.

Muehlenhard, C. L., P. A. Harney, and J. M. Jones. 1992. From "Victim-Precipitated Rape" to "Date Rape": How Far Have We Come? *Annual Review of Sex Research,* 3:219-253.

Muehlenhard, C. L., I. G. Powch, J. L. Phelps, and L. M. Giusti. 1992. "Definitions of Rape: Scientific and Political Implications." *Journal of Social Issues,* 48(1):23-44.

Murdock, G. P. 1949. *Social Structure.* New York: Macmillan.

Murphy, G. J., W. W. Hudson, and P. L. Cheung. 1980. "Marital and Sexual Discord Among Older Couples." *Social Work Research and Abstracts,* 16:11-16.

Murry, V. M. 1995. "An Ecological Analysis of Pregnancy Resolution Decisions Among African American and Hispanic Adolescent Females." *Youth and Society,* 26(3):325-360.

Murstein, B. I. 1974. *Love, Sex, and Marriage Through the Ages.* New York: Springer.

Mussen, P. H., ed. 1983. *Handbook of Child Psychology: Volume 1, History, Theory, and Methods* (4th ed.). New York: J. Wiley.

NARAL. 1995. *Sexuality Education in America: A State-by-State Review.* Washington, DC: NARAL and the NARAL Foundation.

National Council of la Raza. 1992 (February). *State of Hispanic America 1991: An Overview.* Washington, DC: National Council of la Raza.

National Council of la Raza. 1993. *State of Hispanic America: Toward a Latino Anti-Poverty Agenda.* Washington, DC: National Council of la Raza.

National Research Council. Panel on Monitoring the Social Impact of the AIDS Epidemic. 1993. *The Social Impact of AIDS in the United States.* Washington, DC: National Academy Press.

Neale, T. H. 1989. *Hispanic Heritage in the U.S.: Tradition, Achievement, and Aspiration.* *CRS Report for Congress 89-532 Gov. Congressional Research Service.* Washington, DC: The Library of Congress.

Nelson, J. B. 1978. *Embodiment.* Minneapolis: Augsburg Publishing House.

Nelson, J. B. 1983. *Between Two Gardens: Reflections on Sexuality and Religious Experience.* New York: Pilgrim Press.

Nelson, J. A. 1986. "Incest: Self-Report Findings from a Nonclinical Sample." *Journal of Sex Research,* 22:463-477.

Nelson, J. B. 1992. *Body Theology.* Louisville, Kentucky: Westminster/John Knox.

Nelson, J. B., and S. P. Longfellow, eds. 1994. *Sexuality and the Sacred: Sources for Theological Reflection.* Louisville, Kentucky: Westminster/John Knox Press.

NetGuide. 1995 (April). "Millions Hooked on the Net," p. 139.

Newcomer, S. F., and J. R. Udry. 1985. "Oral Sex in an Adolescent Population." *Archives of Sexual Behavior,* 14:41-46.

Newman, B. S., and P. G. Muzzonigro. 1993. "The Effects of Traditional Family Values on the Coming Out Process of Gay Male Adolescents." *Adolescence,* 28(109):213-226.

Newman, L. 1989. *Heather Has Two Mommies.* Northampton, MA: In Other Words Publishers.

Newman, L. 1991. *Gloria Goes to Gay Pride.* Boston: Alyson Publications.

Newsweek. 1996 (December 2). "The End of AIDS", pp. 64-73.

The New York Times. 1996 (June 13. "Panel of Three Judges Turns Back Federal Law Intended to Regulate Decency on Internet."

Newsweek. 1993 (August 2). "A Cheeky Protest," p. 6.

Newsweek. 1993 (August 2). "Aspin on Gays in the Military," p. 4.

Newsweek. 1994 (March 14). "Was It Real or Memories?" pp. 54-55.

Nobile, P., and E. Nadler. 1986. *United States of America vs. Sex.* New York: Minotaur Press.

Noonan, R. J. 1995/1984. *Sex Surrogates: A Clarification of Their Functions.* Master's thesis, New York University. Available at World Wide Web site: http://www.SexQuest.com/surrogat.htm. New York: SexQuest/The Sex Institute.

Noonan, R. J. 1996a. "New Directions, New Hope for Sexuality: On the Cutting Edge of Sane Sex." In P. B. Anderson, D. de Mauro, and R. J. Noonan, eds. *Does Anyone Still Remember When Sex Was Fun? Positive Sexuality in the Age of AIDS* (3rd ed.; pp. 144-221). Dubuque, IA: Kendall/Hunt Publishing Co.

Noonan, R. J. 1996b. "Survival Strategies for Lovers in the 1990s." In P. B. Anderson, D. de Mauro, and R. J. Noonan, eds. *Does Anyone Still Remember When Sex Was Fun? Positive Sexuality in the Age of AIDS* (3rd ed.; pp. 1-12). Dubuque, IA: Kendall/Hunt Publishing Co.

North, B. J. 1990. Effectiveness of Vaginal Contraceptives in Prevention of Sexually Transmitted Diseases. In N. J. Alexander, H. L. Gabelnick, & J. M. Spieler, eds. *Heterosexual Transmission of AIDS: Proceedings of the Second Contraceptive Research and Development (CONRAD) Program International Workshop, held in Norfolk, Virginia, February 1-3, 1989* (pp. 273-290). New York: Wiley-Liss.

Norton, A. J., and J. E. Moorman. 1987. "Current Trends in Marriage and Divorce Among American Women." *Journal of Marriage and the Family,* 49:3-14.

O'Brien, R. M. 1987. "The Interracial Nature of Violent Crimes: A Reexamination." *American Journal of Sociology,* 92:817-835.

Ogden, G. 1995. *Women Who Love Sex.* New York: Pocket Books.

Okami, P. 1992. "Child Perpetrators of Sexual Abuse: The Emergence of a Problematic Deviant Category." *Journal of Sex Research,* 29:109-130.

Okami, P. 1995. "Childhood Exposure to Parental Nudity, Parent-Child Co-Sleeping, and 'Primal Scenes:' A Review of Clinical Opinion and Empirical Evidence." *Journal of Sex Research*, 32:51-64.

Okazaki, C. N. 1994 (November). "Rowing Your Boat." *Ensign.* 24(11):92-94.

Oliver, M. B., and J. S. Hyde. 1993. "Gender Differences in Sexuality: A Meta-Analysis." *Psychological Bulletin*, 114:29-51.

O'Neill, N., and G. O'Neill. 1972. *Open Marriage: A New Lifestyle for Couples.* New York: M. Evans.

Padilla, A. M., and T. L. Barids. 1991. "Mexican-American Adolescent Sexuality and Sexual Knowledge: An Exploratory Study." *Hispanic Journal of Behavioral Sciences*, 13(1):95-104.

Palmer, C. T. 1988. "Twelve Reasons Why Rape Is Not Sexually Motivated: A Skeptical Examination." *Journal of Sex Research*, 25:512-530.

Paluszny, M. 1979. "Current Thinking on Children's Sexuality." *Medical Aspects of Human Sexuality*, 13:120-121.

Pankhurst, J., and S. K. Houseknecht. 1983. "The Family, Politics, and Religion in the 1980s." *Journal of Family Issues*, 4:5-34.

Patton, C. 1990. *Inventing AIDS.* New York: Routledge.

Pauly, I. B. 1994. "Transsexualism." In V. L. Bullough and B. Bullough, eds. *Human Sexuality: An Encyclopedia* (pp. 590-598). New York: Garland Publishing.

Pauly, I., and T. Lindgren. 1976. "Body Image and Gender Identity. *Journal of Homosexuality*, 2:133-142.

Pearl, J. 1987. "The Highest Paying Customers: America's Cities and the Costs of Prostitution Control." *Hastings Law Journal*, 38:769-800.

Penner, C., and J. Penner. 1981. *The Gift of Sex: A Guide to Sexual Fulfillment.* Dallas: Word.

Peplau, L. A., Z. Rubin, and C. T. Hill. 1977. "Sexual Intimacy in Dating Relationships." *Journal of Social Issues*, 33:86-109.

Pérez. M. A. In press. "Sexual Communication Among Hispanic Farmworker Adolescents."

Pérez, M. A. and K. Fennelly. 1996. "Risk Factors for HIV and AIDS Among Latino Farmworkers in Pennsylvania." In S. I. Misha, R. F. Conner, and J. R. Magana, eds. *AIDS Crossing Borders: The Spread of HIV Among Migrant Latinos* (pp. 137-156). Boulder, CO: Westview Press.

Perper, T. 1985. *Sex Signals: The Biology of Love.* Philadelphia: ISI Press.

Perper, T., and D. L. Weis. 1987. "Proceptive and Rejective Strategies of U.S. and Canadian College Women." *Journal of Sex Research*, 23:455-480.

Peterson, K. S. 1994 (October 7). "Turns Out We Are 'Sexually Conventional.'" *USA Today*, pp. 1-2A.

Peterson, L. S. 1995 (February). "Contraceptive Use in the United States: 1982-90." *Advance Data, No. 260.* Hyattsville, MD: Centers for Disease Control, U.S. Department of Health and Human Services.

Pettigrew, T. 1964. *A Profile of the Negro American.* Princeton, NJ: Van Nostrand.

Phillips, L., and C. Phillips. 1994. *Survey of Transgenderists.* Bulverde, TX 78163: P.O. Box 17.

Phipps, W. E. 1975. *Recovering Biblical Sensuousness.* Philadelphia: Westminster Press.

Pietropinto, A., and J. Simenauer. 1977. *Beyond the Male Myth: A Nationwide Survey.* New York: New American Library.

Pleck, J. 1981. *The Myth of Masculinity.* Cambridge, MA: MIT Press.

Pomeroy, W. B. 1972. *Dr. Kinsey and the Institute for Sex Research.* New York: Harper and Row.

Prendergast, W. E. 1991. *Treating Sex Offenders in Correctional Institutions and Outpatient Clinics: A Guide to Clinical Practice*. Binghamton, NY: Haworth Press.

Prendergast, W. E. 1993. *The Merry-Go-Round of Sexual Abuse: Identifying and Treating Survivors*. Binghamton, NY: Haworth Press.

Prescott, J. W., and D. Wallace. 1978 (July-August). "Abortion and the 'Right-to-Life.'" *The Humanist*, 18-24.

Prins, K. S., B. P. Buunk, and N. W. VanYperen. 1993. "Equity, Normative Disapproval and Extramarital Relationships. *Journal of Social and Personal Relationships*, 10:39-53.

Purchas, S. 1905. *Haklutus Posthumus, or Prchas His Pilgrimes: Contayning a History of the World in Sea Voyages and Land Travells by Englishmen and Others*. Glascow, Scotland: J. Maclehose and Sons.

Quinttner, Joshua. 1996 (June 24). "Free Speech for the Net." *Time Magazine*, 147(26).

Rainwater, L. 1964. "Marital Sexuality in Four Cultures of Poverty." *Journal of Marriage and the Family*, 26:457-466.

Ramey, J. W. 1976. *Intimate Friendships*. Englewood Cliffs, NJ: Prentice-Hall.

Ramsey, G. V. 1943. "The Sexual Development of Boys." *American Journal of Psychology*, 56:217-233.

Ranke-Heinemann, U. 1990. *Eunuchs for the Kingdom of Heaven: Women, Sexuality, and the Catholic Church*. New York: Doubleday.

Redlich, F. 1977. "The Ethics of Sex Therapy." In W. H. Masters, V. E. Johnson, and R. C. Kolodny, *Ethical Issues in Sex Therapy and Research*. Boston: Little, Brown and Company.

Reibstein, J. A., and M. Richards. 1993. *Sexual Arrangements: Marriage and the Temptation of Infidelity*. New York: Scribner.

Reichelt, P. A., and H. H. Werley. 1975. "Contraception, Abortion and Venereal Disease: Teenagers' Knowledge and the Effect of Education." *Family Planning Perspectives*, 7(2):83-88.

Reiss, I. 1960. *Premarital Sexual Standards in America*. New York: Free Press.

Reiss, I. 1964. "Premarital Sexual Permissiveness Among Negroes and Whites." *American Sociological Review*, 29:688-698.

Reiss, I. 1967. *The Social Context of Premarital Sexual Permissiveness*. New York: Holt, Rinehart and Winston.

Reiss, I. L. 1976/1980. *Family Systems in America* (2nd ed./3rd ed.). New York: Holt, Rinehart and Winston.

Reiss, I. 1981. "Some Observations on Ideology and Sexuality in America." *Journal of Marriage and the Family*, 43(2):271-283.

Reiss, I. L. 1986. *Journey into Sexuality: An Exploratory Voyage*. Englewood Cliffs, NJ: Prentice-Hall.

Reiss, I. L. 1995. "Is This the Definitive Sexual Survey?" Review of E. O. Laumann, J. H. Gagnon, R. T. Michael, and S. Michaels. The Social Organization of Sexuality: Sexual Practices in the United States. *Journal of Sex Research*, 32:77-85.

Reiss, I. L., R. E. Anderson, and G. C. Sponaugle. 1980. "A Multivariate Model of the Determinants of Extramarital Sexual Permissiveness." *Journal of Marriage and the Family*, 42:395-411.

Reiss, I. L., A. Banwart, and H. Foreman. 1975. "Premarital Contraceptive Usage: A Study and Some Theoretical Explorations." *Journal of Marriage and the Family*, 37:619-630.

Relief Society Conference, 1965 (September 29). Salt Lake City: Church of Jesus Christ of the Latter-Day Saints Publication.

Resick, P. A. 1993. "The Psychological Impact of Rape." *Journal of Interpersonal Violence,* 8:223-255.

Resnick, H. S., D. G. Kilpatrick, B. S. Dansky, B. E. Saunders, and C. L. Best. 1993. "Prevalence of Civilian Trauma and Posttraumatic Stress Disorder in a Representative National Sample of Women." *Journal of Consulting and Clinical Psychology,* 61:984-991.

Rheingold, H. 1995 (March/April). "The Virtual Community." *Utne Reader,* 68:61-64.

Richardson, L. W. 1985. *The New Other Woman: Contemporary Single Women in Affairs with Married Men.* New York: Free Press.

Riddle, G. 1989. *Amputees and Devotees.* Sunnyvale, CA: Halcyon Press.

Rimmer, R. H. 1966. *The Harrad Experiment.* New York: Bantam.

Riportella-Muller, R. 1989. "Sexuality in the Elderly: A Review." In K. McKinney and S. Sprecher, eds. *Human Sexuality: The Societal and Interpersonal Context* (pp. 210-236). Norwood, NJ: Ablex.

Roberts, B. 1981. "Surrogate Partners and Their Use in Sex Therapy." In D. A. Brown & C. Chary, eds. *Sexuality in America* (pp. 283-300). Ann Arbor, MI: Greenfield Books.

Roberts, S. V., and G. Cohen. 1995 (April 24). "The Religious Right: Church Meets State; On God's Green Earth; The Heavy Hitter." *U.S. News and World Report,* pp. 26-39.

Robinson, I. E., K. King, and J. O. Balswick. 1972. "The Premarital Sexual Revolution Among College Females." *Family Coordinator,* 21:189-194.

Robinson, P. 1976. *The Modernization of Sex.* New York: Harper and Row.

Roebuck, J. and M. McGee. 1977. "Attitudes Toward Premarital Sex and Sexual Behavior Among Black High School Girls." *Journal of Sex Research,* 13:104-114.

Rogers, J. A. 1967. *Sex and Race: Negro-Caucasian Mixing in All Ages and All Lands.* 9th ed. New York: J. A. Rogers.

Roiphe, K. 1993. *The Morning After: Sex, Fear and Feminism on Campus.* Boston: Little Brown.

Rosen, R. C., and J. G. Beck. 1988. *Patterns of Sexual Arousal: Psychophysiological Processes and Clinical Applications.* New York: Guilford Press.

Ross, M. W., J. A. Paulsen, O. W. Stalstrom. 1988. "Homosexuality and Mental Health: A Cross-Cultural Review." *Journal of Homosexuality,* 15(1):131-152.

Rosser, B. R. S., S. M. Dwyer, E. Coleman, M. Miner, M. Metz, B. Robinson, and W. O. Bockting. 1995. "Using Sexually Explicit Material in Sex Education: An Eighteen Year Comparative Analysis." *Journal of Sex Education and Therapy,* 21(2):118-128.

Rossetti, S. J. 1991. *Slayer of the Soul: Child Sexual Abuse and the Catholic Church.* Mystic, CT: Twenty-Third Publications.

Rotello, G. 1996 (June 24). "To Have and To Hold: The Case for Gay Marriage." *The Nation,* pp. 11-18.

Roth, S., and L. Lebowitz. 1988. "The Experience of Sexual Trauma." *Journal of Traumatic Stress,* 1:79-107.

Rotheram-Borus, M.J., M. Rosario, et al. 1994. "Sexual and Substance Use Acts of Gay and Bisexual Male Adolescents in New York City." *Journal of Sex Research,* 31(1):47-57.

Rotkin, K. 1986. "The Phallacy of Our Sexual Norm." In S. Bem, ed. *Psychology of Sex Roles* (pp. 384-391). Acton, MA: Copley Publishing. (Reprinted from *RT: A Journal of Radical Therapy,* 1972, p. 3.)

Rubenstein, M. 1982. *An In-Depth Study of Bisexuality and Its Relationship to Self-Esteem.* Unpublished doctoral dissertation, The Institute for Advanced Study of Human Sexuality, San Francisco.

Rubin, A. M., and J. R. Adams. 1986. "Outcomes of Sexually Open Marriages." *Journal of Sex Research,* 22:311-319.

Rush, F. 1990. "The Many Faces of Backlash." In: D. Leidholdt and J. Raymond, eds. *The Sexual Liberals and the Attack on Feminism* (pp. 165-174). New York: Pergamon.

Russell, D. E. H. 1990. *Rape In Marriage* (rev. ed.; originally published in 1982). Bloomington: Indiana University Press.

Russell, D. E. H. 1984. *Sexual Exploitation: Rape, Child Sexual Abuse, and Workplace Harassment.* Newbury Park, CA: Sage.

Russo, N., and K. Zierk. 1992. "Abortion, Childbearing, and Women's Well-being." *Professional Psychology: Research and Practice*, 23:269.

Samuels, H. P. 1994. "Race, Sex, and Myths: Images of African-American Men and Women." In V. L. Bullough and B. Bullough, eds. *Human Sexuality: An Encyclopedia.* New York: Garland Press.

Samuels, H. P. 1995. "Sexology, Sexosophy, and African-American Sexuality: Implications for Sex Therapy and Sexuality Education." *SIECUS Report*, 23:3.

Sandoval, A., R. Duran, L. O'Donnel, and C. R. O'Donnell. 1995. "Barriers to Condom Use in Primary and Nonprimary Relationships Among Hispanic STD Clinic Patients." *Hispanic Journal of Behavioral Sciences*, 17(3):385-397.

Sarrel, P. M, and W. H. Masters. 1982. "Sexual Molestation of Men by Women. *Archives of Sexual Behavior*, 11:117-231.

Sarrel, P., and L. Sarrel. 1980 (October) and 1981 (February). "The Redbook Report on Sexual Relationships, Parts 1 and 2." *Redbook*, pp. 73-60 and 140-145.

Saunders, J. M., and J. M. Edwards. 1984. "Extramarital Sexuality: A Predictive Model of Permissive Attitudes. *Journal of Marriage and Family*, 46:825-835.

Savitz, L., and L. Rosen. 1988. "The Sexuality of Prostitutes: Sexual Enjoyment Reported by 'Streetwalkers.'" *Journal of Sex Research*, 24:200-208.

Schmitt, E. 1996 (June 13). "Panel Passes Bill to Let States Refuse to Recognize Gay Marriage." *The New York Times*, p. A15.

Schmalz, J. 1993 (April 16). "Survey Stirs Debate on Number of Gay Men in U.S." *The New York Times*, p. 20.

Schoenborn, C. A., S. L. Marsh, and A. M. Hardy. 1994 (February). "AIDS Knowledge and Attitudes for 1992: Data from the National Health Interview Survey." *Advance Data from Vital and Health Statistics #243. National Center for Health Statistics.* Hyattsville, MD: Government Printing Office.

Schwartz, I. 1993. "Affective Reactions of American and Swedish Women to Their First Premarital Coitus: A Cross-Cultural Comparison." *Journal of Sex Research*, 30:18-26.

Schwartz, John. 1996a (February 9). "Abortion Provision Stirs On-Line Furor." *Washington Post.*

Schwartz, John. 1996b (June 13). "Court Upholds Free Speech on Internet, Blocks Decency Law." *Washington Post.*

Schwartz, M. F. and J. S. Quarterman. 1993. "The Changing Global Internet Service Infrastructure." *Internet Research*, 3(1):8-25.

Schwartz, S. 1973. "Effects of Sex Guilt and Sexual Arousal on the Retention of Birth Control Information." *Journal of Consulting and Clinical Psychology*, 41:61-64.

Scott, J. W. 1976. "Polygamy: A Futuristic Family Arrangement for African-Americans." *Black Books Bulletin*, p. 4.

Scott, J. W. 1986. "From Teenage Parenthood to Polygamy: Case Studies in Black Polygamous Family Formation." *Western Journal of Black Studies*, 10(4):172-179.

Schow, R., W. Schow, and M. Raynes. 1991. *Peculiar People: Mormons and Same-Sex Orientation.* Salt Lake City, UT: Signature Books.

Seaman, B. 1969. *The Doctor's Case Against the Pill.* New York: Peter H. Wyden.

Sears, R. R., E. E. Maccoby, and H. Levin. 1957. "Patterns of Child Rearing." Evanston, IL: Row, Peterson.

Sedway, M. 1992 (February/March). "Far Right Takes Aim at Sexuality Education. *SIECUS Report*, 20(3):13-19.

Segura, D. A. 1991. "Ambivalence or Continuity? Motherhood and Employment Among Chicanas and Mexican Immigrant Women Workers." *Aztlan*, 20(2):150.

Seidman, S. 1991. *Romantic Longings: Love in America, 1830-1980.* New York: Routledge.

Settlage, D., S. Fordney, S. Baroff, and D. Cooper. 1973. "Sexual Experience of Younger Teenage Girls Seeking Contraceptive Assistance for the First Time." *Family Planning Perspectives*, 5:223-226.

Shapiro, L. 1994 (January 24). "They're Daddy's Little Girls." *Newsweek*, p. 66.

Shah, R., and M. Zelnick. 1981. "Parent and Peer Influence on Sexual Behavior, Contraceptive Use, and Pregnancy Experience of Young Women." *Journal of Marriage and the Family*, 43:339-348.

Shilts, R. 1993. *Conduct Unbecoming: Gays and Lesbians in the U.S. Military.* New York: St. Martin's Press.

Shilts, R. 1987. *And the Band Played On: Politics, People, and the AIDS Epidemic.* New York: St. Martin's Press.

Shostak, A. B. 1987. "Singlehood." In M. B. Sussman and S. K. Steinmetz, eds. *Handbook of Marriage and the Family* (pp. 355-368). New York: Plenum.

SIECUS. 1990. *Sex Education 2000. A Call to Action.* New York: SIECUS.

SIECUS. 1991. *Comprehensive Sexuality Education, Kindergarten-12th Grade.* New York: SIECUS.

SIECUS Fact Sheet #2 (on comprehensive sexuality education). 1992. National Coalition to Support Sexuality Education.

Simon, W. 1994. "Deviance as History: The Future of Perversion." *Archives of Sexual Behavior*, 23(1):16.

Simon, W., A. S. Berger, and J. H. Gagnon. 1972. "Beyond Anxiety and Fantasy: The Coital Experiences of College Youth." *Journal of Youth and Adolescence*, 1:203-222.

Singh, B. K., B. L. Walton, and J. J. Williams. 1976. "Extramarital Sexual Permissiveness: Conditions and Contingencies." *Journal of Marriage and the Family*, 38:701-712.

Sipe, A. W. Richard. 1995. *Sex, Priests, and Power: Anatomy of a Crisis.* New York: Brunner/Mazel.

Slowinski, J. W. 1994. "Religious Influence on Sexual Attitudes and Functioning." In V. L. Bullough and B. Bullough, eds. *Human Sexuality: An Encyclopedia* (pp. 520-522). New York: Garland.

Smedes, L. B. 1994. *Sex for Christians: The Limits and Liberties of Sexual Living* (rev. ed.) Grand Rapids, MI: William B. Erdsman.

Smith, L. G., and J. R. Smith. 1974. "Co-Marital Sex: The Incorporation of Extramarital Sex into the Marriage Relationship." In J. R. Smith and L. G. Smith, eds. *Beyond Monogamy* (pp. 84-102). Baltimore: Johns Hopkins Press.

Smith, R. E., C. J. Pine, and M. E. Hawley. 1988. "Social Cognitions about Adult Male Victims of Female Sexual Assault." *Journal of Sex Research*, 24:101-112.

Smith, T. W. 1987 (August). *Unpublished Data from 1972-1987 General Social Surveys* Chicago: National Opinion Research Center.

Smith, T. W. 1990 (February). "Adult Sexual Behavior in 1989: Number of Partners, Frequency, and Risk." Paper presented at the annual meeting of the American Association for the Advancement of Science, New Orleans, LA.

Smith, T. W. 1991. "Adult Sexual Behavior in 1989: Number of Partners, Frequency of Intercourse and Risk of AIDS." *Family Planning Perspectives*, 23(3):102-107.

Smith, T. W. 1996 (December). *Unpublished Data from 1972-1994. General Social Surveys.* Chicago: National Opinion Research Center.

Solomon, J., and S. Miller. 1994 (September 12). "'Hero' or 'Harasser'?" *Newsweek*, pp. 48-50.

Sonestein, F. L., J. H. Pleck, and L. C. Ku. 1991. "Levels of Sexual Activity Among Adolescent Males in the United States. *Family Planning Perspectives*, 23(4):162-167.

Sorensen, R. C. 1973. *Adolescent Sexuality in Contemporary America.* New York: World.

Spaccarelli, S. 1994. "Stress, Appraisal, and Coping in Child Sexual Abuse: A Theoretical and Empirical Review." *Psychological Bulletin,* 116:340-362.

Spanier, G. B. 1975. "Sexualization and Premarital Sexual Behavior." *Family Coordinator,* 24:33-41.

Spanier, G. B. 1976. "Formal and Informal Sex Education as Determinants of Premarital Sexual Behavior." *Archives of Sexual Behavior,* 5:39-67.

Spanier, G. B. 1978. "Sex Education and Premarital Sexual Behavior Among American College Students." *Adolescence,* 8:659-674.

Spanier, G. B., and R. L. Margolis. 1983. "Marital Separation and Extramarital Sexual Behavior." *Journal of Sex Research,* 19:23-48.

Spector, R. E., ed. 1991. *Cultural Diversity in Health and Illness.* Norwalk, CA: Appleton and Lange.

Spong, J. S. 1988. *Living in Sin? A Bishop Rethinks Human Sexuality.* San Francisco: HarperSanFrancisco.

Sprenkle, D. H. and D. L. Weis. 1978. "Extramarital Sexuality: Implications for Marital Therapists." *Journal of Sex and Marital Therapy,* 4:279-291.

Stacy, R. D., M. Prisbell, and K. Tollefsrud. 1992. "A Comparison of Attitudes Among College Students Toward Sexual Violence Committed by Strangers and by Acquaintances: A Research Report." *Journal of Sex Education and Therapy,* 18:257-263.

Stanley, L. A. 1989. "The Child Porn Myth." *Cardozo Arts and Entertainment Law Journal,* 7:295-358.

Sprecher, S., A. Barbee, and P. Schwartz. 1995. "'Was It Good for You, Too?': Gender Differences in First Sexual Intercourse Experiences." *Journal of Sex Research,* 32:3-15.

Staples, R. 1972. "Research on Black Sexuality: Its Implications for Family Life, Sex Education and Public Policy." *The Family Coordinator,* 21:183-188.

Staples, R. 1974. "Black Sexuality." In: M. Calderone, ed. *Sexuality and Human Values* (pp. 62-70). New York: Association Press.

Staples, R. 1977. "The Myth of the Impotent Black Males." In D. Y. Wilkinson and R. L. Taylor, eds. *The Black Male in America.* Chicago: Nelson-Hall.

Staples, R., ed. 1978. *The Black Family: Essays and Studies.* Belmont, CA: Wadsworth Publishing Co.

Staples, R. 1981. *The World of Black Singles: Changing Patterns of Male/Female Relations.* Westport: CT: Greenwood Press.

Staples, R. 1982. *Black Masculinity: The Black Male's Role in American Society.* San Francisco: The Black Scholar Press.

Staples, R. 1986. "The Black Response." In R. T. Francoeur, ed. *Taking Sides: Clashing Views on Controversial Issues in Human Sexuality.* Guilford, CT: Dushkin Publishing.

Staples, R., and L. Boulin Johnson. 1993. *Black Families at the Crossroads: Challenges and Prospects.* San Francisco: Jossey-Bass.

Starr, B. D., and M. Bakur Weiner. 1981. *The Starr-Weiner Report on Sex and Sexuality in the Mature Years.* Briarcliff Manor, NY: Stein and Day.

Stekel, W. 1922. *Bi-Sexual Love.* New York: Emerson Books.

Stern, H. 1993. *Private Parts.* New York: Simon and Schuster.

Stine, G. J. 1995. *AIDS Update: 1994-1995.* Englewood Cliffs, NJ: Prentice-Hall.

Storms, M. D. 1981. "A Theory of Erotic Orientation Development." *Psychological Review,* 88:340-353.

Strong, B., and C. DeVault. 1994. *Human Sexuality.* Mountain View, CA: Mayfield.

Sullivan, A. 1996. *Virtually Normal: An Argument about Homosexuality.* New York: Knopf.

Surra, C. A. 1990. "Research and Theory on Mate Selection and Premarital Relationships in the 1980s." *Journal of Marriage and the Family,* 52:844-865.

Symonds, C. 1973 (September). "Sex Surrogates." *Penthouse Forum.* Quoted in S. Braun, ed. 1975, *Catalog of Sexual Consciousness* (p. 137). New York: Grove Press.

Szapocznik, J. 1995. "Research on Disclosure of HIV Status: Cultural Evolution Finds an Ally in Science." *Health Psychology*, 14(1):4-5.

Taggart, J. M. 1992. "Gender Segregation and Cultural Constructions of Sexuality in Two Hispanic Societies." *American Ethnologist*, 19:75-96.

Talmage, J. E. 1977. *A Study of the Articles of Faith.* Salt Lake City, UT: Church of Jesus Christ of Latter-Day Saints.

Tamosaitis, N. 1995. *net.sex.* Emeryville, CA: Ziff-Davis Press.

Tangri, S., M. R. Burt, and L. B. Johnson. 1982. "Sexual Harassment at Work: Three Explanatory Models." *Journal of Social Issues*, 38(4):33-54.

Tanner, President N. Eldon. 1973. *The Role of Womanhood.* Salt Lake City: Church of Jesus Christ of the Latter-Day Saints Publication.

Tavris, C. 1978, February. "40,000 Men Tell About Their Sexual Behavior, Their Fantasies, Their Ideal Women, and Their Wives." *Redbook*, pp. 111-113 and 178-181.

Tavris, C., and S. Sadd. 1975. *The Redbook Report on Female Sexuality.* New York: Delacorte.

Teevan, J. J. Jr. 1972. "Reference Groups and Premarital Sexual Behavior." *Journal of Marriage and the Family*, 34:283-291.

Terman, L. M. 1938. *Psychological Factors in Marital Happiness.* New York: McGraw-Hill.

Thayer, N. S. T., et al. 1987 (March). "Report of the Task Force on Changing Patterns of Sexuality and Family Life." *The Voice.* Newark, NJ: Episcopal Diocese of Northern New Jersey.

Thompson, A. P. 1983. "Extramarital Sex: A Review of the Research Literature." *Journal of Sex Research*, 19:1-22.

Thompson, A. P. 1984. "Emotional and Sexual Components of Extramarital Relations." *Journal of Marriage and the Family*, 46:35-42.

Thorne, B., and Z. Luria. 1986. "Sexuality and Gender in Children's Daily Worlds." *Social Problems*, 33(3):176-190.

Thornton, B. 1977. "Toward a Linear Prediction Model of Marital Happiness." *Personality and Social Psychology Bulletin*, 3:674-676.

Tiefer, L. 1995. *Sex Is Not a Natural Act and Other Essays.* San Francisco: Westview.

Time Magazine. 1995 (Spring). Special Issue: "Welcome to Cyberspace."

Timmerman, J. 1986. *The Mardi Gras Syndrome: Rethinking Christian Sexuality.* New York: CrossRoads.

Tommy. 1992. "A Theory on Infantilism." Reprint available from DPF. Suite 127. 38 Miller Avenue. Mill Valley, CA 94941.

Tribe, L. H. 1992. *Abortion: The Clash of Absolutes.* New York: W. W. Norton.

Trudell, B., and M. Whatley. 1991. "Sex Respect: A Problematic Public School Sexuality Curriculum." *Journal of Sex Education and Therapy*, 17:125-140.

Trussell, J., and C. Westoff. 1980. "Contraceptive Practice and Trends in Coital Frequency." *Family Planning Perspectives*, 12: 246-249.

Turco, S. A. 1994 (September 22). "Students Admit Sexual Activity." *BG News*, 80(22):1 and 5.

Twining, A. 1983. *Bisexual Women: Identity in Adult Development.* Unpublished Doctoral dissertation, Boston University School of Education.

Tzeng, O. C. S., and H. J. Schwarzin. 1987. "Gender and Race Differences in Child Sexual Abuse Correlates." *International Journal of Intercultural Relation*, 14:135-161.

Udry, J. R. 1980. "Changes in The Frequency of Marital Intercourse from Panel Data." *Archives of Sexual Behavior*, 9:319-325.

Udry, J. R. 1990. "Hormonal and Social Determinants of Adolescent Sexual Initiation." In J. Bancroft and J. M. Reinisch, eds. *Adolescence and Puberty* (pp. 70-87). New York: Oxford Press.

Udry, J. R., K. E. Bauman, and N. M. Morris. 1975. "Changes in Premarital Coital Experience of Recent Decade of Birth Cohorts of Urban American Women." *Journal of Marriage and the Family*, 37:783-787.

Udry, J. R., F. R. Deven, and S. J. Coleman. 1982. "A Cross-National Comparison of the Relative Influence of Male and Female Age on the Frequency of Marital Intercourse." *Journal of Biosocial Science*, 14:1-6.

Udry, J. R., L. M. Tolbert, and N. M. Morris. 1986. "Biosocial Foundations for Adolescent Female Sexuality." *Demography*, 23:217-230.

Ullman, S. E., and Knight, R. A. 1992. "Fighting Back: Women's Resistance to Rape." *Journal of Interpersonal Violence*, 7:31-43.

United Presbyterian Church in the U.S.A. General Assembly Special Committee on Human Sexuality. 1991. *Part 1: Keeping Body and Soul Together: Sexuality, Spirituality, and Social Justice. Part 2: Minority report of the Special Committee on Human Sexuality* (Report to the 203rd General Assembly). Baltimore: Presbyterian Church (U.S.A.).

U.S. Bureau of the Census. 1993. *Hispanic Americans Today. Current Population Reports, P23-183*. Washington, DC: Government Printing Office.

U.S. Department of Commerce. 1991. *Statistical Abstract of the United States 1991. 111th edition. Bureau of the Census*. Washington, DC: Government Printing Office.

U.S. Department of Health and Human Services. 1994 (December). *Sexually Transmitted Disease Surveillance 1993*. Atlanta, GA: Public Health Service, Centers for Disease Control and Prevention.

U.S. News and World Report. 1995 (April 24). "The Religious Right: Church Meets State," pp. 26-39.

Vance, C. S., and C. A. Pollis. 1990. "Introduction: A Special Issue on Feminist Perspectives on Sexuality. *Journal of Sex Research*, 27:1-5.

Van Wyk, P. H. and C. S. Geist. 1984. "Psychosexual Development of Heterosexual, Bisexual, and Homosexual Behavior." *Archives of Sexual Behavior*, 13:505-544.

Vener, A. M., and C. S. Stewart. 1974. "Adolescent Sexual Behavior in Middle America Revisited: 1970-1973." *Journal of Marriage and the Family*, 36:728-735.

Verhovek, S. H. 1995 (August 12). "New Twist for a Landmark Case: Roe v. Wade Becomes Roe v. Roe." *The New York Times*, pp. 1, 9.

Voeller, B. 1991. "AIDS and Heterosexual Anal Intercourse." *Archives of Sexual Behavior*, 20(3):233-276.

Wachowiak. C., and H. Bragg. 1980. "Open Marriage and Marital Adjustment." *Journal of Marriage and the Family*, 42(1):57-62.

Walsh, J. 1993 (July/August). "The New Sexual Revolution: Liberation at Last? or the Same Old Mess?" *Utne Reader*, No. 58:59-65.

Warshaw, R. 1988. *I Never Called It Rape*. New York: Harper & Row.

Waterman, C. K., L. J. Dawson, and M. J. Bologna. 1989. "Sexual Coercion in Gay Male and Lesbian Relationships: Predictors and Implications for Support Services." *Journal of Sex Research*, 26:118-124.

Weaver, A. J. 1995. "Has There Been a Failure to Prepare and Support Parish-Based Clergy in Their Role as Front-Line Community Mental Health Workers: A Review." *Journal of Pastoral Care*, 49(2):129-147.

Weeks, M. R., J. J. Schensul, S. S. Williams, M. Singer, and M. Grier. 1995. "AIDS Prevention for African-American and Latina Women: Building Culturally and Gender-Appropriate Interventions." *AIDS Education and Prevention*, 7(3):251-264.

Weinberg, M., and C. J. Williams. 1994. *Dual Attraction.* New York: Oxford University Press.

Weinberg, M. S., C. J. Williams, and C. Calham. 1994. "Homosexual Foot Fetishism." *Archives of Sexual Behavior,* 23(6):611-626.

Weis, D. L. 1983. "Affective Reactions of Women to Their Initial Experience of Coitus." *Journal of Sex Research,* 19:209-237.

Weis, D. L. 1983. "Open Marriage and Multilateral Relationships: The Emergence of Nonexclusive Models of the Marital Relationship." In E. D. Macklin and R. H. Rubin, eds. *Contemporary Families and Alternative Lifestyles: Handbook on Research and Theory* (pp. 194-216). Beverly Hills, CA: Sage.

Weis, D. L., and J. Jurich. 1985. "Size of Community of Residence as a Predictor of Attitudes Toward Extramarital Sexual Relations." *Journal of Marriage and the Family,* 47(1):173-179.

Weis, D. L., and M. Slosnerick. 1981. "Attitudes Toward Sexual and Nonsexual Extramarital Involvement Among a Sample of College Students." *Journal of Marriage and the Family,* 43:349-358.

Weise, E. R., ed. 1992. *Closer to Home: Bisexuality and Feminism.* Seattle: Seal Press.

Wellman, B. 1992. "Men in Network: Private Communities, Domestic Friendships." In P. M. Nardi, ed. *Men's Friendships* (pp. 74-114). Newbury Park, CA: Sage.

Wellman, B. 1985. "Domestic Work, Paid Work and Net Work. In S.W. Duck and D. Perlman, eds. *Understanding Personal Relationships* (pp. 159-191). Newbury Park, CA: Sage.

Wells, R. V. 1985. *Uncle Sam's Family: Issues and Perspectives on American Demographic History.* Albany, NY: State University of New York Press.

Westheimer, R., and L. Lieberman. 1988. *Sex and Morality: Who Is Teaching Our Sex Standards?* Boston, MA: Harcourt, Brace, Jovanovich.

Westoff, C. 1974. "Coital Frequency and Contraception." *Family Planning Perspectives,* 6:136-141.

Wheat, E., and G. Wheat. 1981. *Intended for Pleasure* (rev. ed.) Grand Rapids, MI: Fleming H. Revell/Baker Book House.

Wheeler, D. L. 1995 (April 7). "A Birth-Control Vaccine." *The Chronicle of Higher Education,* 41(A8):9 & 15.

Whitley, M. P., and S. B. Poulsen. 1975. "Assertiveness and Sexual Satisfaction in Employed Professional Women." *Journal of Marriage and the Family,* 37:573-581.

Wiederman, M. W. 1993. "Demographic and Sexual Characteristics of Nonrespondents to Sexual Experience Items in a National Survey." *Journal of Sex Research,* 30:27-35.

Wiederman, M. W., D. L. Weis, and E. R. Allgeier. 1994. "The Effect of Question Preface on Response Rates to a Telephone Survey of Sexual Experience." *Archives of Sexual Behavior,* 23:203-215.

Wiener, L. S. 1991 (September). "Women and Human Immunodeficiency Virus: A Historical and Personal Psychosocial Perspective." *Social Work,* 36(5):375-378.

Wilkinson, D. 1987. "Ethnicity." In M. B. Sussman & S. K. Steinmetz, eds. *Handbook of Marriage and the Family* (pp. 183-210). New York: Plenum Press.

Wilkinson, D. Y., and R. L. Taylor. 1977. *The Black Male in America.* Chicago: Nelson-Hall.

Wille, W. S. 1961. "Case Study of a Rapist: An Analysis of the Causation of Criminal Behavior." *Journal of Social Therapy,* 7:10-21.

Williams, J. D. 1989. *U.S. Hispanics: A Demographic Profile. CRS Report for Congress 89-460 Gov. Congressional Research Service.* Washington, DC: The Library of Congress.

Williams, M. H. 1978. "Individual Sex Therapy." In J. LoPiccolo & L. LoPiccolo, eds. *Handbook of Sex Therapy* (pp. 477-483). New York: Plenum Press.

Wolfe, L. 1978. "The Question of Surrogates in Sex Therapy." In J. LoPiccolo & L. LoPiccolo, eds. *Handbook of Sex Therapy* (pp. 491-497). New York: Plenum Press.

Wolpe, J., and A. A. Lazarus. 1966. *Behavior Therapy Techniques*. New York: Pergamon Press.

World Almanac and Book of Facts, 1993. New York: World Almanac, Pharos Books.

World Almanac and Book of Facts, 1996. New York: World Almanac, Pharos Books.

Worth, D. and R. Rodriquez. 1987, January/February. "Latina Women and AIDS." *SIECUS Report*, 25(3):5-7.

Wyatt, G. E., and G. J. Powell, eds. 1988. *Lasting Effects of Child Sexual Abuse*. London: Sage Publications.

X, L. 1994. "A Brief Series of Anecdotes about the Backlash Experienced by Those of Us Working on Marital and Date Rape." *Journal of Sex Research*, 31:141-143.

Yllo, K. A. 1978. "Nonmarital Cohabitation: Beyond the College Campus." *Alternative Lifestyles*, 1:37-54.

Zelnik, M., J. F. Kantner, and K. Ford. 1981. *Sex and Pregnancy in Adolescence*. Beverly Hills, CA: Sage.

Zelnik, M., and F. K. Shah. 1983. "First Intercourse Among Young Americans." *Family Planning Perspectives*, 15(2):64-70.

Zilbergeld, B. 1978. *Male Sexuality: A Guide to Sexual Fulfillment*. Boston, MA: Little Brown.

Zilbergeld, B. 1992. *The New Male Sexuality*. New York: Bantam Books.

Zoucha-Jensen, J. M., and A. Coyne. 1993. "The Effects of Resistance Strategies on Rape." *American Journal of Public Health*, 83:1633-1634.

Supplementary References for Updated U.S.A. Volume

American Medical Association. 1992. "Induced Termination of Pregnancy Before and After *Roe v. Wade*." *Journal of the American Medical Association*, 268(22):3237.

Anderson, K. 1996. *Changing Woman: A History of Racial Ethnic Women in Modern America*. New York: Oxford Press.

Arditti, R., E. D. Klein, and S. Minden. 1984. *Test-Tube Women: What Future for Motherhood?* London: Pandora Press.

Atkinson, D. R., G. Morten and D. W. Sue. 1993. *Counseling American Minorities: A Cross Cultural Perspective* (2nd ed.). Dubuque, IA: William C. Brown Company.

Binion, V. J. 1990. "Psychological Androgyny: A Black Female Perspective." *Sex Roles*, 22(7/8):487-507.

Brick, P., and D. M. Roffman. 1993 (November). "'Abstinence, No Buts' Is Simplistic." *Educational Leadership*, 51:90-92.

Broman, C. L. 1991. "Gender, Work-Family Roles and Psychological Well-Being of Blacks." *Journal of Marriage and Family*, 53: 509-520.

Califia, P. 1997. *Sex Changes: The Politics of Transgenderism*. San Francisco, CA: Cleis Press.

Centers for Disease Control and Prevention (CDC). 1996. "1996 HIV/AIDS Trends Provide Evidence of Success in HIV Prevention and Treatment." http://www.cdc.gov/od/oc/medial pressrel/aids-dl.htm.

Centers for Disease Control and Prevention (CDC). 1998. "The Challenge of STD Prevention in the United States." http://www.cdc.gov/nchstp/dstd/STD_Prevention_in_the_United_States.htm.

Chase, C. 1998 (April). "Hermaphrodites with Attitude: Mapping the Emergence of Intersex Political Activism. *Gay and Lesbian Quarterly*, 4(2):189-211.

Christensen, C. P. 1988. "Issues in Sex Therapy with Ethnic and Racial Minority Women." *Women and Therapy*, 7(213):187-205.

Cole, E. 1988. "Sex at Menopause: Each in Her Own Way." *Women and Therapy*, 7:159-168.

Coleman, E., ed. 1991 *John Money: A Tribute*. New York: Haworth Press. Also published as volume 4, number 2 of *Journal of Psychology and Human Sexuality,.*

Corea, G. 1985. *The Mother Machine: Reproductive Technologies from Artificial Insemination to Artificial Wombs*. New York: Harper & Row.

Collins, P. H. 1990. *Black Feminist Thought: Knowledge, Consciousness, and the Politics of Empowerment*. Boston: Unwin Hyman.

Ehrenreich, B., G. Hass, and E. Jacobs. 1987. *Remaking Love: The Feminization of Sex*. New York: Doubleday/Anchor.

Eng, T. R., and W. T. Butler. 1997. *The Hidden Epidemic: Confronting Sexually Transmitted Diseases*. Washington, D.C.: National Academy Press.

Farley, R., and W. R. Allen. 1987. *The Color Line and the Quality of Life in America*. New York: Russell Sage Foundation.

Fineman, H., and K. Breslau. 1998 (February 2). "Sex, Lies and the President." *Newsweek*, pp. 20-29.

Francoeur, R. T. 1977. *Utopian Motherhood: New Trends in Human Reproduction*, third edition. Cranbury NJ: A. S. Barnes/Perpetua Books.

Getman, K. 1984. "Sexual Control in the Slaveholding South: The Implementation and Maintenance of a Racial Caste System." *Harvard Women's Law Review*, 7:115-53.

Guttmacher, S., et al. 1997 (September). "Condom Availability in New York City Public High Schools: Relationships to Condom Use and Sexual Behavior." *American Journal of Public Health*, 87(9):1427-1433.

Herman-Giddens, M. E. 1997 (April). "Secondary Sexual Characteristics and Menses in Young Girls Seen in Office Practice: A Study from the Pediatric Research in Office Settings Network." *Pediatrics*, 99(44):505-12.

Holmes, H. B., B. B. Hoskins, and M. Gross, eds. 1981. *The Custom-Made Child? Women-Centered Perspectives*. Clifton NJ: Humana Press.

Hooks, B. 1990. *Yearning: Race, Gender, and Cultural Politics*. Boston: South End Press.

Irvine, J. 1995. *Sexuality Education Across Cultures: Working With Differences*. San Francisco: Jossey-Bass.

Isikoff, M. 1997 (August 11). "A Twist in Jones v. Clinton." *Newsweek*, pp. 30-31.

Isikoff, M., and H. Fineman. 1997 (July 7). "A Starr-Crossed Probe?" *Newsweek*, p. 31.

Isikoff, M., and E. Thomas. 1997 (June 8). "I Want Him to Admit What He Did." *Newsweek*, pp. 30-38.

Isikoff, M., and E. Thomas. 1998 (February 2). "Clinton and the Intern." *Newsweek*, pp. 30-46.

Koch, P. B. 1997. "The International Encyclopedia of Sexuality." Plenary presented at the Annual Conference of the Midcontinent Region of The Society for the Scientific Study of Sexuality, Chicago, IL.

Lebacqz, K. 1997."Difference or Defect? Intersexuality and the Politics of Difference." *The Annual. Society of Christian Ethics*, 17:213-29.

Levy, S. 1997 (March 31). "U.S. v. the Internet." *Newsweek*, pp. 77-79.

Lorde. A. 1984. *Sister/Outsider: Essays and Speeches*. New York: Crossing Press.

Love, S. 1997. *Dr. Susan Love's Hormone Book*. New York: Random House.

Mansfield, P. K., and P. B. Koch. 1997. "Enhancing Your Sexual Response." *Menopause Management*, 6(2):25.

Mansfield, P. K., A. M. Voda, and P. B. Koch. 1995. "Predictors of Sexual Response Changes in Heterosexual Midlife Women." *Health Values*, 19(1):10-20.

Marin, R., and S. Miller. 1997 (April 14). "Ellen Steps Out." *Newsweek*, pp. 65-67.

Marsh, M., and W. Ronner. 1996. *The Empty Cradle: Infertility in America from Colonial Times to the Present*. Baltimore: Johns Hopkins University Press.

McGoldrick, M., J. K. Pearce, and J. Giordano, eds. 1982. *Ethnicity and Family Therapy.* New York: Guilford Press.

Morganthau, T. 1997 (June 30). "Baptists vs. Mickey." *Newsweek,* pp. 51.

National Abortion Rights Action League (NARAL) 1998. *A State-by-State Review of Abortion and Reproductive Rights: Who Decides?* Washington, D.C.: NARAL.

National Institutes of Health Consensus Development Conference Statement. 1992 (December 7-9). *Impotence. NIH Consensus Statement Dec. 7-9,* 10(4):1-31. (Number 91) *Impotence.*

Nelson, K. L. 1996 (August/September). "The Conflict Over Sexuality Education: Interviews with Participants on Both Sides of the Debate." *SIECUS Report,* pp. 12-16.

Newsweek. 1997 (June 30). "Nude Fight." p. 8.

Nichols, M. 1989. "Sex Therapy with Lesbians, Gay Men, and Bisexuals." In S. R. Leiblum and R. C. Rosen, eds. *Principles and Practice of Sex Therapy.* (2nd edition). New York: Guilford.

Noonan, R. J. 1998 (in press). "The Psychology of Sex: A Mirror from the Internet." In J. Gackenbach (Ed.). *Psychology and the Internet: Intrapersonal, Interpersonal and Transpersonal Implications.* New York: Academic Press.

Ogden, G. 1995. *Women Who Love Sex.* New York: Pocket Books.

Planned Parenthood of Southeastern Pennsylvania v. Casey, 505 U.S. 833, 954 (1992) (Rehnquist, C. J., dissenting and concurring in part).

Richardson, L. 1997 (October 16). "When Sex Is Just a Matter of Fact: To High School Students, Free Condoms Seem Normal, Not Debatable." *The New York Times,* pp. B1 and B6.

Sherwin, B. B. 1991. "The Psychoendocrinolgy of Aging and Female Sexuality." *Annual Review of Sex Research,* 2:181-98.

Simon, W. 1993. *Postmodern Sexualities.* London: Rutledge.

Smart, T. 1996 (February). "Protease Inhibitors Come of Age." *Newsletter of Experimental AIDS Therapies,* 10(2):1.

Spector, I., and M. Carey. 1990. "Incidence and Prevalence of the Sexual Dysfunctions: A Critical Review of the Empirical Literature." *Archives of Sexual Behavior,* 19:389-408.

Staples, R., and L. B. Johnson. 1993. "Black Families at the Crossroads: Challenges and Prospects. San Francisco: Jossey-Bass.

Stipp, D., and R. Whitaker. 1998 (March 16). "The Selling of Impotence." *Fortune,* 137(5):115-24.

Taylor, S. 1997 (June 9). "The Facts of the Matter." *Newsweek,* p. 39.

Tiefer, L. 1995. *Sex Is Not a Natural Act and Other Essays.* San Francisco: Westview.

Weitz, R., and L. Gordon. 1993. "Images of Black Women Among Anglo College Students." *Sex Roles,* 28(1/2):19-34.

West, C. M. 1995. "Mammy, Sapphire, and Jezebel: Historical Images of Black Women and Their Implications for Psychotherapy." *Psychotherapy,* 32(3):458-66.

Wyatt, G. E. 1992. "The Sociocultural Context of African American and White American Women's Rape." *Journal of Social Issues,* 48(1):77-91.

Wyatt, G. E., M. Newcomb, and C. Notgrass. 1990. "Internal and External Mediators of Women's Rape Experiences." *Psychology of Women Quarterly,* 14:153-76.

Contributors and Acknowledgments

The Editors

PATRICIA BARTHALOW KOCH, PH.D., coeditor of this volume, is an associate professor of biobehavioral health and health education at Pennsylvania State University. She earned a master's degree in the Program in Human Sexuality, Marriage, and Family Life Education at New York University, during which time she studied in Japan and Sweden. Her doctorate is in health education from Pennsylvania State University, specializing in sexuality education, sexual health issues, human development, and counseling. She has authored over fifty chapters and scientific articles and contributed to several textbooks on sexual topics. She recently authored a textbook, *Exploring Our Sexuality: An Interactive Text* (Kendall/Hunt). She has conducted numerous research studies in the areas of sexuality education, sexual health issues, and women's health. Recently elected a Fellow of the Society for the Scientific Study of Sexuality (SSSS), she is also past president of the Society's Eastern Region and has served on the Board of Directors of SSSS and the Foundation for the Scientific Study of Sexuality. (Section 2C Sexological Research and Advanced Education—Feminist Issues; Section 3 Sexuality Knowledge and Education; Section 10 Contraception and Abortion; and Section 15 Current Developments.)

DAVID L. WEIS, PH.D., coeditor, received his Ph.D. in family studies in 1979 from Purdue University. He has taught at Rutgers University, and is currently an associate professor of human development and family studies at Bowling Green State University in Ohio. A member of and officer for the National Council on Family Relations, the Society for the Scientific Study of Sexuality, and the International Network on Personal Relationships, he is also an associate editor for the *Journal of Sex Research*. Weis has published numerous research articles in professional journals in such areas as adolescent sexuality, marital exclusivity, marital and sexual belief systems, sexual interaction processes, peer education programming, social services for the homeless and mentally ill, and adolescent drug use. He has also taught and conducted workshops in these areas, as well as in interpersonal communications, intimacy, flirtation behavior, dual-career marriages, and black families. Weis received the Hugo Beigel Award for Outstanding Sexuality Research for his study of the emotional reactions to first intercourse. (Introduction; Section 1 Basic Sexological Premises; and Section 5 Interpersonal Heterosexual Behaviors.)

Biographical Sketches for Section Authors

Most of the following contributors are active members of the Society for the Scientific Study of Sexuality, and several have held national or regional offices in the Society.

DIANE E. BAKER, M.A., PH.D. (cand.) is completing her doctoral dissertation on child sexual abuse in the Psychology Department at Syracuse University, Syracuse, New York. (Section 7A Incest and Child Sexual Abuse.)

SUSAN BARGAINNIER, ED.D., is a certified athletic trainer and assistant professor at the State University of New York in Oswego specializing in wellness promotion. (A Door to the Future: Sexuality on the Information Superhighway.)

SARAH C. CONKLIN, PH.D., received her first three degrees in her native state of Minnesota, a bachelor of science from the University of Minnesota, a master's degree in guidance and counseling from the University of St. Thomas, and a master's degree in theology from United Theological Seminary of the Twin Cities (Minneapolis–St. Paul). She earned her doctorate in human sexuality education from the University of Pennsylvania. She is currently an assistant professor of health and sexuality education at the University of Wyoming (Laramie), College of Health Sciences, School of Physical Health Education, and has done adjunct education in sexuality in Pennsylvania and Minnesota seminaries. (Section 13 Clergy Education.)

MARTHA CORNOG, M.A., M.S., is a linguist and librarian at the American College of Physicians. Her recent work includes a long article on conducting sexological research in *Human Sexuality: An Encyclopedia,* coeditor of *The Complete Dictionary of Sexology,* and coauthoring *For Sex Education: See Librarian.* (Section 13 Sexuality Research and Advanced Education.)

RICHARD CROSS, M.D., pioneered medical school sexuality education while he was a professor at the Robert Wood Johnson School of Medicine at Rutgers University, New Brunswick, New Jersey. (Section 13E Medical School Education.)

MARILYN A. FITHIAN, PH.D., is cofounder of the Center for Marital and Sexual Studies, Long Beach, California, and coauthor of *Treatment of Sexual Dysfunction, Any Man Can,* and other works. (Section 12 Sexual Dysfunctions and Therapies.)

JEANNIE FORREST, M.A., worked for seven years as a family educator with the Church of the Latter-Day Saints and was married to a Mormon. She earned a master's degree in health education in the Human Sexuality Program at New York University. (Section 2A Sexuality and the Church of the Latter-Day Saints.)

ANDREW D. FORSYTH, M.S., is a fifth-year graduate student in clinical psychology in the Department of Psychology at Syracuse University, Syracuse, New York, whose interests include the assessment of high-risk sexual behaviors among at-risk groups. (Section 11 HIV/AIDS.)

ROBERT T. FRANCOEUR, PH.D., A.C.S. (General Editor) Trained in embryology, evolution, theology, and the humanities, Dr. Francoeur's main work has been to synthesize and integrate the findings of primary sexological researchers. He is the author of twenty-two books, contributor to seventy-eight textbooks, handbooks, and encyclopedias, and the author of fifty-eight technical papers on various aspects of sexuality. His books include *The Scent of Eros: Mysteries of Odor in Human Sexuality* (1995), *Becoming a Sexual Person* (1982, 1984, 1991) and *Taking Sides: Clashing Views on Controversial Issues in Human Sexuality* (1987, 1989, 1991, 1993, 1997)—two college textbooks, *Utopian Motherhood: New Trends in Human Reproduction* (1970, 1974, 1977), *Eve's New Rib: 20 Faces of Sex, Marriage, and Family* (1972), *Hot and Cool Sex: Cultures in Conflict* (1974), and *The Future of Sexual Relations* (1974). He is editor-in-chief of *The Complete Dictionary of Sexology* (1991, 1995). A fellow of the Society for the Scientific Study of Sexuality and past president of the Society's Eastern Region, he is also a charter member of the American College of Sexology. He is currently professor of biological and allied health sciences at Fairleigh Dickinson University, Madison, New Jersey, U.S.A., adjunct professor in the doctoral Program in Human Sexuality at New York University, and professor in the New York University "Sexuality in Two Cultures" program in Copenhagen. (Section 2 Religious Values, Section 4 Autoerotic Behavior, Section 5 Sexuality and Older Persons, Section 8 Sexual Harassment, Prostitution, and Pornography, Section 10 STDs, Section 13 Research Assessment, and Section 15 Current Developments.)

BARBARA GARRIS, M.A., earned a bachelor's degree in anthropology and sociology at Mountclair State University and did graduate studies at New York University in women's studies. She works for AT&T. (A Door to the Future: Sexuality on the Information Superhighway.)

PATRICIA GOODSON, PH.D., obtained her bachelor's degree from the Universidade de Campinas, Brazil, and a master's degree in philosophy of education from the Pontificia Universidade Catolica de Campinas, Brazil. After earning a Master of Arts degree in general theological studies from Covenant Theological Seminary in St. Louis, Missouri, she completed her doctorate in health education at the University of Texas at Austin. At present, she is an assistant professor in health at the University of Texas at San Antonio, in the Division of Education. (Section 12 Clergy Education.)

WILLIAM E. HARTMAN, PH.D. is cofounder of the Center for Marital and Sexual Studies, Long Beach, California, and coauthor of *Treatment of Sexual Dysfunction, Any Man Can,* and other works. (Section 12 Sexual Dysfunctions and Therapies.)

ROBERT O. HAWKINS, PH.D., former associate dean of the School of Allied Health Professions at the Health Sciences Center of the State University of New York at Stony Brook, is also coauthor of *Counseling Lesbian Women and Gay Men: A Life-Issues Approach.* (Section 6 Homosexual and Lesbian Issues.)

LINDA L. HENDRIXSON, PH.D., completed her undergraduate studies and master's degree in health education at Montclair State University in New Jersey. She did her doctoral studies in the Human Sexuality Program in the Department of Health Education at New York University. Her dissertation examined issues of HIV-positive women in rural northwestern New Jersey. She has taught at various New Jersey universities and colleges, and published on issues related to sexuality and health education. (Section 11B Emerging Issues in HIV/AIDS.)

BARRIE J. HIGHBY, M.A., is a graduate student in clinical psychology at the University of Kansas, where her research has focused on rape. She has worked at several shelters for battered women. (Section 8A Sexual Coercion and Rape.)

ARIADNE KANE, M.ED., is a nationally known gender specialist, author, and educator, as well as a diplomate of the American Board of Sexology. (Section 7 Cross-Gender Issues.)

SHARON KING, M.S.ED., graduated from the Human Sexuality Program at the University of Pennsylvania where she completed all but her dissertation for the doctorate. Her specialty is survivor therapy. (Section 8A Child Sexual Abuse and Incest.)

ROBERT MORGAN LAWRENCE, D.C., is on the board of advisors of San Francisco Sex Information. He lectures extensively about sexuality and health. (Section 6B Bisexuality.)

BRENDA LOVE is author of the *Encyclopedia of Unusual Sex* and has worked at the Institute for the Advanced Study of Human Sexuality in San Francisco. (Section 8D Paraphilic Behaviors.)

CHARLENE MUEHLENHARD, PH.D., is an associate professor of psychology and women's studies at the University of Kansas. Her research focuses on rape and other forms of sexual coercion, as well as on communication and miscommunication about sex. (Section 8A Sexual Coercion and Rape.)

RAYMOND J. NOONAN, PH.D., is an adjunct instructor of human sexuality and health education at the Fashion Institute of Technology, State University of New York, in Manhattan, and an adjunct lecturer in human sexuality at Brooklyn College of the City University of New York. He is also director of SexQuest/The Sex Institute, providing educational consulting in human sexuality and educational content for the World Wide Web. He is coeditor and author of *Does Anyone Still Remember When Sex Was Fun? Positive Sexuality in the Age of AIDS* (3rd edition, 1996). He recently completed his doctoral dissertation in the Human Sexuality Program at New York University. (Section 11C Impact of AIDS on the Perception of Sexuality and Section 12E Sex Surrogates.)

MIGUEL A. PERÉZ, PH.D., teaches kinesiology at the University of North Texas, where he also pursues an interest in sexuality. (Section 2B Latino Sexuality.)

TIMOTHY PERPER, PH.D. Dr. Perper is a Philadelphia-based, independent sex researcher and writer. Trained as a biologist, with his doctorate from City University of New York, he has studied human courtship and flirtation behaviors for over a decade, assisted by full-support grants from the Harry Guggenheim Foundation. He is author of *Sex Signals: The Biology of Love* (1985), coauthor of *For Sex Education, See Librarian* (1996), author of numerous articles on human and animal sexual behavior, and coeditor of *The Complete Dictionary of Sexology* (1991, 1995). He has served variously as associate, consulting, and book review editor for the *Journal of Sex Research.* He is a long-time member of the Society for the Scientific Study of Sexuality and an elected fellow of the American Anthropological Association. (Section 2A Religious Values and Sexuality.)

HELDA L. PINZÓN, PH.D. is a Colombian-born nurse with wide experience in public health. A professor at Pennsylvania State University, her research interests include Latino health issues, community health, and Latino adolescent health. (Section 2B Latino Sexuality.)

CAROL QUEEN, PH.D. (cand.), has written extensively on bisexuality and other topics related to sexual diversity, including *Exhibitionism for the Shy: Show Off, Dress Up, and Talk Hot* (1995). She is a cultural sexologist in the doctoral program at the Institute for Advanced Study of Human Sexuality. (Section 6B Bisexuality.)

HERBERT P. SAMUELS, PH.D., is assistant professor of natural and applied sciences at the City University of New York/Laguardia Community College. (Section 2B African-American Sexuality.)

JULIAN SLOWINSKI, PSY.D., is a marital and sex therapist at Pennsylvania Hospital and faculty member at the University of Pennsylvania School of Medicine, Department of Psychiatry. (Section 12 Sexual Dysfunctions and Therapies.)

WILLIAM STACKHOUSE, PH.D., is director of the HIV Prevention Program for the Bureau of HIV Program Services at the New York City Department of Health. He is also an adjunct assistant professor in the Graduate Department of Applied Psychology at New York University and maintains a private psychotherapy practice. (Section 6 Male Homosexuality and Lesbianism.)

WILLIAM R. STAYTON, TH.D., is assistant professor of psychiatry and human behavior at Jefferson Medical College and an adjunct professor in the

Human Sexuality Program at the University of Pennsylvania. (Section 12 Sexual Dysfunctions and Therapies.)

MITCHELL S. TEPPER, M.P.H., PH.D., a physically challenged person, earned his doctorate at the University of Pennsylvania, Program in Human Sexuality. (Section 5D Sexuality and People with Disabilities.)

Acknowledgments

We would like to thank the many sexuality professionals who contributed to this volume. As editors, we take full responsibility for the material ultimately included in this analysis of sexual practices and values in the United States. Throughout this book, we emphasize the complexity and diversity of sexuality in America. These concepts apply equally to the range of issues studied by sexual scientists and to the variety of academic disciplines involved with the study of sexuality. The various authors who contributed to this work offered perspectives from such fields as biology, psychology, sociology, health, ethnic studies, women's studies, theology, medicine, and library science. Some of the contributions also came from sexual activists. The topics covered reflect the complexity and diversity of these fields of study, as well as the range of sexual practices described. We greatly appreciate the multiple perspectives that our authors and consultants contributed. The result, we think, is a broader, more varied, and in many cases, more thorough approach than the two of us could have accomplished by ourselves. This collaborative effort makes this work a truly unique assessment of American sexuality.

In addition to the sexologists who authored specific sections of this book, the editors are grateful to other colleagues who served as special consultants: Mark O. Bigler, L.C.S.W., Ph.D., Bonnie Bullough, R.N., Ph.D.; Vern L. Bullough, R.N., Ph.D.; Sandra S. Cole, Ph.D.; Carol A. Darling, Ph.D.; J. Kenneth Davidson, Ph.D.; Clive Davis, Ph.D.; Karen Komisky-Brash, M.A.; Barbara Van Oss Marin, Ph.D.; Ted McIlvenna, Th.D, Ph.D.; John Money, Ph.D.; Gina Ogden, Ph.D.; Paul Okami, Ph.D.; Letitia Anne Peplau, Ph.D.; William J. Taverner, M.Ed.; and Stephanie Wadell, M.A. Although these colleagues generously contributed resource materials and their expertise for chapters or sections in this book, the editors and the general editor of *The International Encyclopedia of Sexuality* accept full responsibility for the final integration of the material presented in this volume.

American Sexological Organizations

The Society for the Scientific
Study of Sexuality (SSSS)
P. O. Box 208
Mt. Vernon, Iowa 52314 USA
Telephone: 319/895-8407
Fax: 319/895-6203

The American Association of
Sex Educators, Counselors, and
Therapists (ASSECT)
P. O. Box 208
Mt. Vernon, Iowa 52314 USA
Telephone: 319/895-8407
Fax: 319/895-6203

The Sexuality Information and
Education Council of the
United States (SIECUS)
130 West 42nd Street. Suite 350
New York, New York 10036 USA
Telephone: 212/819-9770
Fax: 212/819-9776
E-mail: siecus@siecus.org

The Society for Sex Therapy
and Research (SSTAR)
c/o Candyce Risen
The Center for Sexual Health
2320 Chagrin Blvd.
3 Commerce Park
Beachwood, Ohio 44122 USA

International Gay and Lesbian
Human Rights Commission
1360 Mission Street, Suite 200
San Francisco, CA 94103 USA
Telephone: 415/255-8680
Fax: 415/255-8662

United Nations Population
Fund FUND (UNFPA)
Education, Communication and
Youth Branch
220 Eeast 42nd Street
New York, New York 10017 USA
Telephone: 212/297-5236
Fax: 212/297-4915

World Association of Sexology
(WAS)
Eli Coleman, Secretary General
University of Minnesota
Medical School
Program in Human Sexuality
1300 South Second Street, Suite 180
Minneapolis, Minnesota 55454 USA
Telephone: 612/625-1500
Fax: 612/626-8311

Margaret Sanger Center International
Margaret Sanger Square
26 Bleecker Street
New York, New York 10012 USA
Telephone: 212/274-7272
Fax: 212/274-7299

Advocates for Youth
International Center on
Adolescent Fertility
1025 Vermont Avenue N.W.
Washington DC 20005 USA
Telephone: 202/347-5700
Fax: 202/347-2263

YWCA of the USA
624 9th Street N.W. 3rd Floor
Washington, DC 20001 USA
Telephone: 202/628-3636
Fax: 202/783-7123

Office of Minority Health
Resource Center
P. O. Box 37337
Washington, DC 20013-7337 USA
Telephone: 800/444-6472
Fax: 301/589-0884

Instituto Puertorriqueno de
Salud Sexual Integral
Center Building, Oficina 406
Avenida de Diego 312, Santurce
Puerto Rico 00909 USA
Telephone: 809/721-3578

BEBASHI
(Blacks Educating Blacks About
Sexual Health Issues)
1233 Locust Street Suite 401
Philadelphia, PA 19107 USA
Telephone: 215/546-4140
Fax: 215/546-6107

National Asian Women's
Health Organization
250 Montgomery Street, Suite 410
San Francisco, CA 94104 USA
Telephone: 415/989-9747
Fax: 415/989-9758

National Youth Advocacy Coalition—
Bridges Project
1711 ConnecticutAvenue N.W., Suite 206
Washington, DC 20009 USA
Fax: 202/319-7365

National Latina/o Lesbian and
Gay Organization
1612 K Street N.W. Suite 500
Washington, DC 20036 USA
Telephone: 202/466-8240
Fax: 202/466-8530

National Coalition of Hispanic Health
and Human Services Organizations
(COSSMHO)
1030 15th Street N.W Suite 1053
Washington, DC 20005 USA
Telephone: 202/387-5000
Fax: 202/797-4353

National Minority AIDS Council
1931 13th Street N.W.
Washington, DC 20009 USA
Telephone: 202/483-6622
Fax: 202/483-1135

Child Welfare League of America
440 First Street N.W. Suite 310
Washington,DC 20001 USA
Telephone: 202/638-2952
Fax: 202/638-4004

National Native American
AIDS Prevention Center
2100 Lake Shore Avenue Suite A
Oakland, California 94606 USA
Telephone: 510/444-2051
Fax: 510/444-1593

Planned Parenthood
Federation of America
810 Seventh Avenue
New York New York 10019 USA
Telephone: 212/541-7800
Fax: 212/247-6269

Feminists for Free Expression
(FFE)
2525 Times Square Station
New York, NY 10108-2525 USA
Telephone: 212/702-6292

Bay Area Surrogates Association
(BASA)
c/o Stephanie Wadell
P. O. Box 60971
Palo Alto, CA 94306 USA

International Professional
Surrogates Association (IPSA)
P. O. Box 4282
Torrance, CA 90510-4282 USA
Telephone: 213/469-4720
(answering machine)

Index